CHRISTINA PIRELLO

CHRISTINA COOKS

Everything You Ever Wanted

to Know About Whole Foods, but Were

Afraid to Ask

H P Books

Most HPBooks are available at special quantity discounts for bulk purchases for sales promotions, premiums, fund-raising, or educational use. Special books, or book excerpts, can also be created to fit specific needs.

For details, write: Special Markets, The Berkley Publishing Group, 375 Hudson Street, New York, New York 10014.

Notice: The recipes in this book are to be followed exactly as written. Neither the publisher nor the author is responsible for your specific health or allergy needs that may require medical supervision, or for any adverse reactions to the recipes contained in this book.

HPBooks
Published by The Berkley Publishing Group
A division of Penguin Group (USA) Inc.
375 Hudson Street
New York, New York 10014

First HP Books trade-paperback edition: January 2004

Library of Congress Cataloging-in-Publication Data

Pirello, Christina.
    Christina cooks : everything you always wanted to know about whole foods but were afraid to ask / Christina Pirello.—1st ed.
        p. cm.
    ISBN 1-55788-423-4
    1. Cookery (Natural foods). 2. Natural foods. I. Title.

TX741.P5636 2004
641.5'63—dc22

2003056831

Printed in the United States of America

10   9   8   7

To Jon Michaels

Destiny is not to be messed with . . . your passion, your loyalty, your commitment, your laugh, your voice, your talent . . . the perfect mix of ingredients for our truly great freindship.

CONTENTS

ACKNOWLEDGMENTS

This is my fourth cookbook. I sometimes can't believe it. I didn't know I had one book in me, let alone four (with ideas for five and six rolling around in my head). Sure, my voice and knowledge are in these pages, but more important, at least to me, is the support and love that is extended to me—constantly—by the people around me. They work hard to create an atmosphere in which I can do my best work and I would be lost without them. John Keats said "I am certain of nothing, save the holiness of the heart's affections." Truer words were never spoken.

Everybody needs someone who holds it all together. Michele Gambino, the glue of our operations, and my sanity, I am deeply grateful to you. Your skills, wisdom, perseverance, humor and love bless my life.

To Mary, Sue, Tina, Gayle, Elaine, Rob and Lois, for the truest and most loyal friendship. Your counsel, your wisdom, your confidence and your serenity are like fresh air to me.

To Cynthia, my best friend, for your unwavering love and wise advice. Our history has shown us that we can do anything. Every time I see you, I remember that. Thank you.

To Richard, thank you for hearing me. Thank you for your loyal, honest partnership and support, and for your respect and trust. I love you dearly.

To Sue Becker and everyone at Eden Foods. There are no words to express how deeply grateful I am to you for all that you do. Your loving support and friendship has made working together a dream.

To Susan Morano and all the brilliant minds at Suzanne's Specialties: Thanks for sticking with me all these years. I love you guys.

To John Duff and Jeanette Egan and everyone at HPBooks, for all your guidance, encouragement, friendship and support. You have been with me from the start of this journey and I love you all. You are wonderful to work with and bring out the best in me.

To Jon, there are no words to express the joy that your music and friendship have brought to me as I wrote this book. My life has been blessed since you came into it. I love you.

To all my cherished mentors, friends and students, for keeping me true and teaching me to live open in love and place no conditions or judgments on others.

Finally to sweet Robert, my love, my other half, my hero . . . for making me prove myself, for making me the best I can be, for your inspired ideas, for keeping me honest, for holding my heart tenderly in your strong hands, for loving me for who and what I am . . . no matter what.

CHRISTINA COOKS

Everything You Always Wanted

to Know About Whole Foods, but Were

Afraid to Ask

INTRODUCTION

I love cooking. I love life in the kitchen. There isn't one aspect, one piece, one detail of the process of cooking that doesn't enchant me. I recently read an interview with Julia Child during which she was asked her feelings about the new phrase *domestic arts* being used to describe cooking. She said (indignantly) that she felt that it made life in the kitchen seem unimportant. She said cooking should be called what it is "a life skill . . . that its importance should never be marketed nor trivialized."

For me, cooking is about far more than the process of combining ingredients so that we can eat a meal. Cooking is not just a time-consuming means to an end. Cooking itself is a healing, nourishing meditation. Cooking is how we make our love manifest.

By cooking, we share in the work that sustains our lives; we share in Mother Nature's abundance. Gorgeous winter squash, its vibrant orange flesh as vivid as the sun that gave it color, hearty carrots as sweet as the earth that cradles them, leafy greens stretching luxuriously open to the raindrops that quench their thirst, whole cereal grains that wave in the gentle breeze that lifts them to maturity; our food is a gift from the earth that so generously sustains us. We sell ourselves short if we see cooking food as simply a way to feed our hungry tummies. Handling food is an expression of sincerity and appreciation for the gifts of our lives. We honor the ingredients, and each other, by preparing food with mindful consideration and open hearts.

Cooking provides a vehicle for making our lives whole. If we can find pleasure in the process of cooking, the shopping, the cleaning, the slicing and dicing, the sautéing and simmering, instead of thinking that the joy comes only in the eating, when the work is complete, we experience joy for joy's sake, not in anticipation of a reward. The true joy is in the journey. There is no end.

We have forgotten what truly nourishes us. If we disconnect with nature, our life grows dead and empty. To see food only as fuel to operate our bodies is to create profound impoverishment of the spirit. We can achieve intimacy no greater than that with our food. It joins with us, becomes us, helps create our characters. There is nothing more sensual, more delicious than the experience of preparing food for our loved ones. Cooking is the realization of life. Let's taste the flavor of each divine bite, understanding that what enlivens us affords us the blessing of our ability to taste, smell and be aware. Cooking makes us conscious of the gift we give whenever we nourish others or ourselves.

Cooking is not designed to impress with accomplishment, just like it isn't designed to create tight shoulders, clenched fists and knots in our stomachs as we try to put a meal together. Cooking is about freed passion, a tapping into the sensuality that exists in all of us, just waiting to be expressed. As cooks, we need to be reminded, or remind ourselves, that there is no singular way to cook, no right or wrong way. We all have the capacity to take a recipe and infuse it with our own creative energies, to cook with our own sensibilities, desires and tastes. Recipes simply provide a set of guidelines. *We* provide the soul that makes a meal come alive with the passion of creation.

Anyone can cook. The joy of it comes when you realize that we come alive in the kitchen. Entering the kitchen transports you to a world vivid with crisp green leaves, dramatic black beans, pristine white tofu, vibrant carrots and squash, succulent fruit . . . all lush with nature's vitality. The kitchen is alive with cutting boards, sparkling knives, pots and pans, tenderizing flames seducing the food to completion. Cooking takes you from the world of imagination into the reality of passionate awareness. Where you may have previously looked for solace or satisfaction to be provided to you, in the kitchen you realize that nourishment flows from your being. You are alive with vibrant energy, re-creating yourself meal to meal.

A CHANGE OF HEART?

I have lived a macrobiotic lifestyle for over twenty years and I have learned a lot in that time. One of my most valuable lessons was to understand that everything changes. The more I live in the world, the more I am humbled by how little I understand about life's twists and turns. A good friend often says if you want to make God laugh, just tell him your plans for the future.

When I faced my health crisis, I changed my diet drastically to rebalance my body so that it could heal, and it did. I'm here more than twenty years later as proof. My diet was monastic to say the least, but it helped me return to the wonderful health that I now enjoy. I maintained that very austere and restricted diet for more than fifteen years.

In 1998, I found myself, once again, in a life-threatening situation and was forced to examine my dietary choices. My crisis was the direct result of maintaining an extreme diet for too many years. I had to regroup and rethink how I lived my life so that I could, in fact, live.

The results of that reexamination are in these pages. I was forced to change my thinking on many subjects, from the basics like the use of tomatoes and peppers to the amount of good-quality fat needed to maintain a healthy life to the ratio of carbohydrates to other nutrients in my daily diet. For many years I had turned my back on my Italian culinary heritage, eschewing it as unhealthy, embracing only Asian-style cooking. I have come full circle, as we all do and, while I still love Asian wisdom and cooking, I have rediscovered the wonders of natural balance within who I am, culturally, socially, spiritually and, of course, physically.

I have come to the conclusion that there's not a

vegetable on earth that will kill us if eaten in moderation. Most of us don't need to make a change or improve our health because we ate too many tomatoes. Sure they contain scary amounts of solanine, an alkaloid that has been linked to arthritis symptoms, as well as making our blood more acidic. But they are also a great source of magnesium, vitamin C and lycopene. What's a girl to do? I went back to my family and asked. Although they didn't know from solanine, they knew that tomatoes gave them *acida* unless cooked, marinated or dried. My own research shows that those processes neutralize the solanine as well as make the essential nutrients more available to us. So do I use them on occasion? When tomatoes are in season, lush with juices and fresh taste? You bet, but marinated, cooked or dried.

And then there's fat. There's a whole slew of nutrients that we can't assimilate or utilize without it as the vehicle. It's up to us to discover the best-quality fat and use it appropriately for our lifestyle and health. So is it enough that an oil is cold-pressed or unrefined? While those are better than any saturated or hydrogenated fats, I have narrowed the field of oils that I find acceptable for daily use and cooking. Corn oil used to be my choice for baking and even some sautéing, but

genetically modified corn has changed all that. There are no organic corn oils (that I'm aware of) and because I choose not to support genetically modified foods, corn oil is out for me. Smoke points and conversion to trans fats are also considerations, so I choose oils that can withstand cooking at high temperatures for long periods of time. Thus my pantry now contains only extra-virgin olive oil, avocado oil (both with high smoke points) and hempseed oil (for omega-3 content, low temperature cooking and salad dressings). I use sesame oil on occasion, mostly for flavor not for long cooking.

In short, I have come to the conclusion that we have to understand food and how it works in our bodies. Right, wrong, rules, extremes, brown rice, daikon, tomatoes, peppers, chocolate or amasake, it's really about making choices appropriate to human health. Living in harmony with nature around you and enjoying whole, unprocessed, seasonal, organic food that is simply and elegantly prepared are the keys to health and vitality. It's as simple as that.

Change of heart? I prefer to think I'm simply evolving and, I hope, growing wiser in the process. Only time will tell.

EATING WELL *IS* ALL THAT IT'S CRACKED UP TO BE

There is a kind of sorcery in cooking, a magical alchemy in choosing ingredients, in coaxing each nuance of flavor from the foods we prepare. The sensuality of cooking overwhelms my senses. Water sluices over my hands as I wash vegetables, caressing their smooth skin, gently cleansing them. I stir simmering pots, steam rising, sweat beading on my skin, leaving it moist, slightly salty. I spoon finished recipes onto platters and into bowls, pasta mounded, fragrant with the heady scents of fresh herbs. I delight in delicately cooked vegetable stews; soups that warm as cozily as a down quilt; seemingly modest grains, lustily silky under their neutral appearance; crisp, vital salads dance on my tongue, lush with the passion of the season; succulent fruits, juice spurting, dribbling down my chin, through my fingers, over my wrist, demanding to be kissed away.

I move from task to task, completely engaged in the foreplay of preparation. I am intoxicated with the scents and aromas of a meal coming together. I whisk sauces to lusty, smooth perfection. I sauté, simmer and stir dishes to their sensual climax, occasionally brushing a sweat-dampened tendril of hair from my cheek. I am lost to the passion of creation when I cook.

Are you thinking that this doesn't sound like *your* experience in the kitchen or your experience of food? Are you thinking that this *certainly* doesn't sound like the experience you would expect when envisioning natural foods? I know, but this is life in the kitchen, when life in the kitchen is lived with understanding and sensual abandon.

Cooking is an art form being rapidly lost in this country. Whether preparing prime rib or tofu, your love of the kitchen determines if your meals are delicious or pedestrian, sublime or just a way to feed yourself. Of course, I prefer you prepare the tofu, but that's me; more on that later.

THE PASSION OF FOOD

"Please enjoy your food." How often has this simple phrase drawn our attention to the meal we are about to consume? And how ironic it has become. Eating, like cooking, has become a chore for us, another hassle to be endured at the end of a long, frenetic day. In a way, this simple phrase has become a mockery, the pure antithesis of our experience of food. Enjoy it? We can barely stand the thought of it . . . and all that it entails.

In a way, it's not our fault. We try so hard to have fun. We try to do it all the right way; we work hard, dutifully keep our journals, meditate because it's good for us, exercise, sweat and toil at life because we believe that we can have it all. Even intimacy and sex has become a chore to be wedged between everything else we need to accomplish in each twenty-four-hour interval. Seems like a lot of work to be happy and healthy, doesn't it?

Lost in the shuffle of life are the acts of nourishing ourselves, better known as cooking and eating. Lost is the simple pleasure of preparing the food that is responsible for our lives, loves and behavior in the world. Sound dramatic? Maybe, but think about it. Can you imagine anything sweeter or more satisfying than your loved ones gathered around a table, enjoying a delicious meal that you prepared for them? Can you imagine anything lonelier than eating drive-through in the isolation of your car? The way we regard food, from its purchase to the served meal influences the way we feel about the art of nourishment.

THE LOST ART OF EATING WELL

We all know that McDonald's is one of the leading forces in the fast-food industry and that it has become a model for many other sectors of business in an effort to duplicate its overwhelming success. With the focus on efficiency; quantity over quality; and predictable products, settings and experiences, this model has pervaded many arenas of society. With this model, unfortunately, there is a loss of concern for unique goods and services and the decline of humanity's place in how our food is produced and prepared. It's no coincidence that phrases like "fast food" and "junk food" are often associated with this mode of eating. The drive-through mentality has led to a major trade-off: Speed and quantity has all but replaced quality and service. Every increase in speed and efficiency erodes the experience and sensuality of eating food.

Slow Food, a gastronomic movement with its origins in Italy, was founded by Carlo Petrini, a personal hero of mine, in response to the opening of a McDonald's restaurant near the Spanish Steps in Rome. He wanted to create a movement that would preserve the sensual pleasure of dining, nothing more. Over the years, however, this movement has evolved into one of ecological consciousness, dedicated to preserving not only a love of food and its pleasures but also the traditions involved in growing, producing and preparing food. Now everything from preserving heirloom seeds and foods to artisanal cheese and wine making come under the protective hand of the Slow Food movement.

Predictably, this movement is sluggish in the United States, where we have lost touch with the pleasures of a table laden with natural, whole, delicious foods. But more and more, as we feel worse and worse, weaker and weaker, our intuition is taking over and we are beginning to demand more sanity. As consumers, we've begun to notice and to rebel against the fast-food mentality that threatens to destroy forever the joy of eating. We ask more questions, read more labels, demand better quality. Attendance in cooking classes is on the rise, with learning to cook being a favorite leisure activity. We know, deep in our souls, that fast food and fast-paced living will not lead to love, peace, fulfillment and happiness, and we are beginning to do something about it. I love hope.

BUT WHAT'S NATURAL?

Having worked in the natural-food industry for as long as I have, I know the power that words have over our choices. Using terms like, *fresh, in season* and *natural* conjure images of times lost and purity of spirit. They create a kind of nobility to which we can aspire.

The truth is that these terms are relatively new to us, not a product of the good old days. The cuisine of the poor, upon which much of natural cooking is based, had its roots in attempting to defeat the seasons and their whims to avoid starvation. The desire to store, preserve and produce foods that would hold over long periods was paramount to most of the working world. Whole grains, dried beans and preserved foods were staples of the diet, because they could be stored and used when food was scarce. Fresh fruit was turned into jams and marmalades; vegetables were pickled in oil; meat, fish and vegetables were smoked or dried in the heat of the sun. All these techniques were designed by humans to preserve some kind of uniform diet throughout the year. No farmer, no culture has been able to base a diet entirely on fresh foods that are "in season." The biggest difference lies in the use of chemicals in food growing and production; these are not ancient concepts but ones for which modern culture must shoulder all the blame.

For the affluent aristocracy, however, life was different. The privileged took great pride in the abundance of fresh foods they laid on their tables. Aristocratic gluttony was based on the excessive consumption of fresh food. Offering foods from different regions, as well as fruits out of season, was a sought-after luxury that displayed power. Even in this mind-set, however, the wealthy had little interest in natural taste and flavor but spent a great deal of time and effort to create artificial flavor combinations and distortions of natural foods as evidence of man's power over nature. I guess little has really changed.

Bartolomeo Stefani, the great chef from Bologna, who is considered to be one of the foremost culinary experts of the seventeenth century, pointed out that there were no products of the season, since there was nearly always a place where they grew, and to get them, you needed only a "fast horse" and "full purse." Roman emperors boasted that they could have any product in any season, and disliked what they considered "cheap food," which included fruits, vegetables and herbs "of the season," preferring rare and foreign things. It was a sign of affluence to have strawberries in January and grapes in April. It's reasonable to suggest then, that our own enchantment with exotic, rare and out-of-season ingredients is simply a by-product of our ability to obtain, transport and preserve food. Such advancements have simply made available to many what was previously available only to a few. Humanity's attitude has remained essentially the same.

So what about the taste for natural taste? Where did it come from and how does it benefit us? That cabbage should taste like cabbage, carrots like carrots, freshly picked from the earth is a simple, but revolutionary idea that took hold very slowly in European cuisine. Launched by the French and Italians between the seventeenth and eighteenth centuries as a part of a cultural rationalization, one of the main tenets of this thinking was natural simplicity. Culturally stimulating and with the threat of hunger less ominous in society, people were finally ready for the concept of natural, seasonal foods and everything that it entailed.

It was one of the first births, if you will, of the philosophy that less is more and that the quality of the ingredients used determined the quality of the final dish. As this thinking took hold, the beauty of seasonality and locally produced foods grew in value. People came to the realization that foods of the season and of their region were not to be overlooked for the seeming exotic nature of foods from distant reaches of the world. We came to see that the food grown in our backyard was food at its finest.

With modern methods of preservation, refrigeration, canning, and freeze-drying, the quality of the food can actually be preserved. And though modern technology seems to be the opposing force to fresh and natural, these methods seem much more compatible with nature and her rhythms. We should welcome the natural food revolution as the wave of the future of our food and its quality, not as a return to traditions that didn't exist until recently. Fresh food, whole food belongs to the future, not to the past.

WAKE UP AND SMELL THE TOAST

But what about choices? If cooking is so freeing, so passionate, why is what we choose to cook so important? If cooking is about life and sensuality and abandon, why should we worry?

With the passion and sensuality of cooking comes responsibility. The capacity to nourish doesn't give us the freedom to squander the gifts of nature, our health and our community. Cooking is a divine art in which we create life. To leave behind destruction is to fly in the face of the divine that lives in us.

All of this may sound high-minded and esoteric, but each of us carries a small burden. Each of us must remind himself that he is woven into the web of life. We are not, in fact, the weavers of it. Humans have the unique gift of being able to create what we visualize. Dogs don't build bridges. Cats don't plan cities. If we can imagine it, we can manifest it. And it seems that the more we create, the more enchanted with ourselves we become. The more enchanted with ourselves we become, the more arrogant we become. The more arrogant we become, the more we think that we control life and nature. We forget that we live by nature's rules; nature doesn't live by ours. When we ignore nature's rules, she begins to suffer at our hands, and we, at hers.

Which makes our choices important. For me,

the choice is to live my life as a vegan, eating no animal products at all. I also choose to eat no simple sugars, chemicals, additives or preservatives and to limit the use of processed or canned foods, as much for my health as for the health of the environment; they create pollution, rubbish and toxins. But that's me and as much as I would love to see the world embrace a vegetarian diet, I live in reality. I know that many people choose to eat animal products; some even feel as though they need it to survive with strength and vitality. It's not my job or my desire to judge, preach or try to convert anyone. My responsibility is to live life the best way I know, based on my experiences and my truth and to try and do no harm.

The quality of our food supply is in jeopardy. The largest source of pollution in our world today comes from agribusiness. The fatal flaw in today's food production is that it's modeled on the industrial system. No longer even attempting to remain within the bounds of nature, it has been designed to "beat" nature at her game. For much of the last century, an industrial agriculture model has been the one to emulate, with more natural styles of growing, producing and processing being cast aside as "old-fashioned" and considered inefficient. For those in the big business of agriculture, progress has meant bigger machines, bigger corporate farms and more chemical use.

THE HISTORY OF ORGANIC FOOD PRODUCTION

The alternative to this industrialized version of food production is a system in which food trade increases income as well as food safety and security. This system would preserve the environment, give farmers fair access to the means needed to produce food and give consumers fair access to pure food at fair prices. As you might guess, these simple principles create the foundation of organic food production and farming, which have the goal of fair, safe and sane food production for everybody.

To understand the importance of organic growing and production in our lives, we must understand that this is not a modern or scientific concept but rather one that has ancient roots. Not American or European, the credit for organic principles must go to indigenous peoples and their approach to farming. In 1911, F. H. King, (a former head of the U.S. Department of Agriculture's Division of Soil Management), came back from China and wrote about their ancient sustainable methods of farming in his book *Farmers of Forty Centuries*. In the 1940s, Paul Keene and J. I. Rodale came back from India so inspired by the traditional organic farming methods they had witnessed that they began to farm and promote organic growing. Of course, they were seen as somewhat eccentric and organic foods remained on the fringe for a very long time. Even the "back to the land" movements of the 1960s and 1970s, which embraced these pioneers as visionaries and saw their ideas grow in popularity with the counterculture of the time were still practicing what was seen as "hippie" farming.

Many farmers saw the common sense of organic growing as an alternative to the increasing environmental problems they were experiencing with industrial agriculture and as a way to farm with dignity, preserving the land and the local rural economy. Organic farming became a way to combine standards and values with the ability to produce and sell food at fair prices to all. However, it wasn't until 1962 that industrial agriculture took its first big hit and the attention of the consumer was focused on the dangers of the chemicals used to produce our food. The publication of *Silent Spring* by Rachel Carson, a respected and well-published marine biologist, caused a virtual firestorm of controversy. Her historic book on the dangers of chemical pesticides launched an entire movement against the misuse and overuse of pesticides in our food supply. Carson, fighting terminal cancer, created a new public awareness of the profound impact of pesticides on our health and with her book began a consumer movement against the use of chemicals, pesticides, fungicides and herbicides in our food.

The late 1960s saw the advent of Cesar Chavez's United Farm Workers and focused attention on the effect of chemical use on the health of farm workers. His work created a bridge between the consumer and farm worker, a relationship that has served as the cornerstone in the building of the organic food industry.

As time went on, farm organizations formed and research was conducted to determine the quality of organic production. By 1979, California farmers had mobilized and pushed through state legislation defining the first set of organic standards, which still serve as the gold standard today.

The 1980s saw a hostile political climate for organic organizations, with little or no funding being earmarked for organic food production and subsidies. However, in the mid-1980s, the Sustainable Agriculture Research and Education program was formed, with a small amount of research money trickling toward organic farming as a result. With forty different certifiers and a decade of growth in the private sector, there still remained very little public support for organics.

Concern grew among the organic food industry that state levels of certification may not be consistent enough to retain the integrity of organic food production. Credibility was essential to create consumer confidence, support and demand. The Organic Food Production Act of 1990, introduced by Senator Patrick Leahy of Vermont, had the goal of putting research dollars, enforcement and universal standards in place to ensure the continued growth of the organic food movement. As the organic food industry grew from fresh and local to global, confidence in the standards grew in importance.

The result of these many years of work opened the door for the creation of the National Organic Standards Board, whose primary responsibility was to establish national organic standards for the growth and production of safe and pure food. Organic farmers, food producers and retailers, as well as consumer representatives, scientists and environmentalists worked to create the national organic standards that are in place today. And while many organic proponents (me included) think that the standards could be more stringent and fear commercialization of organics, they are a beginning and ensure that anything carrying an organic label has been grown and produced without the use of chemical pesticides, herbicides and fungicides; was produced without any genetically modified organisms; and is free of sewage sludge, growth hormones and antibiotics. The organic food movement has finally arrived, stepping out of the shadows of the industrial food business into the light of consumer demand. And it's here to stay.

With the U.S. Department of Agriculture (USDA) federal organic standards (put into effect October 2002), organic foods have moved into mainstream accessibility. The many people who were reluctant to try organic foods, for whatever reason, with federal government standards are more likely to take the plunge. Where standards could vary from state to state before, now every organic grower and food producer has to meet the same criteria. As I said earlier, and can never say enough, food labeled as *organic* must be produced to strict standards, no herbicides, pesticides or fungicides may be used; no sewage sludge; no antibiotics or growth hormones; and no genetically modified organisms are allowed in the finished product. A USDA label ensures that the food you are consuming has been grown in accordance to the laws of nature.

The only downside to the new standards is corporate takeover. As organic food continues to grow in popularity and demand, will our collective integrity hold true to the core values of organics or will we cave in to corporate greed and excess? Only time will tell.

WHERE DO WE GO FROM HERE?

We walk a fine line now, however. Enchanted by technology and our aspiration to control nature, we have lost touch with the rhythms that govern us. Having moved far beyond the "fast horses" and "full purses" of the Romans, we have moved to a place that is so out of touch with nature that we need completely to rethink our approach to food and the art of eating.

There have been a series of scandals and accidents in the food production industry: mad cow disease in Europe, chickens containing dioxin, the use of sewage sludge from water treatment plants in animal feed. Suddenly, consumers have been rudely awakened to the fact that the growing process, production and processing techniques used to put food on the market shelves is less than stellar.

We have discovered that, organic foods notwithstanding, cows no longer graze lazily on organic grass, industrial residues have been released into the food chain and the vegetables and fruits we buy and eat are cultivated and developed on large farms run by agribusiness, not individual farmers, and are most likely irradiated. Food processing and production has become increasingly mysterious and, as a result, ominous.

Genetically Modified Organisms

As consumers, we are becoming more aware of the divide between our food and nature. Not surprisingly, the introduction into our food of genetically modified organisms (GMOs), manipulated in laboratories by the engineering of genes from different species into vegetables or animals, has become cause for considerable discomfort for us, as consumers.

GMOs are, after all, just the latest disaster waiting to happen in an industrialized agribusiness that has caused phenomenal damage: soil depletion, water and atmospheric pollution, a decrease in biodiversity and sustainability, toxic residues in and on our crops, a dissolution of the bond between a product and its area of origin and the loss of farms and farm markets, to name but a few. I find it ironic that the very chemical companies that have given rise to GMOs, promoting them as an alternative to chemical food pollutants, are the very same companies that produce the chemicals sprayed on our foods causing pollution.

Here's the deal with GMOs. The promoters of this aberration of nature would have us believe that they are in the same vein as hybridizing, a method used by farmers since the inception of agriculture, to create varietal improvements that strengthened and improved species. Farmers have always strived to create new varieties by crossbreeding characteristics of the same or similar species, but always within the natural boundaries of reproduction and the natural compass of the

GENETICALLY ENGINEERED CROPS OPEN-FIELD PLANTED IN THE UNITED STATES AND EUROPE

Alfalfa	Papayas
Apples	Plums
Barley	Potatoes
Broccoli	Pumpkins
Carrots	Rapeseed
Cauliflower	(canola)
Chicory	Rice
Cotton (46 percent of	Soybeans
U.S. cotton is GMO)	Strawberries
Corn	Sugar beets
Cucumbers	Sunflowers
Eggplants	Sweet potatoes
Grapes	Tobacco
Lettuce	Tomatoes
Mountain	Walnuts
cranberries	Watermelons
Peas	Wheat
Onions	

ecosystem. GMOs remove an important barrier that exists between species, but rather than an advance, this creates less-than-natural situations for our already fragile environment.

This radically new and untested technology is based on scientific research that is still in its infancy. With yet to be discovered risks, whose long-term consequences can only be imagined, how can we allow these foods to be released into the market-place? With little testing, genetically modified crops have been allowed to spread over millions of acres of our farmland and are present, directly and indirectly, as ingredients in tens of thousands of food products that are on our tables every day.

Like other forms of pollution, genetic pollution is spread through the dissemination of a particular substance into the environment. In the case of GMOs, artificially produced genetic material is being released into our air, water and soil. All plants, cultivated and wild, exchange their genetic material, primarily through pollination. In this manner, sooner or later, the genes of each plant will find their way into another of the same species. Unlike chemical pollution, genetic pollution, the contamination of a plant's genetic makeup, is irreversible and self-multiplying. Contaminated plants are certain to multiply, producing more contaminated plants. The consequences for the environment are unpredictable and potentially disastrous. The funding for research to study the risks and consequences of genetic pollution is paltry at best.

Why GMOs? The promoters will tell us that genetic modification will reduce the use of pesticides (yet to be proven true), increase yield (yet to be proven true) and concentrate nutrition (yet to be proven true, unless artificially enriched). It seems that quantitative yield has become the sole objective in food production, with little consideration for anything else, including quality and biodiversity. The introduction of GMOs poses a dilemma of mammoth proportion. Will our future food supply reflect the bond between plant and soil, air, water and sun and the farmer who plows the field, or will it be the product of a laboratory, devoid of its natural inheritance? Do we want to continue to embrace the gifts of nature, the beautiful and the ugly, or embrace the sterile, codified, industrial products created in an environment devoid of nature?

In organic agriculture, on the other hand, there is energy and vitality between the cultivated plants and the ecosystems where they are developed. Cultures that see nature as life have always considered the divine presence in nature and nature as an expression of the divine. Cultures that see nature as a living organism respect its diversity and variety, recognizing that everything grows out of itself, by itself; creatures develop by themselves. Organic food is produced by methods that respect the power of nature and respect the diversity of every ecosystem, thereby preserving the biodiversity that makes nature, well, nature.

Is organic food actually better? Nutritionally, you'll find very little variance in most of the nutrients present in food. Carbohydrates, protein and most vitamins will be the same in commercially produced foods as in organic foods. The true difference, however, is vast. Organic foods are grown in mineral-rich soil and those minerals make their way into the food. Organic food is grown free of any chemical additives and pesticides, which also make their way into the food. Recent studies show significantly higher amounts of magnesium, potassium and iron in organic produce. Organic food is sustainable, meaning that the planet and humanity can be sustained by the methods used to produce food, a huge point in organic's favor; looks to me like the choice is obvious.

FROM MARKET TO TABLE

Okay, so you've decided to reconnect with your food and the earth. Where to begin? Natural foods stores offer a wide array of organic choices and most are friendly, comfortable places to shop and to get information. But as natural food stores grow in popularity and size, they can take on a Disneyland-like quality, and we, the consumer, are once again caught up in the circus of excessive packaging, loss of quality and marketing objectives.

Want to really connect with your food and the earth that spawned it? Go to a farm market. You'll find more than bins overflowing with seasonal, fresh, spectacular foods. You'll find a way of life. A farm market places on our tables food that has the vitality, flavor and beauty of that which is infused with the energy of the sun, air, water and soil.

Shopping at a farm market takes the innocent shopper on a journey. Shopping at a farm market is more than buying new potatoes or apples. Quite often, the foods we find at a farm market are grown and produced by sustainable methods. Fields and orchards are planted and maintained by natural methods. Animals are raised naturally, without the use of antibiotics and hormones. Food is produced with respect for nature, without the use of compounds that can damage the food, the planet and humans.

Very often, the food found at a farm market will be produced traditionally from heirloom seeds and stock and chosen for optimal flavor and diversity, as opposed to the demands of distant marketplaces. Foods from a farm market have an integrity that far surpasses that which we find in a supermarket. A regular farm market shopper will develop a fine sense of quality and of the phrase *in season,* understanding that these two little words refer to where we live, our community, not the never-changing, eternal season we find on supermarket shelves.

But there's more to a farm market than fine food. A successful community farm market ensures a healthy rural economy. Even better, a farm market fosters a connection between the urban and the rural communities of a region, connecting people at the most primal level, their food. Knowing where our food is grown and produced provides us with a sense of connection to nature. A civilized existence depends on the sense of community that comes from connecting with the people who produce what we consume.

With the connection created between farmer and consumer, a deep respect for the farm and the land that produces our food becomes a part of our lives in a very personal way. Suddenly the environment and our food supply are not distant and intangible but something to care for and protect. We begin to see how interdependent we are on each other and how we are all woven into life's tapestry.

Shopping at a farm market has always been, for me, a way to ease the pace of an all too modern lifestyle. It allows me to move in a more harmonious rhythm. Farm market shopping is not an experience to race through but one to savor and relish in all its sensual nature. A farm market allows me to plan my menus around the fresh abundance of the season, ensuring that the freshest, most delicious food will find its way to my table. For me, shopping at my local market, chatting up the farmers I meet every week, is a source of inspiration and joy. I feel involved in the bigger picture of contributing to the sustainable production of food. It creates in me a reverence for the planet and those who care for it. It shows me how important it is for me to vote with my dollar, that the way I choose to spend my money on food directly affects the way food is produced. It is in the farm market that I have the unique opportunity to participate in sustaining a way of life and a way of producing food that can endure, ensuring the quality of food that I enjoy will be enjoyed by generations after me.

GO BACK TO THE KITCHEN... NOW!

To really develop a passion for food and an appreciation for its effect on our life and health, you must cook. Sorry. I know, I know, we're all so busy. And I'm asking you to go back into the kitchen, work up a sweat, get your hands dirty and cook. I'm asking that you reprioritize your life and make the space you need to nourish yourself and those you love. I'm asking you to skip some of your ever-important extra-curricular activities and go home and prepare a meal. Not a popular stance, I'm told, but one that can change your life.

You must be wondering why I put such emphasis on getting back in the kitchen. Every aspect of our lives is affected by what we choose to eat. Sound a bit dramatic? Not really. The food we choose determines how we look, how we feel, how we act and react on a daily basis. Sure, there are other influences that contribute to who we are, but food is the foundation on which we build the rest of our lives.

Let me tell you how this all began for me. I grew up in a wildly dramatic Italian household, with lots of yelling, kissing, hugging, arguing, cooking and eating. There was one room in the house where, amid the chaos that was the signature of my family, there was a joy that was tangible—yep, the kitchen. In this humble room, my mother worked her magic, seducing everyone with the perfume of nourishment. In this room, I learned about life, just by watching the activity—how people related to each other over food, how deeply food impacted each of us, how specific foods created certain moods and responses, how so much of our lives centered around nourishment.

When I was a child and teenager, my mother dragged me to farm market after farm market, sometimes driving miles from the city where we lived to the countryside so that she could get the freshest seasonal ingredients for the meals she would cook for our family. As a kid, I was frustrated by what I saw as constant lecturing about quality and freshness and how important it was to the meal. I rolled my eyes as she coaxed my hands, teaching me to discern properly ripened tomatoes, lush melons, crisp greens, the freshest corn. She taught this reluctant child not to pick fruit that was bruised or out of its season. Truthfully, I would have rather been roller-skating with my friends than wandering through rows of fruit and vegetables with my mother, listening to her talk about the importance of freshness and how valuable the farmer was to our sustenance; how it was important to choose locally grown foods, since the planet's resources weren't infinite and should not to be wasted or poisoned. We had to preserve what we had and respect the environment. She was ahead of her time with her depth of social conscience, but she created a reverence for nature in me that I have come to be eternally grateful to possess. I never had to catch up with the environmental movement; I have lived in it most of my life, following my mother to demonstrations, meetings, recycling plants and community clean-ups.

After shopping, we'd return home with our bundles and the counter would be filled with an array of stunning beauty and freshness. Even as a reluctant participant, I was always taken back by what nature provided us. Even as a kid, I was impressed with how my mother (and under her tutelage, I) could transform nature's finest ingredients into meals fit for royalty.

And so the process of cooking would begin. First the vegetables for the meal would be carefully washed, glistening in the sink in all their colorful glory. The careful slicing and dicing would create shapes and sizes that would bring each dish together. Cooking was easy, with my mother choosing only the finest oils and vinegars, spices and salt, herbs, nuts and seeds. With simplicity in mind, she relied on the exquisite natural flavors of the ingredients, with tender enhancements used only to make them sparkle. A drizzle of olive oil, a sprinkle of salt and a touch of lemon juice could change a dish from simple to sublime.

After my mother passed away, I turned my back on the kitchen, choosing a more "modern" existence away from cooking and in the world of business. Facing a health crisis that I wanted to deal with on my own terms, I decided to return to the kitchen, where, for me, life began, to see if I could regain my footing. That was almost twenty years ago and there have been many occasions where I have smiled to myself in deep gratitude to the woman who instilled such values and standards of excellence in me. As I stand over a hot stove today, completely contented to be there, I realize that she taught me the most valuable life skills—how to cook and nourish. With her influence, I had the knowledge and intuition to regain my health and rediscover my love of cooking.

In the kitchen, I changed everything about myself, curing my cancer and finding my true self, and continue to do so even today. If I feel weak or tired, I know what to do. If I feel nervous or anxious, I know what to do. You name it and there's probably a dish that can help somehow. Okay, okay, I'm not saying that everything in our lives can be cured in the kitchen, but it's a pretty good place to start. In the kitchen, we lay a foundation.

When we cook for ourselves, we decide how we'll feel every day. We decide how we'll behave, how we'll handle stress, how we'll interact with our families and friends. The kind of food we choose and prepare is the fuel that operates us. Think about it. We put superior gasoline in our cars so they'll run smoothly. But we think we can subsist on drive-through. Make sense? Not to me.

But we're busy. How do we return to the kitchen in a society that looks down its nose at the kitchen, unless of course, you're a celebrity chef, whose social status has grown akin to a rock star? I think that it's time that we see food and its preparation as something sacred and sensual. It's how we create life every day. It's hard work and we'll sweat and toil at it, but the payoff is just amazing. Imagine feeling strong and vital most of the time, happy and at peace, clear-minded and grounded, joyful at the thought of life. Can all this come from cooking? All this and more.

BUT WAIT! THERE'S MORE TO THE KITCHEN THAN A HOT STOVE

Just as there are ethics essential to the growing and producing of our food, there are ethics in the preparation and eating of our food. I know, more responsibility. As we become more aware of *what* we eat, we must become aware of *how* we eat. The ritual of coming together and breaking bread together was once the foundation of community, and remains so today. At the table, values are taught and senses heightened to the delight of the sensual experience of eating.

We no longer see ourselves as passive consumers. We are beginning to understand that our food choices help create the future and its quality. Will we create a future of chemical poisoning that destroys human and planetary health or one of sustainable, natural living? We decide with every purchase.

With the decision to live sustainably comes a deep respect for the world, nature and those we love. In that respect, we feel a need to eat together, to commune over the beauty of the food we create. When we eat together, we share in the process of the meal creation. Shared meals honor the ingredients, the cook, the farmer, the art of cooking and the people who eat them.

At the table, we reap the reward of family living. Humanistic values are learned, more than anywhere else, at the dinner table. Eating together passes on the ideas of courtesy, kindness, sharing, thrift, respect, reverence and gratitude. The shared meal is the core of civilized being, cultivating a capacity for thoughtfulness.

In modern America, over fifty percent of families no longer share meals together on a regular basis. With the advent of frozen dinners, instant food, drive-through, take-away and our growing need to be active and away from the home, sharing meals has dropped dramatically on our list of essentials.

Speed dishonors our food and us, replacing quality and joy with quantity and lack of sensitivity. It's time to recover and rediscover the joys of the shared meal, to embrace the seduction of the richness of the aromas of a food-scented kitchen. Fast food and all that it embodies threatens the fabric of our lives and well-being, poisons the environment and robs us of our health and our future.

As our children embrace the fast-food mentality of our culture, we must fight to get them back. They grow lethargic, obese and sick, with degenerative diseases growing to epidemic proportions among our young. Our greatest challenge lies in luring our children back to the table. We must teach our children the sensuality of eating, or they will settle for the mediocre and mundane in every aspect of their lives. If we awaken their senses to good, wholesome food, we can awaken their senses to the world around them. Of course, we have the challenge of advertising, which seduces our children away from the natural, toward the slick, packaged and shiny. And then there are the schools, where natural food has taken a distant back seat to processed inexpensive meals and fast-food franchises. But if we can teach our children to use their senses, to enliven their smell, taste and touch, we will see an improved ability to relate and communicate, not just about food but about everything. We can help create wiser, happier, more loving and open people.

LIVING WELL IS YOUR BEST DEFENSE

Chronobiology, or the study of natural rhythms, was pioneered in about 1931, when the first case of jetlag was diagnosed and studied. Since that discovery, scientists have widened their research to many of the body's natural rhythms. Did you know that our threshold for tooth pain is highest between one and three in the afternoon? And that our senses of taste and smell are sharpest between five and seven in the evening? Or that our skin is 100 percent more sensitive at midnight than at high noon?

Interestingly, thousands of years ago, before science and monitoring systems, India's Vedic philosophers took note of the relationship of people to outside influences like time of day, season, work, rest and eating patterns. Out of their teachings sprang Ayurveda, the knowledge of life, a philosophy of achieving natural balance for each individual based on tendencies and lifestyle.

At the same time as Ayurveda was developing, Chinese physicians were working on a more complex system, the Five Transformations of Energy, the study of yin and yang. Natural law, it is believed, governs everything, and so time of day,

season changes, sleep patterns and diet directly affect the health and behavior of each person. Strong influences in my life, these systems have been the basis of much of my work.

For instance, in both Ayurveda and Chinese medicine, it is believed that the time of day when we think most clearly is in the morning. Modern science has come to the same conclusion, identifying cortisol, the human hormone that brightens thought processes after a night of rest. The Chinese have long held the belief that high noon is the time of day for joy, laughter and activity. Interestingly, science has proven that a natural surge in seratonin (the feel-good compound in our brain) occurs at that time of day. Both systems also identify late afternoon as the time of day when fatigue will naturally occur as the body prepares itself for evening and rest. I think all of us have experienced this one; we don't need science to validate it for us.

Ancient wisdom teaches us that we are connected body and soul to nature and are subject to her whims and moods. We do not control nature, but live in her graces. If we can but reconnect with her, our intuition will guide us to a more balanced existence. Each day, people grow more aware of the connection between health and diet. In the same manner, we must embrace the idea that health is something that we create in our day-to-day lives.

Achieving glowing health is quite simple. The only tools required are a balanced diet, exercise, natural body care and a positive attitude. Understanding the power of our daily choices enables us to create the life we want to live. We must realize that when we balance our bodies with nature, we become our best selves. We are simply the sum result of the foods we choose to eat, the activities we pursue and the way we see the world around us.

We exist in an environment and how we interact with that environment contributes to the quality of life around us. It's not news that surrounding ourselves with elements of nature's purity is essential to life. Clean air to breathe, clean water to drink, cook with and bathe in, pure sunlight, lush green plant life and serene surroundings create an environment in which natural vitality is easier to achieve and maintain. We control these factors, to some degree, with our choices—how we live, play and work and impact nature. The environmental factor over which we have the most control, however, is the food we choose to eat.

I've been know to say, and do believe, that food is simply a condensed version of our larger environment and is the material that nature uses to construct our bodies. New cells, muscles, tissue, body fluids and bone are constantly being created and affected by what we choose to eat and drink. While I won't go so far as to say that we are truly the creation of what we put in our mouths every day, I will say that what we choose to eat, drink, smell, listen to and surround ourselves with are the strongest influences over who we are. Our health, our discomfort, our vitality and our disease are the end results of what we consume on every level of consumption. However, understanding how to choose and balance daily food is the essential foundation to our radiant vitality.

IT'S NOT JUST A DIET

Good, you've made it this far . . . I didn't scare you off with wild visions of having to slave over a hot stove to create health and happiness or traveling far and wide to find ingredients good enough for your table. Well, this chapter has only good news. What if I say you need never think about a "diet" again, never count another calorie? What if I tell you that it would be the greatest culinary adventure of your life, that you'd be satisfied, sated, contented and absolutely delighted with how simple, elegant and absolutely yummy your food will be? You'd laugh. You'd say, no way. Well, read on.

When I talk about eating well, I don't mean turning the experience of food into a clinical, stuffy, self-absorbed, no-fun-at-all chore. I mean dining on food that's whole and wholesome, that's so delightful to prepare and eat that you can't wait until the next meal.

I'm talking about nourishing yourself with food that's delicious and at the same time serves our body's needs to function with strength and vitality. Remember, though, food is a great source of comfort as well as the way to fuel our body's needs. I believe that in addition to serving us for basic survival, our food can also reduce the risks of disease, fortify our immune function and trigger our inherent mechanisms of healing. I believe that our food choices play a dramatic role in how we feel and how we age. I believe that food can work in the body as a powerful medicine, influencing a variety of ailments: severe, chronic and common.

I also believe, perhaps more than anything else, that food is a source of joy and passionate abandon. And while I am a proponent of whole, natural, organic food, I am not a proponent of deprivation. No wonder we hate to cook. Fanatics have taken all the fun out of it, turning our sensual kitchens into makeshift labs, where we tinker with our health, rather than nourish ourselves deeply and fully, creating our health through love.

While I personally believe that certain foods have no place in our diet, I also believe that we all need to make our own choices. My only agenda, if you will, is to provide sensible information, from my own study and experience, and let you decide for yourself. Ultimately, the only expert on you and your health is you.

WHAT IS FOOD, ANYWAY?

First, it's important to understand why we eat. Sure, it's fun and delicious, but those are just fringe benefits. Our body requires energy to function, for our organs to work properly, to think clearly—basically for the will to get out of bed in the morning. Our energy source is our food. By eating and metabolizing nutrients, our body derives fuel to work. Our food contains energy from the sun, stores it in green plants, which in turn, pass it on to fruits, animals and seeds. We eat the food, combine it with oxygen and release and use the stored solar energy. So we can conclude that to live, we need to eat.

Our bodies need nutrients from three categories of what science calls macronutrients. These three groups of food—carbohydrates, fat and protein—provide the body with all of its calorie needs. (Protein also provides elements for the growth and repair of tissue.) Our body also needs small amounts of micronutrients, vitamins, minerals and a variety of protective compounds found in plants. The roles of these three groups of food have caused more controversy than the law should

allow. And the experts, both medical and self-proclaimed, have jumped on our insecurities about nutrition and left us breathless and confused, with diet plan after diet plan designed to make us "perfect."

Before we discuss individual diets and their values, first we need to understand nutrients. The role of fat, carbohydrates and protein in our health and well-being, while sources of our strength, have also become sources of stress. Although I will take the time here to address the facts of these three macronutrients, the truth is that just a little common sense and intuition are all we really need. No more experts—wouldn't that be fun? We could just enjoy healthy, delicious food, free of anxiety. Problem is, to regain that freedom, we need to understand, so hang in there with me so you can become your own personal expert.

There seem to be very important questions to be answered surrounding these foods and their value to us. Interestingly, amid all the expert opinions, scientific data are inconclusive. Plus, there are indications that many of the prevailing ideas about conventional nutrition are up for discussion. It would seem that we still have much to learn about nutrition and its influence on our health, but there is some sensible speculation out there based on facts and common sense.

THE TRUTH ABOUT FAT

Fat is one of the most discussed and perplexing foods. Should we eat it? Should we not? The truth is, we need some fat for normal body function. But hardened, saturated fats will accumulate in various organs and tissue, clog blood vessels and inhibit body functions. With fat accumulating and hardening in various places within our system, the flow of vitalizing energy is inhibited and blocked, leaving the body hard and inflexible, among other things.

But we love fat. We love what it does for our food and its ability to satisfy our desires. Fat makes our food flavorful; it's responsible for much of the taste of food. When we refer to food as "rich" or "decadent," it's simply a primal response to its fat content. And primal it is, as our Paleolithic ancestors knew that fat was the difference between feast and famine. When they came across fat, it was party time. Why? Somewhere, deep in their intuitive nature, ancient humans knew that fat was essential to their survival.

Fat is the determining factor in satisfaction, how a food feels in our mouth, its sensuality. So many flavor components of foods, in particular spices are fat soluble, with fat as the vehicle that carries the intensity of flavor and satisfaction to our waiting taste buds. Concentrated flavor is directly linked to fat content. Think about it this way. Which idea causes shudders of delicious anticipation, bakery-baked chocolate chip cookies or a packaged low-fat imitator? See my point?

Should we eat fat or not eat fat? It's a question that has plagued modern man for as long as I can remember. With Americans becoming the fattest people on earth, we have every right to be concerned. Obesity is an epidemic that gets worse every year. Even our children are plagued by it. Not only do we eat too much in general but about half our diet comes from fat. And it's not just that we eat fat, it's the kind of fat we choose in our diets that makes the difference in our health. Here are some facts about fat that can help you decide for yourself how to incorporate this vital macronutrient into your diet appropriately.

Animals condense energy by turning glucose into fat for storage. What exactly is fat? Fat is a mixture of fatty acids, chains of carbon atoms linked together by hydrogen atoms, with a distinctive oxygen-containing group at the end of the chain. Fatty acids have more energy than carbohydrates and protein and, as a result, have more calories (almost twice, actually) than carbohydrates. I know it's complicated, but it'll mean something in a minute. Let's look at recipes. We have a bowl of brown rice, topped with crisp, steamed vegetables, a delicious, hearty, carbohydrate-rich dish that'll keep your energy on a lovely simmer. Add some baked tofu to this dish and you add protein for strength and some more calories. Now take this same bowl of brown rice and add fried tofu and tempura-style vegetables. Delicious? Absolutely. And calories? There're about twice the amount of the original brown rice and steamed vegetables. None of these dishes is better than another for us. All are tasty and good for us, but they are as different as night and day in terms of how they behave in our body. Fat gives us the most energy and delicious satisfaction and, yes, calories.

What about oils? Oils are simply liquid fats. Plants store oils in seeds, nuts and in some fruits, like olives and avocados and pretty much nowhere else. The purpose of the fats in seeds is to provide concentrated energy for growth of the embryonic seed into a mature plant. As humans, we store fat under our skin as energy stores, in anticipation of famine, to insulate our body from the weather and to cushion our delicate, vital organs.

We can make fat from glucose, so we need to understand that any food that can be broken down into glucose (sugar), can be converted into fat (but not the reverse, hence obesity). When our caloric intake is more than we expend, the fat is simply stored for later use, which turns into excess, in the form of adipose and cellulite, on our hips, tummies, thighs, upper arms. When our expenditure of energy is more than our caloric intake, the stores of glycogen (sugar) in our liver and muscles grow depleted and fat reserves are tapped for the process better known as weight loss.

Fat stored in the body, on the hips for instance, isn't used for energy as quickly as glycogen (sugar). So, to turn fat into energy to be burned for weight loss, fat is combined with oxygen, producing carbon dioxide (such as that exhaled from our lungs) and water (such as sweat and urine). This process, called *fatty acid oxidation,* happens in almost all the cells in our body, all the time, 24/7! Muscle cells are more efficient, which is why people with more muscle than fat tend to lose weight faster than those with more fat than muscle. Is all this science beginning to make some sense now? The bottom line: Muscle is a great burner of calories, even at rest. Fat cells aren't. So, having more muscle is important for weight loss. Get out those barbells!

Fat Class 101

There are three basic types of fatty acids: saturated fat, monounsaturated fat, and polyunsaturated fat. *Saturated fat,* found in animal food, margarine and hydrogenated oils, contains carbon bonds that are covered with hydrogen atoms. These are the fat molecules that our body prefers to use, so these are the fat molecules we store first. When we consume saturated fat, it's stored in our tissue and on the outside of most organs (like our heart and lungs) and as plaque in our arteries. In America, saturated fat is the main contributor to obesity, heart attack, stroke, and many other diseases and conditions. Another fatty acid, *trans-fatty acid,* is chemically similar to saturated fat but is made by "hydrogenating" or heating a polyunsaturated fat. Although similar, trans-fatty acids are far more harmful to the health than even the butter or cheese they replace in our bid for a healthier diet.

Monounsaturated fat, like that found in avocado, olive, canola, almond and peanut oils, have a molecular structure that allows them to remain more fluid or slippery than saturated fat. This lets them be burned for energy more easily. This is a better oil to use for cooking, since monounsaturated fat can't be converted to a *trans*-fatty acid by heating or cooking, unlike polyunsaturated fat.

While most foods have a blend of these three kinds of fats, only one group, *polyunsaturated fats,* is critically needed to sustain life. Polyunsaturated fat is found in flax, sunflower, sesame, safflower, soy, walnut, corn, and hempseed oils. This is where omega-3, omega-6 and omega-9 (actually a category of nonessential fatty acids, including oleic acid, which makes up 75 to 80 percent of olive oil) are found, those "essential" fatty acids required by the body.

Essential Fatty Acids

What are essential fatty acids? Sometimes called "the good fats," these are the two polyunsaturated fatty acids that must come from our diet, as our body cannot manufacture them. They are omega-3 (alpha-linolenic acid) and omega-6 (linoleic acid).

A derivative of linoleic acid is gamma-linolenic acid (GLA). Good sources of GLA include hempseed and hempseed oil, blue green algae, spirulina, evening primrose oil, black currant seed oil, borage oil and some fungal oils. Research has shown GLA to alleviate symptoms of psoriasis, atopic eczema and mastalgia. It has also been under investigation for its beneficial effects on cardiovascular, psychiatric and immunological disorders.

Essential fatty acids are the raw materials for the cells and are needed for all of the body's functions. Essential fatty acids are vital to the long-term maintenance of healthy human tissue, promoting the healthy function of our brain, heart, digestive and immune systems. The ideal balance of these essential fats is one key to our health. The recommended ratio, three parts omega-6 to one part omega-3, is not as easy to obtain as it sounds.

Omega-6 is very common, found in most foods from meat and dairy products to nuts and seeds. We really have no problem getting enough omega-6 in our diet, unless of course we are eating a low-fat diet. Omega-6 is needed for blood clotting, proper circulation, healthy kidney and liver function and proper healing of internal injury. A deficiency in omega-6 can result in increased blood pressure and cholesterol levels, hardening of the arteries and artery obstruction, arthritis, poor circulation, premenstrual syndrome, reduced sperm production, slow growth and wound healing and a variety of skin disorders. However, because it's abundantly found in most people's diets, there isn't much worry about getting it. Most American diets have too much omega-6 and too little omega-3, throwing off the delicate balance necessary to health.

Omega-3 is a fatty acid not as easy to get. Found only in fish and some vegetables, nuts and seeds, the effects of omega-3 deficiencies are becoming an epidemic in our modern world. Although we need only small amounts of this powerful essential fat, it is responsible for all vital body functions, including the fluidity of our blood, increased immune function, balance of cholesterol production, proper growth, fetal development, mental acuity and cell renewal. A deficiency of omega-3 can cause such problems as arrhythmia, asthma, arteriosclerosis, attention deficit disorder, bipolar disorder, breast cancer, colon cancer, diabetes, hypertension, inflammation, immune disorder, migraine headaches, obesity, prostate cancer and psoriasis, to name but a few!

Fat-free and low-fat diets further reduce the amount of omega-3, making us feel hungry and deprived. We might binge on high-calorie foods to compensate for the deficiency of fat and omega-3, and eating less fat inhibits the absorption of fat-soluble nutrients (including vitamins A, D, E and K). But a diet high in omega-3 can result in softer skin and stronger hair, natural weight loss, improved memory, improved vision, faster wound healing, more energy, improved vitality, and more.

Just about everyone is aware that a diet high in saturated fats, like those found in meat, dairy foods and hydrogenated oils, causes plaque in the arteries, reduces blood flow, and increases the risk of heart attack and stroke. If a polyunsaturated fat has been hydrogenated or partially hydrogenated, the oil becomes a trans-fat and will not have the benefits to our health of the essential fatty acids, plus it is seen by our body as a saturated fat. All in all, a waste of a good polyunsaturated fat, I'd say.

Essential fatty acids make blood platelets less sticky, so they don't cause hardening of the arteries, like trans-fat and saturated fat. Essential fatty acids are too important to the body to be used for mere energy storage, like the other fats. It would seem that there's only good news here! The building blocks for all of the body's biochemicals, including hormones and prostaglandins, are essential fatty acids. They also help carry toxins from the skin, kidneys, lungs and intestinal tract and create energy within the cells by delivering oxygen from red blood cells.

Essential fatty acids are made into the hormone prostaglandin, which controls cholesterol production and blood platelet aggregation. As the different prostaglandins made from the different essential fatty acids often have opposite effects in the body, their delicate balance is best obtained from a source closest to the three to one omega-6 to omega-3 ratio.

So how do we get these essential fatty acids in our diet? As I mentioned earlier, omega-6 isn't much of a problem to get, but omega-3 is. In addition, it's important that we eat the proper balance of these two fats. Coldwater fish, and especially salmon, are rich in both essential fatty acids but in particular the illusive omega-3. But as the controversy around fish continues to grow, it needs to be rethought. Our oceans and rivers grow more polluted, and the toxins from the water can be found in the fatty flesh of the fish. Fish is increasingly farm raised, with diminished levels of the omega-3 we desperately need.

For vegetarians and vegans, sources of omega-3 are even scarcer. With small amounts in avocados, walnuts and pumpkin seeds, many have looked to flax oil, flaxseed and other supplements. However, that's changing. For the last several years, there has been a slow resurgence of the ancient food hempseed, which supplies as much as 20 percent of the recommended amount of omega-3 and in the optimal three to one ratio to omega-6 for best health. High in complete protein and amino acids, this super plant food has become the primary source of essential fatty acids in my diet. Delicious, easy to use and completely versatile (which you'll see in a variety of the recipes in this book), hempseed and hempseed oil can help us obtain the fats essential to our good health and vitality.

Whether or not you grasp the science of fat, it's easy to see that without good fat in our diet, good health is more difficult to come by. With less fat having a regular place at our tables, the body has difficulty absorbing fat-soluble nutrients so vital to good health, such as vitamin D and calcium. So don't be so quick to adopt the latest no-fat craze; instead educate yourself on the type of fat you choose and what you need for your lifestyle, and discover for yourself the key to good health and vitality.

AND THEN THERE'S PROTEIN

Too little protein? Sure, we've all seen it, but only in advertisements for aid for Third World countries. However, for most of us, our problems with health and appearance come from too much protein, rarely too little.

As adults, our primary requirement for nutrition is fuel to carry us through our lives, with the secondary job of forming and maintaining cells, which is one of the primary jobs of nutrients in children. In general terms, complex carbohydrates are the fuel and protein is used to repair, construct and maintain tissue. It would seem sensible to conclude, then, that most of us require more carbohydrate energy than protein energy to maintain our vitality through our days. In our modern way of eating, however, protein has become an obsession, with carbohydrates being neglected, diminished and even feared.

Here's the deal with protein, as I understand it. We require it for strength and for the maintenance of our muscles. Without sufficient protein, we can grow weak and become overly thin, because our body will begin to feed on its own muscle for maintenance and strength. The question is how much protein is enough and when is it too much? Interestingly, with all we know of nutrition, we are still perplexed by protein and how much we require. We have no explanation, for instance, as to why people need different amounts to be vital and healthy. Why do some of us need protein at both lunch and dinner to maintain our energy level, while others will feel sluggish and dull all afternoon after a protein lunch? It seems that protein is quite personal and that to determine what we need, we must look at our lifestyle, activity level and needs. Only then can we figure out what we need to stay healthy, vital and strong.

We all know that protein is important to our nutrition and maintenance of our vitality. We've been hammered with information about it. As with everything in nature, though, there is a front and back to the miracle of protein. For instance, compared to carbohydrates, protein is inefficient as a fuel, making our body toil to assimilate it and utilize the nutrients in it. High-protein diets are so incredibly effective for quick weight loss for just this reason. But before you run out for a big, juicy steak, read on. Our body kicks into high gear and burns tremendous amounts of resources to break down the density of protein-rich foods. I suppose as a quick fix for weight loss, there is actually some logic here, but the reality of the situation is that protein, in large quantities, can have negative long-term effects on our health. So what about high-protein diet plans? Hang on, we'll get to that subject.

Meats and other animal products, the most popular source of protein in our modern culture, are highly unstable. They decompose rapidly, becoming toxic, with a virtual plethora of poisons being created in our body as a result. From uric acid to ammonia to sulfates, animal protein can create an internal environment not unlike a toxic waste dump. The kidneys and intestines, our body's key organs for discharge of waste, are overworked and exhausted, growing too weak to do their job effectively. The result? Toxins build up in the bloodstream and in various organs and tissue, leaving us depleted and tired, with sluggish circulation and clogged arteries.

It only gets worse with animal food. As animal protein and fat harden in the body, a layer of saturated fat builds up under the surface of the skin, clogging the pores, inhibiting waste release and blocking moisture intake. As a result, our skin hardens and wrinkles, starved for moisture. As this toxic buildup of fat and waste continues in its accumulation, our skin dries and toughens and we age far more quickly than we might otherwise.

The downside of excessive protein consumption, especially animal protein, can have an even darker side, especially when it comes to the health of our bones and their calcium content. The more protein we eat, the more calcium the body will use in the digestion process. As more protein is consumed, more calcium is taken from the bones. The more calcium we lose to this process, the thinner and weaker our bones become, with the risk of osteoporosis rising. In a culture in which we consume so much protein, we are plagued by calcium deficiencies. We supplement our diet with more and more milligrams of precious calcium, yet it seems to no avail. Studies have shown that women consuming a vegetarian or, even better, vegan diet demonstrate far less bone degeneration than women consuming more protein. Ironically, as simplistic as it sounds, if we would simply cut back our intake of animal protein, we wouldn't require such dramatic supplementation of calcium, simply because we wouldn't lose as much. Our bodies would make a natural balance and our bones would be healthy for our entire lifetime.

But where to get the protein we all crave, especially as a vegetarian or vegan? For starters, did you know that there is protein in almost everything you eat, except fruit? And did you know that plants are the original source of protein on the planet? Think about it. Cows eat grass.

So what's a tree hugger to do? I can tell you from my own experience, abstaining from animal food for over twenty years, life goes on without meat, poultry, eggs, dairy or fish—and deliciously, I might add. With so many varieties of beans to choose from, tofu and tempeh, as well as hempseed (31 percent complete protein), I never lack protein sources that are varied and satisfying. And the payoff? Enjoying a happy and healthy existence. How does that sound? A woman once approached me after a cooking class and announced that she had been eating a vegetarian diet for two months and that the only way she could describe how she felt, was "light inside." She had never felt better, had more energy, slept more soundly or had more patience for life. You decide—drive-through food, steaks, burgers, bone loss, lethargy, obesity and heart disease or fresh delicious food that leaves you vital and happy?

WHICH BRINGS US TO CARBOHYDRATES…

I don't think I've seen anything that can create as much terror in people since *The Exorcist*. The thought of carbohydrates can send people from the room screaming. I often wonder how something that used to be referred to as the "staff of life" has grown to be so misunderstood.

Perhaps you should run screaming from white flour, white sugar, white bread and white rice. Highly refined carbohydrate sources are responsible for many health problems, from obesity to diabetes. The carbohydrates that I want to discuss are those from whole grain sources.

There are anticarbohydrate advocates who will tell us that all the ills we suffer today—cancer, obesity, diabetes and heart disease—are a result of carbohydrates. They wax rhapsodic about the Paleolithic diet, one of wild game, fish and some fruit and seeds, as optimal. They will tell us that the cultivation of cereal grain, the advent of agriculture was the beginning of the end of our health.

(Come to think of it, in terms of pollution from commercial agribusiness, they might not be far from the truth, but it has little to do with grain.)

Here's their reasoning. With the cultivation of grain and then of starchy tubers and roots, large quantities of carbohydrates were introduced into our diet on a regular basis. Before that, starch and its resulting sugar were taken in only occasionally, through the use of wild honeycomb, fruit and nuts. This diet change caused the pancreas to work harder than it had in the past to manage the glucose levels of the bloodstream. High levels of glucose, remaining in the blood for too long, can be toxic and must be cleared to avoid trouble.

Which brings us to insulin, the hormone charged with the primary job of transporting glucose from our blood to our cells. In addition, insulin has the secondary responsibility of storing calories as fat. Imbalances of insulin can also promote arterial damage and even encourage the growth of tumors. In some people, frequent releases of insulin can cause them to become insulin resistant. Insulin resistance has been associated with obesity, abnormal blood fats, high blood pressure, adult-onset diabetes and cardiovascular disease.

So you're thinking, they're right. We must be nuts to eat carbohydrates. I'm not through yet. Life-sustaining, satisfying carbohydrates do, indeed, have a place on our tables and in our bodies, but like other foods, understanding is the key to deciding how, why and what to choose.

One tool that has become valuable (and much misunderstood) is the glycemic index, a way to measure the effects of various carbohydrate foods on our blood glucose. The logic is that the higher the glycemic index, the faster the glucose level will rise in our blood, which means a stronger insulin response. The conclusion is that high glycemic index foods increase our exposure to the harmful effects of excess glucose far more than low glycemic index foods.

Where we have gone awry in our understanding of carbohydrates and their effect on our health is by assuming that high glycemic index foods are bad for our health and low glycemic index foods are better. Nothing could be further from the truth. The chemical makeup of the carbohydrate food is a large determining factor. Our body is tremendously efficient at assimilating and using glucose, our preferred fuel, but we don't handle fructose (the common simple sugar in fruit and honey) very well. Even though fructose has a relatively low glycemic index, we just don't use it well.

More important, however, is that we have taken the glycemic index at face value and lumped all carbohydrates into the same category. We rarely eat just carbohydrates as an entire meal. We tend to eat them as a part of a meal and that dramatically affects how the carbohydrate food affects our blood chemistry. Fat, fiber, protein and other nutrients that would be present in a meal all change the effects of carbohydrates on our blood chemistry.

So do we need to chart every meal with tables and calculators to balance our blood? Don't be silly. By simply eating a wide and varied diet, with carbohydrates sensibly balanced with protein and fat to suit our personal needs, we can relax and enjoy delicious whole meals that nourish us body and soul.

What to do about carbohydrates? It's important to pay attention to the the quality as well as the quantity that we consume. The problem with carbohydrate foods is not that we eat them but that the quality of them has declined rapidly in our modern mode of eating. Refined and processed carbohydrates serve no purpose save turning into fat in our systems. Think about the carbohydrates of our grandparents' days. Whole grains, gruels and porridges and dark, hearty breads were common fare, rounded out nicely with vegetables and beans and, if they could afford it, some meat.

To maintain our health, some carbohydrate foods are essential. These macronutrient foods are a source of efficient fuel, using fewer of our precious resources to break them into energy. Balanced properly with other nutrients, they keep our burners on simmer, ensuring that we have energy to draw on when we need it.

For me the choices are obvious, and varied. I don't eat just brown rice every day. Choosing from the many whole grains and whole grain products that nature provides us, we can maintain a balanced diet and state of health. Brown rice, millet, barley, quinoa, teff, corn, oats, wheat, rye, spelt, kamut, whole wheat pasta and whole grain breads are in my pantry all the time, so that I always have a variety of complex carbohydrate foods to choose from to round out my meals.

Ah, Sugar

There's a lot of controversy about sugar and because we're talking carbohydrates, we might just as well talk sugar. Simple sugars, from those sparkling little crystals, to fruit and juices, are simple carbohydrates, composed of loosely bound molecules of glucose, unlike complex carbohydrates, composed of tightly bound chains of glucose molecules. The difference in our bodies is like night and day and the difficulty lies in the amount of simple carbohydrates that we consume versus the amount of complex carbohydrates.

Sugar is found in all the obvious places, candies, chocolate bars, soft drinks and other snack foods. While you may say that these foods don't have a place in your diet, just try reading a few labels. Sugar is an ingredient in so many products, from breads and pasta to cereals to salad dressings and sauces and other processed foods, that we are consuming tremendous amounts of simple, refined sugar unconsciously. And if you think shopping in a natural foods store is your salvation, think again; in most cases, you'll need to read labels as diligently as you do in any supermarket. From maple syrup, high fructose corn syrup, fructose, sucrose, molasses, honey and organic cane juice (which is just a fancy name for sugar), many natural products contain as much simple sugar as any snack you can pick up in your local convenience store.

The molecular structure of simple sugar causes it to be rapidly absorbed into the bloodstream, causing the glucose level to rise very quickly. When this happens, the pancreas (the organ that regulates blood sugar) secretes insulin that moves excess sugar from the blood to the cells. With this, blood sugar drops, resulting in rapid fluctuations in metabolism. We know this sensation as sugar "highs" and "lows," as the levels of glucose in the blood rise and fall erratically. We experience a burst of energy as the levels of glucose rise, followed by the inevitable crash, as the glucose levels drop, leaving us feeling depleted and tired.

Over time, with this pattern continuing, our body becomes exhausted from the extreme changes in energy levels. Is sugar all bad? While not a fan of refined white sugar and all of its counterparts, I sometimes wonder if all the fuss about sweet taste doesn't stem from the fact that we love it so much, so it must be bad for us. Of course, we consume far too many sweets, which is truly a problem, especially for our children. The problem lies more with the technology of sugar than sugar itself. The fact that it has made its way into so many foods, at such a concentrated level has made sugar a problem. Sugar makes food taste great, but at what cost to our health and well-being?

We are born with a natural attraction to sweet tastes, with our affinity or aversion to other tastes developing through our cultural conditioning. In Asia, the Five Transformations of Energy define five flavors, that when in balance, create health. Those five flavors are sweet, spicy/pungent, salty, sour and bitter. In Chinese medicine, it's said that sweet taste will predominate but the others are vital to round out our health; the most important one is bitter taste. They say that without bitter, we crave sweet taste in excess. Most of us, with the exception of Italians, who thrive on bitter greens and bitter aperitifs, have an aversion to bitter flavor, driving us to sweets more and more. What's that old saying? Without the bitter, the sweet just isn't as sweet.

With few exceptions, it's important to understand that in terms of the glycemic index, most natural sugars are the same. It doesn't matter if it's honey, fruit, fruit juice, maple syrup, molasses or organic cane juice, your blood sugar will react almost the same to any of these simple sugars. Of course, with honey, you also get the benefit of antioxidants and some minerals and with fruit there are some vitamins and precious fiber, but your reaction to the sugar will be virtually the same.

The exceptions to the sugar dilemma come in the form of whole grain sweeteners, barley malt, wheat malt and my personal favorite, brown rice syrup. Made by cooking sprouted grains until they form syrups, the complex carbohydrates in the whole grains remain largely intact. What this means to us is that we get to have our cake and eat it too. We get a delicious sweet taste with less drama for our blood chemistry. So relax. You're not doomed to grim endurance of a life of good health with no fun. I use these grain sweeteners in every form of dessert, from puddings and custards to cookies, pies and cakes, all with wonderful results. Life has never been sweeter.

DAIRY FOODS

We see them everywhere, beautiful, milk-mustached people in ads telling us how wonderful life will be if we drink it. In my opinion, milk should be placed on the official hazardous food list with its own surgeon general's warning.

Milk is considered to be the perfect food, rich in calcium and protein. We even made it into a food group. Many experts now question the wisdom of this thinking. Studies are beginning to show that dairy food is instrumental in causing compromised immune function, allergies, brittle bones, obesity, a variety of reproductive disorders and early onset of puberty.

Mother's milk is our first food, imprinting on us the characteristics and behavior patterns that make us who we are. Does milk contain all the nutrients vital to life? Yes. Species create the perfect milk for their young—*their* young. We are the only species that drinks the milk of another after weaning, with the exception of domesticated animals.

The problems associated with drinking whole milk after infancy reads like a laundry list. Saturated fat and cholesterol in milk clog arteries, contributing to heart disease. The basic milk molecule, casein, is dense, stressing the liver, pancreas, stomach and intestines in the milk drinker. To combat udder infection, commercial dairy cows are fed antibiotics, which in turn attack the flora and villi in the intestines of the consumer, contributing to digestive trouble, just the way secondhand smoke affects the lungs of nonsmokers. The estrogen being fed to commercial dairy cows has been directly linked to breast and prostate cancer.

Commercial dairy cows are pushed to produce more milk than is natural and are fed hormones, including estrogen, prolactin and progesterone. In a recent study, it was concluded that the onset of puberty, as early as age ten, is caused by excessive amounts of hormones that children are ingesting in meat and dairy foods. Our children are having children because their bodies are ready too soon. What about organic milk? Isn't it better? Of course it is. At the very least, we aren't taking in antibiotics, herbicides, pesticides and hormones, but it's still milk; and even without additives, it is the root of many problems, including osteoporosis. It's not a natural food for mature adults to be consuming. It's for babies, to help them mature and grow.

What about calcium? Milk is loaded with it, but it doesn't do us much good. The calcium present in dairy is bonded to casein and, although abundant, is largely unavailable to us, since milk lacks magnesium, potassium and vitamin D, unless artificially enriched with these added nutrients.

There's more to it than calcium. Milk protein is dense, designed to build a huge, heavy animal that matures quickly and is difficult to digest. Animal proteins cause a greater excretion of urea from the kidneys, depleting the body of calcium, magnesium and potassium. The excessive intake of protein causes the blood to become highly acidic. The body relies on serum calcium in the blood to balance that acid, depleting our store of calcium and creating need for supplementation to replenish our loss.

By removing the fat to make skim or nonfat milk, you concentrate the proteins and remove the very component needed for assimilation—fat. By removing the fat, we inhibit our body's ability to assimilate vitamin D, which is vital to our utilization of calcium. Does a body good? Don't be too sure. Lactose intolerance is the least of our worries with milk.

So is there life without dairy? Yes, a healthy one. By reducing animal fats and choosing plant foods, especially dark leafy greens, broccoli, beans, nuts, seeds and soyfoods, including tofu and soymilk with calcium, we can create a diet rich in calcium that is usable, with protein and fat that nourishes rather than weakens us. Interestingly, studies show that in dairy-reliant women and cultures in which dairy products are a major food source, osteoporosis and other degenerative diseases have become epidemic. Coincidence? Not likely.

Although ingrained in our culinary history, dairy foods have no regular place in our diets; and in the final analysis, you will only understand the effect dairy has had on your health by eliminating it and experiencing the difference in your daily well-being.

A SPRINKLE A DAY

For most of us, salt is as confusing and trying as any other vital nutrient. How did we become so neurotic about our food? While a necessary ingredient to life, salt has two very different sides to its nature. Vital to our existence, natural sea salt is rich in trace minerals and sodium chloride, which maintain the health of our blood. Then there's processed, refined salt—the kind found in commercial table salt, snack foods (like potato chips, popcorn and salted nuts) as well as processed foods and meats. Far removed from its natural state in the sea, commercial salt has been stripped of nutrients, reenriched and laced through with chemicals and preservatives. Eaten or used in this state, even small amounts of salt will have a most dramatic effect on our blood chemistry and overall health.

Salt has a specific purpose in the cooking and enjoyment of food. We use it so that foods taste like themselves. This is why we miss salt so much when it's absent. Specifically, salt causes contraction, so in food and cooking, it seals in the flavor (and nutrients) of each ingredient, while squeezing the magnificent juices from the food, enhancing the taste. In our body, consumption of natural sea salt, in appropriate quantities in cooking, aids the body in staying strong, as our muscles and body tissue contract slightly.

There is a downside to salt and it use, however. Commercial salt, and even natural sea salt can have a dramatic effect on how we feel and look if used inappropriately. Excessive use of salt or poor-quality commercial salt will cause tissues in our body to tighten and constrict, inhibiting the flow of blood to our various organs. Our energy flow can become blocked and we begin to feel tightening throughout the body. Our muscles begin to contract, growing stiff and hard. Our skin dries, tightens and wrinkles. Our blood pressure can rise, as blood vessels constrict. Our joints grow stiff and immoveable. Our hair dries and loses its color. We will also see, over time, signs of degeneration in our bones, as the salt dries the body, inhibiting the absorption of vitamins essential to bone health and strength.

So do we employ salt or not? Moderate use of natural salt in cooking, not only adds to the pleasure of eating food but helps start the process of digestion. Salt causes the food to soften as we apply the heat of cooking. Natural, unrefined sea salt, naturally aged soy sauce and naturally fermented miso are your best choices for salt flavors.

One old rule holds true: no sprinkling of salt or soy sauce on cooked food at the table. All you'll taste is salt, as it hasn't had a chance to be assimilated into the food. Over time, the use of added salt can cause cravings for sugar, excessive amounts of fluid and more food than we need, as our body tries to relax the tension created by the salt. However, used delicately in cooking, salt makes eating a pleasure and our bodies strong and vital.

JUNK FOOD, AT LEAST THEY NAMED IT CORRECTLY...

Not long ago, our meals were centered around foods that were seasonal, naturally processed and whole. Our diet was easier on our bodies, with few artificial ingredients and additives that made food difficult to digest and utilize. Sadly, our modern culture has replaced fresh, vital foods with processed, refined versions. While these foods may be easy on our lifestyle, they're murder on our health. They, too, should carry a surgeon general's warning.

Processed foods have been stripped of the light of the sun, the kiss of the breeze, the refreshment of natural water and the nourishment of the soil. We eat them and our bodies may receive the vitamins, protein and carbohydrates, but these kinds of foods—canned, processed, refined, frozen—are devoid of the life energy that sustains us. How can life flow through us, when the food we eat has been stripped of its very essence? Eating foods like these leave us looking and feeling as stale as they are, dull and lifeless, with lethargic energy.

Processed foods also leave us hungry, starving, in fact. When we eat foods devoid of life, we are left dissatisfied with our meals for a very specific reason. We eat for life and so we need food that is alive to nourish ourselves. When we eat dead food, animals, canned vegetables, processed foods, foods stripped of their natural nutrients, we are eating food devoid of what is most essential to us, life. Not sated, we look for more and more food. Everything we eat is "super-size" to fill the void. This cycle continues: We eat more and more quantity, with less and less satisfaction. The result is obvious. The more refined foods we eat, the more calories we consume, the heavier we get. We're starving ourselves to obesity.

When we eat fresh food, elegantly and simply prepared, the vitality comes through. We are almost overwhelmed by the symphony of flavors that nature provides for our nourishment. Each bite reminds us of the wonder of our world and we are satisfied quite easily. Can you even imagine finishing dinner and being so content that your head isn't in the refrigerator an hour later, looking for something to satisfy that deep well of desire that never seems to be filled? We sleep more soundly and wake refreshed, with the energy we need to carry on effectively throughout the day.

So recognize junk food and fast food for what they are, the fastest and most efficient way to gain weight and lose your health.

WEIGHT A MINUTE

You know, I'm always fascinated by the latest diet crazes that sweep the nation. *Craze* is the operative word for me. Each one seems nuttier than the one that precedes it. And we fall for them all. We want desperately to lose weight—now—with no effort, sacrifice or change to our lifestyle and eating habits. We buy book after book, choke down powders and pills and potions, all in an attempt to find that one magic bullet to do the job. Well, the next time one of these "miracle diets" comes along, read the fine print. You know the disclaimers by heart, "results not typical" or "when combined with a sensible diet and exercise." When will we stop being so gullible? Education is the key, just like anything else. Let's take a look at the most popular diets that guarantee you results for life.

High-Protein Diets

First let's look at high-protein diets. The first known diet book was published in 1864 by an English casket-maker, William Banting. He knew he needed a change when he could no longer tie his shoes and had gotten so fat he had to walk down the stairs backward. His book, *Letter of Corpulence*, called for low-carbohydrate foods and a daily portion of alcohol and sold fifty-eight thousand copies. In 1961 Herman Taller wrote *Calories Don't Count,* which was against the intake of carbohydrates and sugar and sold two million copies. Then in 1967, Irwin Stillman published *The Quick Weight-Loss Diet* and sold twenty million copies of his version of a high-protein, low-carbohydrate diet. In 1972 Robert Atkins published his first version of this diet, *The Diet Revolution*. In 1978 *The Scarsdale Diet* became a national best-seller, advocating a 700-calorie-a-day, high-protein diet. In 1992 Dr. Atkins reissued his book as *The New Diet Revolution*, again a best-seller and the most popular of the ketogenic diet plans. Other currently popular high-protein, nonketogenic diets such as *The Carbohydrate Addicts Diet, Sugar Busters!, Enter the Zone, The Schwarzheim Principle, Suzanne Somers' Get Skinny on Fabulous Food, Protein Power*, and *Healthy for Life* simply restrict your caloric intake through various convoluted rules based on little or no science.

Medical doctors and diet gurus are touting the glories of high-protein and fat-laden diets and are grabbing the attention of millions of desperate dieters. The truth about these types of fad "diets" is that people can temporarily lose large amounts of weight and can even lower their blood cholesterol, blood sugar and triglycerides, but the method is unhealthy on a long-term basis, to say the least.

Before we name names and call a spade a spade, let's talk about high-protein diets in general, with the focus on what effects these kinds of foods can have on our overall health.

The foods recommended for a high-protein diet are mainly meat, eggs, and dairy products, which are high in cholesterol, fat, and animal protein. These foods are deficient in dietary fiber and carbohydrates, are often contaminated with chemicals and microbes and have serious vitamin and mineral imbalances.

In 1988 *Nutrition and Health in the United States,* published under the direction of Surgeon General C. Everett Koop, put to rest all controversy (or so we hoped) concerning whether or not diet is fundamental in the cause, prevention and treatment of common diseases. The main conclusion of the report was that excessive consumption of certain foods was a major concern for Americans. While many foods are involved, chief among them was the disproportionate consumption of foods high in fats and protein, often minimizing foods high in complex carbohydrates and fiber that may be more conducive to health.

Recommendations to eat fewer animal products and more plant foods have been made by just about every health organization, including the American Heart Association, the American Cancer Society, The Diabetic Association, and the American Dietetic Association. All of these respected organizations agree, to some degree, that many of the chronic illnesses plaguing modern Western society are caused by an unhealthy diet and lifestyle and that improved and maintained health comes from eating fewer animal products and a more plant-based diet.

Among the diseases believed to be caused by meats, eggs, and dairy products include most cases of obesity; heart diseases; adult on-set diabetes; breast, colon and prostate cancer; gallbladder disease; osteoporosis; kidney failure; kidney stones; multiple sclerosis; rheumatoid arthritis; constipation; diverticulosis; hemorrhoids and hiatal hernias. You don't have to be a rocket scientist to see that the risk of becoming sick increases as our intake of these foods is increased . . . as they are, on high-protein diets.

Among other things, high-protein diets cause serious metabolic changes that lead to bone loss and kidney stones. Red meat, poultry, fish, shellfish and eggs tend to be more acidic in structure. Plant foods are alkaline by nature. Our body fiercely guards its acid–alkaline balance (pH) so all of our pH-driven biochemical functions take place smoothly. The acid overload that results from high-protein animal foods must be somehow buffered. The primary buffer? The bones. They literally dissolve into phosphates and calcium for just this purpose. This is the first step in the loss of bone density that leads to osteoporosis. The second step consists of altered kidney physiology caused by the acid, increasing the acid load, resulting in the loss of substantial quantities of bone material, including calcium into the urine. The presence of this bone material in our kidneys also lays the foundation for calcium-based kidney stones. Getting the picture on high protein yet?

So let's take a look at what these high-protein experts are saying and what it all really means. We'll travel to the Zone, break the Carbohydrate Addicts' addiction, discover the connection between our blood type and our food choices and see what's so revolutionary about Dr. Atkins's approach to health.

Two kinds of high-protein diets are popular today: ones that limit calorie intake by causing our body to move into a toxic metabolic state known as *ketosis,* and ones that impose stringent rules that limit our intake of food.

The first type of high-protein diet, known as a "ketogenic diet," like Dr. Atkins's *The Diet Revolution*, causes our body to produce ketones (acidic by-products of metabolism) by severely restricting the intake of carbohydrates, while allowing for the unlimited consumption of fat and protein. With an insufficient intake of its primary fuel, carbohydrates, our body turns to the fat from food as well as body fat for its energy source. The resulting condition is known as ketosis, a toxic state associated with loss of appetite, nausea, fatigue, and low blood pressure. The obvious result is a decrease in food (calorie) intake. Therefore, ketosis is the key to the diet's success; our body starves while reducing the suffering of severe hunger pangs. This same condition, ketosis, occurs naturally when people are starving to death or seriously ill. When starving, this state is nature's blessing, because the victim notices dramatically reduced hunger pains while dying. During a life-threatening illness, appetite suppression allows us to rest rather then be forced by hunger to worry about food and its preparation. On top of this, these diets contain significant amounts of the very foods, meat, eggs, poultry, dairy, saturated fats, that most nutrition experts tell us contribute dramatically to our most common causes of death and disability.

Why does this version of the high-protein diet work? The initial weight loss is rapid (and elating for the desperate dieter). However, most of the initial weight loss is water loss, rather than fat loss. With reduced stores of carbohydrate in the diet, our body resorts to using its glycogen stores of glucose. Glycogen, which we store in our liver and muscles, can meet our glucose needs for 12 to 18 hours. With each gram of glycogen is stored 2.7 grams of water. An average body stores 300 grams of glycogen. Depletion of our glycogen stores will result in an almost overnight weight loss of 3 pounds. Combined with the strong diuretic effect caused by the ketones, you're looking at the quick and dramatic weight loss that's so seductive when you're desperate.

The drama grows. People who somehow manage to remain on high-protein diets also lose weight because the restriction of carbohydrate calories—like those in fruits, vegetables, breads, pasta, cereals, and beans—eliminates so many foods from their diet, they have no choice but to reduce their calorie intake. This negative calorie balance will naturally result in weight loss. Once again, no magic potion, no magic pill, just calories in versus calories out, but with a high price tag on health. As they reach their ideal weight, dieters add some carbohydrate calories back into their meals, but should their weight begin to creep up (as it naturally will, since they're adding calories), it's right back to the restricted diet. Is this method of weight maintenance sustainable? You decide.

The second style of high-protein diets uses strict rules for choosing foods to limit calorie intake. *Enter the Zone* asks that you limit your protein intake to about 100 grams a day. You then distribute the rest of the calories as 30 percent protein, 30 percent fat, and 40 percent carbohydrate. Following this plan an average man would be eating about 1,300 calories a day, when he actually needs 2,300 calories a day to maintain his energy. The book tells us that we won't feel hungry because this diet plan puts us in "the Zone" of properly balanced insulin levels. I suggest you give it a go and see just how hungry you are.

Enter the Zone claims, among other things, that the problem with our weight and health, specifically heart disease, is that diets that are rich in carbohydrate calories promote excessive production of specific hormones—insulin and "bad" eicosanoids (our body's superhormones). The book claims that the secret to weight loss and preventing heart disease is keeping these hormones in a narrow range, known as the Zone. We do this by adding more protein to our diet than is normally consumed or recommended, a whopping 30 percent versus the usual 12 to 15 percent. And, of course, suckers for marketing that we are, we love hearing that there's magic; we enter the Zone, which mysteriously tricks our body into losing ugly fat without giving up the foods we love or, heaven forbid, having to exercise. We also like hearing that being fat just isn't our fault. It's our hormones. We have no need to shift from gluttony to sensible eating. We can remain couch potatoes and look like Adonis.

Here's why this type of diet works but also why it is nearly impossible to sustain for a lifetime. The Zone diet translates into 400 calories of protein (1 gram of protein = 4 calories). Because the proportions of the diet are 30/30/40, this means that we should also consume 400 calories of fat and about 500 calories of carbohydrate, for a total of 1,300 calories per day. Conservative estimates of average caloric needs are over 2,300 calories a day, and that's with only sedentary activity. Every day our average man is on the diet, he is about 1,000 calories short of his needs. Take away that many calories from a diet, and you lose weight. So why all the double talk? Why not just tell us that the truth hasn't changed, you need to eat less to lose weight? Why to sell books, of course.

Like all calorie-restricted diets, the Zone diet is next to impossible to sustain because it hurts to be hungry. I also find the rules to be impossibly complicated and the recommended foods to be unappealing—and, as a vegetarian, I am without resources to enter the Zone. The book claims that a vegetarian diet is as far as you can get from the Zone . . . one step farther than if you ate nothing but Snickers bars, to be precise.

Interestingly, every scientific diet study published points to the health and longevity of vegetarian cultures, while a diet centered around beef, pork, poultry, lamb, eggs, bacon, shrimp, lobster and dairy foods has been linked to just about every degenerative disease known. The author of *Enter the Zone* has yet to publish a single diet study of his own.

While many high-protein diets make nonsensical claims about health maintenance, here are the most common and dangerous.

They say eating fat doesn't make you fat. The thinking is that we're consuming less fat than we did ten years ago and are still getting fatter, so dietary fat must not be to blame. The truth is that we're consuming just a little more fat now than before. In addition, we consume, on average, over 250 more calories of refined flours and sugars than we did fifteen years ago. Because of the added refined carbohydrates, the percentage of fat in the American diet may have been reduced between 1980 and 1990 (a drop for men from 38 to 34 percent, for women from 37 to 34 percent), but the actual grams or amount of fat consumed has remained the same (men 99.8 vs. 98.8 grams, women 62.6 vs. 67.8 grams). On top of that, we Americans eat more calories than we need (men 2,457 to 2,684, women 1,531 to 1,805). The reason for the rise in obesity is no mystery—Americans eat a high-calorie, high-fat diet and do not get enough exercise.

Another myth put about by high-protein diet gurus is that a carbohydrate-rich diet can be dangerous to cardiovascular patients. They tell us that experiments have shown that high carbohydrate diets increase the risk factors for heart disease by raising cholesterol and triglycerides and lowering HDL cholesterol. In studies in which the subjects eat refined carbohydrates and are overfed, the triglycerides do go up. When subjects ate only until they were full (not overfed) cholesterol levels fell, their triglyceride levels didn't go up significantly and they lost weight.

Proponents of high-protein diets say that athletes perform better on a high-fat diet and that a carbohydrate-rich diet doesn't serve elite athletes. They report that a carbohydrate-rich diet actually inhibits the performance of highly trained endurance athletes. The truth is that carbohydrates, not fat, is the primary fuel for exercise at or above 70 percent of aerobic capacity, the intensity at which most people train and compete. We need to remember that fat becomes available for fuel only after 20 minutes of continuous exercise. Average people never exercise enough to lose body fat. Almost every study of trained athletes shows that consuming carbohydrates before and during an event improves their performance. Consuming carbohydrates after an event replenishes their glycogen (sugar) stores for the next challenge.

Now it gets really interesting. The Zone requires precise control of the protein to carbohydrate ratio, which is said to counteract the carbohydrates you eat, keeping insulin levels in balance. High levels of insulin generated by too many calories from carbohydrates remove you from the Zone. Again, the truth is that there is no evidence that eating equal amounts of protein and carbohydrates at every meal, as this plan suggests, lowers insulin. Research shows that protein increases insulin secretion and that there is no difference in insulin production if it is eaten with carbohydrates or not.

On to eicosanoids, the body's superhormones, which when imbalanced are responsible for every disease, from heart disease, cancer, obesity to autoimmune diseases, like arthritis and multiple sclerosis, according to The Zone. To keep the eicosanoids in a healthy balance you need to eat

3 grams of protein for every 4 grams of carbohydrates. Once again the truth is that, although the entire diet plan is based on this theory, the author has never measured the eicosanoid levels in people, so the response to this diet is unknown. Most research shows that it is highly unlikely that eicosanoids are the keys to health and disease.

The *Carbohydrate Addicts Diet* is another personal "favorite" of mine. This diet reduces your calorie intake by asking you to eat two carbohydrate-restricted meals and one well-balanced Reward Meal (containing carbohydrates), which is limited to 1 hour of eating, each day. The carbohydrate-restricted meals drastically limit your food choices to meats, poultry, fish, oils and many high-fat dairy products, with the not so surprising results that you take in fewer calories.

The Reward Meal is what really gets me, and it has been modified over the years since its inception in 1991. Originally, the meal description read: "All foods are allowed on the Reward Meal and quantities are not limited" and included unlimited amounts of alcohol. In 1999, the new Reward Meal began with 2 cups of fresh salad followed by equal portions of protein, low-carbohydrate vegetables, and high-carbohydrate foods along with modest amounts of alcohol. Hmmmmmm . . .

So What's the Deal?

The resurgent popularity of high-protein diets is based on the misconception that carbohydrates alone induce weight gain. Actually, the quality and amount of fat in the American diet is the true culprit. Fat is already in the chemical form for storage and is almost effortlessly transferred to our body's fat cells. This transfer is so easy and smooth that the chemical structure of the dietary fat remains largely unchanged as it is stored. To convert carbohydrate into fat takes about 30 percent of our calories, so this conversion is relatively limited in the typical Western diet.

Refined or simple carbohydrates do raise insulin levels. As a result, when combined with fat, as they are for the Western diet, they do promote obesity. One extremely healthy recommendation made by proponents of a low-carbohydrate diet plan is their consistent advice to avoid sugar, white flour, milk, ice cream, cakes, pies, soft drinks and low-fat diet products that contain highly refined carbohydrates. They also recommend a relatively high intake of healthy green and yellow vegetables, like asparagus. Where they fail is by restricting our intake of essential complex carbohydrates, like rice, corn, and beans and by recommending butter, eggs, meats and other very high fat, high-cholesterol and/or high-protein foods.

And Then There's Our Blood Type

The "blood-type diet" theory has gained widespread attention from the public since the release of *Eat Right for Your Type* in 1996. The book's premise? That our blood antigens determine the kinds of foods we should be eating. For instance, people with type O blood are said to be the dominant, hunter caveman type who require meat in their diet, whereas type As are mild-mannered vegetarians. Type Bs are dairy-eating omnivores able to eat anything, anytime.

Much of the theory of this book rests on the action of lectins, sugar-containing proteins found on the surface of certain foods that can cause various molecules and some types of cells to stick together. Lectins are blamed for serious disruptions throughout the body, from agglutination of the blood cells to cirrhosis of the liver and kidney failure. The book states that "certain beans and legumes, especially lentils and kidney beans, contain lectins that deposit in your muscle tissues, making them more alkaline and less charged for physical activity." This is quite an alarming thought, especially if you are unfortunate enough to have blood type O (which constitutes a large portion of the population). So does this mean that a bowl of chili with beans will render a type O person helpless and weak? If you're going to make a statement like this and publish it in a book with the intent of changing the way people eat, wouldn't you think that solid scientific evidence should be presented to support these assertions? This book repeatedly fails in such evidence. Without clearly citing the scientific references that demonstrate such proof, the credibility of this theory is severely diminished. In the manner that this theory is presented, millions of people can be potentially terrified to eat foods loaded with valuable nutrients for fear of upsetting their blood type profile. If a type O individual eats a wheat cracker, does he double over with agonizing pain? Does a type A person eat a piece of chicken with life-threatening results?

What pushes the blood type theory beyond the limits of believability for me is what the author deems to be the true criminal—namely, lectin proteins in some foods that cause blood agglutination (red blood cells in the vessels irreversibly sticking together and forming clumps) in certain people of blood types who are "not genetically/ evolutionarily suited" to eat those foods. It is a very serious and potentially life-threatening phenomenon that this book proposes. According to the author, once the red cells in your blood begin to clump together, they don't separate again.★

Having your blood agglutinate is not a good thing . . . for health or long-term survival. Because red blood cells deliver oxygen to all the tissues of the body, they must flow easily through the tiniest of blood vessels. If the red blood cells are being clumped together by lectins (or anything else), they will clog up the capillaries and block the blood flow. The bloodstream will be prevented from delivering its precious cargo of oxygen and nutrients to the tissues served by those obstructed capillaries. Cells deprived of oxygen become damaged and soon die. Based on the theory in this book, most people (because we eat food that is "evolutionarily inappropriate") are experiencing showers of clumped-together cells, resulting in epidemic proportions of dying cells. If true, this spells disaster for millions of people. Don't you think we'd see a number of studies supporting this theory?

I've lived my life as a vegan for many years. The most upsetting part of *Eat Right for Your Blood Type* is the portrayal of people who choose to live a vegetarian lifestyle. He tells us that flesh-eating type O individuals have a "genetic memory of strength, endurance, self-reliance, daring, intuition, and innate optimism," are "the epitome of focus, drive" and are "hardy and strong, fueled by a high protein diet." The book then paints the "more vegetarian" type A person as a submissive tofu eater, "biologically predisposed to heart disease, cancer and diabetes." Vegetarian type As are portrayed as having

★This is very different from blood *sludging*, a phenomenon seen when the surface of the red blood cells becomes coated with fat or other substances that make them sticky enough to adhere to each other temporarily; they do not become permanently bonded through irreversible intertwining of surface proteins, which is what happens in agglutination.

personalities "poorly suited for the intense, high pressured leadership positions at which Type Os excel" and that in pressure situations, people with type A blood "tend to unravel" and "become anxious and paranoid, taking everything personally." Finally, and infuriatingly, he calls Adolf Hitler, "a mutated Type A personality." Yuck.

In my opinion, this diet plan spins a fairy tale that leaves many unanswered questions. It seems as thin on logic as it does on researched evidence, but that's me.

SO WHAT DO WE DO?

So what is the natural way to achieve your ideal weight and keep it under control without another "perfect" plan that can compromise your health?

Look at the cultures, societies and groups that maintain their weight without effort or diets. The Japanese eat a diet abundant in rice, vegetables and fermented foods with only small amounts of animal protein, and have a very low incidence of heart disease and breast, colon and prostate cancer and have the world's greatest longevity. Of course, this is rapidly changing as Asian cultures adopt Western eating patterns of high-fat diets with lots of animal protein. Then they, too, grow fat.

Seventh-Day Adventists, many of whom are strict vegetarians, eat a diet that is mainly grains, legumes, fruits and vegetables. As a result research shows that they have a lower incidence of heart disease and colon cancer compared to the general population. A recent study of Seventh-Day Adventists, and vegetarians in general, found that they lived longer and healthier and were not obese.

A diet based on the complex carbohydrates of whole grains, beans, vegetables, some fruit, nuts and seeds, a moderate intake of healthy desserts and appropriate amounts of superior quality fat will ensure effortless, permanent, healthful weight loss without restricting food or causing hunger. And delicious? Check out the recipes! You'll never starve or restrict yourself, count a calorie, measure a portion or compromise your health again.

In spite of great marketing by proponents of high-protein diets, the link between animal protein and various cancers is as solid as the link between smoking and lung cancer. Of course, animal foods are not the sole cause of cancer, but clearly the increased consumption of animal products and the decreased consumption of fresh produce has had the most powerful impact on cancer risks.

What makes up the best diet? I know I won't surprise you. Almost every expert of note agrees that, to stay healthy, we should eat a diet that is low in saturated and trans-fat, which means cutting way back on red meat, poultry, dairy food, hydrogenated fats and fast foods. A healthy diet is rich in vegetables and beans, whole cereal grains and pasta, whole wheat breads and crackers, fruits, nuts and seeds. The only real debate is how much oil or nuts or other foods rich in unsaturated fat is necessary for good health. Some good fat is necessary, not only for assimilation of fat-soluble nutrients but to ensure that we obtain appropriate amounts of essential fatty acids. How much we need depends on our current condition of health, our activity level and our ancestry.

The conclusion? Listen to that little voice inside you that always tells you the truth—your intuition. You'll discover your path to health and vitality is not rocket science and is paved with delicious food along the way.

BEYOND THE PERIMETER OF YOUR PLATE

Radiant good health, in my opinion, results from our attention to three important areas of our life: what we eat, moving our body and our emotions.

Food

Clearly, by now you know that I believe that switching to a naturally wholesome plant-based diet is one of the most positive steps we can take for our health. We'll find ourselves achieving our optimal weight and condition when we feed our body the delicious fuel it was ideally designed to run on.

Exercise

Do we need to sweat at a gym for hours to be healthy? If that works for you, then go for it. Whatever makes you feel strong and healthy is what you should do in your life. If it's barbells and treadmills, then it's barbells and treadmills. If it's a long run along trails, roadways or city streets, then it's a long run. If it's bicycling up hills and mountain trails, it's biking. Surfing, swimming, group classes, dancing, salsa, throwing a Frisbee in the park, all good, and good for you. For me, it's yoga, some light weights and walking as my primary mode of transportation. Your workout can be as simple as taking a daily brisk walk or jog or any kind of regular aerobic workout. It not only improves cardiovascular fitness and helps win the battle of the bulge but improves our psychological outlook, too. Just 30 minutes out in nature does wonders for our attitude. Deep breathing, moving our body, stimulating our senses will always improve our mood.

Emotional Health

Our state of mind and emotional outlook also play an important role in our body's ability to maintain and even regain our vibrant good health. Meditation and relaxation techniques have been proven to provide significant health benefits. Most important, at least for me, and the best way to maintain your health, is to live open in love. Successful relationships with friends, family and lovers open us to experience the world in ways unique to us. By opening ourselves to each other, from intimate relationships with our partners to intimate relationships with our fellow humans, we change the way we see the world. Connecting with each other in deep, open communication helps us see the bigger picture of life. Everything changes when we connect with each other in truth, from our hearts. We can create truly joyful community with our friends and neighbors, true love with our families and deep abiding passion with our partners and mates.

Closing ourselves in fear will surely lead us down the path to ill health. As we clench our bodies tightly against the possibility of hurt or pain, we lose our ability to see the wonders of life around us. By remaining open and experiencing deeply, we feel our way to a relaxed, receptive life. As we allow the energy of the world to move through us, the depth of feeling of our beloved family and friends fills us with joy and vitalizing energy. Sure, we'll get hurt; we might even get battered by trusting and feeling deeply. But we'll recover, stronger than ever and open even more deeply to our fellow humans. Open and relaxed or clenched and fearful, which sounds healthier to you?

A DAY IN THE LIFE

We live a life at a frenetic pace in the United States. We want it all, faster, bigger and better. We work more hours, make more money, grow more enchanted with our toys and technology and own big houses and fancy cars. We race—often dragging our exhausted, over-scheduled children behind us—from activity to activity. We'll live well if it kills us. If this makes your life healthy and blissful, then you might just want to skip to the recipes. Mazel tov. But if you're like most of the people who I talk with, you're wondering what happened. How did we get here? How did our lives get reduced to minuscule intervals of rest between inhuman levels of racing against the clock?

I know what you're thinking. Oh, sure, she has a television show, writes cookbooks, teaches, owns her own business and has independence. She probably has twelve assistants doing it all for her. What about normal people who go to a job every day? Well, let me set the record straight. I have worked for myself for most of my professional life, either in the food

business or in the arts. Twenty-hour days were the norm for me for many years, just trying to keep it all together, the work, the house, the meals. I began to wonder. I thought that there was a delicious independence that came with working for myself. I was as much a slave to work as any company employee, and I had no benefits or retirement fund. My husband and I had to stop and get

off the roller coaster of business long enough to reflect on what it was that we wanted our lives to be about. We love our work, it's fulfilling, rewarding, does no harm and is good fun, but it's not who we are. Our friends, family and community are far more important to us than one more phone call or one more appearance or class.

Our country and the lifestyle here isn't particularly suited to more natural rhythms. So to choose to live more naturally, more whole, means going against the grain of society. It's definitely a choice that you will or won't make. It means different priorities, different goals. It means less stuff, smaller cars, fewer toys—but more love, more joy, more serenity, more fulfillment in your life.

Even with my seemingly glamorous life, I still do it all, clean the house, cook the meals, bundle the recycling. I also produce and host my television show, write books, teach all over the world, serve as a partner in a natural food business and live as a loving wife. I work hard, sometimes too hard, and must consciously scale back when it feels out of control. Every day, I choose how I will be in the world. Every day, I choose to resist the treadmill that has trapped so many of us, robbing us of our joy and health. I choose to live a more simple life, respecting nature and her natural cycles, respecting my nature and natural cycles. I choose sanity over stuff.

It isn't always easy. I look around and observe how we work in the world, especially women. We try to have it all. We want to work, have a family, run a perfect home and have a blissful social and romantic life. Working women count seconds like others count calories. I'm not sure we can have it all, and I'm not sure why we want it all anyway. Rising at five in the morning and collapsing into bed after eleven each night is not a fulfilling way to live. You may get to the gym, work a full day, drag everyone to soccer practice and dance class, gulp down some kind of food and spend exhausted "quality time" with your family, but is it worth it? Really worth it? We have moved far past necessities, deep into the realm of excess. Single parents fall into a class by themselves, nobly toiling to keep their families fed. I wish our world supported them more to make their lives easier.

We see them here and there, those calm people, just sailing through their day, moving at a slower pace, stress free. We assume they're lazy, insane, unemployed or wealthy. But what if they've just made other choices? Maybe they want a different kind of life. Wouldn't we just love to know their secrets?

It all begins at home, specifically in the kitchen. To manage our lives in the society we have created, we must have strength and vitality. We need clarity of thought and good, solid health. Without these assets, the world will steamroller right over us and toss us aside like used tissues. But how do we make it all work in this runaway world? Where do we find the time to go back to the kitchen, when everything in our lives drags us farther and farther from that sacred room? Well, I could lie to you and tell you it's a snap, but the truth is not so easy. To regain and maintain our health and sanity, we need to cook for ourselves. We need to prepare whole, natural, minimally processed foods in our kitchens for our beloved families and friends. For most of us, that means reprioritizing a bit to make space in our lives for cooking.

While sweating over a hot stove and scrubbing pots may not seem glamorous, it is one of the more sensual activities you can undertake. Be mindful. Watch the colors dance as you wash vegetables. Feel the silken texture of grains sliding through your fingers. Allow the tickle of sweat slipping down your back to delight you. Come alive as the aromas of cooking fill your senses, drawing you seductively into their embrace, thrilling you with anticipation of the meal to come. Feel fully and openly present as you serve the meal you have prepared and enjoy the contentment of your beloved family and friends as they nourish themselves with your love through the food they eat. If we could only think of the art of cooking like this, we'd race home so that we could cook for those who mean the most to us. Fast food, slapping a meal together from take-away deli food, opening cans and frozen dinners would lose their hold on us. The importance of nourishment would take its rightful place on our list of things we love to do, and life would change completely. Our home would take on a new vibrance. It would become our sacred haven, our place to feel whole, to regain our footing before facing the onslaught of life outside again. We would reconnect with our loved ones, communing over yummy meals. Sound unrealistic? It's not, really. You just have to want it. Let's begin at the beginning.

GETTING STARTED

It all begins in the kitchen, the heart of any home. And just like all of us, kitchens come in all shapes and sizes, with varying equipment. None of that matters. What's important is that you create, in your kitchen, an atmosphere that attracts you and makes you comfortable and content to be in it.

If you're new to the whole "comfy in the kitchen" thing, then I suggest you begin by cleaning it, from top to bottom. Get the piles of old mail off the countertops, organize the cabinets, toss out anything you can't identify and scrub the whole room down. This ritual gives you the sense of a new start, a new beginning. It also makes for a clean kitchen, a pleasant environment in which to create.

Organization will be your key to success. Whether in a large country kitchen or a compact urban space, having your essential tools and ingredients at your fingertips will allow your work to go smoothly, with little chaos. Decide where your primary work area will be and set up your pantry close by (if possible). In my kitchen, I have my prep area between the stove and sink, so that I can move easily from cleaning ingredients to slicing and dicing to cooking. Above my work area is my mini-pantry, with all my condiments right at hand. Oils, vinegars, salt, seasonings, herbs and spices are stored just a reach away. On the other side of my stove is my full pantry, with larger quantities of ingredients and less-used items. Pots and pans are stored in the cabinet just beneath my work area and larger cooking pots are stored in the island just behind me. My recycling bin is near the back door, also in easy reach, so my sink and counter don't get cluttered with empty containers, and my small compost bucket is next to my cutting board. I can put my hands on anything I need for my meal preparation with just a few steps. This may not sound like much, but when you're cooking, if you're running all over the kitchen searching for ingredients and utensils, you'll exhaust and frustrate yourself. So much for the sensual experience of cooking! You want to create a space that's comfortable and efficient so you can do your best work.

TOOLS OF THE TRADE

The good news about natural cooking is that it requires very few gadgets. Unless you love them, you'll find most gadgets simply take up precious space. But again, whatever makes cooking a great experience for you is what you should have handy. Here are what I consider to be the absolute essentials, anything else you'd like is up to you and your artistic taste.

I regard the **chef's knife** (vegetable knife) as the most valuable tool you can have at hand and recommend that you invest wisely in this one. You will be using it every day. It should suit you, feel comfortable in your hand, work efficiently and sharpen easily. I recommend you go to a kitchen shop that will allow you to hold the knives on display. This will sound weird, but trust me. When the knife that is right for you slips into your palm, you will know it. It will feel like coming home. The weight will feel right, the handle comfortable. This baby's yours. A quality knife is a bit of an investment; you'll want to spend a decent amount of money on your knife to ensure quality. Stay away from the $19.95 sets of six knives, please; you know what they say about too good to be true.

You'll also need, depending on your style of cooking, a **paring knife**. And every kitchen needs a **serrated bread knife**. You never want to use your chef knife for slicing bread; it dulls the blade quickly.

For knife maintenance, you'll need a **sharpening stone** and **a steel.** The stone is used to give your knife a real edge. You'll need to sharpen on a stone only once a month or so, depending on the kind and amount of work you do. The steel is for everyday use. Just a few strokes on the steel before cooking will ensure efficient, accurate work.

Storing your knives is important. Clean them, dry them and put them away. I prefer to keep them in a block or in their boxes in a drawer. Just tossing them in the junk drawer could result in damage. Take care of these precious tools.

Cutting boards are most likely your second most important tool. Wooden boards will serve natural cooking the best. Plastic and glass boards will dull your knives quickly. Wooden boards have a "relaxing" energy, less noisy as knives don't clang against them. Wooden boards also hold fewer bacteria than their synthetic counterparts. I prefer a very thick and large cutting board. Because I use it so much, it's wet a lot of the time, so a thick board won't warp or crack. Clean it with warm water only. Soap will leave a residue that can leach into your food. I also don't rub oil into my board. My experience is that it can develop a rancid flavor. Here's my big maintenance tip: About once a month, to freshen my wooden board, I wet it thoroughly, sprinkle it with salt and rub a lemon half over the surface, rinse and that's that.

Some people like a small board for garlic, but I don't find it necessary. If you choose to cook fish or, heaven forbid, meat or chicken, you'll need a separate board for that (a separate kitchen in my book, but that's me).

You'll need a variety of **strainers,** fine ones for rinsing grains and more coarse ones for sauces and such. **Colanders** are needed for washing vegetables and draining pasta, so you'll need a couple of sizes.

Many people like vegetable **brushes** for washing vegetables. I don't use them. I just wash vegetables under water, but if you like a brush, use one made from natural fiber. Other brushes that are essential in a kitchen are simply natural fiber paintbrushes in various widths, for brushing pans, baking dishes and griddles with oil.

You'll need a variety of **pots and pans** to accommodate your cooking. I prefer stainless steel for everyday work, cast iron for heavier cooking (they provide such even heat) and clay, for roasting and long, slow stews. Look for pots that are good quality, that are pleasing to your eye and that feel good in your hand. Again, you have to look at them every day; they should delight you aesthetically.

Basic pot and pan needs include a large soup pot (a gallon or more) with a lid; a small or medium pressure cooker for grains and beans; large and small skillets with lids; several small and medium pots with lids for sauces, puddings, soups, stews and boiling vegetables; and if you like, a pasta pot.

I recommend you have a couple of **flame deflectors** on hand for low simmering.

Some miscellaneous, but necessary (at least to me) pots and pans include a bamboo steamer, a stainless steel steamer and a wok.

If you bake, you'll also want several **baking sheets, muffin tins, pie plates** and **cake pans** on hand for when your creative juices are flowing. I like to keep both full-size and miniature cake pans, so I can make smaller servings as well as special occasion bigger cakes.

You'll also need several **baking dishes**, small, medium and large. I prefer glass, stainless steel or clay, with lids if possible, so you can avoid using aluminum foil as much as possible, for your health and for the environment.

You will need some **utensils**, including all the little detail necessities that may seem obvious but without them, cooking will be much harder. Wooden spoons of every shape and size make cooking a pleasure. I choose elegant, graceful spoons because they're beautiful as well as functional and I love to cook amid lovely things. I like longer spoons for deeper pots and high heat and shorter, more delicate spoons for sauces and delicate cooking. Spatulas and whisks make cooking sauces a pleasure as you whip them to silky perfection. A melon baller, food mill for straining soups and sauces, ginger grater, hand juicer, mandolin and for some a garlic press and measuring cups are simple little gadgets that make cooking a breeze. I have

one kitchen indulgence that I just adore, a tiny salad spinner for delicate greens and fresh herbs, and I can't live without it. Rounding out the utensil list I'll add kitchen towels, sponges and mixing bowls.

I don't use many **small appliances,** but a well-equipped kitchen will often include a food processor, blender, juicer, mixer and toaster oven. Choose what you like and will use.

I love to set a beautiful table, nothing fancy or expensive, just lovely. It's important that we take the joy of cooking and eating to every level of sensual pleasure and that includes **beautiful service**. I keep a variety of bowls, platters, plates, napkins and placemats to ensure that I have whatever I'll need for whatever dish and mood.

Other than these essentials, whatever makes you feel happy, secure and delicious should be in your kitchen. I like to keep my windowsills lined with flowering plants and herbs, small paintings on the walls and very little clutter on my countertops. I like order and space in my kitchen, with touches of natural beauty. Next to my bedroom, it's my favorite room in the house.

STOCKING THE PANTRY

Okay, the kitchen is clean and your pots and pans are ready for use. Time to fill the pantry shelves. What's a novice whole-foods chef to do? Take a deep breath and relax. We're heading off to a natural food store.

Grains

As you know, a whole, healthy diet centers around whole grains and whole grain products. So let's get some basic ingredients on your pantry shelves. Short, medium, long and basmati brown rice are essential grains to have for everyday variety. Then you'll need yellow millet, barley, quinoa, kasha, corn grits and cracked wheat. We eat a lot of pasta, so I keep several cuts of both semolina and whole grain pasta in the pantry all the time for quick, easy meals.

Beans

Because I choose to live a vegan lifestyle, beans play a big role in my diet. I keep green, brown, red and baby lentils; chickpeas; split peas (both green and yellow); black turtle beans; cannellini beans; red adzuki beans; kidney and pinto beans; black soybeans and fava beans. It seems like a lot, but I like variety in my cooking. You can choose what you like; there are so many more than these types of beans. Don't overwhelm yourself, but keep a few kinds of beans around so you aren't at a loss for inspiration.

Condiments and Seasonings

Condiments are my greatest luxury. I'm a total sucker for exotic oils, vinegars and seasonings. For the basic essentials, however, choose as many organic ingredients as you can. You'll need extra-virgin and light olive oils (for baking); avocado oil; light and toasted sesame oils; hempseed oil; unrefined natural sea salt; umeboshi plums and paste; and umeboshi, brown rice, red wine and balsamic vinegars. Dried herbs and spices have their own special shelf in my pantry, as I use them frequently to make simple dishes sparkle with flavor. Take care to purchase only the amounts of herbs and

spices you'll use in a six-month period to ensure fresh flavor. I keep herbs and spices simple—basil, rosemary, thyme, cinnamon, nutmeg, black pepper, ginger, wasabi, curry powder, chili powders, cloves and poppy seeds. Natural soy sauce, tamari and several varieties of miso (which I keep in the refrigerator) add dramatic flavor to any dish. I keep kuzu and arrowroot on the shelf for thickening sauces and glazes. I round out my spice pantry with a few extracts: pure vanilla, almond, hazelnut, lemon, orange and anise seed.

Sweeteners and Chocolate

The sweetener shelf is sparse, holding only barley malt, wheat malt and various flavors of brown rice syrup (strawberry, raspberry, blueberry, maple, chocolate and original). They serve me in every sweet instance, from desserts to sauces to balancing savory dishes. I couldn't do without them. You'll find no simple sugars in my pantry, no maple syrup, honey or sugar (organic or otherwise). You will, however, find organic unsweetened cocoa powder, nondairy grain-sweetened chocolate chips and baking chocolate.

Nuts and Seeds

In the coolest part of the pantry, I store nut butters, sesame seeds (tan and black), pumpkin seeds, sunflower seeds, hempseeds, walnuts, pecans, almonds and hazelnuts. For nut butters, I keep just the basics—peanut, almond and sesame tahini.

Include anything else that makes you smile and feel inspired when you open the pantry doors readying yourself to cook; go for it.

THE REFRIGERATOR

As you'll hear me say quite often, one of my favorite places in the world to shop for fresh, seasonal food is at a farm market. More than just locally grown foods, farm markets are a community, a place where I can connect with the people who grow and process my food. I get to play a part in creating a thriving rural economy. I know that not everyone has the luxury of a farm market, but if you can get to one, your life . . . at least when it comes to food and the environmental impact of your choices . . . will never be the same.

Short of a farm market, where do we find fresh seasonal produce? Natural food stores are a primary source of food for me because there is such a large selection of organic produce (and other foods) available. Since organic vegetables and fruit are my first choice, I fare far better in natural markets. I shop in supermarkets to fill in my produce choices with nonorganic items that I just can't seem to find organically grown.

What to buy? Choose what's seasonal and fresh . . . and what you like. I keep basic ingredients on hand at all times so I can walk in the door and cook. Garlic, onions, carrots, scallions, parsley, some kind of green leafy vegetables, cabbage, broccoli, cauliflower, lemons, cucumbers and radishes and some fresh fruit give me lots of creative breathing room.

Okay, so you don't want to travel to two or three locations for vegetables? Then start at the supermarket. If you've been to one recently, you surely have noticed that the produce section looks like Disneyland. Pause a minute as you race through your shopping and take in the life around you. Let your eyes feast on the colors; breathe in the fragrances, enjoy the vibrance. Look for what's seasonal and seems to be freshest; that's what you

want to buy. Be brave and try new vegetables. Take your tummy on a culinary adventure. The more you cook, the more confidence you'll develop. And with supermarkets bringing in more and more organic foods, your choices are growing and growing.

Once home, you'll want your vegetables and fruit to stay just-picked fresh for as long as possible, so you can enjoy their peak flavors. For me, I have had the best luck storing produce without washing it. I clean it as I use it. I remove all rubber bands and ties that might hold bunches together, so that air can circulate. Root vegetables, like carrots, parsnips and turnips and heartier ground vegetables, like winter squash and onions, I store in the crisper drawers without wrapping them. Head cabbage, Brussels sprouts and Chinese cabbage are kept well wrapped for freshness. Hearty dark greens and delicate herb and salad greens are kept loosely wrapped in plastic produce bags. This keeps them freshest. Fresh fruit is kept in crisper drawers, also unwrapped.

MEAL PLANS

Okay, so now you have all this fresh, organic food, all these wonderful pots and pans in your clean, orderly kitchen, what's next? After years, or even a lifetime of junk food, frozen dinners and take-away meals, where do you start?

When new to whole natural cooking, a bit more thought and planning may be needed so you can manage your meals without losing your sanity. Balance is the key to success. Learn to balance with the seasons, the weather, individual tastes, what's available, your abilities and work schedule and the health needs of your family. Don't panic, you don't need to be a nutritionist, you just need to keep a few things in mind. In the beginning, I recommend that you write out a weekly menu plan, of course, allowing flexibility for what might strike your fancy at the market. With a plan, you're not wandering aimlessly from aisle to aisle trying to imagine how you'll pull it all together.

The best news about whole natural foods is that they are extremely versatile. For instance, if you know that you have a particularly busy week coming up, cook a few dishes ahead. I cook a pot of beans, without seasoning, so that I can use them in a variety of ways for two or three meals. Soups, salads, pâté and stews can all be made with cooked beans as the base, with fresh vegetables and various seasonings to create new tastes. I also might pressure cook a bit of extra rice, so I can create salads, a soup or simple fried rice to put a nutritious meal on the table quickly.

No matter the time, no matter how late, I always cook vegetable dishes fresh, even if it means that we eat a bit later than planned. For me, there's just no substitute and frankly, nothing tastes quite as stale to me as leftover vegetables. I might use them as soup starters or whip them up with some seasonings into creamy spreads for bread.

Tofu and tempeh are versatile, easy to cook and ready in minutes; these two delicious soyfoods have been my saving grace on more than one occasion. Marinated for a few minutes and then fried or baked, they can stand boldly on their own with simple side dishes to create a hearty and satisfying protein-rich meal in no time flat.

For my own menu plans, I take into account our activities, our workweek and our travel schedules. I base my menus on what will serve us best, but mostly on what sounds good to me. Bottom line is that the cook really cooks for his or her own desires and needs, but a good cook knows how to take everyone's needs into consideration.

Generally speaking, throughout a day, I incorporate whole grains and pasta, beans or some other protein and lots of seasonal vegetables—not all in one meal but over the course of the day. A typical day might include a breakfast of polenta with lightly cooked greens, a lunch of lentil soup with bread and a dinner of brown rice or pasta with lots of vegetables. There's always a bit of dessert in the evening, a lovely way to end the day, I say.

SO WHAT'S FOR DINNER?

We can all seem to manage breakfast and lunch. Breakfast can be a quick porridge and lunch can be pulled together pretty easily from leftovers, but dinner is more difficult. As busy people, the biggest challenge of our day is creating a healthy, delicious dinner for our beloved families. It's all too easy to fall into the take-away meal and drive-through habit.

It's important to instill in yourself a sense of timing, of how things work in the kitchen. Learning to estimate how long dishes will take to cook will aid immeasurably in planning evening meals. You'll be able to figure which nights you'll have the time to relax and really create from scratch and which nights you'll need some leftovers to make cooking a bit easier for you.

I try to vary my dinners. On leisurely nights, I'll cook elaborate dinners so I'll have leftovers to work with the next day. I'll make condiments, bake cookies or miniature cakes or muffins, cook a pot of beans that I can use as my week gets more hectic. I have more flexibility this way. I'll take leftover beans, sauté some onions and spices, wrap them in corn tortillas and serve them with a crisp, fresh salad, for a delicious quick dinner. Cooked grains and beans can be turned into hearty winter stews as well as fresh, flavorful summer salads. Quickly cooked greens will round out any dinner menu.

MAKING THE CHANGE TO EATING WELL

I know what you're thinking. It all sounds good, from fresh shopping to cleaning and organizing the kitchen to cooking and serving whole delicious meals to our grateful families. But it doesn't always work that way. One of our biggest challenges is getting people to eat the food we have lovingly prepared. You know I'm right. So, what to do? First, don't turn into the food police; that would be bad. My best advice is to cook deliciously. Because your meals are short on saturated fat, dairy fat and sugar, there's no need for them to be short on flavor. Natural meals are as tasty as you allow them to be.

Tastes do, in fact, change. You may meet resistance in the beginning, as you attempt to replace foods that are not serving your family's health with foods that are more, shall we say, human-friendly. Move slowly, making gradual changes; people tend to resist change. Children, reluctant spouses and friends want delicious meals that leave them feeling nourished and contented. Many people are used to strong, artificial flavors, heavy seasonings and saturated fats and sugar. It will take time for those tendencies to change. Be patient and continue to cook wonderful meals.

Here's another tip that I have found successful. While your introduction of whole, natural foods needs to be delicious, it's important that it be familiar. Look at the home-cooked meals that your family loves the best and try to emulate that feeling. You'll never succeed if you try to take your family directly from the Golden Arches to steaming bowls of brown rice and hiziki!

What do they love? Italian food? Center your meals around Italian flavors, using fresh herbs, pasta, lots of vegetables and beans, cooked in a Mediterranean style. Is Mexican food their weakness? Go for organic beans and vegetables, with soy cheese, creating tacos, enchiladas and burritos. Are they all-American, not-the-least-bit-adventurous, don't-feed-me-anything-weird types? Try pasta dishes, fresh, crisp salads, with a few cooked broccoli spears and some chickpeas with a delicious dressing and sandwiches. Hummus with vegetable sticks and corn chips are a pretty safe bet as a snack for this crowd. If they don't like vegetables at all, it's a bit trickier, but you can manage to throw a few fresh vegetables into just about any dish without creating too much of a fuss.

I would also recommend that you make a gradual change to healthful eating. Begin with one meal a week, and again, keep it familiar. Create a themed dinner so it seems more an adventure than the Inquisition. Keep it all very low key. Just serve dinner. Don't announce that tonight is vegetarian night. If your food is delicious, your family won't miss the meat.

You can also try the old trick of cooking and eating well at home, but when the family is away from your table, they can eat and order what they like. My experience has been that the most reluctant diner returns to the table more often as tastes change and the realization dawns about what good food tastes like. Remember that the more relaxed and open you are about the meals you serve, the more relaxed and open your reluctant family will be to try them. All in all, a gentle and loving approach to serving healthier foods to your family will be the key to success.

One last thing you probably want to know. Is this more work? Will you cook more and spend more time in the kitchen? Will you shop more frequently and stock your pantry more fully? Yes, to all the questions. Will it be worth that extra effort? Yes, completely. Don't give up. Your health depends on it.

WHAT A DIFFERENCE A DAY MAKES

There isn't much more I can tell you about getting through your day, except this one thing. And it's a big one. As important as it is to shop frequently for fresh organic food and as important as it is to cook yummy, nutritious meals for your beloveds, it's equally important that you take care of your spirit. If all your good intentions to live well are reduced to the stress and tension of "what you have to do," so much for health and balance.

Food is merely the foundation on which we build the rest of our lives. We live in a world where it is quite difficult to maintain a natural balance. Everything around us pushes us to work harder, make more money, move more quickly. Even our leisure time is frenetic with activity.

Think about how you feel when you take a holiday to a beach or camping. By returning to natural surroundings and rhythms, the body is allowed to shift into a more natural way of being. That's why, even a weekend away with no agenda, is so incredibly refreshing. If we observe nature, we will notice that she is wiser than us. She maintains periods of activity and periods of rest—in perfect balance.

I am not, by any means, suggesting that we all vacate our lives, move to the country and accom-plish nothing. I am suggesting, instead, that we strive for a bit of balance in our lives, that we take care of ourselves, so that we can accomplish our goals and realize our dreams.

TEN TIPS TO GET YOU STARTED

1. Try to retire before midnight and rise early in the day for the most restful sleep.

2. Try to get outdoors each day, regardless of the weather.

3. Keep your home environment clean and orderly. Orderly surroundings make us feel calm and safe, while a chaotic home agitates our frazzled nerves. Think of your home, be it simple or palatial, as your sacred haven.

4. As much as possible, use natural materials in your home, like cotton sheets, pillowcases and towels, incandescent (rather than florescent) lighting and natural carpeting and flooring. Use stainless steel, earthenware or cast-iron cookware. Avoid aluminum and nonstick pots and pans for your cooking. Clean your home with nontoxic products. Bring nature into every aspect of your life.

5. Open the windows every day, if possible. Open a window or two just a crack for 10 to 15 minutes each day to freshen and enliven the air in your home.

6. Place several green plants throughout your home. They freshen the air in our homes and enrich the oxygen content in the air we breathe, and they add beauty. If you work on a computer, keep a green plant close by to help you to stay a bit more hydrated, as computers make you feel dry and tired.

7. Take a break. If you are working at a desk or at a computer, take a stretch break for about 10 minutes every hour or two. This will prevent tight back muscles and stiff joints, refocus your energy and keep you from feeling exhausted.

8. Indulge in some quiet time each day. Meditate, take a bath, read a book, or drink a cup of fragrant tea.

9. Exercise at least three days a week, but five is best to achieve your best overall health and radiance.

10. Be grateful for your life and all that it entails, even your difficulties. Show gratitude for the many blessings you have, family, friends, neighbors, your life and work, the food you eat, even your challenges. Each day, each breath you take is a blessing for which you must be deeply grateful.

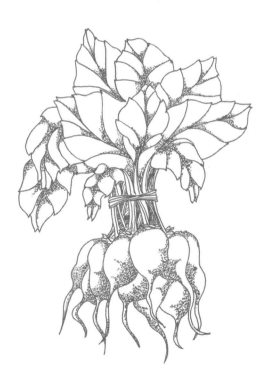

THE ELEVENTH TIP

I know I said ten tips, but one this works so well, you'll find you can't live without it, and it's easy. We all have to bathe, right? Just add this practice to your bath or shower. It will change your life, your perspective, your attitude, how well you sleep, how beautiful your skin and hair look each day, how balanced your energy feels. All you need is a washcloth and access to hot water. Sound simplistic? Try it for thirty days. Trust me.

Fold a cotton washcloth in quarters (or use a cloth spa glove from the pharmacy). Using hot water, wet the cloth and begin to scrub your body (without soap), rubbing gently with just the weight of your hand, until your skin turns pink all over. Start with your hands, rubbing palm and backside, between your fingers and work your way up your arms toward your chest. Next, rub your chest and back—but women should avoid the breasts and both men and women should avoid the genitals. Work your way down your belly, scrub your groin area and your buttocks and then work your way down your legs, front and back to your feet, scrubbing the tops of your feet, between your toes and even the soles of your feet.

At first, you'll notice that your skin turns a mottled pink. As the body breaks down accumulated, hardened fats, your skin will turn a uniform, rosy pink in minutes.

One month of faithful scrubbing and you'll notice a new softness to your skin, and you'll be addicted. In about two months, you'll find that you no longer need to slather on moisturizer. Oh, you'll still love the luxury of fragrant natural lotions on your silky skin, but you won't need them. You'll notice that you don't have flaky shins or crusty heels, dry elbows and itchy patches, oily areas or frequent breakouts. You'll find that you have more energy, sleep more soundly and feel more flexible in attitude and spirit. For the best results, scrub every day.

And if you forget all of this—or feel that it's just too much, simply smile, scrub your skin and enjoy your day. It will change your life. And if it's *still* too much, simply do what one of my greatest mentors, Michio Kushi, advises, sing a happy song every day.

THE TWENTY QUESTIONS I GET ASKED MOST OFTEN

I teach cooking and lecture all over the world. In every class, in every lecture hall, I end my presentations with a question-and-answer period. And since my television show began airing, I'm bombarded with letters and e-mails, which actually spawned this book. Throughout the years, I've noticed a pattern. Here are my Top Twenty, just like David Letterman, but ten more . . .

20. What about chocolate?

What about it? As far as I'm concerned, it's a food group. Seriously, there is a place for healthy chocolate in a healthy diet. It's not the chocolate that creates the problems; it's what we do to it, adding dairy, sugar and chemicals, and the volume we consume. Check out the dessert chapter for some great uses of this food of the gods.

19. What's so bad about dairy?

So much information, so little time. Unless you're a nursing infant, dairy is the least natural food you can choose to consume. See page 25 for details, and to have your boat rocked.

18. What do you substitute for milk, cheese and butter?

This is an easy one; there are so many substitutes for dairy products that yield delicious results.

For milk, try these: soymilk, which is a bit sweeter than milk, but behaves in recipes like whole milk and is extremely versatile with a creamy richness; almond milk, which is rich, but light and a little sweet, not good in tea or coffee, but good in desserts, like cakes for a moist crumb; grain milks, which if they aren't too refined act like skim milk, very light, not sweet, bland, great on cold cereal.

For cheese, look for soy cheese. While some of them are highly refined and still contain a dairy product called casein, there are quite a few vegan cheese substitutes that work very well in any recipe calling for cheese. For a less refined, more whole cheese substitute, try tofu, pickled, marinated or baked for a great cheeselike texture—but it won't melt.

Butter, another easy substitute, to create the buttery richness you crave, try olive oil or avocado oil. Both have high smoke points, resist conversion to trans-fats and give foods such incredible richness, you'll never use anything else. For bread, try dipping into lovely olive oil or look for the nonhydrogenated solid spread made from olive oil. Avoid canola spreads because they're made from canola oil, which has no place in our diets, in my opinion.

17. As a vegetarian, do you eat fish?

Well, when they start planting fish 12 inches apart in soil, maybe I'll consider it. Fish is a form of animal protein and for many people who are proponents of healthy eating, fish may be a great choice. As animal protein goes, fish is the easiest to digest and depletes us the least. If you eat fish, buy fish from unpolluted water and preferably wild fish, not farmed. Much of the fish we eat is farm raised, meaning they are grown with the use of antibiotics and as we farm raise more and more of our fish, the amount of the essential fatty acid, omega-3 and other ntrients will be dramatically reduced. Might want to think about this a bit.

16. What do you eat for breakfast?

Remember that our first meal of the day is literally breaking the fast after sleeping all night. What we choose to eat sets the tone for our whole day, how we'll feel, act and react. For me, breakfast is soft-grain porridge and lightly cooked vegetables, with lots of variations and some special occasion treats. Check out the breakfast chapter for some ideas to rev your engines.

15. How do I take lunch to work?

If you like substantial lunches, cook a bit extra for dinner and package it up for work. Of course, it may mean you'll be eating food at room temperature, but that can be quite nice. You can always make sandwiches or enjoy instant noodles in a cup or ramen for lighter fare. And soup in a thermos can be lovely on chilly days.

For eating out, lunch or dinner, choose pasta, grilled vegetables, vegetarian entrées, vegetable soups and salads or grilled fish, should you choose to eat it.

There are lots of ideas in this book to help you create delicious lunches and snacks.

14. What do you eat for Thanksgiving? And what about guests?

Holidays can be challenging, if we want them to be. I choose not to make a political or personal stand when I have family and loved ones sharing a meal around my table. For me, the holidays are meant to bring us all together in harmony. I cook delicious dishes, some traditional, some not. And if a few of my guests simply cannot live without the stuffed bird, I invite them to bring it along. Everybody's happy. See page 279 for my Thanksgiving dinner, vegan style.

13. How do I get my kids to eat healthy food?

My advice is to take it a meal at a time. Remember that our kids are bombarded with advertising and peer pressure and want so very much to fit in. For them to embrace healthier eating, keep the food familiar . . . and above all delicious. Oh, and don't be the food police. Try some of the recipes in the chapter that talks about our kids and their health and read the section "Healthy Kids" (page 254), and good luck!

12. What about ice cream?

I know it tastes great, but the only word I can use to describe ice cream is *deadly*. Frozen, loaded with dairy fat, sugar, and in many cases chemicals and additives, ice cream will make us fat and unhealthy. There are some nondairy substitutes that are delicious but they're highly refined—not the best choices, but okay for a treat on occasion.

11. Where do I buy tofu and how do I cook it?

Tofu has gone mainstream, yep, you heard me, mainstream. Found everywhere from Asian markets to supermarkets to natural foods stores, tofu is commonplace. In supermarkets, look in the produce section for tofu, while natural foods stores will keep it in a refrigerator case with other soy products. Tofu comes in various textures, from silken to extra firm and each one is used differently.

10. Isn't chicken healthier?

Healthier than what? All you need to do is study how commercial chicken is processed and you'll have your answer. From toxins to antibiotics to unsanitary living and processing conditions to saturated fat and cholesterol. Chicken? I don't think so.

9. Can we have pizza, ever?

I could tell you to never, ever eat pizza. The combination of white flour, cheese, salt and acid-producing tomato sauce is not one that I recommend as a food group (which it was for me at one time). However, the occasional treat would be just fine and if you'd like to enjoy pizza and not wreak havoc on your tummy, try a tomato pie, all the delight of pizza without the cheese. Better yet, make whole wheat, veggie pizza at home.

8. How do I get my husband to eat this food?

A big one. In many cases, the choice to eat a more healthful diet is made by the woman in a relationship, because she wishes to keep the family healthy or someone is sick and needs care. Either way, the choice can be challenging for the family. See the section "Making the Change to Eating Well" (page 44). Just like with children, you need to create delicious meals, without torturing him with lectures and plain, boring, bland food. Change your way of cooking slowly and introduce new foods gradually. Cook with joy and sensual abandon, and he'll eat it.

7. Where do I get protein if I don't eat meat?

There's some protein in everything we eat, except fruit. Remember that cows are vegetarian; they eat grass. I'm just saying let's skip the middle man—er, cow. With grains, beans and vegetables at the core of your diet, you'll never need to worry about protein. Any more questions? See pages 20–22 for more answers.

6. What about calcium?

Of course we all know that there is a tremendous amount of calcium in milk. What we fail to realize is that most of that calcium is not available to us for use; we can assimilate only about 10 percent. On top of that, milk is a very concentrated form of protein, which requires calcium to digest it, so we lose more than we gain. People choosing a plant-based diet lose far less calcium than their carnivorous counterparts and usually require very little supplementation to keep their bones strong.

Where do vegetarians get calcium? Dark leafy greens—like kale, collard greens, bok choy, watercress and broccoli—are rich sources of precious calcium, as are soyfoods, beans and sea plants.

5. Which diets work best?

I can't think of any of the popular diets that are sustainable over a long period of time. There is no new news here; it's calories in versus calories out, with a diet rich in whole grains, beans, vegetables and fruit as the foundation of long-term health and weight maintenance. For a breakdown of all the current fad diets, see the chapter "It's Not Just a Diet."

4. Will I ever get sick if I eat healthy food?

Yep. Eating a healthy diet is your best insurance for overall health maintenance, but if you think that you'll never get a pesky cold or ache with the flu because you eat tofu, you're in for a big surprise. The good news is that while most people are languishing in the misery of their cold and flu for weeks on end, you'll recover quickly, regaining strength in a matter of days. While even the healthiest of diets can't ensure that you'll never struggle with a degenerative disease, you'll have more strength in reserve to help you cope.

3. Can your desserts make me fat?

Even the healthiest desserts, eaten in excess, will pack on the pounds. I'm a big advocate of eating dessert regularly, so we aren't inclined to binge on sweets or overeat. I recommend regular sweets but in small portions. You'll find your sweet tooth satisfied and your hips still slender.

2. Is sugar really that bad?

Dramatically affecting our blood chemistry and glucose levels, simple sugars make us fat, lethargic, rob us of minerals, rot our teeth, suppress immune function and exhaust us. And there are healthier options. Any other questions?

1. Why do your skin and hair look so good?

My mother had the most exquisite skin and luxurious hair, so genetics have certainly been good to me in that department. But the real truth is choosing a diet rich in whole, natural foods, by minimizing processed foods, simple sugars and saturated fats and choosing pure natural body care products and cosmetics have resulted in problem-free skin and strong, shiny hair. My biggest secret though, is scrubbing my skin every day (page 47). I tell you, it will change your life.

FOR LOVE OF SOUP

When you think of soup, the picture is usually one of comfort and solace but not necessarily hip and cool. More like hot and steamy as in chicken soup for your cold and flu. The truth is that soup is about as hip as it gets.

Soup has a profound effect in our body, especially in how we feel, inside and out. Soup determines how well we digest the meal we eat. And what does that have to do with lives? Our vitality? Our relationships? With realizing our dreams? Plenty.

Soup works to draw energy and warmth into the digestive tract, relaxing and stimulating its function, so that digestion is eased and made more efficient. The body relaxes and is less stressed. When your body doesn't work so hard to nourish itself, you have strength and stamina, important components in our lives, wouldn't you agree?

Soup is magic for all aspects of our lives. When our bodies relax, they can open and allow our life force to flow to our organs, to our skin, to the tips of our toes, enlivening us with energy. We feel stimulated, yet softened. Soup is primal, its very nature taking us back to the warm, liquid comfort of the womb, the very spark of life.

With grains or beans, rich with vegetables, a simple consommé or a hearty stew, soup is generally served as the kick-off to the meal. Will it be a feast or simple repast? A humble broth serves as an indicator that your taste buds will be tantalized with course after course of richly flavored dishes, while a hearty soup, thick with ingredients tells you that the main course will be simple, light. Sipped slowly or sampled by the spoonful, soup sets the tone for the meal and the evening to follow, as you relax, melting into the satisfaction of eating, open in your being.

So make a fresh pot of soup for dinner. It will start the meal gently, softening your body, stimulating conversation and ensuring that you have the strength and stamina to enjoy the next day.

WHITE BEAN AND PASTA SOUP

Creamy, rich and sensual, this starter soup is sure to please. You would never guess from its mild, pearl white color and subtle sweet flavor the soup has not-so-subtle staying power.

MAKES 4 TO 6 SERVINGS

About 1 tablespoon extra-virgin olive oil
4 shallots, finely diced
3 cloves fresh garlic, finely minced
Sea salt
3 parsnips, diced
1 cup cooked cannellini beans (see note below)
3 cups plain soymilk
1 cup spring or filtered water
2 teaspoons sweet white miso
¾ cup small pasta (mini shells or elbows)
Small handful fresh flat-leaf parsley, finely minced, for garnish

Place the oil, shallots and garlic in a medium soup pot over medium heat. When the shallots begin to sizzle, add a pinch of salt and sauté until the shallots are translucent, about 2 minutes, taking care not to brown the garlic. Stir in the parsnips and sauté just until shiny with oil. Spread the vegetables over the bottom of the pan and top with the beans. Add the soymilk and water, cover and bring to a boil over medium heat. Reduce the heat to low and cook until the parsnips are quite soft, about 25 minutes. Remove a small amount of broth and use to dissolve the miso. Stir the miso mixture into the soup and simmer, uncovered, for 3 to 4 minutes to activate the enzymes in the miso. Transfer the soup, by ladlefuls, to a food processor and purée until smooth. Return to the stovetop and keep warm over very low heat.

While the soup cooks, bring a pot of water to a boil and cook the pasta al dente. Drain well, but do not rinse. Immediately stir the cooked pasta into the soup and serve garnished with the parsley.

Note: To prepare the beans, rinse and sort about ⅓ cup dried cannellini beans. Soak the beans for 1 hour in warm water. Cook, with a 1-inch piece of kombu or 1 bay leaf until tender, about 1 hour. You may also used canned, organic beans, but freshly cooked ones, if you have the time, have more vitality.

ADZUKI BEAN AND FARRO SOUP

Like Romeo and Juliet, these little red beans and ancient grain adore each other, coming together to support your tired, overworked kidneys. With sweet carrots and stimulating ginger, this delicate soup gives us the courage we need to take a chance in life.

MAKES 4 TO 5 SERVINGS

1 tablespoon extra-virgin olive oil
4 to 5 slices fresh ginger, finely minced
1 small leek, split lengthwise, rinsed well, thinly sliced
3 small carrots, diced
1 cup dried adzuki beans, sorted and rinsed well, soaked for 1 hour
½ cup farro, rinsed well

4 cups spring or filtered water

2 teaspoons barley miso

2 to 3 scallions, thinly sliced on the diagonal,
  for garnish

Place the oil, ginger and leek in a small soup pot over medium heat. When the vegetables begin to sizzle, sauté until the leek is just limp, about 1 minute. Stir in the carrots and sauté until shiny with oil. Add the beans, farro and water, cover and bring to a boil. Reduce the heat to low and simmer until the beans are tender, about 45 minutes.

Remove a small amount of broth and use to dissolve the miso. Stir the miso mixture into the soup and simmer, uncovered, for 3 to 4 minutes to activate the enzymes in the miso. Stir well and serve garnished with the scallions.

ROASTED PUMPKIN AND CARROT SOUP

This soup creates a serene strength and a calm disposition. By normalizing our blood sugars, this soup keeps our emotions on an even keel, keeping operalike drama out of our lives and on the stage.
MAKES 3 OR 4 SERVINGS

2 small sugar pumpkins, halved and seeded

2 tablespoons extra-virgin olive oil, plus extra
  for coating the pumpkins

Sea salt

1 small yellow onion, diced

3 to 4 carrots, diced

Grated zest of 1 lemon

1 tablespoon mirin or white wine

2 cups spring or filtered water

1 cup plain soymilk, plus extra if needed

2 teaspoons sweet white miso

2 to 3 tablespoons pumpkin seeds, pan-
  toasted, for garnish

2 to 3 sprigs fresh parsley, minced, for garnish

Preheat the oven to 375°F. Generously rub the outside skin of the sugar pumpkins with oil and place, cut sides down, in a shallow baking pan. Sprinkle lightly with salt and add ⅛ inch water to the baking pan. Cover loosely with foil and bake about 40 minutes, until the pumpkins are tender (baking time depends on the size of the pumpkins). Remove from oven and set aside to cool.

Place the 2 tablespoons oil and the onion in a medium soup pot over medium-high heat. When the onion begins to sizzle, add a pinch of salt and sauté for 2 minutes. Stir in the carrots, a pinch of salt, the lemon zest and mirin. Sauté for 1 to 2 minutes.

Scoop the pumpkin flesh out of the skins and add to the vegetables in the soup pot. Add the water and soymilk, cover and bring to a boil. Reduce the heat to low and cook the soup until the carrots are quite soft, about 25 minutes.

Transfer the soup, by ladlefuls, to a food mill and puree until smooth. Add a small amount of soymilk to thin the soup as desired. Return the soup to the pot and place over very low heat.

Remove a small amount of broth and use to dissolve the miso. Stir the miso mixture into the soup and simmer, uncovered, for 3 to 4 minutes to activate the enzymes in the miso. Serve garnished with the pumpkin seeds and parsley.

LEEK, PARSNIP AND GINGER SOUP

Sweet and spicy . . . we love soups like that. With leek for light energy, parsnip for sweet strength and ginger to stimulate circulation, this creamy bisque is all you've ever dreamed of in a soup.
MAKES 3 TO 4 SERVINGS OF SOUP AND
4 TABLESPOONS OF CANDIED ORANGE PEEL

Soup
About 2 tablespoons extra-virgin olive oil
2 to 3 cloves fresh garlic, minced
1 small leek, halved lengthwise, rinsed well, diced
Sea salt
4 to 5 parsnips, diced
3 to 4 cups plain soymilk
1-inch piece fresh ginger, grated, juice extracted

Candied Orange Peel
2 oranges
3 tablespoons brown rice syrup
Sea salt

To make the soup: Place the oil, garlic and leek in a small soup pot over medium-high heat. When the vegetables begin to sizzle, add a pinch of salt and sauté for 1 to 2 minutes. Stir in the parsnips and a pinch of salt and sauté for 1 to 2 minutes. Add the soymilk, cover and bring to a boil. Reduce the heat to low and cook the soup until the parsnips are quite soft, about 25 minutes. Stir in the ginger juice, season to taste with salt and simmer for 7 to 10 minutes.

Transfer the soup, by ladlefuls, to a food mill and purée until smooth. Return the soup to the pot and simmer over very low heat.

While the soup simmers, prepare the peel: remove the zest of the oranges, using a zester to create long ribbons. Place the zest, rice syrup and pinch of salt in a saucepan. Place over high heat, and cook, stirring, until the syrup foams. Remove from the heat.

Serve the soup, garnished with the orange peel.

RIBOLLITA

A Tuscan tradition, this soup has its roots in poverty, because it is made by adding stale bread to the previous day's vegetable minestra, so there will be enough for today. Farm wives created this soup to keep their men big and strong. Interesting how modern life hasn't changed so much after all.
MAKES 4 TO 5 SERVINGS

1 to 2 tablespoons extra-virgin olive oil
2 to 3 cloves fresh garlic, minced
1 small yellow onion, diced
Sea salt
1 carrot, diced
1 to 2 small turnips, diced
¼ head green cabbage, diced
1 cup white wine
1 medium loaf whole-grain sourdough bread, coarsely crumbled
3 to 4 cups spring or filtered water
2 teaspoons sweet white miso

3 to 4 sprigs flat-leaf parsley, finely minced, for garnish
Fruity olive oil, for drizzling

Place the extra-virgin olive oil, garlic and onion in a small soup pot over medium-high heat. When the vegetables begin to sizzle, add a pinch of salt and sauté for 1 to 2 minutes. Stir in the carrot, turnips and a pinch of salt and sauté for 1 to 2 minutes. Stir in the cabbage and sauté until limp, about 2 minutes.

Pour in the white wine and top with the bread. Add the water, cover and bring to a boil. Reduce the heat to low and cook until the vegetables and bread are quite tender, 25 to 35 minutes. Remove a small amount of broth and use to dissolve the miso. Stir the miso mixture into soup and simmer, uncovered, for 3 to 4 minutes to activate the enzymes in the miso. Serve garnished with the parsley and a drizzle of fruity olive oil.

Variation: You may add cooked lentils or chickpeas to this soup for added energy and protein.

TUSCAN KALE SOUP

Silky, white and smooth—this creamy soup is rich with oil and garlic and laced through with energizing leafy green vegetables to create beautiful skin.
MAKES 4 TO 5 SERVINGS

About 2 tablespoons extra-virgin olive oil
1 to 2 cloves fresh garlic, finely minced

1 yellow onion, finely diced
Sea salt
½ cup white Arborio rice (do not rinse)
4 cups spring or filtered water
4 to 5 leaves fresh kale, rinsed well
½ red bell pepper, roasted over an open flame, peeled, seeded and minced (see sidebar below)

Place the oil, garlic and onion in a small soup pot over medium heat. When the vegetables begin to sizzle, add a pinch of salt and sauté until the onions are translucent, about 3 minutes. Stir in the rice to coat with oil. Add the water, cover and bring to a boil. Reduce the heat to low and cook for 20 to 25 minutes, until the rice is quite soft. Season to taste with salt.

Slice the kale into bite-size pieces just before stirring it into the soup. Simmer, uncovered, until the kale is just tender, about 3 minutes. Serve garnished with the bell pepper.

ROASTING PEPPERS

To roast a bell or chile pepper, rinse and dry the pepper and place over an open flame. Cook, turning with tongs, until the outer skin of the pepper is completely charred. Transfer the pepper to a paper sack, seal and allow the pepper to steam for about 10 minutes. Gently rub the charred skin from the pepper and rinse gently to remove any charred residue. Roasted peppers will keep, refrigerated, for about a week.

HARMONY SOUP

Sure, you have to actually make two soups for this recipe, but isn't harmony in your life worth a little extra effort?

MAKES 3 TO 4 SERVINGS

Black Soybean Soup
About 2 tablespoons extra-virgin olive oil
1 yellow onion, finely diced
2 small carrots, finely diced
1 stalk celery, finely diced
1 cup cooked black soybeans
Grated zest of 1 lemon
2 cups spring or filtered water
1 teaspoon barley miso

Squash Soup
1 yellow onion, finely diced
1 small butternut squash, peeled, seeded and finely diced
3 cups plain soymilk
2 teaspoons mirin
Grated zest of 1 orange
Sea salt

6 to 8 thin carrot rounds, for garnish

To make the soybean soup: Place the oil and onion in a medium saucepan over medium heat. When the onion begins to sizzle, sauté for 1 minute. Add the carrots and celery and sauté for 2 minutes. Stir in the soybeans, lemon zest and water. Cover and bring to a boil. Reduce the heat to low and cook until the vegetables and beans are quite soft, about 20 minutes. Remove a small amount of broth from the pot and use to dissolve the miso. Stir the miso mixture into the soup and simmer, uncov-ered, for 3 to 4 minutes to activate the enzymes in the miso.

To make the squash soup while the soybean soup cooks: place the onion, squash, soymilk, mirin and orange zest in a saucepan and add a pinch of salt. Cover and bring to a boil over medium heat. Reduce the heat to low and simmer until the squash is quite soft, about 20 minutes. Season lightly with salt and simmer for 3 to 4 minutes.

Transfer the soybean soup, by ladlefuls, to a food mill and purée until smooth. Return the soup to the pot over low heat. Purée the squash soup. Return it to the pot over low heat.

To serve, transfer each soup to a large glass measuring cup with a pouring spout or to a pitcher. Pour both soups, simultaneously, into individual bowls, so that a "seam" forms in the middle of the bowls. Using a wooden skewer, pull and push the seam of the soups to create a yin/yang symbol. Place a carrot round on each side of the soup and serve.

CORN SOUP WITH RED BELL PEPPER SALSA

This soup is a midsummer's night dream, fresh corn in a creamy broth, topped with a slightly spicy salsa. Its sweet and spicy flavors dance on the tongue, sensual, with just a hint of the heat of the season.

MAKES 4 TO 5 SERVINGS OF SOUP AND 1 CUP OF SALSA

Red Bell Pepper Salsa
1 small tomato, diced
1 small red bell pepper, seeded and diced

2 to 3 leaves fresh basil, minced, or ½
  teaspoon dried basil
Extra-virgin olive oil
Sea salt
¼ teaspoon red pepper flakes

Corn Soup
About 1 tablespoon extra-virgin olive oil
2 cloves fresh garlic, finely minced
½ yellow onion, finely diced
Sea salt
2 small carrots, finely diced
1 stalk celery, finely diced
2½ cups fresh corn kernels
2 teaspoons mirin
3 cups plain soymilk
1 cup spring or filtered water
Fruity olive oil, for drizzling

To make the salsa: Preheat the oven to 400°F and line a baking sheet with parchment paper.

Combine the tomato and bell pepper in a mixing bowl. Toss in the basil and drizzle generously with oil. Sprinkle lightly with salt and red pepper flakes. Gently mix to coat the vegetables. Spread the tomato mixture on the baking sheet and bake, uncovered, tossing occasionally, until the vegetables brown slightly, 15 to 20 minutes. Mix well to combine and set aside. The salsa will keep, refrigerated, for about 4 days.

To make the soup: Place the extra-virgin olive oil, garlic and onion in a small soup pot over medium heat. When the vegetables begin to sizzle, add a pinch of salt and sauté for 1 to 2 minutes. Stir in the carrots, celery and a pinch of salt and sauté for 1 minute. Stir in the corn, mirin, soymilk and water. Cover and bring to a boil. Reduce the heat to low and cook until the corn and other vegetables are just tender, about 15 min-

utes. Season to taste with salt, but remember this is a sweet soup, so go easy with the salt. Simmer for 3 to 4 minutes. Serve garnished with a generous spoonful of salsa and a drizzle of fruity olive oil.

FAVA BEAN AND SPRING VEGETABLE SOUP

A soup reflective of the rites of spring, when a young man's mind turns to thoughts of love. If you can find fresh favas, you can create a pale green soup as delicate as the sprouting shoots of the season.
MAKES 4 TO 5 SERVINGS

1 pound fresh fava beans, in the shell (see note below)
About 1 tablespoon extra-virgin olive oil
2 to 3 cloves fresh garlic
1 small leek, split lengthwise, rinsed well, diced
Sea salt
8 to 10 asparagus spears, tough ends snapped off and stalks sliced into ½-inch pieces
2 teaspoons mirin
3 cups plain soymilk
1 cup spring or filtered water
Small handful fresh flat-leaf parsley, minced, for garnish

Bring a small pot of water to a boil. Shell the fava beans and blanch them for 1 minute. Drain and set aside to cool. Peel off and discard the skin surrounding the beans.

Place the oil, garlic and leek in a small soup pot over medium heat. When the vegetables begin to sizzle, add a pinch of salt and sauté for 1 minute. Stir in the asparagus, mirin, soymilk and water. Stir in the favas. Cover and bring to a boil. Reduce the heat to low and simmer until the vegetables are just tender, but still green, 7 to 10 minutes. Season to taste with salt and simmer for 2 to 3 minutes. Transfer the soup, by ladlefuls, to a food mill and purée until smooth. Return to the pot and warm over low heat. Serve garnished with a sprinkle of parsley.

Note: If fresh fava beans are not available, you may use frozen or substitute 1 cup dried baby lima beans. Cook the limas by soaking them in lightly salted water for 3 hours, draining and cooking in 3 cups of water until tender, about 45 minutes. When the limas are tender, drain the remaining cooking liquid and proceed with the recipe.

MISO SOUP WITH SAUTÉED GREENS

This may be a basic recipe, but nothing starts your engine quite like miso soup. Laced through with fresh vegetables and topped with richly sautéed greens, this could be the start of something big.

MAKES 2 TO 3 SERVINGS

> **2-inch piece wakame, soaked until tender**
> **4 dried shiitake mushrooms, soaked until tender**
> **Spring or filtered water**
> **½ yellow onion, cut into thin half-moon slices**
> **1 carrot, cut into thin oblong slices**
> **2 teaspoons barley miso**

> **3 to 4 leaves kale or collard greens, rinsed well**
> **About 1 tablespoon extra-virgin olive oil**
> **½ red onion, finely minced**
> **¼ red bell pepper, roasted over an open flame (page 57), peeled, seeded and sliced into thin ribbons**

Drain the wakame, reserving the soaking water, and slice into bite-size pieces. Drain the mushrooms, reserving the soaking water, and slice into bite-size pieces. Place the wakame, mushrooms and all the soaking water in a medium soup pot, along with enough additional water to equal 4 cups. Cover and bring to a boil over medium heat. Add the yellow onion and carrot, cover and return to a boil. Reduce the heat to low and cook until the carrot is tender, about 6 minutes. Remove a small amount of broth and use to dissolve the miso. Stir the miso mixture into the soup and simmer, uncovered, for 3 to 4 minutes to activate the enzymes in the miso.

While the soup simmers, slice the greens into small pieces. Place the oil, red onion and bell pepper in a small sauté pan and place over high heat. When the vegetables begin to sizzle, sauté for 1 minute. Stir in the greens and sauté until just wilted, about 2 minutes.

To serve, ladle the soup into individual serving bowls and top with a generous amount of sautéed greens. Serve immediately.

TOMATO-FENNEL SOUP

A delicious soup at the end of summer, those golden days just before autumn, when tomatoes are freshest and the fennel is just coming in. The lively energy of late-season tomatoes says farewell to summer as fennel ushers autumn in.

MAKES 4 TO 5 SERVINGS

1 to 2 tablespoons extra-virgin olive oil

1 yellow onion, diced

Sea salt

1 carrot, diced

1 small fennel bulb, tops removed, 4 tablespoons reserved for garnish, and bulb diced

5 to 6 fresh vine-ripened tomatoes, diced (do not peel or seed)

4 cups spring or filtered water

2 teaspoons white miso

1½ cups cooked small pasta (orzo, pastina, small shells)

Place the oil and onion in a soup pot over medium heat. When the onion begins to sizzle, add a pinch of salt and sauté for 2 minutes. Add the carrot and a pinch of salt and sauté for 1 minute. Add the fennel, tomatoes and a pinch of salt and sauté just until the fennel is shiny with oil. Add the water, cover and bring to a boil. Reduce the heat to low and simmer until the fennel is soft, 20 to 25 minutes.

Remove a small amount of broth and use to dissolve the miso. Stir the miso mixture into the soup along with the cooked pasta and simmer, uncovered, for 3 to 4 minutes to activate the enzymes in the miso. Finely mince the reserved fennel tops and use to garnish the soup.

MISO

A fermented soybean paste used traditionally to flavor soups, it's prized in Asia for its ability to strengthen the digestive system. A great source of protein, miso is rich in digestive enzymes and friendly bacteria, both key ingredients to the health of the microvilli in our intestinal tracts.

PAPPA AL POMODORO

Visions of a Tuscan summer come in each spoonful of this simple, richly flavored Italian tradition. Using only the freshest tomatoes at the peak of their flavor, this simple soup is summer at its best.

MAKES 4 TO 5 SERVINGS

1 to 2 tablespoons extra-virgin olive oil

2 to 3 cloves fresh garlic, finely minced

2 to 3 pounds vine-ripened tomatoes, diced (do not peel or seed)

4 to 5 cups spring or filtered water

1 whole carrot, unpeeled

Sea salt

1 small loaf whole-grain sourdough bread, coarsely crumbled

2 teaspoons sweet white miso

1 small bunch fresh basil, finely minced

Place the oil and the garlic in a soup pot over medium heat. As soon as the garlic begins to sizzle (do not let it burn), add the tomatoes and water. Bring to a boil and add the carrot, several pinches of salt and the bread. Stir well, cover and return to a boil. Reduce the heat to low and simmer until the bread is quite soft, 35 to 40 minutes. Remove the carrot from the pot and discard.

Remove a small amount of broth and use to dissolve the miso. Stir the miso mixture into the soup and simmer, uncovered, for 3 to 4 minutes to activate the enzymes in the miso. Stir in the basil and serve.

Cook's Tip: Adding the whole carrot to the soup will draw excess acid from the tomatoes into itself, making them easier to digest. A whole carrot can be added to any tomato soup or sauce to ease digestion.

SPICY LENTIL SOUP

A comforting, thick soup, it's sweet with an underlying spicy flavor. Serve with a crisp, fresh salad and a chunk of whole-grain bread and you have created the perfect light meal.
MAKES 5 TO 6 SERVINGS

1 to 2 tablespoons extra-virgin olive oil
2 to 3 cloves fresh garlic, finely minced
1 small yellow onion, diced
Sea salt
1 carrot, diced
1 small sweet potato, diced
1 small dried red chile, crushed
1 teaspoon ground cumin
1 teaspoon turmeric
1 cup green or brown lentils, sorted and rinsed well
1 bay leaf
4 cups spring or filtered water
2 teaspoons white miso
2 to 3 sprigs fresh basil, finely minced

Place the oil, garlic and onion in a soup pot over medium heat. When the onion begins to sizzle, add a pinch of salt and sauté for 2 minutes. Add the carrot, sweet potato and another pinch of salt and sauté, stirring occasionally, until shiny with oil. Add the chili, cumin and turmeric and stir well. Add the lentils, bay leaf and water, cover and bring to a boil. Reduce the heat to low and simmer until the lentils are quite soft, about 45 minutes. Remove a small amount of broth and use to dissolve the miso. Stir the miso mixture into the soup, remove the bay leaf and simmer the soup, uncovered, for 3 to 4 minutes to activate the enzymes in the miso. Stir the basil into the soup and serve immediately.

SUMMER MINESTRA

I know what you're thinking . . . hot soup in the summer? The warmth of the broth keeps your body in even balance with the external heat of the season; with the moisture from the fresh vegetables, you remain calm, cool and collected.
MAKES 4 TO 5 SERVINGS

1 to 2 tablespoons extra-virgin olive oil
1 to 2 cloves fresh garlic, thinly sliced
1 small leek, split lengthwise, rinsed well, thinly sliced
Sea salt
2 stalks celery, diced
1 carrot, diced
2 small zucchini, diced
3 fresh vine-ripened tomatoes, diced (do not peel or seed)
1 bay leaf
4 cups spring or filtered water

1 cup cooked chickpeas (see note below)

2 teaspoons white miso

3 sprigs fresh basil, finely shredded

Place the oil, garlic and leek in a soup pot over medium heat. When the leek begins to sizzle, add a pinch of salt and sauté for 1 minute. Add the celery, carrot, zucchini and a pinch of salt and sauté for 1 minute. Stir in the tomatoes and bay leaf. Add the water, cover and bring to a boil. Reduce the heat to low and simmer for 20 minutes. Add the chickpeas. Remove a small amount of broth and use to dissolve the miso. Stir the miso mixture into the soup and simmer, uncovered, for 3 to 4 minutes to activate the enzymes in the miso. Remove the bay leaf and stir in the basil. Serve immediately.

Note: You may cook organic chickpeas from scratch or use canned organic chickpeas.

~~~~~~

HOT, HOT, HOT BLACK BEAN SOUP

There's something about beans that just screams for spicy flavors. Perhaps it's the intuitive knowledge that adding a bit of spice makes the protein easier to digest and less heavy in our tummies. Or maybe it's just that it's a fabulous combination. Truth? It doesn't matter; it's delicious.

MAKES 5 TO 6 SERVINGS

1 to 2 tablespoons extra-virgin olive oil

2 to 3 cloves fresh garlic, thinly sliced

1 dried red chile, crushed

1 teaspoon minced fresh ginger

1 red onion, diced

Sea salt

1 carrot, diced

1 cup diced butternut squash

Mirin

1 cup fresh or frozen corn kernels

2 cups cooked black turtle beans

5 cups spring or filtered water

2 scallions, thinly sliced on the diagonal, for garnish

Place the oil, garlic, chile, ginger and onion in a soup pot over medium heat. When the onion begins to sizzle, add a pinch of salt and sauté for 2 minutes. Stir in the carrot, squash, a pinch of salt and a generous sprinkle of mirin. Sauté, stirring occasionally, until just shiny with oil. Add the corn and beans and stir gently. Add the water, cover and bring to a boil. Reduce the heat to low and cook for 30 minutes. Season to taste with salt and simmer for 5 minutes. Serve garnished with the scallions.

MIRIN

A Japanese rice wine with a sweet taste and very low alcohol content, it's made by fermenting sweet brown rice with koji (cultured rice) and water. Mirin adds a depth and dimension to sauces, glazes, soups and stews.

CURRIED SWEET POTATO SOUP

Sweet and spicy . . . sounds like a great date. Don't get too excited; this is only the starter course for an autumn feast. The earthy taste of the curry lifts the natural sweetness of the soup high onto your palate for the most delicious, creamy bisque you can imagine.

MAKES 4 TO 5 SERVINGS

1 to 2 tablespoons extra-virgin olive oil
2 to 3 cloves fresh garlic, finely minced
1 yellow onion, diced
½ to 1 teaspoon curry powder
Sea salt
3 to 4 medium sweet potatoes, peeled and diced
2 cups plain soymilk
2 cups spring or filtered water
2 teaspoons sweet white miso
2 to 3 sprigs fresh flat-leaf parsley, finely minced, for garnish

Place the oil, garlic, onion and curry powder in a soup pot over medium heat. When the onion begins to sizzle, add a pinch of salt and sauté for 1 minute. Stir in the sweet potatoes and a pinch of salt and sauté for 1 minute. Add the soymilk and water, cover and bring to a boil. Reduce the heat to low and simmer until the sweet potatoes are quite soft, 40 minutes.

Transfer the soup, by ladlefuls, to a food processor and purée until smooth. Return the soup to the pot over low heat. Remove a small amount of broth and use to dissolve the miso. Stir the miso mixture into the soup and simmer, uncovered, for 3 to 4 minutes to activate the enzymes in the miso. Serve garnished with the parsley.

CREAMY SHIITAKE SOUP

Not just any creamy mushroom soup, this one is jammed with nutrition and energy. And in case shiitake and barley aren't strong enough for you, I've upped the ante with a touch of hempseeds, one of the most ancient and nutritious forms of food known.

MAKES 4 TO 5 SERVINGS

1 yellow onion, diced
8 to 10 dried shiitake mushrooms, soaked until tender and thinly sliced
½ cup pearl barley, rinsed well
4 cups spring or filtered water
Sea salt
2 teaspoons barley miso
⅓ cup shelled hempseeds
2 to 3 scallions, thinly sliced on the diagonal, for garnish

Place the onion, shiitake mushrooms and barley in a soup pot with the water and a pinch of salt. Cover and bring to a boil over medium heat. Reduce the heat to low and simmer for 35 minutes. Remove a small amount of broth and use to dissolve the miso. Stir the miso mixture into the soup and simmer, uncovered, for 3 to 4 minutes to activate the enzymes in the miso. Stir in the hempseeds and serve, garnished with the scallions.

WHAT'S UP WITH HEMP?

Let's get the jokes over with straight away. Hemp is not marijuana. Industrial hemp is one of the oldest cultivated plants, valued by many cultures for its ability to nourish so completely. Hempseeds have been enjoyed throughout the world for thousands of years, staving off hunger, used in traditional medicine and eaten by hardworking peasants for strength and endurance. Still widely used in Asia and Europe, hempseeds have been pretty much off the radar screen in the United States, thanks to politics and special-interest groups. Until recently, that is. A small, but tenacious group of environmentally aware entrepreneurs have worked tirelessly to create a market for shelled hempseeds as food. I have to admit that I was unaware of the value of hempseed as food until a couple of years ago. I knew that hemp and hempseeds existed, but I didn't think much about them, except from an environmental standpoint. I wished that our farmers could still cultivate this valuable crop, yielding fiber for cloth and paper, nourishing the soil and requiring little or no pesticides. I loved the fabric that came from hemp, loved its durability and soft texture. I loved that it didn't harm our fragile planet. But food? Over the next couple of years, as I became educated about this incredible plant, I came to be a true believer that hempseeds are, indeed, the hope of the future. Why? Made up of more than 30 percent complete protein, with all of the essential amino acids necessary for digestion, rich in essential fatty acids, omega-3 and omega-6 (occurring in the biologically optimal ratio for long-term maintenance of healthy human tissue), respectable amounts of omega-9, trace minerals, vitamins, fiber and other essential nutrients, hempseeds and their oil are powerhouses of nutrition.

WILD THING SOUP

I got this recipe from the original wild thing himself, my friend Richard Rose, a great vegan chef and food innovator. From soyfoods to his current passion, hempseed foods, Richard never takes the safe route but is always interesting . . . just like this soup.

MAKES 4 TO 5 SERVINGS

1 tablespoon extra-virgin olive oil
1 clove fresh garlic, finely minced
1 yellow onion, diced
Sea salt
1 cup finely diced Yukon Gold potatoes
4 cups spring or filtered water
4 cups mixed wild greens (dandelion, nettle, violet, lamb's quarter or a mixture)
2 teaspoons sweet white miso
½ cup shelled hempseeds
½ red bell pepper, roasted over an open flame (page 57), peeled, seeded and sliced into thin ribbons

Place the oil, garlic and onion in a soup pot over medium heat. When the onion begins to sizzle, add a pinch of salt and sauté for 1 minute. Add the potatoes and sauté briefly. Add the water, cover and bring to a boil. Reduce heat and simmer until the potatoes are soft, about 25 minutes. Finely chop the greens and stir into the soup. Remove a small amount of broth and use to dissolve the miso. Stir the miso mixture into the soup and simmer, uncovered for 3 to 4 minutes to activate the enzymes in the miso. Stir in the hempseeds just before serving and serve garnished with the bell pepper.

PASTA AND PESTO SOUP

Nothing says summer quite like fresh basil pesto, and as the crowning glory of this simple soup, it's at its earthy, decadent best.

MAKES 4 TO 5 SERVINGS OF SOUP AND I CUP OF PESTO

Soup
1 to 2 tablespoons extra-virgin olive oil
2 to 3 cloves fresh garlic, thinly sliced
1 yellow onion, diced
Sea salt
1 yellow summer squash, diced
1 zucchini, diced
1 cup fresh or frozen corn kernels
4 cups spring or filtered water
2 to 3 sprigs fresh flat-leaf parsley, finely
 minced
1 cup cooked tiny pasta (small shells, orzo,
 pastina)

Basil Pesto
1 cup loosely packed fresh basil leaves
1 cup pine nuts and/or walnuts
1 tablespoon white miso
¼ cup extra-virgin olive oil
2 teaspoons brown rice syrup
1 teaspoon umeboshi plum vinegar
Spring or filtered water, if needed

To make the soup: Place the oil, garlic and onion in a soup pot over medium heat. When the onion begins to sizzle, add a pinch of salt and sauté for 1 minute. Stir in the summer squash and zucchini, add another pinch of salt and sauté for 1 minute. Stir in the corn, add the water, cover and bring to a boil. Reduce the heat to low and cook for 20 minutes. Season to taste with salt and sim-mer for 5 minutes. Stir in the parsley and cooked pasta.

While the soup cooks, make the pesto: Bring a small pot of water to a boil and quickly dip the basil leaves into the boiling water (this helps the pesto hold its color) and drain well. Place the basil, nuts, miso, oil, rice syrup and vinegar in a food processor. Purée until smooth, adding a small amount of water only if needed to smooth the pesto. The thicker the pesto, the better the flavor.

Ladle the soup into individual bowls and place a generous spoon of pesto in the center of each bowl.

LEMONY ASPARAGUS SOUP

Spring in a bowl, this soup, light and slightly tart, with a creamy richness and elegant pale green hue satisfies us as deeply as seeing the first tulips of the season break through the frozen earth.

MAKES 4 TO 5 SERVINGS

1 small leek, split lengthwise, rinsed well,
 thinly sliced
1 bunch asparagus, tough ends snapped off
 and stalks cut into 1-inch pieces
2 stalks celery, diced
Grated zest of 1 lemon
2 cups plain soymilk
2 cups spring or filtered water
2 tablespoons mirin or white wine
Sea salt
2 to 3 scallions, thinly sliced on the diagonal,
 for garnish
Thin lemon slices, for garnish

Place the leek, asparagus, celery and lemon zest in a soup pot. Add the soymilk, water, mirin and a pinch of salt. Cover and bring to a boil over medium heat. Reduce the heat to low and cook for 15 minutes. Season to taste with salt and simmer for 5 minutes.

Transfer the soup, by ladlefuls, to a food processor and purée until smooth. Return the soup to the pot and simmer for 1 to 2 minutes. Serve garnished with the scallions and lemon slices.

CREAMY CAULIFLOWER BISQUE WITH PUMPKIN SEED PESTO

Smooth as silk and mildly sweet, this creamy bisque comes to life with a generous dollop of spicy pumpkin seed pesto. The old theory that opposites attract holds true here, as sweet and spicy join forces for a great starter course.

MAKES 5 TO 6 SERVINGS OF SOUP AND 1⅓ CUPS OF PESTO

Bisque
1 yellow onion, diced
1 head cauliflower, florets removed, stem discarded
½ cup Arborio rice
5 cups spring or filtered water
Mirin
Sea salt

Pumpkin Seed Pesto
1 cup pumpkin seeds
1 cup loosely packed fresh basil leaves
½ cup loosely packed fresh flat-leaf parsley
⅓ cup extra-virgin olive oil
1 tablespoon white miso
¼ teaspoon chili powder
Juice of 2 lemons
Spring or filtered water, if needed

½ red bell pepper, roasted over an open flame (page 57), peeled, seeded and finely diced, for garnish

To make the bisque: Place the onion, cauliflower and rice in a soup pot. Add the water, a generous splash of mirin and a pinch of salt. Cover and bring to a boil over medium heat. Reduce the heat to low and cook until the cauliflower is soft, about 30 minutes. Season to taste with salt and simmer for 5 minutes. Transfer the soup, by ladlefuls, to a food processor and purée until smooth. Return the soup to the pot and keep the soup at a simmer, while making the pesto.

To make the pesto: Place the pumpkin seeds, basil, parsley and olive oil in a food processor and pulse into a coarse paste. Add the miso, chili powder and lemon juice. Purée until smooth. You may need to add a small amount of water to purée properly, but keep the pesto thick, so that it holds its shape in the soup.

To serve, spoon the soup into individual bowls and scoop a generous dollop of pesto in the center of each bowl and sprinkle with the bell pepper.

POLENTA SOUP

Simple and delicious, this soup will get any meal off to a great start. Just a few ingredients come together to create a dish that is creamy, richly flavored, relaxing to our digestion and oh so easy to make.

MAKES 5 TO 6 SERVINGS

1 to 2 tablespoons extra-virgin olive oil
2 to 3 cloves fresh garlic, finely minced
1 yellow onion, diced
Sea salt
¼ head green cabbage, cut into small dice
5 cups spring or filtered water
⅔ cup yellow cornmeal
2 teaspoons sweet white miso
2 to 3 sprigs fresh flat-leaf parsley, finely
   minced, for garnish

Place the oil, garlic and onion in a soup pot over medium heat. When the onion begins to sizzle, add a pinch of salt and sauté for 1 to 2 minutes. Stir in the cabbage and a pinch of salt and sauté for 1 minute. Add the water and slowly whisk in the cornmeal, to prevent lumping. Cover and bring to a boil. Reduce the heat to low and cook for 20 minutes. Remove a small amount of broth and use to dissolve the miso. Stir the miso mixture into the soup and simmer, uncovered, for 3 to 4 minutes to activate the enzymes in the miso. Serve garnished with the parsley.

GARLICKY CARROT SOUP

There is nothing quite like intensely flavored soups. In this one, we enhance the delicate sweetness of the carrots with the strong, earthy taste of garlic. Energizing but, at the same time, relaxing, this soup will get everyone's attention.

MAKES 5 TO 6 SERVINGS

1 to 2 tablespoons extra-virgin olive oil
4 to 5 cloves fresh garlic, finely minced
1 yellow onion, diced
Sea salt
6 to 7 carrots, diced
½ small butternut squash, diced
Mirin
4 to 5 cups spring or filtered water
2 teaspoons sweet white miso
3 to 4 sprigs fresh basil, leaves removed, finely
   shredded

Place the oil, garlic and onion in a soup pot over medium heat. When the onion begins to sizzle, add a pinch of salt and sauté for 1 minute. Stir in the carrots, squash and another pinch of salt and sauté just until shiny with oil. Add a generous splash of mirin and the water. Cover and bring to a boil. Reduce the heat to low and cook until the carrots are quite soft, about 45 minutes. Remove a small amount of broth and use to dissolve the miso. Stir the miso mixture into the soup and simmer, uncovered, for 3 to 4 minutes to activate the enzymes in the miso. Serve garnished with the basil.

BARBADOS SPLIT-PEA SOUP

I spend a lot of time in Barbados, cooking for our travel company. When I was making split-pea soup one day Cally, a friend of mine who is a resident of Worthing, Christ Church (and a brilliant wind-surfer), asked if I was planning to add okra to my soup for flavor and vitality. I gave it a try and have never looked back. Hope you love it, too.

MAKES 4 TO 6 SERVINGS

1 yellow onion, diced
2 to 3 stalks celery, diced
1 to 2 carrots, diced
⅔ cup sliced okra
1 cup split peas, sorted and rinsed well
2 bay leaves
1-inch piece kombu
1 dried chiptole chile (smoked jalapeño), left whole
Grated zest of 1 lemon
4 cups spring or filtered water
Sea salt
2 to 3 scallions, thinly sliced on the diagonal, for garnish

Layer the onion, celery, carrots and okra in a soup pot. Top with the split peas. Work the bay leaves and kombu to the bottom with your finger. Add the chile, lemon zest and water, cover and bring to a boil over medium heat. Reduce the heat to low and cook for 45 to 60 minutes. Season to taste with salt and remove the bay leaves and chile. Using a hand blender, purée the soup until smooth. Serve garnished with the scallions.

CREAM OF WATERCRESS SOUP

Creamy, smooth and just a bit peppery, this simple soup is the perfect starter for a spring feast. It's relaxing but with a gentle kick to get our energy moving in sync with the season.

MAKES 4 TO 6 SERVINGS

1 yellow onion, diced
1 (14-ounce) package silken tofu, boiled for 4 minutes, coarsely crumbled
4 cups plain soymilk
Sea salt
1 large bunch watercress, rinsed well, diced
Mirin
2 teaspoons sweet white miso
1 red bell pepper, roasted over an open flame (page 57), peeled, seeded and diced
Several sprigs of watercress, for garnish

Place the onion, tofu and soymilk in a soup pot. Add a pinch of salt, cover and bring to a boil over medium heat. Reduce the heat to low and simmer for 10 minutes. Stir in the watercress and season lightly with mirin. Cover and cook for 10 minutes. Transfer the soup, by ladlefuls, to a food processor and purée until smooth. Return the soup to the pot and place over low heat. Remove a small amount of broth and use to dissolve the miso. Stir the miso mixture into the soup and simmer, uncovered, for 3 to 4 minutes to activate the enzymes in the miso. Serve garnished with a sprinkle of roasted pepper and a few sprigs of watercress.

NOODLES AND BROTH WITH FRIED TOFU AND SCALLIONS

This comforting, satisfying and delicious one-dish meal can serve as a light lunch or a quick dinner for those days when we're on the run. And its effect on our energy? It gives us the vitality to keep up with our hectic lives without losing our grip.

MAKES 4 TO 6 SERVINGS

2 small leeks, split lengthwise, rinsed well, thinly sliced
1 carrot, cut into fine matchstick pieces
½ cup fine matchstick pieces fresh daikon
4 to 5 dried shiitake mushrooms, soaked until tender and thinly sliced
4 cups spring or filtered water
3 to 4 tablespoons soy sauce
1 teaspoon brown rice syrup
1 cup shredded Chinese cabbage
Avocado or light olive oil, for frying
½ block extra-firm tofu, cut into 1-inch cubes
4 ounces udon or soba noodles, cooked al dente
2 to 3 scallions, thinly sliced on the diagonal, for garnish

Layer the leeks, carrot, daikon and mushrooms, in order, in a soup pot. Add the water, cover and bring to a boil over medium heat. Reduce the heat to low and cook for 15 minutes. Add the soy sauce, rice syrup and cabbage and simmer for 5 to 7 minutes.

Meanwhile, fry the tofu. Heat about 1 inch oil in a deep skillet over medium heat. When the oil is hot (patterns will form, known as "dancing"), increase the heat to high and fry a few cubes of tofu at a time until golden brown, 2 to 3 minutes. Drain on parchment paper. Repeat with remaining tofu cubes until all are fried.

To serve, place some noodles in individual bowls. Spoon vegetables and broth over the noodles and top with fried tofu and scallions. Serve immediately.

DAIKON

A long white radish root with a refreshingly clean and peppery taste, it is prized in Asian healing for its ability to aid the body in the digestion of fats and protein, as well as cleansing organ tissue.

KALE AND BLACK-EYED PEA SOUP

A splendidly hearty soup to warm you down to your tippy toes, it has its very own yummy energy. With beans for enduring strength and greens to keep it on the lighter side, this starter course will start your engines and keep them humming.

MAKES 4 TO 6 SERVINGS

1 to 2 tablespoons extra-virgin olive oil
2 to 3 cloves fresh garlic, thinly sliced
1 yellow onion, diced
Sea salt
2 to 3 stalks celery, diced
1 carrot, diced

1 teaspoon sweet paprika

1 bay leaf

4 cups spring or filtered water

1¼ cups canned diced tomatoes with liquid

2 cups cooked black-eyed peas

2 teaspoons white miso

1 cup cooked brown rice

2 cups finely shredded fresh kale

Place the oil, garlic and onion in a soup pot over medium heat. When the onion begins to sizzle, add a pinch of salt and sauté for 1 minute. Add the celery, carrot, paprika, bay leaf and another pinch of salt and sauté for 1 minute. Add the water and tomatoes, cover and bring to a boil. Reduce the heat to low and cook for 15 minutes. Add the black-eyed peas and cook for 5 minutes. Remove a small amount of broth and use to dissolve the miso. Stir the miso mixture into the soup and remove the bay leaf. Stir in the brown rice and kale and simmer, uncovered, for 3 to 4 minutes to activate the enzymes in the miso, heat the rice and lightly cook the kale.

CORN CHOWDER WITH GARLIC CROUTONS

Summer means fresh, sweet corn in our home; we have it so often, it becomes a food group. From salads to stir-fry dishes to this rich, seasonal soup, there is nothing like fresh corn, on the cob or swimming in this delicious chowder. And the garlic croutons? They just make it sweeter, baby.

MAKES 4 TO 6 SERVINGS

Garlic Croutons

3 to 4 slices whole-grain sourdough bread

Extra-virgin olive oil

4 cloves fresh garlic, split lengthwise

Corn Chowder

1 yellow onion, diced

1 cup diced yellow summer squash

3 cups fresh corn kernels

4 cups plain soymilk

Sea salt

Mirin

4 to 5 sprigs fresh flat-leaf parsley, finely minced

To make the croutons: Preheat the oven to 400°F and line a baking sheet with parchment paper. Lightly brush the bread slices with olive oil and rub each side with the cut side of a garlic clove. Cut the coated bread into cubes and place on the lined baking sheet. Bake about 15 minutes, until crisp and golden brown.

To make the chowder: Place the onion, squash and corn in a soup pot. Add the soymilk, a pinch of salt and a generous splash of mirin. Cover and bring to a boil over medium heat. Reduce the heat to low and simmer for 15 minutes. Season lightly with salt and simmer for 5 to 7 minutes. Stir in the parsley and serve garnished with several garlic croutons.

SPICY VEGETABLE SOUP WITH CORN TORTILLAS

There's nothing quite like seasonal vegetables in a savory broth, and this soup has a zippy hint of spice to get your attention and keep you alert. Crispy corn tortillas on the side keep it all interesting.

MAKES 5 TO 6 SERVINGS

1 to 2 tablespoons extra-virgin
  olive oil
3 to 4 cloves fresh garlic, finely minced
1 yellow onion, diced
Sea salt
½ jalapeño chile, split lengthwise, minced
  (with seeds)
1 carrot, diced
1 yellow summer squash, diced
1 small zucchini, diced
4 to 6 fresh plum tomatoes, diced
  (do not peel or seed)
1 cup cooked chickpeas
4 cups spring or filtered water
Avocado or light olive oil
4 to 6 soft corn tortillas
3 to 4 sprigs fresh basil, leaves removed and
  finely shredded

Place the extra-virgin olive oil, garlic and onion in a soup pot over medium heat. When the onion begins to sizzle, add a pinch of salt and sauté for 1 minute. Stir in the chile, carrot and another pinch of salt and sauté for 1 minute. Add the yellow squash, zucchini and another pinch of salt and sauté for 1 minute. Stir in the tomatoes and chick-peas. Add the water, cover and bring to a boil. Reduce the heat to low and simmer for 30 min-

utes. Season to taste with salt and simmer for 5 to 7 minutes.

When the soup is nearly ready, heat about 2 inches avocado oil in a deep skillet over medium heat. Slice each tortilla into 8 wedges. When the oil is hot, increase the heat to high and fry the tortillas, in batches, until golden brown, 1 to 2 minutes. Drain on parchment paper and repeat until all tortilla pieces are fried. Sprinkle the tortillas lightly with salt.

To serve, stir the basil into the soup and ladle into individual bowls. You may top the soup with a handful of tortilla chips or serve them on the side.

Note: You may substitute organic corn chips if you don't have the time to fry your own.

CARAMELIZED ONION SOUP WITH ROASTED PORTOBELLO MUSHROOMS

Sweet, rich, delicious and satisfying, all this in a bowl of soup. It takes bit of effort, but it's worth the extra steps. Just think how grateful your tummy will be when it relaxes under the influence of this warming soup. You'll be so calm, everyone will think you've been on holiday.

MAKES 4 TO 6 SERVINGS

2 portobello mushrooms, stems removed and
  brushed free of dirt
About 2 tablespoons extra-virgin olive oil
Sea salt
Mirin or white wine

6 to 8 red onions, thinly sliced into half-
    moon pieces

3 to 4 cipolline onions, thinly sliced into half-
    moon pieces

4 cups spring or filtered water

2 teaspoons white miso

3 to 4 sprigs fresh flat-leaf parsley, finely
    minced, for garnish

Preheat the oven to 400°F. Lightly brush the mushrooms with some of the oil and place on a shallow baking sheet. Sprinkle lightly with salt and mirin. Bake, uncovered, about 20 minutes, until browned. Remove from the oven and when they are cool enough to handle, finely dice and set aside.

While the mushrooms bake, begin the rest of the soup. Place the remaining oil and the red and cipolline onions in a soup pot over medium heat. When the onions begin to sizzle, add a pinch of salt and sauté, stirring, until the onions have browned and begun to caramelize; this can take as long as 40 minutes. Add the water and roasted mushrooms, cover and bring to a boil. Reduce the heat and simmer for 25 to 30 minutes to develop the flavors. Remove a small amount of broth and use to dissolve the miso. Stir the miso mixture into the soup and simmer, uncovered, for 3 to 4 minutes to activate the enzymes in the miso. Serve garnished with the parsley.

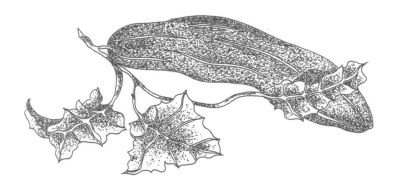

GREAT GRAINS, GREAT STRENGTH

Silky risotto, moist cornbread melting in your mouth, creamy polenta smothered in richly sautéed vegetables, crunchy crostini and grain salads dancing on your tongue and pasta so rich in flavor, each bite feels like a tease of pleasure to come. What? These aren't exactly the visuals that spring to mind when you think of whole grains?

Not only delicious, whole cereal grains are the foundation of our strength, instrumental in creating the vitality and stamina we all desire. I know, I know, they're so beige and neutral, like Clark Kent. Well, don't let their mild-mannered exterior fool you. Underneath hides a supernatural character. Within the humble grain lies the key to our physical strength.

Let's get clinical for just a minute. Whole grains are composed of complex carbohydrates, long-chain molecules that break down quite slowly in the body. Complex carbohydrates, essential components to leading a strong, vital life, keep us feeling nourished and stable. We need energy to fuel our bodies and spirits if we are to follow our dreams and desires.

We all know that the fiber in whole grains is an important factor in the prevention of digestive disorders, including colon cancer and diverticulitis. In Chinese medicine, intestinal function is said to govern our strength. Think of the clichés. "What a gutsy move." "Oh him? Gutless wonder." While funny to us, these sayings have their roots in the truth. Our strength and fortitude depend largely on the functioning of the microvilli in the small intestine and the overall function of the large intestine. The quality of nutrients taken into the body, along with how well they are assimilated, is responsible for nourishment or starvation of our other organs, resulting in our strength or weakness.

The soluble fiber in whole grains is linked to

our life blood in a more direct way. Not only responsible for digestive function, fiber has been found to lower cholesterol and reduce the buildup of plaque in arteries, reducing the risk of coronary diseases. To have drive of any kind, your heart needs to be well, beating strongly.

There's more to strengthening grain, however. The complex carbohydrates in whole grains break down slowly and are not absorbed into the bloodstream from the small intestine very quickly. Simple sugars, like refined sugar, honey, maple syrup and organic cane juice, raw sugar, date sugar, turbinado sugar and even fruit sugar are rapidly absorbed. Complex carbohydrates, however,

strengthen the ability of the digestive system to distribute nutrients essential to life.

But wait! There's more. Other important jobs of the intestines are to regulate our internal moisture and to influence the quality of the blood that will nourish all of our organs, determining their health and ours. If the intestines are working well, because we nourish them with nutrient-rich foods, then we stand straight, walk confidently, have courage, stay focused, and radiate vitality.

Rich in soluble fiber, complex sugars, minerals, protein and B vitamins, whole grains may look beige, but baby, they're as hot as it gets.

CORN AND CHANTERELLES

Just saying "chanterelles" sounds special, but it's the relaxing quality of these richly flavored mushrooms that will enchant you. With fresh corn adding a bit of vitality to the mix, you have the perfect side dish.
MAKES 4 TO 5 SERVINGS

> About 1 tablespoon extra-virgin olive oil
> 2 to 3 cloves fresh garlic, finely minced
> 1 small leek, split lengthwise, rinsed well, diced
> Sea salt
> 2 cups thinly sliced fresh chanterelles
> 2 cups fresh or frozen corn kernels
> Small handful fresh flat-leaf parsley, finely minced, for garnish
> Juice of 1 lemon

Place the oil, garlic and leek in a sauté pan over medium heat. When the leeks begin to sizzle, add a pinch of salt and sauté for 1 to 2 minutes. Stir in the chanterelles and a pinch of salt and sauté until the mushrooms release their juices and begin to reabsorb them. Stir in the corn, season to taste with salt and sauté for 2 to 3 minutes. Remove from the heat and stir in the parsley and lemon juice. Serve immediately.

CORNBREAD WITH GREEN BEAN SALAD

Moist cornbread, delicately sweet and smothered with the freshest green beans of the season, is sensual and easy to digest. This combination of grain and vegetables is a delicious light lunch.
MAKES 8 CORNBREAD SERVINGS AND ABOUT 4 SALAD SERVINGS

> *Cornbread*
> **2 cups whole wheat pastry flour**
> **1 cup yellow cornmeal**
> **2½ teaspoons baking powder**
> **Generous pinch sea salt**
> **½ teaspoon ground cinnamon**
> **½ cup extra-virgin olive oil**
> **2 tablespoons brown rice syrup**
> **⅔ to 1 cup plain soymilk**
> **½ cup fresh or frozen corn kernels**

> *Green Bean Salad*
> **About 1 tablespoon extra-virgin olive oil**
> **3 to 4 shallots, cut into thin slices**
> **2 cloves fresh garlic, minced**
> **Sea salt**
> **1 small carrot, cut into fine matchstick pieces**
> **Grated zest of 1 lemon**
> **2 to 3 cups green beans, tips trimmed, left whole**
> **Balsamic vinegar**

To make the cornbread: Preheat the oven to 350°F and lightly oil and flour a 9-inch-square glass baking dish.

Combine the flour, cornmeal, baking powder, salt and cinnamon in a mixing bowl. Whisk to impart air into the mixture. Stir in the oil and rice syrup. Slowly add the soymilk, mixing to create a smooth, spoonable batter. Fold in the corn. Spoon the batter evenly into prepared dish and bake for about 35 minutes, until the center springs back to the touch. Remove from the oven and set aside to cool before slicing.

To make the salad: Combine the oil, shallots and garlic in a sauté pan and place over medium heat. When the shallots begin to sizzle, add a pinch of salt and sauté until the shallots are just limp, about 1 minute. Add the carrot, lemon zest and a pinch of salt and sauté for 1 minute. Stir in the green beans, cover and reduce the heat to low. Cook until the beans are bright green and crisp-tender, about 4 minutes. Remove from the heat, sprinkle lightly with vinegar and stir gently to combine.

To serve, cut the cornbread into 8 pieces. Reserve 4 pieces for another use and place the remaining pieces on individual salad plates. Mound the green beans over the top of the cornbread and serve hot.

CARAMELIZED ONION AND ROSEMARY FOCACCIA

Soft, pillowy focaccia, topped with richly cooked onions, is balanced with sensible rosemary. More than just bread, focaccia strikes the perfect chord—sweet, savory, light, substantial—like a symphony.

MAKES 1 (10-INCH) FOCACCIA

Dough
1¾ teaspoons active dry yeast
¾ cup warm spring or filtered water
⅛ cup extra-virgin olive oil, plus extra for brushing
1 cup whole wheat bread flour
1 cup semolina flour
1¼ teaspoons sea salt

Topping
About 4 tablespoons extra-virgin olive oil
3 yellow onions, cut into thin half-moon slices
2 sprigs fresh rosemary, leaves removed, or 2 teaspoons dried rosemary, ground
Sea salt
Balsamic vinegar

1 fresh tomato, diced, for garnish

To make the dough: Stir the yeast into the warm water in a large mixing bowl. Allow to stand until foamy, about 10 minutes. Stir in the oil, then the flours and salt. Mix until the ingredients come together. Transfer to a lightly floured surface and knead until smooth and elastic, about 10 minutes.

Place the dough in an oiled bowl, cover tightly with plastic and set aside to rise until doubled, about 1 hour.

Flatten the dough into a disk. Lightly oil a 10-inch pie plate. Flatten and stretch the dough to mostly cover the bottom of the pie plate. Dimple the top of the focaccia with your fingertips, creating an uneven surface. Cover with a towel and set aside to rest for 10 minutes. Dimple and stretch the dough again, so that it completely covers the bottom of the pie plate. Brush lightly with oil, cover with a towel and set aside to rise until very puffy, about 50 minutes.

To prepare the topping: While the dough rises, place the oil and onions in a skillet over medium-high heat. When the onions begin to sizzle, add the rosemary and a generous pinch of salt and sauté for 2 minutes. Drizzle lightly with balsamic vinegar and reduce the heat to low. Cook, stirring frequently, until the onions are deeply browned, 15 to 20 minutes. Season to taste with salt and sauté for 2 to 3 minutes.

Preheat the oven to 425°F. Spoon the onions and cooking oil over the focaccia dough, covering generously, but allowing the dough to peek through.

Bake for 10 minutes. Reduce the heat to 375°F and bake 15 to 20 minutes, until the topping is browned and the focaccia is firm and the edges browned. Garnish with the tomato, slice into wedges and serve hot.

WILD MUSHROOM AND BLACK OLIVE PIZZA

Nothing says "Friday-night date" quite like pizza, but nothing diminishes the glow of an evening quite like fatty, oily cheese over the top of gluelike white-flour crusts. On the other hand, a whole-grain crust, smothered in silky, rich mushrooms and olives, with just a touch of spice creates a superb starter course.
MAKES I LARGE PIZZA

Pizza Dough
1 package active dry yeast
2 cups warm spring or filtered water
3 tablespoons extra-virgin olive oil
2 teaspoons sea salt
2½ cups semolina flour
2½ cups whole wheat flour

Topping
1 to 2 tablespoons extra-virgin olive oil, plus additional for drizzling
2 to 3 cloves fresh garlic, finely minced
½ yellow onion, diced
Sea salt
½ teaspoon red pepper flakes
1 cup loosely packed dried porcini mushrooms, soaked until tender
8 to 10 dried shiitake mushrooms, soaked until tender, thinly sliced
10 to 12 oil-cured black olives, pitted, finely minced

To make the dough: In a large bowl, dissolve the yeast in the warm water. Let stand until foamy, about 10 minutes. Stir in the oil and salt. Using a wooden spoon, slowly stir in the semolina flour.

Slowly stir in the whole wheat flour to form a soft, moist dough (which makes a crispy crust). Turn the dough out onto a lightly floured surface and knead for 10 to 15 minutes to achieve a smooth, elastic dough. Add flour as needed for kneading, but not too much or the dough will become dry. Transfer the dough to a lightly oiled bowl and oil the surface of the dough to prevent a crust from forming. Cover tightly with plastic wrap and set in a warm place to rise until doubled in size, about 2 hours.

While the dough rises, prepare the topping: Place the oil, garlic and onions in a skillet over medium-high heat. When the onions begin to sizzle, add a pinch of salt and the red pepper flakes and sauté for 2 to 3 minutes. Add the mushrooms, season lightly with salt and sauté until the mushrooms release their juices into the pan and reabsorb them, about 10 minutes. Remove from heat and stir in the olives.

Preheat the oven to 450°F. Lightly flour a round baking stone or lightly oil a pizza pan. Punch down the dough and, on a lightly floured surface, roll out to the size of the stone. Transfer the dough to the prepared stone and spread the topping over the dough, leaving about 1 inch around the rim. Drizzle with oil and bake for about 30 minutes, until the crust is golden brown. Remove from oven and allow to cool for about 10 minutes before slicing.

BRAISED LEEKS AND GARLIC CROSTINI

A light starter course, this slightly spicy crostini can really start your engines. The strong upward lift of leeks and the intensely strengthening energy of the condensed, gathered, rooted garlic bulb are cooked to perfection and piled atop crusty whole grain bread to create strong, vital energy in us.

MAKES 2 OR 3 SERVINGS

About 3 tablespoons extra-virgin olive oil
2 teaspoons balsamic vinegar
Sea salt
3 to 4 cloves fresh garlic, thinly sliced
1 small leek, split lengthwise, rinsed well, thinly sliced diagonally
¼ fresh lemon
4 to 6 thick slices whole-grain baguette
Fresh flat-leaf parsley, finely minced, for garnish

Preheat the oven to 400°F. Line a baking sheet with parchment.

Place the oil, vinegar and 3 to 4 pinches salt in a skillet over medium heat. Add the garlic and leek. Cover the pan and when you hear sizzling, gently shake the skillet, holding the lid in place. Reduce the heat to low and braise until the leek is quite tender and deeply browned, 15 to 20 minutes. Remove the lid and allow any remaining liquid to reduce. Remove from heat and squeeze the lemon over the vegetables and stir gently to combine.

Brush the bread lightly with oil on both sides. Arrange the bread on the baking sheet and sprinkle lightly with salt. Bake until the bread is lightly browned and crispy at the edges.

Remove the bread from the oven and spoon the leek mixture generously onto each slice. Arrange on a platter and serve immediately.

≈≈ *Did You Know?* ≈≈
BALSAMIC VINEGAR

Legend The vinegar was used by Roman legions to maintain strength and vitality.

Fact Aged traditionally from 4 to 40 years, balsamic vinegar is unpasteurized so varying amounts of enzymes are preserved. In addition, it contains phosphorus and potassium. A high concentration of acid makes balsamic vinegar a great natural wound salve and relieves insect bites.

BLACK OLIVE BRUSCHETTA

It's said in Italian folklore that olives are the food of love. Perhaps this bruschetta will show if it's truth or legend. Food of love or not, this sensual, richly flavored starter course is a delicious way to begin a meal.
MAKES 2 OR 3 SERVINGS

    2 to 3 tablespoons extra-virgin olive oil
    1 to 2 cloves fresh garlic, finely minced
    1 to 2 shallots, finely minced
    Sea salt
    Mirin
    ¼ cup coarsely chopped pine nuts
    ½ cup pitted, finely minced oil-cured black
       olives

    4 to 6 thick slices whole-grain baguette
    Fresh flat-leaf parsley, finely minced

Preheat the oven to 400°F and line a baking sheet with parchment.

Place the oil, garlic, shallots and a generous pinch of salt in a skillet over medium heat. When the shallots begin to sizzle, sprinkle lightly with mirin and sauté for 2 to 3 minutes. Stir in the pine nuts and olives, season lightly with salt (taste first, remember the salt in the olives) and sauté for 2 to 3 minutes.

Brush the bread lightly with oil on both sides. Arrange the bread on the baking sheet and sprinkle lightly with salt. Bake until the bread is lightly browned and crispy at the edges.

Remove the bread from the oven and spoon the olive mixture onto each slice. This topping is strongly flavored, so use it to each person's taste.

Note: You may have extra topping. It will keep, refrigerated, for 1 week.

ENDIVE RISOTTO WITH WALNUTS

So smooth and silky, this rich risotto is a sinfully delicious main course. Its neutral character is brought to life with the vitality of the walnuts and the clean, bitterness of the endive.
MAKES 4 OR 5 SERVINGS

    5 cups spring or filtered water
    3 tablespoons extra-virgin olive oil

1 to 2 cloves fresh garlic, finely minced

½ yellow onion, finely diced

Sea salt

½ cup white wine

1 cup Arborio rice, do not rinse

2 to 3 medium Belgian endives, quartered

½ cup pan-toasted walnuts, coarsely diced
(see note)

1 red bell pepper, roasted over an open flame
(page 57), peeled, seeded and finely diced

Pour the water into a saucepan over low heat and keep warm throughout the cooking.

Place 2 tablespoons of the oil, the garlic and onion in a deep skillet over medium-high heat. When the onion begins to sizzle, add a dash of salt and sauté for 1 to 2 minutes. Stir in the wine and rice and sauté until the rice absorbs the liquid. Turn the heat to medium-low and begin adding the warm water, by ladlefuls, and stirring it into the risotto, adding more liquid only as quickly as the rice absorbs it. When the dish is about 80 percent cooked, season to taste with salt. The total cooking time should be 25 to 30 minutes. The risotto will be creamy, but the rice will retain some firmness.

While the risotto cooks, heat the remaining 1 tablespoon oil in a small sauté pan and lay the endive, cut sides down, in the oil. Sprinkle lightly with salt and cook, uncovered, until the endive is tender and the edges are richly browned, about 7 minutes. Set aside.

To serve, spoon the risotto onto a platter and arrange the endive, cut sides up, around the rim. Stir in the walnuts and garnish with bell pepper.

Note: To pan-toast the walnuts, heat a dry skillet over medium heat. Toast the walnuts, stirring con-

stantly, until fragrant and lightly browned, a. minutes.

GREEN RISOTTO WITH FAVA BEANS AND PEAS

Silky, rich and the color of spring, this risotto is just lovely. In spring, as we turn our faces toward the sun, we are reawakened like the buds on the trees. This brilliantly simple grain dish, laced through with fresh beans and peas, is nourishing, yet gentle in its effect on us.
MAKES 4 OR 5 SERVINGS

5 cups spring or filtered water

1 to 2 tablespoons extra-virgin olive oil

1 to 2 cloves fresh garlic, minced

½ yellow onion, finely diced

Sea salt

1 cup Arborio rice, do not rinse

Grated zest of 1 lemon

½ cup mirin or white wine

1 cup fresh fava beans

1 cup fresh peas

4 to 5 sprigs fresh flat-leaf parsley, finely
minced, for garnish

Place the water in a saucepan over low heat and keep warm throughout the cooking.

Place the oil, garlic and onion in a deep skillet over medium heat. When the onion begins to sizzle, add a pinch of salt and sauté until the onion is translucent, about 2 minutes. Stir in the rice and lemon zest and sauté until just coated with oil. Add the mirin and reduce the heat to low. When the rice has absorbed the mirin, begin adding the warm water, by ladlefuls, stirring the rice frequently, and only adding more liquid as it is absorbed. The total cooking time should be 25 to 30 minutes. The risotto will be creamy, but the rice will retain some firmness.

While the rice is cooking, bring a pot of water to a boil and cook the fava beans until tender, 7 to 10 minutes. Lift out the beans with a strainer or slotted spoon, and in the same water, boil the peas about 1 minute. Drain the peas. Remove the skins from the fava beans and mix gently with the peas.

When you have added the final ladle of water to the risotto, season to taste with salt and stir in the fava beans and peas, allowing them to cook in the risotto for the final few minutes. Remove from heat, transfer to a serving platter and serve garnished with the parsley.

SAFFRON POLENTA WITH SAUTÉED VEGETABLES

Richly flavored and silky smooth, this main course will fill you with pleasure. Creamy, yes, but not mild-mannered, this dish is loaded with the kind of energy that will make you sparkle. Corn polenta, with its sunny disposition, joins with vigorously sautéed vegetables and stimulating herbs, creating a symphony of vitality.

MAKES 5 TO 6 SERVINGS

Saffron Polenta
5 cups spring or filtered water
½ cup yellow cornmeal
2½ cups yellow corn grits
Pinch sea salt

2 to 3 teaspoons extra-virgin olive oil
1 teaspoon saffron threads

Sautéed Vegetables
1 to 2 tablespoons extra-virgin olive oil
2 to 3 cloves fresh garlic, finely minced
1 yellow onion, cut into thin half-moon slices
Sea salt
6 to 8 cremini mushrooms, thinly sliced
½ small fennel bulb, stalks trimmed flush to the bulb and bulb thinly sliced
1 carrot, cut into fine matchstick pieces
½ cup mirin or white wine
3 fresh vine-ripened tomatoes, diced
1 small bunch broccoli rabe, finely cut
½ cup loosely packed fresh basil leaves, shredded

To make the polenta: Whisk together the water, cornmeal, grits, salt, oil and saffron in a large saucepan. Bring to a boil over medium-low heat, whisking constantly. Reduce the heat to low and cook, stirring frequently, until the center of the polenta bubbles and pops, about 35 minutes. Transfer the polenta to a lightly oiled, shallow dish and set aside until firm, about 1 hour.

To make the vegetables: Place the oil, garlic and onion in a wok or skillet over medium heat. When the vegetables begin to sizzle, add a pinch of salt and sauté for 2 minutes. Stir in the mushrooms and a pinch of salt and sauté until the mushrooms release their juices into the pan. Stir in the fennel, carrot and a pinch of salt and sauté for 1 minute. Add the mirin and tomatoes, cover and cook over low heat until the vegetables are quite soft, about 25 minutes. Season to taste with salt and add the broccoli rabe on top. Cover and cook until the rabe is bright green. Remove the cover and simmer until any remaining cooking liquid has been absorbed into the vegetables. Remove from heat and stir in shredded basil.

To serve, either cut or scoop polenta onto individual plates and mound vegetables on top. Serve immediately.

≈≈≈ *Did You Know?* ≈≈≈
SAFFRON

Legend The value of saffron is the same, per pound, as gold.

Fact Hand harvested, from the stigmas of a crocus, it takes 100,000 flowers to produce less than a pound of saffron, making it the most expensive spice in the world.

~~~~~~~~~~~~~~~~~~~~~~~

LETTUCE ROLLS WITH PLUM SAUCE

A lovely starter course, the spicy rice filling is tenderly wrapped in delicate lettuce leaves, gently steamed to develop the flavor and served in a pool of richly flavored plum sauce.

MAKES 4 OR 5 SERVINGS AND ABOUT 2 CUPS OF SAUCE

Rolls
1 to 2 tablespoons extra-virgin olive oil
5 to 6 slices fresh ginger, cut into fine matchstick pieces
5 to 6 scallions, thinly sliced on the diagonal
Sea salt
2 cups cooked brown basmati rice
6 to 8 leaves romaine lettuce, rinsed and towel dried

Plum Sauce
2 cloves fresh garlic, finely minced
¼ jalapeño chile, seeded and finely minced
2 teaspoons sesame tahini
2 teaspoons finely minced fresh ginger
1 teaspoon soy sauce
1 tablespoon brown rice syrup
Generous pinch red pepper flakes
Grated zest and juice of 1 lemon
2 to 3 dark-fleshed plums, peeled, pitted, diced

To make the rolls: Place the oil, ginger and scallions, (reserving a few scallion slices for garnish) in a skillet over medium heat. When the vegetables begin to sizzle, add a pinch of salt and sauté until the scallions are limp, but still bright green, about 3 minutes. Remove from the heat and stir the sautéed vegetables into the rice.

Lay the lettuce leaves on a dry surface. Spoon the filling generously onto each leaf and wrap the lettuce around the filling, sealing completely. Place each roll, seam side down, on a bamboo steamer. Place over a shallow pot of boiling water and steam the rolls, uncovered, until the lettuce just wilts, about 4 minutes. Remove from the heat and set aside to cool on the bamboo rack.

To make the plum sauce: Place the garlic, chile, tahini and ginger in a saucepan and simmer, stir-

ring constantly, over low heat for about 2 minutes, to release the heat in the chile. Add the remaining ingredients to the pan and cook over low heat until the plums are quite soft, about 30 minutes. Transfer to a food processor and purée until smooth. Adjust the seasonings to your taste.

To serve, pool some plum sauce on individual salad plates. Using a sharp knife, slice each lettuce roll in half on the diagonal. Arrange two to three diagonal pieces on each plate and serve, garnished with the reserved scallions. The unused plum sauce will keep, refrigerated, for about 1 week.

SPICE-LACQUERED SEITAN

Seitan is a great substitute for those who just love the thought of sinking their teeth into something a bit "meatier" than, say, tofu or tempeh. Made from wheat gluten and densely textured, the seitan medallions in this recipe are glazed with a sweet spicy mixture.
MAKES 3 TO 4 APPETIZER SERVINGS

3 tablespoons extra-virgin olive oil
½ cup Suzanne's Specialties Maple Rice
  Nectar
Pinch sea salt
Generous pinch ground cinnamon
Scant pinch ground cumin
Scant pinch ground coriander
10 ounces seitan, cut into bite-size medallions
1 bunch watercress, stem tips trimmed and
  left whole
1 to 2 scallions, thinly sliced on the diagonal

Place the oil, maple rice nectar, salt and spices in a deep skillet over medium heat. When the mixture begins to foam at the edges, gently add the seitan, taking care that pieces do not touch each other. Cook, turning frequently, until the glaze begins to stick to the seitan, 5 to 7 minutes.

Bring a small pot of water to a boil. Add the watercress and boil just until it wilts, about 30 seconds. Drain and cut into bite-size pieces and arrange on a platter. When seitan is shiny with glaze, arrange on the watercress, sprinkle with the scallions and serve immediately.

FRIED SEITAN WITH GINGERED COUSCOUS

Hearty and a bit spicy, this dish will add some pep to your step. It's a main course with some teeth. With the powerful protein in the seitan and circulation-stimulating ginger, all balanced by mild-mannered couscous, this is a combination to be reckoned with, as you stride confidently from task to task.
MAKES 4 TO 6 SERVINGS

Gingered Couscous
2 cups spring or filtered water
Sea salt
1 cup couscous
About 1 teaspoon extra-virgin olive oil
2 to 3 cloves fresh garlic, finely minced
4 to 5 slices fresh ginger, finely minced
2 to 3 scallions, thinly sliced on the diagonal

Shiitake Gravy

2 to 3 dried shiitake mushrooms, soaked until tender in 1 cup spring or filtered water, stems trimmed and thinly sliced

1 cup spring or filtered water

Soy sauce

1 teaspoon kuzu, dissolved in 2 tablespoons cold water

Fried Seitan

Avocado or light olive oil, for frying

½ cup yellow cornmeal

Pinch sea salt

1 pound seitan, cut into bite-size pieces

To prepare the couscous: Bring the water and salt to a boil over high heat. Stir in the couscous, turn off the heat and cover the pan. Set aside for 5 to 7 minutes.

Place the oil, garlic and ginger in a small skillet and turn the heat to medium. When the vegetables begin to sizzle, add a pinch of salt and sauté for 1 minute. Stir in the scallions and a pinch of salt and sauté until the scallions are bright green, 2 to 3 minutes. Stir the vegetables into the couscous and set aside, loosely covered, so the flavor can develop.

To make the gravy: Drain the mushrooms, reserving the soaking water. Strain the soaking water and add to a small saucepan along with the 1 cup water and soy sauce to taste. Bring to a boil over medium heat. Reduce the heat to low and simmer, uncovered, until the mushrooms are tender, about 10 minutes. Stir in the dissolved kuzu and simmer, stirring, until the gravy thickens and turns clear, 2 to 3 minutes.

To prepare the seitan: Heat about ½ inch oil in a skillet over medium heat. While the oil heats, mix together the cornmeal and salt. Dredge the seitan in the cornmeal, coating it very well. When the oil is hot (patterns will form, known as "dancing"), shallow-fry the seitan, in batches, turning until golden on all sides. Drain on paper towels.

To serve, arrange the couscous on a serving platter with the fried seitan on top. Spoon the gravy over the seitan.

SEITAN WITH BROCCOLI RABE

Looking to spice things up a bit? Then this is the dish for you. Combining richly sautéed vegetables and seitan with lightly cooked bitter greens is perfect. The heartiness of the seitan, the richness of the sauté and the touch of hot spices make us strong, beautiful, open-hearted and ready for adventure.

MAKES 4 TO 6 SERVINGS

1 to 2 tablespoons extra-virgin olive oil

2 to 3 cloves fresh garlic, finely minced

1 red onion, cut into thin half-moon slices

Generous pinch red pepper flakes

Sea salt

1 red bell pepper, roasted over an open flame (page 57), peeled, seeded and sliced into thin ribbons

1 pound seitan, sliced into thin strips

Mirin or white wine

Grated zest of 1 lemon

1 large bunch broccoli rabe, rinsed well

Place the oil, garlic and onion in a deep skillet over medium heat. When the vegetables begin to sizzle, add the red pepper flakes and a pinch of salt and sauté for 2 to 3 minutes. Stir in bell pepper and a pinch of salt and sauté for 1 minute. Stir in the seitan and add a splash of mirin and the lemon zest. Cover and reduce the heat to low, simmering until the vegetables and seitan are tender, about 10 minutes. Season to taste with salt.

Just before adding it to the skillet, slice the broccoli rabe into bite-size pieces. Lay the greens on top of the ingredients in the skillet, cover and cook until the greens are bright green and just wilted, 3 to 4 minutes. Toss gently to combine and transfer to a serving platter. Serve immediately.

STUFFED ROASTED RED BELL PEPPERS

Savory rice stuffing wrapped in the embrace of smoky roasted peppers is a delicious way to serve grain. With the stability we get from brown rice and with a touch of fiery vitality from the peppers and spices, you create a dish that'll make you oh so strong.

MAKES 4 MAIN-COURSE SERVINGS OR 8 FIRST COURSES

Stuffing
1 to 2 tablespoons extra-virgin olive oil
2 to 3 cloves fresh garlic, finely minced
½ red onion, finely diced
Sea salt
Generous pinch red pepper flakes
1 carrot, finely diced
2 to 3 stalks celery, finely diced
1 cup fresh or frozen corn kernels
2 to 3 teaspoons mirin or white wine
1½ cups cooked short-grain brown rice

Red Bell Peppers
4 red bell peppers
Extra-virgin olive oil, for coating
Fruity olive oil, for drizzling

To make the stuffing: Place the oil, garlic and onion in a small skillet over medium heat. When the vegetables begin to sizzle, add a pinch of salt and red pepper flakes and sauté for 1 to 2 minutes. Add the carrot, celery and a pinch of salt and sauté for 1 to 2 minutes. Stir in the corn, season lightly with salt and add the mirin. Cover and cook over low heat for 3 to 4 minutes. Stir in the rice until ingredients are well combined. Transfer to a mixing bowl to cool.

To prepare the bell peppers: Lightly coat each bell pepper with extra-virgin olive oil and place each over an open flame on the stove. Turn each pepper, charring the skin completely. When the peppers are blackened, transfer them to a paper sack and seal shut to allow the peppers to steam. After 10 minutes, carefully remove the peppers and, with your fingers, gently remove the charred skin, taking care to keep the peppers intact. Once all the charred skin is removed, carefully pull the seeds out of the tops of the peppers, keeping the peppers intact. Clean any remaining seeds from the peppers.

Preheat the oven to 300°F. Carefully spoon the filling into each bell pepper, filling abundantly, but taking care not to split the skins. Place the stuffed peppers on a baking sheet and bake for about 10 minutes, until warmed through. Serve drizzled with fruity olive oil.

BULGUR PILAF WITH PAN-BRAISED TOMATOES

This dish is a light take on a Mediterranean-style grain dish. Laced through with vitalizing almonds and rich with braised tomatoes, with a touch of parsley and lemon to lend a bit of sparkle to the mix, this main course will have you dreaming of the magical isle of Capri.

MAKES 2 OR 3 SERVINGS

    2 cups spring or filtered water
    Sea salt
    1 cup bulgur
    ½ cup blanched almonds
    2 to 3 stalks celery, diced
    ½ cucumber, diced
    3 tablespoons extra-virgin olive oil
    2 to 3 cloves fresh garlic, thinly sliced
    1 tablespoon balsamic vinegar
    6 to 8 fresh vine-ripened tomatoes, cut in half
        lengthwise (do not peel or seed)
    Grated zest of 1 lemon
    ½ cup white wine
    Juice of 1 lemon
    3 to 4 sprigs fresh flat-leaf parsley, minced

Bring the water to a boil with a pinch of salt. Stir in the bulgur, cover and turn off the heat. Allow to stand for 5 to 7 minutes. Gently fold in the almonds, celery and cucumber until combined. Transfer to a mixing bowl and set aside, loosely covered.

Place the oil, garlic, vinegar and a generous pinch of salt in a small skillet over medium-low heat. Lay the tomato halves, cut sides down, in the oil mixture. Sprinkle with the lemon zest, cover and cook until the tomatoes have wilted and are quite tender, about 10 minutes. Carefully remove the tomato halves and arrange them around the rim of a shallow bowl or serving platter, reserving any remaining liquid from cooking in the skillet.

Add the white wine to the skillet, increase the heat to medium and reduce the wine until it thickens. Stir into the pilaf, along with lemon juice and parsley. Mound the pilaf in the center of a platter and serve.

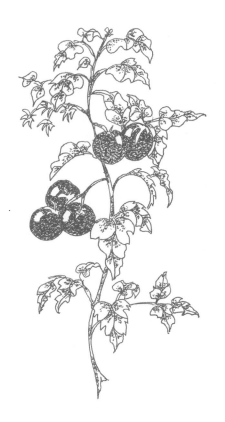

RICE PILAF WITH CARAMELIZED ONIONS

Mild-mannered rice serves as the Clark Kent in this powerful dish. Nuts, seeds and strengthening root vegetables are made sweetly gentle with richly flavored onions, creating vitality in a cup.

MAKES 4 TO 6 SERVINGS

> 2 tablespoons plus 2 teaspoons extra-virgin olive oil
>
> ½ red onion, cut into thin half-moon slices
>
> Sea salt
>
> Mirin or white wine
>
> 4 to 5 slices fresh ginger, cut into fine matchstick pieces
>
> 1 small carrot, finely diced
>
> 1 small parsnip, finely diced
>
> ½ cup pecans, lightly oven-roasted, coarsely chopped
>
> 3 tablespoons pumpkin seeds, lightly pan-toasted
>
> 2 cups cooked short-grain brown rice
>
> Brown rice vinegar
>
> 2 to 3 scallions, thinly sliced on the diagonal, for garnish

Place 2 tablespoons of the oil and the onion in a skillet over medium heat. When the onion begins to sizzle, add a generous pinch of salt and sauté for 3 to 4 minutes. Add a generous sprinkle of mirin and reduce the heat to low. Cook, stirring frequently, until the onion begins to caramelize; this can take as long as 20 minutes.

While the onion cooks, place the remaining 2 teaspoons of the oil, the ginger, carrot, parsnip and a generous pinch of salt in a skillet over medium heat. When the vegetables begin to sizzle, add a pinch of salt and sauté until just tender, about 10 minutes. Turn off the heat and stir in the pecans and pumpkin seeds, just to coat with oil. Add the rice, a generous splash of vinegar and stir to combine. Transfer to a serving bowl and top with caramelized onions. Serve garnished with scallion slices.

SEA SALT

Not all salts are created equal. For the best health, choose a white, unrefined sea salt with no additives. Unrefined sea salt is rich in the trace minerals that are destroyed in processed salts.

SWEET CORN AND BASMATI SALAD

Don't we love it when we have a soft place to fall when we need it? Sweetly strengthening, this grain dish creates a strong, confident stride, a quiet passion for life and a gentle, compassionate nature.

MAKES 4 OR 5 SERVINGS

> 1 cup brown basmati rice, rinsed well and soaked for 2 to 3 hours
>
> 1½ cups spring or filtered water
>
> Sea salt
>
> About 1 tablespoon extra-virgin olive oil
>
> 2 to 3 cloves fresh garlic, finely minced
>
> 1 yellow onion, finely diced
>
> 1 cup fresh or frozen corn kernels
>
> Mirin

5 to 6 leaves fresh basil, shredded

Parsley sprigs, for garnish

Drain the rice. Place the rice and water in a heavy pot and bring to a boil over medium heat, loosely covered. Add a pinch of salt, reduce the heat to low and simmer, covered, until the liquid has been absorbed into the rice, about 45 minutes.

Place the oil, garlic and onion in a small skillet over medium heat. When the vegetables begin to sizzle, add a pinch of salt and sauté until the onion is translucent, 3 to 4 minutes. Stir in the corn and add a generous splash of mirin. Sauté for 1 to 2 minutes. Turn off the heat and stir in the basil.

To serve, stir sautéed vegetables into the cooked rice. Garnish with parsley sprigs and serve hot.

~~~~~~~~~~~~~~~~~~~~~~~~~~~~~~~~~~~~~~

RICE AND LENTIL SALAD

Rice and beans are true soul mates. A complete protein, these two ingredients are far from star-crossed but rather come together for the perfect nutritional marriage. The power of protein joins forces with the simmering strength that we get from complex carbohydrates to help us feel strong and passionate about our lives.

MAKES 4 TO 6 SERVINGS

About 1 tablespoon extra-virgin olive oil

1 to 2 cloves fresh garlic, finely minced

1 small yellow onion, finely diced

Sea salt

1 small carrot, finely diced

½ cup small green lentils, sorted and rinsed well

¼ cup mirin or white wine

1½ cups spring or filtered water

1 bay leaf

2 cups cooked brown basmati rice

Balsamic vinegar

Juice of lemon

3 to 4 sprigs fresh flat-leaf parsley, finely minced

1 red bell pepper, roasted over an open flame (page 57), peeled, seeded and finely diced

4 to 6 leaves romaine lettuce, rinsed well, trimmed, left whole and well chilled

Place the oil, garlic and onion in a deep skillet over medium heat. When the vegetables begin to sizzle, add a pinch of salt and sauté until the onion is translucent, about 2 minutes. Stir in the carrot and sauté until coated with oil. Top with the lentils, add the mirin and water, toss in the bay leaf and bring the mixture to a boil, uncovered. Cover, reduce the heat to low and cook until the lentils are tender, about 40 minutes. Remove the cover, discard the bay leaf, season to taste with salt and increase the heat to high to cook off any remaining liquid. When the liquid has disappeared, turn off heat and stir in the rice, a generous splash of vinegar and the lemon juice, parsley and bell pepper. Stir gently to combine. Arrange the lettuce leaves on a plate and mound the rice mixture in the center. Serve hot.

Note: A more informal way to serve this dish is to shred the lettuce leaves and mound the lentil-and-rice mixture on individual plates.

~~~~~~~~~~~~~~~~~~~~~~~~~~~~~~~~

FRIED RICE

Fried rice is the perfect dish. Basic and simple but richly flavored and slightly spicy, this dish is wondrous on so many levels, from ease of preparation, to strength and stamina, to soft skin and hair. With complex carbohydrates, a hit of protein and just the richest touch of oil, this dish shines a whole new light on mild-mannered brown rice.
MAKES 4 TO 6 SERVINGS

About 1 tablespoon avocado or light olive oil
3 to 4 slices fresh ginger, cut into fine
    matchstick pieces
2 to 3 cloves fresh garlic, finely minced
1 small leek, split lengthwise, rinsed well,
    thinly sliced on the diagonal
Soy sauce
3 to 4 dried shiitake mushrooms, soaked until
    tender and thinly sliced
1 carrot, cut into fine matchstick pieces
¼ small head green head cabbage, finely
    shredded
Mirin
½ pound extra-firm tofu, cut into small cubes
1½ cups cooked short-grain brown rice
About 2 cups spring or filtered water
Toasted sesame oil
Brown rice vinegar
2 to 3 scallions, thinly sliced on the diagonal,
    for ganish

Place the oil, ginger, garlic and leek in a deep skillet over medium heat. When the vegetables begin to sizzle, add a dash of soy sauce and sauté for 2 to 3 minutes. Stir in the mushrooms, carrot and another dash soy sauce and sauté for 2 minutes. Add the cabbage, a dash soy sauce and a generous splash of mirin. Sauté until the cabbage just wilts.

Top with tofu and brown rice. Season lightly with soy sauce and add the water. Cover, reduce the heat to low and simmer until water is absorbed into the dish, 7 to 10 minutes.

Remove from the heat and stir in a modest drizzle of sesame oil and vinegar. Serve garnished with the scallions.

SOY SAUCE

Soy sauce or shoyu is the name for a traditionally brewed condiment made from cracked wheat as the fermenting starter and soybeans. The best soy sauces are those aged for at least two years. A lighter seasoning flavor than tamari, soy sauce is great for everyday use for a different flavor of salt.

~~~~~~~~~~~~~~~~~~~~~~~~~~~~~~~~

SPRING VEGETABLE PAELLA

This vegan version of the Spanish classic has all the spice and satisfaction combined with the lighter energy of vegetables. The varying flavors and textures make this dish come alive.
MAKES 5 TO 6 SERVINGS

1 small fennel bulb, cut into 1-inch chunks; 2
    tablespoons minced fronds
2 to 3 bunches baby carrots, left whole and
    tops minced
3 to 4 spring turnips, cut into large dice
3 to 4 new potatoes, cut into large dice
1 tablespoon extra-virgin olive oil, plus extra
    for drizzling

6 or 7 sprigs fresh flat-leaf parsley

3 to 4 cloves fresh garlic, finely minced

½ tablespoon sweet paprika

1 teaspoon saffron threads

Sea salt

1 yellow onion, diced

4 ripe plum tomatoes, diced (do not peel or seed)

2 cups brown Arborio rice

4 cups spring or filtered water

¾ cup dry white wine

10 to 12 asparagus spears, tough ends snapped off and stalks cut into 1-inch pieces

1 cup cooked chickpeas

Preheat the oven to 450°F. Place the fennel bulb, whole carrots, turnips and potatoes in a mixing bowl. Drizzle with olive oil and toss to coat. Transfer to a shallow baking dish and bake, uncovered, about 1 hour, until tender and lightly browned.

Take about 5 sprigs of the parsley and finely mince them. Mix with the garlic, paprika, saffron and about 1 teaspoon salt. Stir well to combine and set aside.

Place 1 tablespoon oil and the onion in a deep skillet over medium heat. When the onion begins to sizzle, add a pinch of salt and sauté for 1 minute. Stir in the tomatoes, rice and the parsley mixture. Add the water and wine, cover and bring to a boil. Reduce the heat to low and simmer for about 15 minutes. Stir in the asparagus, chickpeas and roasted vegetables. Increase heat to medium, cover and cook until liquid has been absorbed into the rice mixture, stirring often, about 20 minutes. Season lightly with salt and stir in the fennel leaves and carrot tops. Serve garnished with remaining parsley sprigs.

≈≈≈ *Did You Know?* ≈≈≈
BROWN RICE

Legend Brown rice helps to create a healthy heart.

Fact One of the richest sources of thiamine, brown rice has been linked to reducing hypertension, cholesterol levels and creating vascular strength.

LEMONY COUSCOUS WITH PEAS AND CARROTS

Light as a spring breeze, this grain course is delicious, easy to make and relaxing to our poor overworked livers. When food is fresh, light and colorful, we can't wait to eat it. And as the weather warms and we long to be outside, this dish will get you out of the kitchen fast . . . and keep you well nourished.

MAKES 4 OR 5 SERVINGS

2 cups spring or filtered water

2 carrots, diced

1 cup fresh or frozen peas

1 cup couscous

Grated zest of 1 lemon

Sea salt

2 teaspoons extra-virgin olive oil

Juice of ½ lemon

1 to 2 sprigs fresh basil, leaves removed and finely shredded

Bring the water to a boil. Add the carrots and cook for 2 minutes. Add the peas and cook for 3 minutes. Stir in the couscous, lemon zest and a light sprinkle of salt. Cover and turn off heat.

Allow to stand, undisturbed, for 7 minutes. Stir in the oil, lemon juice and basil, fluff with a fork and transfer to a serving bowl.

~~~~~~~~~~~~~~~~~~~~~~~~~~~

JASMINE RICE WITH SCALLIONS AND LEMON

Fragrant and delicious, this rice dish is perfect for spring cooking. Because it's light and easy to prepare, with the freshest of ingredients, you can cook dinner and still have time to dance around the maypole.

MAKES 4 TO 6 SERVINGS

1¾ cups spring or filtered water
1¼ cups jasmine rice, rinsed very well
Sea salt
½ cup freshly shelled peas or frozen petite peas
About 1 tablespoon extra-virgin olive oil
1 to 2 cloves fresh garlic, finely minced
6 to 8 scallions, thinly sliced on the diagonal
Juice of ½ lemon
4 or 5 sprigs fresh flat-leaf parsley, finely minced
Grated zest of 2 lemons

Place the water and rice in a saucepan and bring to a boil, loosely covered. Add a generous pinch of salt, cover and reduce heat to low. Simmer until the rice is tender, 15 to 20 minutes. Remove from the heat and allow to stand, undisturbed, for 15 minutes more. Fluff with a fork and set aside.

Bring a pot of water with a pinch of salt to a boil and cook the peas until bright green and just tender, about 1 minute. Drain well and set aside to cool.

Place the oil, garlic and scallions in a skillet over medium heat. When the scallions begin to sizzle, add a pinch of salt and sauté for about 30 seconds. Stir in the cooked rice and sauté for 3 to 4 minutes. Add the peas, lemon juice, parsley and lemon zest. Stir to combine, season lightly with salt and stir well. Transfer to a serving platter and serve immediately.

~~~~~~~~~~~~~~~~~~~~~~~~~~~

RISOTTO WITH BEET GREENS AND LEEKS

Slightly pink and delicately sweet, this risotto is silky smooth and oh so satisfying. As a main course or a hearty side dish, this risotto is refined and elegant and its sweet nature will relax our middle organs, so that we are, too.

MAKES 4 OR 5 SERVINGS

5 cups spring or filtered water
About 1 tablespoon extra-virgin olive oil
1 medium leek, split lengthwise, rinsed well, thinly sliced
Sea salt
1 cup Arborio rice (do not rinse)
¼ cup mirin or white wine
1 small bunch beet greens, diced
1 teaspoon white miso
Grated zest of 1 lemon
Lemon wedges, for garnish

Bring the water to a simmer and keep it warm over low heat throughout the cooking.

Place the oil and leek in a deep skillet over medium heat. When the leek begins to sizzle, add a pinch of salt and sauté until the leek is bright green, 1 to 2 minutes. Stir in the rice and mirin. Sauté until the mirin is absorbed into the rice. Stir in the beet greens. Add the water, ½ cup at a time, stirring frequently and adding more only when the water has been absorbed into the rice. The total cooking time is about 25 minutes.

Dissolve the miso into the final ½ cup water before stirring into the rice, along with the lemon zest. When the rice has absorbed the last of the liquid, it will be creamy, but still retain its shape; transfer to a serving bowl and serve garnished with lemon wedges.

POLENTA WITH SWEET SQUASH

Creamy polenta is smothered in sensually smooth and delicately sweet squash purée with just of touch of herbs to make an interesting side dish.
MAKES 5 TO 6 SERVINGS

   1 large butternut squash, halved lengthwise, seeded
   6 fresh garlic cloves, unpeeled
   Extra-virgin olive oil, for drizzling
   Dried basil
   Sea salt
   5 cups spring or filtered water
   1½ cups yellow cornmeal or polenta
   Several leaves fresh basil, finely shredded

Preheat the oven to 375°F. Arrange the squash, cut sides up, in a shallow baking pan. Place 3 garlic cloves in each seed cavity, drizzle generously with oil and sprinkle lightly with dried basil and salt. Cover tightly and bake 60 to 90 minutes, until the squash is tender. Remove from the oven and cool slightly. Scoop the squash from the peel and transfer to a food processor. Add the peeled garlic. Purée until smooth.

Place the water, a generous pinch of salt and the cornmeal in a saucepan. Whisking, bring to a boil over medium heat. Reduce the heat to low and cook, whisking frequently, until the polenta thickens and the center of it bubbles and pops, about 25 minutes.

Remove the polenta from the heat and stir in about 3 cups of the squash purée and the fresh basil. Return to low heat and cook, stirring constantly, until heated through. Transfer to a serving bowl and serve immediately.

MINTED MEDITERRANEAN COUSCOUS

A salad that will have you dreaming of the Greek isles, it's light, fresh, fragrant with herbs and the perfect side dish to grace any festive summer table. I love to serve it with whole steamed artichokes and crusty whole-grain bread.

MAKES 4 OR 5 SERVINGS

2 cups spring or filtered water

Sea salt

1 cup couscous

1 red bell pepper, roasted over an open flame (page 57), peeled, seeded and diced

½ cup oil-cured black olives, pitted and diced

½ cup fresh mint leaves, finely shredded

3 tablespoons extra-virgin olive oil

Juice of 1 orange

Juice of 1 lemon

½ cup cooked chickpeas

1 large bunch arugula, rinsed well, stemmed and left whole

Bring the water and a generous pinch of salt to a boil. Stir in the couscous, cover and turn off the heat. Set aside for 5 to 7 minutes. Remove the cover and fluff with a fork.

Stir the bell pepper, olives and mint into the couscous and season lightly with salt. Stir in the olive oil, orange juice, lemon juice and chickpeas.

Arrange the arugula on a salad platter and mound the couscous on top. Serve warm or chilled.

BULGUR SALAD WITH CUCUMBER AND DILL

Summer is a time to be outdoors, enjoying the splendid weather, not a time to spend endless hours slaving over a hot stove. This quick and easy salad doesn't even require cooking, just a bit of planning, but it will keep your family satisfied and well nourished.

MAKES 4 OR 5 SERVINGS

1 cup bulgur

1 cup freshly squeezed lemon juice

⅔ cup extra-virgin olive oil

4 or 5 fresh garlic cloves, finely minced

2 medium cucumbers, diced (do not peel, unless cucumber is not organic)

1 small bunch fresh flat-leaf parsley, finely minced

6 to 8 scallions, thinly sliced on the diagonal

½ cup finely minced fresh dill

Sea salt

Lettuce (optional)

Black olives (optional)

Place the bulgur in a glass bowl. Whisk the lemon juice, oil and garlic together in another bowl. Spoon the lemon mixture over the bulgur and stir in the cucumbers, parsley, scallions and dill. Cover and chill until bulgur has absorbed the fluids, about 6 hours. Just before serving, season to taste with salt and stir well. Serve chilled, as is, or on a bed of lettuce, with some black olives on the side.

MARINATED COUSCOUS WITH PAN-ROASTED TOMATOES

Is couscous not interesting enough for you? It will be after trying this recipe. Richly seasoned and served with intensely flavored pan-roasted tomatoes, the couscous serves as the mild-mannered backdrop for the rest of the drama.

MAKES 4 TO 6 SERVINGS

2 cups spring or filtered water

Sea salt

1 cup couscous

4 to 6 oil-packed sun-dried tomatoes, drained, diced

½ cup oil-cured black olives, pitted and diced

1 tablespoon capers, drained

3 to 4 sprigs fresh basil, leaves removed and finely shredded

About 1 tablespoon extra-virgin olive oil

2 teaspoons chili paste

6 to 8 plum tomatoes, split lengthwise (do not peel or seed)

1 bunch arugula, rinsed well, stemmed and left whole

Fruity olive oil, for drizzling

Bring the water and a pinch of salt to a boil. Stir in the couscous, cover, turn off the heat and set aside for 5 to 7 minutes. Fluff with a fork. Stir in the sun-dried tomatoes, olives, capers and basil. Set aside, loosely covered.

Place the extra-virgin olive oil in a skillet over medium heat. Stir in the chili paste and spread the mixture over the pan bottom. Arrange the plum tomatoes, cut sides down, in the skillet and sprinkle with salt. Cover and reduce heat to low. Cook until the skin wrinkles and the cut sides of the tomatoes are lightly browned, 3 to 4 minutes.

To serve, arrange the arugula on a platter, spoon the couscous in the center and arrange the tomatoes on top. Drizzle with a fruity olive oil and serve.

STUFFED PORTOBELLOS WITH GREEN BEANS

So rich, so delicious, no one will miss the meat in this vegan main course. Sensual, sweet and savory ingredients aid in relaxing tension. With a sweet and spicy filling to keep our engines running, these stuffed mushrooms are real attention-getters.

MAKES 4 SERVINGS

> 4 large portobello mushrooms, brushed free of dirt
> Spring or filtered water
> Sea salt
> About 2 tablespoons extra-virgin olive oil
> 2 to 3 cloves fresh garlic, finely minced
> 2 jalapeño chiles, seeded and diced
> 1 red onion, diced
> 1 red bell pepper, roasted over an open flame (page 57), peeled, seeded and diced
> 3 to 4 sprigs fresh basil, leaves removed and finely minced
> 3 to 4 sprigs fresh flat-leaf parsley, finely minced
> 1 cup diced dried apricots
> Grated zest and juice of 1 lemon
> 1 cup whole wheat bread crumbs
> 3 cups whole green beans, tips trimmed, left whole
> 2 to 3 tablespoons sun-dried tomato paste

Preheat the oven to 400°F.

Remove the stems from the mushrooms, dice the stems and set aside. Scoop the gills from the mushrooms and discard. Arrange the mushroom caps in a shallow baking dish, add enough water to cover the bottom and sprinkle with salt. Bake, uncovered, for 10 to 15 minutes, just until tender. Leave oven on.

Place about 1 tablespoon of the oil, the garlic, chiles and onion in a deep skillet over medium heat. When the onion begins to sizzle, add a pinch of salt and sauté for 1 to 2 minutes. Stir in the mushroom stems, bell pepper, basil and parsley, season lightly with salt and sauté for 3 minutes. Remove from the heat and stir in the apricots, lemon zest and juice and bread crumbs. Mix well and divide stuffing among the mushroom caps. Return to the oven for 5 to 7 minutes to brown.

Bring a small pot of water to a boil and cook the beans for 3 to 4 minutes. Drain well. Place the remaining 1 tablespoon of the oil in a skillet and stir in the sun-dried tomato paste and a generous pinch of salt. Cook, stirring, for 2 minutes. Stir in the beans until coated with tomato paste and just tender, 2 to 3 minutes.

To serve, divide the beans among four individual plates, spooning any tomato juices over the beans. Place a mushroom cap on each plate and serve immediately.

SWEET BASIL PILAF

Packed full of fragrant flavors, this summer grain dish is simple, elegant and deliciously gorgeous. It's strengthening without being heavy, relaxing without making us comatose and laced through with the vitalizing energy of fresh herbs and spices.

MAKES 4 OR 5 SERVINGS

> About 1 tablespoon extra-virgin olive oil

3 to 4 cloves fresh garlic, finely minced

1 red onion, finely diced

1 teaspoon red pepper flakes

Sea salt

Grated zest of 1 lemon

1 cup brown basmati rice

2 cups spring or filtered water

1 cup sugar snap peas, strings removed, left whole

1 bunch fresh basil, leaves removed and shredded

Juice of 1 lemon

1 red bell pepper, roasted over an open flame (page 57), peeled, seeded and sliced into thin ribbons

Place the oil, garlic and onion in a deep skillet over medium heat. When the onion begins to sizzle, add the red pepper flakes, a generous pinch of salt and the lemon zest and sauté for 2 to 3 minutes, until the onion is quite limp.

Stir in the rice and water, cover and bring to a boil. Reduce the heat to low and simmer until the rice is tender and the liquid has been absorbed, 35 to 40 minutes. Add the peas and a light seasoning of salt. Cover tightly, turn off the heat and allow rice to stand for 5 minutes to cook the peas.

To serve, fluff the rice, stir in the basil and lemon juice and top with roasted bell pepper.

SAFFRON RISOTTO

The ultimate Italian-style comfort food, this creamy, rich and delicious main dish or side dish risotto is brilliantly relaxing. But just so you don't fall into an enchanted sleep, I've topped it with braised tomatoes and some fresh basil. Yummy.

MAKES 4 OR 5 SERVINGS

5 cups spring or filtered water

Sea salt

Large pinch saffron threads

About 1 tablespoon extra-virgin olive oil, plus extra

2 to 3 cloves fresh garlic, thinly sliced

1 yellow onion, diced

1 cup Arborio rice (do not rinse)

½ cup dry white wine

2 teaspoons sweet white miso

4 ripe tomatoes, quartered (do not peel or seed)

3 to 4 sprigs fresh basil, leaves removed and shredded

Freshly ground black pepper

Place the water, a generous pinch of salt and the saffron in a saucepan and bring to a simmer over medium heat. Reduce the heat and keep it warm throughout the cooking.

Place 1 tablespoon of the oil, the garlic and onion in a deep skillet over medium heat. As soon as the onion sizzles, add a pinch of salt and sauté for 1 minute. Stir in the rice and sauté just until shiny with oil. Add the wine, reduce the heat to medium-low and stir until the rice has absorbed the liquid. Add a ladle of the saffron broth, stirring occasionally, until it has been almost completely absorbed. Continue adding the saffron broth in this manner, a ladleful at a time, until all of it has been used. The total cooking time will be 20 to 25 minutes. The resulting rice should be tender and creamy but retain some firmness. Dissolve the miso in a small amount of warm water and stir into the finished rice. Keep the rice over very low heat while preparing the tomatoes.

Brush a griddle pan generously with oil and heat until very hot. Add the tomatoes and cook over high heat until they are lightly scorched and beginning to wilt. Sprinkle with basil and season lightly with salt and pepper.

To serve, spoon the risotto into a shallow bowl and mound the tomatoes on top. Serve immediately.

LEMON RISOTTO

A Sicilian tradition, this risotto is so delicious, you'll never be able to make enough. Light, creamy, with a hint of lemony delight that will have you feeling the warm volcanic breezes that are as natural to Sicily as the Nostrali lemons that are the pride of the island.

MAKES 4 TO 6 SERVINGS

5 cups spring or filtered water
About 1 tablespoon extra-virgin olive oil
2 to 3 cloves fresh garlic, thinly sliced
1 yellow onion, diced
Zest of 1 lemon
½ teaspoon red pepper flakes
Sea salt
1 cup Arborio rice (do not rinse)
½ cup dry white wine
1 cup whole fresh sugar snap peas
Juice of 1 lemon
2 to 3 sprigs fresh flat-leaf parsley, finely minced
Lemon wedges, for garnish

Place the water in a saucepan and bring to a simmer and keep it warm over low heat throughout the cooking.

Place the oil, garlic and onion in a deep skillet over medium heat. When the onion begins to sizzle, add the lemon zest, red pepper flakes and a pinch of salt and sauté for 1 to 2 minutes. Do not let the onion color.

Stir in the rice, another pinch of salt and the wine. Stir the rice until the wine is absorbed. By ladlefuls, add the water, stirring occasionally, until it is absorbed. Continue until all the water is used. Total cooking time will be 20 to 25 minutes. The rice should be tender and creamy but retain some firmness. About 5 minutes before the rice is done, add the snap peas and cook the risotto to completion. Remove from the heat, season lightly with salt and stir in the lemon juice and parsley. Transfer to a shallow serving bowl and serve garnished with lemon wedges.

QUINOA WITH MUSHROOMS

Ah, quinoa . . . a wonder of the grain kingdom. Used by the Aztecs, quinoa seems to have it all—the perfect balance of amino acids to make it a complete protein, plus it's rich in lysine. Perfect for active people because it is so rich in protein, quinoa cooks quickly and has a nutty flavor that is without compare.

MAKES 4 OR 5 SERVINGS

1 cup quinoa, rinsed very well, drained
3 cups spring or filtered water
Sea salt

About 1 tablespoon extra-virgin olive oil

2 to 3 cloves fresh garlic, finely minced

1 red bell pepper, roasted over an open flame (page 57), peeled, seeded and diced

1 teaspoon dried basil

1 cup dried shiitake mushrooms, soaked until tender and thinly sliced

1 cup button mushrooms, brushed free of dirt and thinly sliced

2 to 3 scallions, thinly sliced on the diagonal, for ganish

Place the quinoa and 2 cups of the water in a saucepan and bring to a boil over medium heat, loosely covered. Add a pinch of salt, cover, reduce the heat to low and simmer until all the liquid has been absorbed and the quinoa has opened up, about 25 minutes.

While the quinoa cooks, place the oil, garlic and bell pepper in a skillet over medium heat. When the bell pepper begins to sizzle, add a pinch of salt and the basil and sauté for 1 to 2 minutes. Stir in the shiitake and button mushrooms, add a pinch of salt and sauté for 2 minutes. Reduce the heat to low and add about 1 cup of the water. Cover and simmer until shiitake mushrooms are tender, stirring occasionally, about 15 minutes.

When the quinoa is cooked, stir in the mushroom mixture and serve garnished with scallions.

≈≈ Did You Know? ≈≈
QUINOA

Legend The mother seed of the Andean people, the cultivation of quinoa was banned by Spanish conquerors, as it was believed to be the source of immortality.

Fact Maybe not immortality, but the strength and vitality we get from quinoa is unparalleled, an excellent source of magnesium, iron, potassium, copper and phosphorous, riboflavin, thiamine and niacin. Quinoa is just about perfect. It is higher in protein than cereal grains, with a more balanced concentration of amino acids.

WINTER QUINOA SALAD

Quinoa is a great light whole grain and, as a result, many of us associate it only with summer. But during cold weather, there is nothing like the light energy of this grain. In this recipe, richly roasted winter vegetables turn this delicious grain into the ultimate comfort food.

MAKES 4 OR 5 SERVINGS

2 red onions, diced

2 to 3 stalks celery, diced

2 carrots, diced

1 cup diced daikon

1 cup diced butternut squash

Extra-virgin olive oil, for drizzling

Brown rice syrup, for drizzling

Sea salt

Zest of 1 lemon

2 cups spring or filtered water

1 cup quinoa, rinsed very well

Juice of 1 lemon

2 to 3 sprigs fresh flat-leaf parsley, finely minced

Preheat the oven to 400°F.

Place the vegetables in a mixing bowl. Drizzle generously with oil and rice syrup, sprinkle with salt and add the lemon zest. Mix well to coat the vegetables. Arrange the vegetables in a shallow baking dish and cover tightly. Bake for 40 minutes. Remove the cover and return to the oven for 15 minutes to brown the vegetables.

While the vegetables roast, place the water and quinoa in a saucepan, loosely cover and bring to a boil over medium heat. Add a pinch of salt, cover and reduce the heat to low. Cook until all the liquid has been absorbed and the quinoa opens, about 25 minutes.

To serve, toss the vegetables with the cooked quinoa and gently stir in the lemon juice and parsley.

~~~~~~~~~~~~~~~~~~~~~~~~

WILD MUSHROOM BRUSCHETTA

A richer, more sensual first course is not to be had. Smoky flavors come together atop crispy whole-grain bread to create a starter that is not only delicious but helps relax tension in our shoulders and calves. It's simple to make, easy on the body and delicious . . . yummy.

MAKES 8 TO 10 SERVINGS

Toast
1 whole-grain baguette, cut into 2-inch-thick diagonal slices
Extra-virgin olive oil, for brushing
2 cloves fresh garlic, split in half
Sea salt

Topping
About 1 tablespoon extra-virgin olive oil
2 to 3 cloves fresh garlic, finely minced
5 to 6 shallots, thinly sliced

Sea salt
1 cup dried shiitake mushrooms, soaked until tender and thinly sliced
1 cup cremini mushrooms, brushed free of dirt and thinly sliced
1 cup oyster mushrooms, coarsely chopped
2 medium portobello mushrooms, brushed free of dirt and coarsely chopped
3 to 4 sprigs fresh basil, leaves removed and shredded
1 cup mirin
Juice of ½ lemon
Several stalks fresh chives, finely minced

To make the toast: Preheat the oven to 375°F and line a baking sheet with parchment. Lightly brush both sides of the baguette slices with oil, rub each with the cut side of the garlic and arrange on the baking sheet. Sprinkle very lightly with salt and bake for about 12 minutes until crisp, and lightly browned at the edges.

To make the topping: Heat the oil in a skillet and sauté the minced garlic and shallots with a pinch of salt for 2 to 3 minutes. Stir in the shiitake mushrooms and sauté for 1 minute. Add the remaining mushrooms and a generous pinch of salt and sauté until the mushrooms release their juices, reabsorb them and are golden brown, about 15 minutes. Stir in the basil. Add the mirin and bring to a boil, uncovered. Reduce the heat to low and simmer until the mirin is absorbed into the mushrooms, 3 to 5 minutes. Season to taste with salt, stir well and remove from the heat. Stir in the lemon juice and most of the chives, reserving about 2 tablespoons for garnish.

To serve, spoon mushrooms generously onto the bread slices and serve garnished with the reserved chives.

CROSTINI WITH ARUGULA AND SUN-DRIED TOMATOES

Italian cooking is simply brilliant in its understanding of how tastes work together. A simple starter course, crostini creates a symphony of flavors that burst on the tongue, making us weak with pleasure. Sweet, savory and satisfying, it has just a hint of bitter to lift the flavors to our palates and our spirits to food heaven. A snap to make, it's best to prepare this just before serving.

MAKES 8 TO 10 SERVINGS

1 whole-grain baguette, cut into 2-inch diagonal slices

About 1 tablespoon extra-virgin olive oil, plus extra for brushing

Sea salt

6 to 7 cups fresh arugula, rinsed very well and stems trimmed

¼ teaspoon red pepper flakes

1 cup oil-packed sun-dried tomatoes, drained well and coarsely chopped

½ cup walnut pieces, lightly pan-toasted (page 81), coarsely chopped

4 to 5 sprigs fresh flat-leaf parsley, finely minced

Preheat the oven to 375°F and line a baking sheet with parchment.

Lightly brush both sides of the baguette slices with oil and arrange on the baking sheet. Sprinkle lightly with salt and bake for about 12 minutes, until crisp and lightly browned at the edges.

Towel dry and hand shred the arugula. Do not cut, because it can take on a metallic aftertaste.

Place about 1 tablespoon of the oil, the red pepper flakes and tomatoes in a skillet over medium heat. When the tomatoes begin to sizzle, add a pinch of salt and sauté for 1 minute. Add the walnuts and arugula, season lightly with salt and sauté until the arugula begins to wilt, 1 to 2 minutes. Do not overcook the greens.

Spoon the cooked vegetables onto the bread slices, sprinkle with parsley and serve immediately.

TABOULI SALAD

A traditional Mediterranean grain salad, tabouli makes a wonderfully light lunch on its own or a great side dish for a buffet party. But there's nothing traditional about this recipe. Enhanced by hempseeds, my version of tabouli is packed with protein, essential fatty acids and a nutty flavor that will win rave reviews.

MAKES 4 OR 5 SERVINGS

2 cups spring or filtered water

1 cup bulgur (cracked wheat)

Sea salt

1 small cucumber, diced (do not peel unless cucumber is not organic)

1 tomato, diced (do not peel or seed)

1 cup finely minced fresh flat-leaf parsley

⅓ cup finely minced fresh mint

½ red onion, finely diced

⅓ cup shelled hempseeds

¼ cup extra-virgin olive oil

Grated zest and juice of 1 lemon

10 to 12 oil-cured black olives, pitted and coarsely minced

Bring the water to a boil and stir in the bulgur and a pinch of salt. Turn off the heat and allow to stand, covered, for 15 minutes. Fluff with a fork and set aside.

Mix together the cucumber, tomato, parsley, mint, onion and hempseeds. Stir in the bulgur to combine. Whisk the oil, lemon zest and juice together with a light seasoning of salt. Fold the dressing and the olives into the bulgur mixture. Serve warm or lightly chilled.

NOT-YOUR-ORDINARY NORI ROLLS

Seen one nori roll, seen 'em all? We've given this Japanese favorite a bit of jazz by adding hempseeds to the rice and filling the rolls with richly flavored tempeh and pickled vegetables. Worth the extra bit of work? Just ask your party guests.
MAKES 32 PIECES

2 cups cooked short-grain brown rice
½ cup shelled hempseeds
4 ounces tempeh, sliced into thin strips
3 tablespoons soy sauce
2 tablespoons ginger juice extracted from grated fresh ginger
1 teaspoon brown rice vinegar
1 teaspoon mirin
Spring or filtered water, as needed
1 cucumber, peeled, halved lengthwise and sliced into thin spears
1 cup shredded red cabbage, blanched for 30 seconds and drained
Umeboshi plum vinegar, as needed

Juice of ½ lemon
Extra-virgin olive oil, for frying
4 sheets toasted sushi nori
2 to 3 scallions, split lengthwise into thin ribbons
Wasabi paste (optional)

Mix the rice and hempseeds together and set aside, covered with a sushi mat or a damp towel to maintain the moisture.

Place the tempeh in a shallow baking dish. Mix together the soy sauce, ginger juice, brown rice vinegar and mirin. Pour over the tempeh, adding enough water just to cover. Marinate for 15 minutes. Drain the tempeh, reserving the marinade to serve as the base for a dipping sauce for the nori rolls.

While the tempeh marinates, pickle the vegetables. Place the cucumbers in a shallow dish and sprinkle with umeboshi vinegar. Toss the cabbage with a generous sprinkle of umeboshi vinegar and the lemon juice and set both aside to pickle for 15 to 20 minutes.

Pour enough oil into a skillet to generously cover the bottom. Heat over medium heat. When the oil is hot, fry the tempeh, turning once, until browned on each side, about 2 minutes total cooking time. Drain on paper and set aside.

To make the sushi, lay a bamboo sushi mat or kitchen towel on a flat, dry work surface. Lay the nori lengthwise on the mat, with the shiny side down. With damp hands, press one-quarter of the rice and hempseed mixture onto the nori, covering lengthwise from edge to edge, but leaving approximately 2 inches nori exposed on the edges closest to and farthest away from you. The rice should be about ¼ inch thick on the nori.

Lay the scallions, cabbage, cucumbers and tempeh along the edge of the rice closest to you. Using the mat as a guide, wrap the nori around the rice and tempeh filling, pressing as you roll, to create a firm cylinder. Set the completed roll, seam side down, on a dry surface and repeat with remaining ingredients to create 4 nori rolls.

To serve, use a wet knife and slice each nori roll into 8 equal pieces. Arrange, cut side up, on a platter. Use the leftover tempeh marinade as a dipping sauce, adding some wasabi if desired for a spicier flavor.

In a mixing bowl, combine the flour, cornmeal, baking powder, salt and rosemary, and whisk to combine. Add the oil and rice syrup, mix well and slowly stir in enough soymilk to create a thick, spoonable batter. Spoon the batter evenly into prepared muffin cups and bake 25 to 35 minutes, until the tops have peaked and spring back to the touch.

ROSEMARY-SCENTED MUFFINS

Serve these savory quick muffins with soups and salads for a light lunch or dinner. They add a lovely earthy flavor to a buffet dinner, a party table or dining al fresco. For that matter, they're great in the morning, when sugary sweets just won't do—so maybe they're just great anytime.

MAKES 1 DOZEN MUFFINS

   2 cups whole wheat pastry flour
   2 cups yellow cornmeal
   3 teaspoons baking powder
   Generous pinch sea salt
   2 teaspoons ground dried rosemary
   ½ cup avocado or light olive oil
   2 tablespoons brown rice syrup
   ¾ to 1 cup soymilk

Preheat the oven to 350°F and lightly oil a 12-cup (2½-inch) muffin pan.

~~~~~~~~~~~~~~~~~~~~~~~~~~~~~~~~~~~~~

BISCUITS D'ORO

Moist and with a delicious golden color, you'd never guess that these simple biscuits pack such a powerful nutritional punch. From winter squash to hempseeds, there's nothing humble about the energy you'll get from these heavenly, delicately sweet biscuits.

MAKES ABOUT 24 BISCUITS

1½ cups whole wheat pastry flour
1½ teaspoons baking powder
Generous pinch sea salt
Generous pinch ground cinnamon
⅓ cup avocado or light olive oil
2 teaspoons Suzanne's Specialties Maple Rice Nectar
1 cup cooked puréed butternut squash or carrots
½ cup shelled hempseeds

Preheat oven to 375°F and line a baking sheet with parchment.

In a mixing bowl, combine the flour, baking powder, salt and cinnamon, and whisk well to combine. Add the oil and maple rice nectar and mix well. Stir in the squash and hempseeds and mix to combine. Turn the dough onto a dry work surface and knead for 2 to 3 minutes to create a soft dough.

Roll out the dough to ¾ inch thick and cut into 3-inch rounds, using a cookie cutter or water glass. Arrange the biscuits on prepared baking sheet, about 1 inch apart and bake 20 to 25 minutes, until they puff slightly and are lightly browned.

Note: When cutting biscuits, take care not to turn the cutter as you press into the dough, as this will take air from the batter, leaving you with heavy, dense biscuits.

BROWN RICE SYRUP

There's brown rice syrup and then there's brown rice syrup. For many recipes, original brown rice syrup will create the delicate sweet flavor we all crave with no compromise to our health. But there are those special times when you want just a bit more than simple sweet flavor. That's where flavored rice syrups come in, like those from Suzanne's Specialties (see Resources, page 295). The brilliance of brown rice syrup is slightly enhanced by whole raspberries, strawberries or blueberries, resulting in a delicate fruity essence. Maple syrup is a simple sugar and I choose to minimize that in my cooking, so maple-flavored rice syrup, made by adding fenugreek to the original syrup is just perfect. What is there to say about chocolate rice syrup? Really.

PASSIONATE ABOUT PASTA

Who isn't in love with pasta? Macaroni (as I grew up calling it) conjures images of Italy, passionate dinners, passionate love, intimate evenings spent feeding each other sensually sauced noodles. What is it about pasta that has us so completely enchanted?

Of course, being a grain product, pasta is carbohydrate heaven. It is also a great source of fiber, an important ingredient in the prevention of colon cancer, diverticulitis, ulcers, appendicitis, hemorrhoids and many other digestive disorders, but if that doesn't take the glamour out of macaroni, nothing will. Being rich in carbohydrates is the gift of pasta.

We live in a culture that is absolutely obsessed with protein and with minimizing or eliminating carbohydrates from our diets. Funny how we want to get rid of the prime ingredient needed to maintain our vitality. Protein has the principal function of building new muscle and tissue; a job of paramount import when we are growing to maturity and for those of us who are physically active. We all need protein; we all need to rebuild, to a degree.

Ah, but carbohydrates. Their primary function in the body is to repair and maintain tissue and cells. Without them, we break down, fall apart, grow weak, no matter how much protein we consume. Without carbohydrate nutrients in our bodies, our muscles grow stiff and hard, bulky, rather than long, flexible and lean.

Carbohydrates serve us best when they are complex in structure, meaning that their molecules are tightly bound, like chains, which break down slowly in our bloodstream. The result is that our blood chemistry is gently nudged, rather than dramatically affected. White flour, white sugar, potatoes—these kinds of carbohydrates turn instantly into blood sugar in the body, triggering insulin responses that cause us to crave more and more, which is how carbohydrates got such a bad rap.

Pasta, in particular whole-grain and semolina pasta, will have a similar effect in our bodies to that of whole grains. We feel sated and contented after eating, with little desire for snacking an hour after dinner. Put pasta together with vegetables and you create the perfect feel-good food. The nutrients in pasta–vegetable combinations release serotonin into the brain; you feel happy and contented, soft and relaxed.

If this isn't enough for you, pasta is the food of our dreams. Easy to prepare and wildly versatile, pasta allows you to create splendid feasts with little effort. Pasta dishes are limited only by what you can imagine. From hearty winter noodles, smothered in richly flavored, thick sauces to the simplest summer feasts of pasta with olive oil with fresh herbs and vegetables from the garden, noodles are heaven on earth.

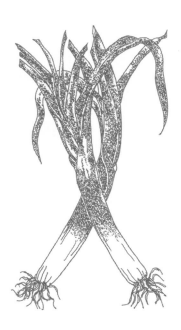

ASPARAGUS AND ARTICHOKE HEART PASTA

In the spring, when young men's hearts turn to flights of fancy, this dish is the stuff of dreams. As fresh as a morning breeze, it's a main course that's light and quick to prepare. And with the weather warming, we are desperate to be outdoors, so this is the perfect dinner.
MAKES 2 TO 4 SERVINGS

  4 to 6 small artichokes, preferably small
    purple ones
  About 1 tablespoon extra-virgin olive oil
  1 to 2 cloves fresh garlic, thinly sliced
  Generous pinch red pepper flakes
  2 to 3 shallots, finely minced
  Sea salt
  Grated zest of 1 lemon
  ½ cup white wine
  6 to 8 stems asparagus, tough ends snapped
    off and stalks cut into 1-inch pieces
  8 ounces orecchiette
  1 red bell pepper, roasted over an open flame
    (page 57), peeled, seeded and sliced into
    ribbons
  Fruity olive oil, for drizzling

Cut off the artichoke stems flush with the bottoms of the globes. Peel and cut away the outer leaves until the tender inner leaves are exposed. Trim the tips of the leaves. Split the artichokes in half lengthwise. Using a grapefruit spoon, clean the choke out of each one, preserving the shape of the artichoke half.

Place the extra-virgin olive oil, garlic, red pepper flakes and shallots in a skillet over medium heat. When the shallots begin to sizzle, add a pinch of salt and sauté for 2 to 3 minutes. Stir in the artichoke hearts, lemon zest and wine, cover and reduce the heat to low. Simmer until the artichoke hearts are tender, about 12 minutes. Add the asparagus, season to taste with salt, cover and cook just until the asparagus is bright green and tender. Do not overcook.

While the vegetables cook, bring a pot of water to a boil and cook the pasta al dente. Drain well, reserving 1 cup pasta cooking water, but do not rinse. Stir the reserved pasta cooking water into the vegetable mixture and cook for 1 to 2 minutes. A thin sauce will form.

Transfer the pasta to a platter and spoon the artichokes and asparagus over the top. Garnish with the bell pepper, drizzle with fruity olive oil to finish and serve immediately.

TAGLIATELLE WITH FAVA BEANS

This dish is the epitome of seasonal cooking. Without fresh fava beans, available only during the tender months of spring, the flavor of this dish will pale. Sure, there are frozen fava beans, but only fresh beans will have the sparkle that makes this dish taste like spring on your plate.

MAKES 2 TO 4 SERVINGS

15 to 20 fresh whole fava beans
About 2 tablespoons extra-virgin olive oil
1 to 2 cloves fresh garlic, thinly sliced
1 red onion, thinly sliced into half-moon
   pieces
Sea salt
Grated zest of 1 lemon
8 ounces penne pasta
2 to 3 sprigs fresh flat-leaf parsley, finely
   minced
Fruity olive oil, for drizzling

Shell the fava beans and parboil them for 1 minute. Drain and cool. Peel the fava beans to reveal the inner beans.

Place a small amount of the oil, the garlic and onion in a skillet over medium heat. When the onions sizzle, add a pinch of salt and the lemon zest and sauté for 2 minutes. Stir in the beans, reduce heat to low, cover and cook until the beans are just tender, about 7 minutes.

While the vegetables cook, bring a pot of water to a boil

and cook the penne al dente. Drain well, but do not rinse. Transfer the pasta to a platter and spoon the fava bean mixture over the top, finishing the dish with a sprinkle of the parsley and a drizzle of fruity olive oil.

ROASTED VEGETABLE PASTA

Rich, satisfying and luscious are only a few of the words that describe this hearty pasta dish. Roasted vegetables are sweet, their natural flavors intensified in the confined heat of the oven. Beautifully diced and spooned over penne pasta creates heaven on a plate.

MAKES 2 TO 3 SERVINGS

1 to 2 cloves fresh garlic, thinly sliced
1 red onion, cut into ¼-inch dice
1 carrot, cut into ¼-inch dice
1 cup ¼-inch-diced butternut squash
1 cup ¼-inch-diced sweet potato
Grated zest of 1 lemon
Extra-virgin olive oil, for drizzling
Sea salt
Mirin
10 to 12 oil-cured black olives, pitted and
   minced
8 ounces penne pasta
Juice of ½ lemon
2 to 3 sprigs fresh basil, leaves removed and
   finely minced
Fruity olive oil, for drizzling

Preheat the oven to 375°F.

Place the garlic, onion, carrot, squash and sweet potato in a mixing bowl. Stir in the lemon zest, a generous drizzle of extra-virgin olive oil, a light sprinkle of salt and a light drizzle of mirin. Mix well to coat the vegetables. Transfer to a shallow baking dish, avoiding a lot of overlap. Bake, covered, for 45 minutes, then remove cover, add the olives and bake until vegetables are lightly browned, about 15 minutes more.

When the vegetables are nearly ready, bring a pot of water to a boil and cook the penne al dente, about 8 minutes. Drain well, but do not rinse. Transfer to a mixing bowl.

Remove vegetables from the oven and gently stir in the lemon juice. Spoon the vegetables into the pasta and mix well. Transfer to a serving bowl and serve garnished with basil and a drizzle of fruity olive oil.

SOBA WITH ENDIVE AND RADICCHIO

Strong and bitter, with buckwheat soba as the foundation for this tower of strength, I add the delicate bitter taste of endive to keep you alert, with the minerals in radicchio to ensure you have strength. Just to make sure you don't become bull-headed, I add a touch of sweet taste to keep you receptive and compassionate.
MAKES 4 OR 5 SERVINGS

8 ounces buckwheat soba
About 2 tablespoons extra-virgin olive oil
2 to 3 cloves fresh garlic, finely minced
½ yellow onion, diced
Sea salt
Mirin
Balsamic vinegar

3 Belgian endive, quartered lengthwise
1 radicchio, shredded
Juice of ½ lemon
3 to 4 sprigs fresh flat-leaf parsley, finely minced, for garnish

Bring a pot of water to a boil and cook the soba noodles al dente, about 12 minutes. Drain and rinse very well, as Japanese noodles are generally coated with salt in the drying process, which can alter the taste of the final dish.

Place the oil, garlic and onions in a deep skillet over medium heat. When the onions begin to sizzle, add a pinch of salt and sauté for 1 to 2 minutes. Spread the onions evenly over the bottom of the skillet. Sprinkle generously with mirin and vinegar and then lay the endive, cut side down, on top. Add the radicchio, cover and reduce the heat to low. Cook until the endive is quite limp and beginning to brown, about 20 minutes. Remove from the heat and add the lemon juice. Add noodles and stir gently to combine. Transfer to a serving platter and garnish with the parsley.

≈ *Did You Know?* ≈
BELGIAN ENDIVE

Legend Eating Belgian endive will make us patient and compassionate.

Fact Belgian endive is rich in folic acid, potassium, vitamin C, pantothenic acid, riboflavin and zinc, all good compounds for cleansing and relaxing the liver, the organ, according to Chinese medicine, that determines whether we keep our cool or not.

WILD MUSHROOM-PINE NUT PENNE

If you want to impress your guests with pasta, you might as well really knock them out with this rich, spicy and earthy dish. They'll be oohing and aahing as this sensual entrée makes their knees weak, and no one need know that you're dissolving all their neck tension with the deliciously creamy mushroom sauce. What a good friend you are.

MAKES 4 TO 6 SERVINGS

About 2 tablespoons extra-virgin olive oil
2 to 3 cloves fresh garlic, thinly sliced
1 red onion, diced
Generous pinch red pepper flakes
Sea salt
1 cup dried shiitake mushrooms, soaked until
    tender, stemmed and thinly sliced
1 cup dried lobster mushrooms, soaked until
    tender and thinly sliced
1 cup cremini mushrooms, brushed free of
    dirt and thinly sliced
1 cup oyster mushrooms, coarsely chopped
2 to 3 portobello mushrooms, brushed free of
    dirt, stemmed and thinly sliced
½ cup dry white wine
1 cup pine nuts
10 ounces penne pasta
2 teaspoons sweet white miso
Grated zest of 1 lemon
3 to 4 sprigs fresh flat-leaf parsley, finely
    minced

Place the oil, garlic and onion in a deep skillet over medium heat. When the onion begins to sizzle, add the red pepper flakes and a pinch of salt and sauté for 2 to 3 minutes. Stir in the shiitake and lobster mushrooms and a pinch of salt and sauté for 1 to 2 minutes. Stir in the cremini, oyster and portobello mushrooms and a pinch of salt and sauté until the mushrooms begin to release their juices. Add the wine, season lightly with salt, cover and reduce the heat to low. Simmer over low heat until the mushrooms are quite tender, 20 to 25 minutes. Stir in the pine nuts.

While the mushrooms cook, bring a pot of water to a boil and cook the penne al dente, 8 to 10 minutes. Drain well, reserving a small amount of pasta cooking water, but do not rinse the pasta. Arrange on a serving platter. Dissolve the miso in the reserved pasta water and stir into the mushroom mixture, along with the lemon zest. Continue to stir for 2 minutes. Remove from the heat and spoon over the pasta. Serve garnished with the parsley.

BROCCOLI RABE PASTA WITH TEMPEH SAUSAGE

I'm not much of a fan of fake foods like veggie lunchmeats. They are usually highly processed, with lots of compromise. Once in a while, though, a spectacular item comes along that just enchants me. I found a version of spicy sausage that I loved as a child; only this one is soy based, with a richly spiced, exotic flavor that is simply delicious. It's made with tempeh, and it's great quality.

MAKES 4 TO 6 SERVINGS

About 2 tablespoons extra-virgin olive oil
1 red onion, cut into thin half-moon slices
Sea salt

½ cup mirin

2 (8-ounce) packages tempeh sausage, sliced
into ¼-inch-thick half-moon slices

1 bunch broccoli rabe, rinsed well and stems
trimmed

10 ounces linguine

Juice of 1 lemon

1 red bell pepper, roasted over an open flame
(page 57), peeled, seeded and diced

4 lemon wedges, for garnish

Place the oil and onion in a deep skillet over medium heat. When the onion begins to sizzle, add a pinch of salt and sauté for 1 to 2 minutes. Add the mirin and tempeh sausage and stir gently. Season lightly with salt, cover and reduce the heat to very low, braising the tempeh for 7 to 9 minutes. Slice the broccoli rabe into bite-size pieces, add to the skillet with a sprinkle of salt and re-cover. Cook over low heat until the rabe wilts completely, 7 to 10 minutes.

While the tempeh sausage cooks, bring a pot of water to a boil and cook the linguine al dente. Drain well but do not rinse the pasta.

Remove the tempeh sausage mixture from the heat, stir in the lemon juice and combine with the cooked pasta, stirring well. Serve garnished with the bell pepper and lemon wedges.

GREENS-FILLED RAVIOLI

The filling in these delicate little pasta pillows is so luscious, you might want to serve it on its own, but make the effort to create these little beauties. This is the perfect pasta course for an elegant dinner, as a light repast for a cocktail party, or when you're making dinner, just because.

MAKES 2 TO 4 SERVINGS OF RAVIOLI AND 1 POUND OF DOUGH

Pasta Dough

1 cup whole wheat pastry flour

2 cups semolina flour

1 teaspoon sea salt

2 tablespoons extra-virgin olive oil

1 cup warm spring or filtered water

Filling

About 1 tablespoon extra-virgin olive oil

3 to 4 cloves fresh garlic, finely minced

½ yellow onion, diced

Generous pinch red pepper flakes

Scant pinch nutmeg

Sea salt

1 cup pine nuts, ground into a course meal

1 small bunch kale, rinsed well, finely minced

4 to 5 sprigs fresh basil, leaves removed and
finely minced

Finishing

Fruit olive oil, for drizzling

Sea salt

Juice of ½ lemon

2 to 3 sprigs fresh flat-leaf parsley, finely
minced

To make the dough by hand: Sift the flours onto a clean, dry work surface. Make a well in the center of the flour and add the salt, oil and ⅔ cup water. Mix gradually, kneading into a smooth, soft dough, bringing in more flour from the edges and slowly adding the balance of the water as needed. Add more flour if necessary. Continue kneading until the dough is a workable ball, about 10 minutes.

To make the dough in a food processor: Place the steel blade in the processor. Combine the flours in a mixing bowl. Blend the salt and oil with ½ cup water in the bowl. With the machine running, slowly add the flour mixture and the remaining ½ cup water. Process until the dough is soft enough to handle. If the dough seems too dry, add water by ½ teaspoons until you achieve a soft, workable dough.

To make the filling: Place the oil, garlic and onion in a deep skillet over medium heat. When the onion begins to sizzle, add the red pepper flakes, nutmeg and a pinch of salt and sauté for 1 to 2 minutes. Stir in the pine nuts and kale, season lightly with salt and sauté until the kale wilts, about 4 minutes. Stir in the basil and sauté for 30 seconds more. Transfer to a mixing bowl and set aside to cool.

To make the ravioli: When the filling has completely cooled, roll out the dough into a thin rectangle, about 6 × 24 inches. Place spoonfuls of filling on the dough about 1 inch apart, along one side of the rectangle. Brush the edges and in between the filling with water and fold the dough over the filling, creating a long thin cylinder. Press the dough together between the mounds of filling. Using a pasta cutter, cut out the ravioli. Using your fingers or a fork, press the dough together around the four edges, sealing the ravioli.

To cook: Bring a pot of water to a boil and drop the ravioli into the water. Cook over medium-high heat until the ravioli float to the top of the water. Drain well. Transfer the ravioli to a serving platter and drizzle generously with a fruity olive oil, a sprinkle of salt and the lemon juice. Sprinkle with the parsley and serve.

GEMELLI WITH CAULIFLOWER AND WALNUTS

Simplicity is the key to any great dish and pasta is no exception. Italy has built its reputation on simply prepared food that makes us feel as if we've died and gone to heaven. This one is no exception. Based on a classic northern Italian dish, I've reduced the amount of saturated fat without losing a smidge of flavor.

MAKES 4 TO 6 SERVINGS

About 2 tablespoons extra-virgin olive oil
1 red onion, cut into thin half-moon slices
Sea salt
½ cup golden raisins, soaked in warm water for 15 minutes
½ cup mirin
½ head cauliflower, cut into small florets
½ cup walnut pieces, lightly pan-toasted (page 81), coarsely chopped
10 ounces gemelli pasta
2 teaspoons sweet white miso
Juice of ½ lemon
3 to 4 sprigs fresh flat-leaf parsley, finely minced

Place the oil and onion in a deep skillet over high heat. When the onion begins to sizzle, add a pinch of salt and sauté until the onion begins to brown slightly, 3 to 4 minutes. Drain the raisins and stir the raisins and mirin into the onion. Sauté for 1 minute. Add the cauliflower and walnuts, cover, reduce the heat to low and simmer until the cauliflower is tender, 5 to 7 minutes.

While the cauliflower cooks, bring a pot of water to a boil and cook the gemelli al dente, 8 to 10 minutes. Drain the pasta, reserving a small amount of cooking liquid. Do not rinse the pasta.

Dissolve the miso in the reserved cooking liquid and stir it into the cauliflower mixture. Simmer for 1 to 2 minutes; it will thicken slightly. Remove from the heat and stir in the lemon juice.

To serve, stir the pasta and cauliflower mixture together and mound on a platter. Garnish with the parsley.

≈ *Did You Know?* ≈
MISO

Legend Given to man by the gods to help humanity find physical health and enlightenment.

Fact Rich in live bacteria and enzymes, miso is the key to strong digestion, promoting the vitality of our digestive tract. Miso also rids the body of heavy metals and free radicals. Think about it—on those days you feel vital and strong, it's like having a glimpse of nirvana.

SUMMER PASTA WITH OLIVES AND ROASTED PEPPERS

There's nothing quite like a summer repast of pasta. It's so easy to prepare, no slaving over a hot stove for hours on end, when every bone in your body wants to languish in the garden. But you don't want to starve either; this dish has it all.

MAKES 4 OR 5 SERVINGS

About 2 tablespoons extra-virgin olive oil
2 to 3 cloves fresh garlic, thinly sliced
1 red onion, cut into thin half-moon slices
Sea salt
½ cup dry white wine
1 bunch arugula or dandelion or other bitter greens, rinsed very well, thinly sliced
Zest of 1 lemon
10 ounces orecchiette
½ cup oil-cured black olives, pitted and coarsely chopped
1 red bell pepper, roasted over an open flame (page 57), peeled, seeded and sliced into thin ribbons
2 to 3 sprigs fresh basil, leaves removed and shredded

Place the oil, garlic and onion in a deep skillet over medium heat. When the onion begins to sizzle, add a pinch of salt and sauté for 2 to 3 minutes. Add the wine, cover, reduce heat to low and simmer the onion until quite soft, about 10 minutes.

While the onion cooks, bring a pot of water to a boil. When the onion is ready, add the arugula and lemon zest to the skillet, season lightly with salt and cover. Cook until the greens have just wilted but are still bright green, about 4 to 5 minutes.

While the greens cook, add the pasta to the boiling water and cook al dente, about 9 minutes. Drain well, but do not rinse the pasta.

To serve, stir the olives into the cooked greens, add the pasta and stir well to combine. Spoon the pasta onto a serving platter and top with the bell pepper and basil.

TOASTED ORZO WITH PEAS

Light, sweet and delicate are the best words to describe this elegant side dish. Perfect for a simple dinner or as a colorful addition to a party . . . not to mention the perfect picnic food. Toasting the orzo helps it hold up so it won't wilt or get mushy as it graces your buffet.

MAKES 3 TO 4 SERVINGS

    2 cups spring or filtered water
    1 cup orzo
    Sea salt
    About 2 tablespoons extra-virgin olive oil
    1 to 2 cloves fresh garlic, thinly sliced
    1 red onion, cut into thin half-moon slices
    1½ cups fresh or frozen peas
    Zest of ½ lemon
    2 to 3 sprigs fresh flat-leaf parsley, finely
        minced, for garnish

Bring the water to a boil and add the orzo and a pinch of salt. Cook until tender, about 5 minutes. Drain well, but do not rinse.

Heat 1 tablespoon of the oil in a skillet over medium heat and sauté the orzo. Cook, stirring frequently, until the orzo begins to brown, about 7 minutes. Transfer to a mixing bowl and set aside.

Wipe out the skillet. Place the remaining 1 tablespoon of oil, the garlic and onion in the same skillet over medium heat. When the onion begins to sizzle, add a pinch of salt and sauté until quite soft, 5 to 7 minutes. Stir in the peas, season lightly with salt and cook, stirring often, just until the peas are bright green and tender, 3 to 4 minutes. Remove from the heat and stir the orzo into the peas, along with the lemon zest and parsley. Serve warm or chilled.

CAPPELLINI WITH PEAS AND LEMON

A delicious lemony pasta is ideal served with a fresh salad of bitter greens and ripe tomatoes. Rich, yet light, this colorful dish makes the perfect centerpiece as the pasta course for an elegant dinner party or as a quick summer dinner on its own.

MAKES 4 OR 5 SERVINGS

    1 pound cappellini (angel hair)
    1 cup plain soymilk
    Grated zest of 2 lemons
    1 teaspoon kuzu, dissolved in 2 tablespoons
        soymilk or water
    1 cup fresh or frozen peas
    1 cup diced packaged smoked tofu (see note
        below)
    ¼ cup mirin
    Juice of ½ lemon
    2 teaspoons white miso
    3 to 4 sprigs fresh flat-leaf parsley, finely
        minced

Bring a pot of water to a boil and cook the cappellini al dente, about 8 minutes. Drain well, but do not rinse.

While the pasta cooks, bring the soymilk and lemon zest to a boil in a deep skillet over low heat.

Stir in the dissolved kuzu, stirring until thickened, about 2 minutes. The sauce will be quite thick. Stir in the peas, tofu and mirin and simmer for 2 minutes. Mix the lemon juice and miso together to dissolve the miso. Stir into the sauce and simmer for 2 minutes.

Stir the pasta and parsley into the pea mixture in the skillet and toss gently to coat.

Note: Smoked tofu comes prepackaged in natural food stores.

PUMPKIN FETTUCINE WITH PESTO AND OLIVES

As summer turns to autumn, we begin the transition from the lightness of summer fare to the heartier dishes that will take us comfortably into the cooler days of autumn. With fresh basil still growing in the garden and the first squash of the fall coming in, this dish is as perfect as the season change.
MAKES 4 OR 5 SERVINGS

Pumpkin Pasta Dough
2 cups semolina flour
1 cup whole wheat pastry flour
1 teaspoon sea salt
2 tablespoons extra-virgin olive oil
1 cup puréed cooked butternut squash or canned pumpkin
Spring or filtered water, as needed

Basil Pesto
1 cup loosely packed fresh basil leaves
1 cup pine nuts

⅓ cup extra-virgin olive oil
1 teaspoon umeboshi plum vinegar
2 teaspoons brown rice syrup
2 teaspoons white miso
Spring or filtered water, as needed

1 cup oil-cured black olives, pitted, left whole, for garnish
1 ripe tomato, diced, for garnish

To make the dough: Sift the flours onto a dry work surface. Make a well in the center of the flour and add the salt, oil and squash. Mix gradually, kneading into a smooth, soft dough by drawing small amounts of flour in from the edges as you knead. Add more flour if the dough seems too sticky or water if it feels too dry; in both cases, add small amounts very slowly so as not to jeopardize the quality of the dough. Continue kneading until the dough is a soft, workable ball, about 10 minutes. Cover the dough with plastic wrap and set aside to rest for about 30 minutes, or refrigerate the dough for up to 2 days. Divide the dough into 3 equal pieces. Roll each piece into a ⅛-inch-thick sheet. Allow to rest for 5 minutes. Cut the dough into wide fettucine strips or run through a pasta cutting machine to create fettucine. Lay the noodles on a dry kitchen towel for at least 1 hour before cooking or you can drape the fettucine over a drying rack and dry completely for 1 to 2 days.

To make the pesto: Bring a pot of water to a boil and quickly dip the basil leaves into the water. Drain well and transfer to a food processor. Add the pine nuts and pulse to begin puréeing the nuts. Add the oil, vinegar, rice syrup and miso. Purée until smooth, adding a small amount of water to thin the pesto, if desired, but do not thin too much.

Bring a pot of water to a boil and cook the pasta al dente, 2 to 3 minutes, stirring frequently to prevent sticking. Fresh pasta dough will not take as long to cook as dried pasta; keep your eye on it during cooking or it will get too soft. Drain well, but do not rinse.

As soon as the pasta is cooked, toss with the pesto and transfer to a serving platter. Garnish with the olives and tomato.

Notes: If umeboshi plum vinegar is unavailable, use 1 teaspoon lemon juice with ¼ teaspoon sea salt.

You can make pesto the traditional way by grinding it in a mortar and pestle, which is my favorite method. Give it a try.

MUSHROOM, RADICCHIO AND SMOKED TOFU LASAGNE

Rich, smoky, with a gentle tangy bite from radicchio, there will be no mistaking this version of lasagne for anything traditional. We have layered noodles and fill-ing, but the similarities end there, with the exception of spectacular flavor.
MAKES 8 TO 12 SERVINGS

10 tablespoons extra-virgin olive oil
3 heads radicchio, diced
Sea salt
4 cups button mushrooms, brushed free of dirt and thinly sliced
4 tablespoons whole wheat pastry flour
2½ cups plain soymilk
2 to 3 cloves fresh garlic, finely minced
1 red onion, cut into thin half-moon slices
5 to 6 sprigs fresh flat-leaf parsley, finely minced
Juice of ½ fresh lemon
8 ounces smoked tofu, very thinly sliced
12 uncooked, no-boil lasagne noodles
4 ounces nondairy soy mozzarella, grated

Place 4 tablespoons of the oil and radicchio in a deep skillet over medium heat. When the radic-chio begins to sizzle, add a pinch of salt and sauté until the radicchio begins to turn golden, about 5 minutes. Stir in the mushrooms, season lightly with salt and sauté until the mushrooms release their juices and reabsorb them.

In a small saucepan, heat another 4 tablespoons of the oil over low heat. Whisk in the flour until smooth. Cook, whisking, over low heat for 3 min-utes. Whisk in the soymilk and season to taste with salt. Cook over low heat, whisking occasion-ally, for 5 minutes, until thickened. Stir the soymilk mixture into the mushrooms and simmer for 2 minutes.

Place about 2 tablespoons of the oil, the garlic and onion in a deep skillet over medium heat. When the onion begins to sizzle, add a pinch of salt and sauté until the onion is quite limp, 4 to 5 minutes. Stir in the parsley and season to taste with salt; simmer for 2 minutes. Remove from the heat and stir in the lemon juice and tofu. Set aside.

Preheat the oven to 375°F and lightly oil a deep 9 × 13-inch baking dish. Spoon 1 cup mushroom sauce over the bottom of the dish; it will not cover the bottom completely. Lay 3 lasagne noodles on the bottom of the pan. Top with half of the remaining mushroom sauce. Lay 3 lasagne noodles on top of the mushroom sauce. Spoon the onion mixture evenly over the noodles. Top with 3 more lasagne noodles and spoon 1 cup of the sauce over the top of the noodles. Lay the final 3 lasagne noodles on top. Spoon remaining sauce over the lasagne and sprinkle evenly with the soy mozzarella.

Cover the dish tightly with foil, tenting slightly to prevent it from sticking to the top. Bake for 35 minutes. Remove the foil and bake the lasagne for another 10 minutes, until the top is lightly browned and bubbling. Remove from the oven and allow the lasagne to stand, undisturbed, for 10 minutes before serving.

ROASTED BUTTERNUT SQUASH, ROSEMARY AND GARLIC LASAGNE

Want to stay toasty warm this winter? Give this delicious, hearty, rustic lasagne a try. Baked with sweet, warming winter squash, smothered in a creamy sauce, this beautiful main course will satisfy, strengthen and help us relax and hold on to our much-needed warmth during chilly winter months.

MAKES 8 TO 12 SERVINGS

9 cups 2-inch-diced butternut squash
¼ cup extra-virgin olive oil, plus extra for
    drizzling
Sea salt
4 cups plain soymilk
1 to 2 tablespoons dried rosemary, ground in
    a mortar and pestle
1 to 2 cloves fresh garlic, finely minced
4 tablespoons whole wheat pastry flour
6 uncooked, no-boil lasagne noodles
8 ounces nondairy soy mozzarella, grated

Preheat the oven to 400°F and lightly oil a large, shallow baking sheet.

Toss the squash with a generous drizzle of oil and salt. Mix well to coat the squash. Spread the squash over the shallow pan and bake, covered, for 15 minutes. Remove cover and bake about 20 minutes more, until the squash is tender and beginning to brown.

While the squash bakes, bring the soymilk and rosemary to a boil in a saucepan over medium heat. Reduce the heat to low and simmer for 10 minutes. Pour through a fine strainer and set aside.

Place oil and garlic in a large pan over low heat. When the oil is warm, stir in the flour and cook, whisking until smooth, for 3 minutes. Remove from the heat and whisk in the rosemary-scented soymilk. Return the pan to low heat and cook the sauce, whisking occasionally, until the sauce thickens, about 10 minutes. Stir in the squash and season lightly with salt. Simmer for 2 minutes.

Reduce the oven temperature to 375°F and lightly oil a deep 9 × 13-inch baking dish. Spoon about 1 cup of the squash sauce over the bottom of the dish. It will not cover the bottom completely. Lay 3 lasagne noodles on top of the sauce. Spread half the remaining sauce over the noodles. Sprinkle with half the grated soy mozzarella. Lay the last 3 sheets lasagne on top, spoon the remaining sauce over the noodles and sprinkle with remaining mozzarella.

Cover tightly with foil, tenting slightly to prevent it from sticking to the top. Bake for 35 minutes. Remove the foil and return to the oven for 10 minutes, until the top is golden and bubbling. Allow the lasagne to stand, undisturbed, for 10 minutes before serving.

≈≈ *Did You Know?* ≈≈
ROSEMARY

Legend Rosemary makes the skin look young and fresh.

Fact Rosemary's Latin name means "dew of the sea" and it has been used for thousands of years as an antiseptic, diuretic, liver tonic and digestive cleanser, all responsible for creating clean, strong blood to nourish our skin.

BROCCOLI RABE AND TOMATO LASAGNE

With this lasagne, it can be summer all year long. The rich-flavored sun-dried tomatoes are in perfect balance with the delicate bitter essence of broccoli rabe. Hearty, satisfying and magnificently flavored, this main course brings a wee bit of July into dreary winter days.
MAKES 8 TO 12 SERVINGS

½ cup densely packed dry-pack sun-dried tomatoes
1¼ cups boiling spring or filtered water
About 6 tablespoons extra-virgin olive oil
2 to 3 cloves fresh garlic, thinly sliced
2 medium leeks, split lengthwise, rinsed well, thinly sliced
Sea salt
3 tablespoons whole wheat pastry flour
1 cup plain soymilk
2 cups canned tomato purée
9 to 10 cups diced broccoli rabe (remove tough stems before dicing)
½ teaspoon red pepper flakes
¼ cup spring or filtered water
12 uncooked, no-boil lasagne noodles
2 to 3 cups nondairy soy mozzarella, grated

Place the sun-dried tomatoes in a small bowl and pour the boiling water over them to soak. When the tomatoes are soft, drain them well, reserving the soaking liquid. Mince the tomatoes. Set aside.

Place about 1 tablespoon of the oil, the garlic and leeks in a deep skillet over medium heat. When the leeks begin to sizzle, add a pinch of salt and sauté for 3 to 4 minutes. Transfer to a bowl and set aside. Wipe out skillet and set aside.

Place 4 tablespoons of the oil in a saucepan over low heat. Whisk in the flour and a pinch of salt and cook, whisking, for 3 minutes. Season lightly with salt and slowly add the reserved tomato soaking liquid and soymilk, whisking frequently. Cook, whisking until thickened, about 5 minutes. Stir in the sun-dried tomatoes and tomato purée and set aside.

Place about 1 tablespoon of the oil in the wiped-out skillet over medium heat. Stir in the rabe, season lightly with salt and add the red pepper flakes. Sauté until wilted, about 2 minutes. Pour water over the rabe, cover the skillet and cook until the rabe is just tender, about 2 minutes. Remove from the heat and remove the cover. Set aside.

Preheat the oven to 375°F and lightly oil a deep 9 × 13-inch baking dish.

Spoon 1 cup of the sauce over the bottom of the baking dish. Lay 3 lasagne noodles over the sauce. Stir the broccoli rabe into the remaining sauce and spoon half of it over the noodles. Sprinkle about one-third of the soy mozzarella over the sauce. Lay 3 lasagne noodles on top and cover with half the remaining sauce. Sprinkle with half the remaining soy mozzarella. Lay the final 3 lasagne noodles over the cheese, spoon the remaining sauce over the noodles and sprinkle with the remaining soy mozzarella.

Cover tightly with foil, tenting slightly to prevent it from sticking to the top. Bake for 35 minutes. Remove cover and bake until the top is golden and bubbling. Allow the lasagne to stand for 10 minutes before serving.

NETTLE GNOCCHI WITH BASIL OIL

Gathering wild greens in the spring says it all. Astringent and bitter, these greens open our energy, rid us of winter's accumulation and ready us for the warmth of the fast-approaching summer. But relax, I've shrouded the bitterness in the most sensual pasta dough and smothered it in richly scented basil oil, delicious and good for us—perfect.
MAKES 4 TO 6 SERVINGS

6 cups nettle leaves, rinsed well (see note below)
½ cup white sushi rice
1 cup plus ¼ cup spring or filtered water
1½ cups semolina flour

1 cup whole wheat pastry flour
Sea salt
½ cup extra-virgin olive oil
Generous pinch red pepper flakes
1 small bunch fresh basil, leaves removed and shredded
Juice of ½ fresh lemon

Bring a pot of water to a boil and quickly blanch the nettles by plunging them into the hot water and draining well. Towel dry and finely mince. Set aside.

Cook the rice in 1 cup of the water over low heat until soft and all liquid is absorbed, about 30 minutes. Purée the rice in a food processor until creamy. Combine the rice, semolina and pastry flours and a generous pinch of salt, mixing until a stiff dough forms, slowly adding water if necessary. Knead the nettles into the dough and continue kneading about 10 minutes, to create a soft, workable dough.

Lightly flour a work surface and pinch off a piece of dough. Roll into a thick rope, about ¼ inch thick. Cut into 1-inch lengths. Lightly flour a fork or gnocchi comb and roll each length across the fork to create ridges. Arrange the gnocchi on a lightly floured baking sheet. Repeat this process until all the pasta dough has been used.

Bring a pot of water to a boil. Add a generous pinch of salt and the gnocchi. Cook until the gnocchi begin to rise to the surface of the cooking water, 2 to 3 minutes. Drain well, but do not rinse.

While the gnocchi cook, heat the olive oil with a generous pinch of salt and the red pepper flakes over medium heat for 2 to 3 minutes. Remove from heat and stir in the basil.

Toss the gnocchi with the warm basil oil and arrange on a serving platter. Serve with a drizzle of fresh lemon juice.

Note: If you are unable to get nettle leaves or tips, try arugula, sorrel or baby spinach greens—but always fresh, not frozen. If you can find nettles, harvest and clean the greens while wearing rubber gloves to avoid the tiny thorns that earn the plant its name, stinging nettles.

≈≈ *Did You Know?* ≈≈
NETTLE

Legend Nettle can relieve the symptoms of common hay fever.

Fact Stinging nettle, with its peppery flavor and astringent character aids in drying out the sinuses, thus relieving allergy congestion and sneezing.

PENNE WITH BEER-STEWED ARTICHOKE HEARTS

While it's lovely to take artichokes down to their hearts, sometimes there's simply no time. So if you keep a jar of prepared artichoke hearts in the pantry, you can put together a delicious masterpiece, like this one, in the blink of an eye for a quick dinner.

MAKES 4 TO 6 SERVINGS

About 2 tablespoons extra-virgin olive oil
2 to 3 cloves fresh garlic, thinly sliced
1 red onion, cut into thin half-moon slices
Generous pinch red pepper flakes
Sea salt

1 (8-ounce) jar marinated artichoke hearts, drained well and oil reserved
1 (12-ounce) bottle dark beer
10 ounces uncooked penne
1 small bunch arugula, rinsed well
Balsamic vinegar
½ ripe tomato, diced (do not peel or seed), for garnish

Place the oil, garlic and onion in a deep skillet over medium heat. When the onion begins to sizzle, add the red pepper flakes and a pinch of salt and sauté until the onion is quite soft and beginning to brown, 5 to 6 minutes. Stir in the artichoke hearts, a pinch of salt and the beer. Cover and bring to a boil. Reduce the heat to low, season lightly with salt and cook for 15 minutes.

While the artichokes cook, bring a pot of water to a boil and cook the penne al dente. Drain well, but do not rinse. Toss the penne with a small amount of the reserved artichoke oil.

When the artichokes are ready, finely shred the arugula and add to the skillet. Remove from the heat and stir gently to incorporate the arugula into the artichokes. Fold in the penne and a light sprinkle of balsamic vinegar and transfer to a serving platter. Serve garnished with the tomato.

FUSILLI CARBONARA WITH SPRING VEGETABLES

Hearty, delicious and oh so easy to prepare, if you want to keep making excuses for not cooking, then skip this recipe. But if you want to wow your family with your culinary skills, without killing yourself in the preparation, this dish is for you. Caution: You may get hooked on cooking.

MAKES 4 TO 6 SERVINGS

10 ounces spiral pasta

2 cups baby carrots, halved lengthwise

1 bunch asparagus, tough ends snapped off and stalks cut into 1-inch lengths

1 large zucchini, cut into long matchstick pieces

2 cups plain soymilk

Sea salt

1½ tablespoons kuzu, dissolved in a small amount cold water

⅔ cup oil-packed sun-dried tomatoes, drained well, diced

3 to 4 sprigs fresh flat-leaf parsley, finely minced

Fruity olive oil, for drizzling

Bring a large pot of water to a boil. Add the pasta and cook for 4 minutes. Add the baby carrots to the pasta and cook for 2 to 3 minutes more. Add the asparagus and cook for 2 to 3 minutes more. Adjust the cooking of the vegetables to the texture of the pasta, which should be al dente. Just before draining the pasta, stir in the zucchini. Drain well, but do not rinse; return the pasta and vegetables to the pot over very low heat.

Warm the soymilk in a saucepan over low heat. Season lightly with salt. Stir in the dissolved kuzu, and cook, stirring constantly, until thickened, about 4 minutes.

Stir the sauce, sun-dried tomatoes and parsley into the pasta and vegetables, transfer to a serving bowl and serve with a drizzle of fruity olive oil.

PAPPARDELLE WITH ROSEMARY-SCENTED WHITE BEANS

A lovely, richly flavored pasta dish creates satisfaction with its complete protein. Strengthening beans join with the stamina of pasta to make you feel big and strong. And easy? Check it out.

MAKES 4 TO 6 SERVINGS

> About 2 tablespoons extra-virgin olive oil
>
> 2 to 3 cloves fresh garlic, thinly sliced
>
> 2 red onions, halved and each half sliced into quarters
>
> Sea salt
>
> Grated zest of ½ lemon
>
> 2 cups cooked cannellini, navy or Great Northern beans (see note)
>
> 1 tablespoon minced fresh rosemary or 1 teaspoon dried rosemary
>
> 1 cup dry white wine
>
> 10 ounces pappardelle
>
> 2 teaspoons sweet white miso
>
> 1 cup diced green beans
>
> Juice of ½ fresh lemon
>
> 1 red bell pepper, roasted over an open flame (page 57), peeled, seeded and diced
>
> 2 to 3 sprigs fresh flat-leaf parsley, finely minced

Place the oil, garlic and onions in a deep skillet over medium heat. When the onions begin to sizzle, add a pinch of salt and the lemon zest and sauté for 3 to 4 minutes. Add the cannellini beans, rosemary, a pinch of salt and the wine. Cover, reduce the heat to low and cook for 15 minutes. Season lightly with salt.

While the beans cook, bring a pot of water to a boil. Cook the pasta al dente, about 11 minutes. Drain, reserving ⅔ cup cooking liquid, but do not rinse.

When the beans are quite soft, dissolve the miso in the reserved pasta liquid. Stir the dissolved miso and green beans into the cannellini beans. Simmer until the greens beans are bright green, and still crisp, about 3 minutes. Remove from the heat and stir in the lemon juice. Transfer the pasta to a serving platter, spoon beans and sauce and serve garnished with the bell pepper and parsley.

Note: You can cook dried beans in three parts water to one part beans, with a small bay leaf to aid in tenderizing them, or use canned organic beans.

FARFALLE WITH ASPARAGUS AND ROASTED SHALLOTS

Spring into spring with this elegantly simple and oh so delicious pasta course. As a light luncheon centerpiece or the pasta course of an elegant dinner party, this dish is like a breath of fresh air.

MAKES 5 TO 7 SERVINGS

> 24 to 30 shallots, peeled, halved lengthwise
>
> 4 to 5 tablespoons extra-virgin olive oil
>
> 1 teaspoon sea salt
>
> 1 tablespoon balsamic vinegar
>
> 1 pound farfalle
>
> 2 to 3 cloves fresh garlic, thinly sliced
>
> Grated zest of 1 fresh lemon

2 bunches asparagus, tough ends snapped off and stalks sliced diagonally into 1-inch lengths

¼ cup spring or filtered water

3 to 4 sprigs fresh flat-leaf parsley, finely minced

⅔ cup whole wheat bread crumbs

½ ripe tomato, diced (do not peel or seed)

Preheat the oven to 375°F.

Place the shallots in a mixing bowl and add 3 to 4 tablespoons of the olive oil, the salt and vinegar. Toss well to coat and spread evenly in a shallow baking pan. Bake, uncovered, about 40 minutes, stirring occasionally, until tender and lightly browned.

When the shallots are nearly cooked, bring a pot of water to a boil. Cook the pasta al dente, about 12 minutes. Drain well, but do not rinse.

While the pasta cooks, place about 1 tablespoon of the oil, the garlic and lemon zest in a skillet over medium heat. Add the aspara-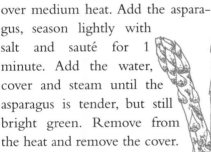gus, season lightly with salt and sauté for 1 minute. Add the water, cover and steam until the asparagus is tender, but still bright green. Remove from the heat and remove the cover.

Toss the cooked pasta with the shallots, asparagus, parsley and bread crumbs. Serve garnished with the tomato.

PASTA WITH SUMMER VEGETABLES AND CHICKPEAS

I love, love, love to serve this main course in my garden on a sultry summer evening. Laced through with fresh vegetables and richly flavored olives, this sensual, colorful dish is the perfect centerpiece with a crisp fresh salad and whole-grain bread on the side. Summer doesn't get better than this.

MAKES 4 TO 6 SERVINGS

About 2 tablespoons extra-virgin olive oil

2 to 3 cloves fresh garlic, thinly sliced

1 red onion, diced

Sea salt

2 small yellow summer squash, diced

2 small zucchini, diced

1 red bell pepper, roasted over an open flame (page 57), peeled, seeded and diced

3 tablespoons capers, drained

½ cup dry white wine

10 ounces medium shells

2 ripe tomatoes, diced (do not peel or seed)

½ cup coarsely minced, pitted, oil-cured black olives

3 to 4 sprigs fresh basil, leaves removed from stems and finely minced

Lemon wedges, for garnish

Place the oil, garlic and onion in a deep skillet over medium heat. When the onion begins to sizzle, add a pinch of salt and sauté for 2 minutes. Stir in the yellow squash, zucchini and a generous pinch of salt and sauté for 2 minutes. Stir in the bell pepper, capers and wine. Cover and cook over low heat for 15 minutes.

While the vegetables cook, bring a pot of water to a boil and cook the shells al dente, 11 to 12 minutes. Drain well, but do not rinse.

When the vegetables are ready, adjust the seasoning and stir in the tomatoes, olives and basil. Finally, fold in cooked shells and transfer to a serving platter. Serve garnished with lemon wedges.

Note: Take care when seasoning this dish as the capers and olives are already salty—don't use a heavy hand with the salt pinches.

RIGATONI WITH CANNELLINI BEANS AND SPICY TEMPEH SAUSAGE

Pairing sausage and white beans is a classic Tuscan combination, like Romeo and Juliet. Lightly spiced and hearty, pasta and beans make the perfect marriage, keeping you feeling nourished and sated, strong, yet free of tension. Ah, harmony.
MAKES 4 TO 6 SERVINGS

About 2 tablespoons extra-virgin olive oil
3 to 4 cloves fresh garlic, thinly sliced
1 yellow onion, diced
Sea salt
8 ounces tempeh sausage, crumbled
1 cup dry red wine
1 cup canned diced tomatoes
Generous pinch red pepper flakes
1 pound rigatoni
2 cups cooked cannellini beans

3 to 4 sprigs fresh basil, leaves removed and finely shredded, plus extra sprigs for garnish
Juice of 1 fresh lemon

Place the oil, garlic and onion in a deep skillet over medium heat. When the onion begins to sizzle, add a pinch of salt and sauté for 2 minutes. Stir in the tempeh sausage, breaking it up with a wooden spoon. Add a pinch of salt and sauté until the tempeh sausage begins to brown, about 3 minutes. Add the wine, tomatoes and red pepper flakes, bring to a boil, cover and reduce the heat to low. Simmer for 15 minutes.

While the tempeh sausage mixture cooks, bring a pot of water to a boil and cook the rigatoni al dente, 8 to 10 minutes. Drain well, but do not rinse.

Stir the beans into the tempeh sausage mixture, season lightly with salt and remove from the heat. Stir in the basil, lemon juice and rigatoni, mixing well to combine. Serve garnished with basil sprigs.

ORECCHIETTE WITH CAULIFLOWER, PISTACHIOS AND CAPERS

Ah, lovely Sicily, this version of a Sicilian classic was taught to me by my husband's family. Part of me is convinced that if pistachios could be a part of every Sicilian dish, they would be. Nutty and earthy, this brilliant pasta course will have people moaning with pleasure.
MAKES 4 TO 6 SERVINGS

⅔ cup unsalted, shelled pistachios

1 small head cauliflower, cut into small florets

About 2 tablespoons extra-virgin olive oil

2 to 3 cloves fresh garlic, finely minced

½ cup capers, drained well

1½ cups plain soymilk

1 pound orecchiette

1 teaspoon sweet white miso

3 to 4 sprigs fresh flat-leaf parsley, finely
   minced

Grated zest of 1 fresh lemon

Preheat the oven to 375°F. Spread the pistachios on a baking sheet. Bake for 5 to 7 minutes, remove from the oven, cool and coarsely mince. Set aside.

Bring a medium pot of water to a boil and cook the cauliflower florets for 2 minutes. Drain well and set aside.

Place the oil, garlic, capers and cauliflower in a deep skillet over medium heat. At the first sign of sizzle, add the soymilk and bring to a boil. Cover, reduce the heat to low and simmer for 12 minutes.

While the sauce simmers, bring a pot of water to a boil and cook the pasta al dente, about 12 minutes. Drain well, but do not rinse.

When the sauce is ready, remove a small amount of liquid and use to dissolve the miso. Stir the dissolved miso, the parsley and lemon zest into the sauce. Fold the pasta and pistachios, reserving 1 to 2 tablespoons for garnish, into the sauce and transfer to a serving platter. Garnish with the reserved pistachios.

FUSILLI WITH BROCCOLI RABE AND FRIED CHICKPEAS

Yummy is the best word for this pasta dish. Fried chickpeas are just the best, rich, slightly crunchy and oh so satisfying. But too much oil? Never fear; I've balanced it all quite nicely with the delicate, bitter flavor of the broccoli rabe, so our livers stay relaxed and so do our tempers.

MAKES 4 TO 6 SERVINGS

1 pound fusilli

About ½ cup extra-virgin olive oil

4 to 5 cloves fresh garlic, finely minced

3 cups cooked chickpeas, drained

2 sprigs fresh basil, leaves removed and finely
   minced, plus extra sprigs for garnish

1 bunch broccoli rabe, stems trimmed and
   shredded

1 cup dry white wine

2 teaspoons white miso

Fruity olive oil, for drizzling

Bring a pot of water to a boil and cook the fusilli al dente, about 10 minutes. Drain well, reserving about 1 cup cooking water, but do not rinse.

Place the extra-virgin olive oil and garlic in a skillet over high heat. Sauté for 30 seconds. Add the chickpeas and sauté until they begin to lightly brown, 8 to 9 minutes. Stir in the basil and sauté for about 30 seconds to blend the flavors. Stir in the broccoli rabe, wine and reserved pasta cooking water. Cover and cook until the broccoli rabe just wilts, 6 to 7 minutes. Remove a small amount of the liquid and use to dissolve the miso. Stir the miso mixture into the chickpea mixture. Stir in the pasta and mix gently. Transfer to a serving platter, drizzle with fruity olive oil and garnish with basil sprigs.

~~~~~~~~~~~~~~~~~~~~~~~~~~~~~~~~~~

CARAMELIZED SHALLOT AND ROASTED PEPPER LINGUINE

Peppery fennel, sweetly caramelized shallots and roasted red bell peppers come together to create a stunning pasta course. Whether the main attraction or an elegant side dish, the energy of this dish will keep you on a relaxed simmer, with just enough sass to keep things interesting.
MAKES 4 OR 5 SERVINGS

About ½ cup extra-virgin olive oil
2 to 3 cloves fresh garlic, thinly sliced
15 to 20 shallots, cut into thin half-moon slices
Sea salt
Generous pinch red pepper flakes
2 small fennel bulbs, tops trimmed, thinly sliced, reserving 2 to 3 tablespoons minced feathery tops
2 red bell peppers, roasted over an open flame (page 57), peeled, seeded, sliced into thin ribbons

1 cup plain soymilk
1 tablespoon brown rice syrup
10 ounces linguine
2 to 3 sprigs fresh flat-leaf parsley, finely minced, for garnish

Place the oil, garlic and shallots in a deep skillet over medium heat. When the shallots begin to sizzle, add a pinch of salt and the red pepper flakes and sauté until the shallots begin to brown, 15 to 20 minutes. Stir in the fennel bulb and a pinch of salt and sauté for 1 minute. Stir in the bell peppers, and season lightly with salt. Stir in the soymilk and rice syrup. Cover and reduce the heat to low. Simmer for 15 minutes.

While the sauce cooks, bring a pot of water to a boil and cook the linguine al dente, about 10 minutes. Drain well, but do not rinse.

Mix the linguine into the sauce with the minced fennel tops and stir well to combine. Transfer to a serving bowl and serve garnished with parsley.

≈≈ *Did You Know?* ≈≈
FENNEL

Legend Fennel is widely used in folk medicine to aid in digestion and relieve stomach upset.

Fact Fennel is a rich source of an essential oil containing anethole, a substance known to ease gastric pain and smooth digestion.

BEANS: THE FOOD OF VITALITY

I know what you're thinking. Beans, simple, humble beans? The stuff of vitality? Most of us think of beans as, at best, musical and, at worst, slow to cook with little pay-off in terms of flavor. Beans are powerhouses of nutrition, the perfect food for creating strength and stamina, without saturated fats to gum up the works. When properly prepared, beans nourish us deeply and deliciously, keeping us sated and strong.

Protein from plant sources, dismissed in conventional nutrition as incomplete is the best source of protein overall. Protein is present in all foods, except fruit, but is especially abundant in beans, bean products and seeds. Plants are the original source of protein. After all, cows eat grass, so it makes perfect sense to go right to the source, as it were, for the purest form of protein.

There is only good news about beans and bean products. Rich in protein, they also contain complex carbohydrates, fat, fiber, folic acid and phytochemicals. Plant proteins are less perishable, lower in saturated fatty acids than animal flesh, making them better for our health. (Okay, there is a bit of bad news; if not cooked properly, they will, in fact, cause people to make up little those songs about your beans, but we'll get to that.)

The bottom line is pretty simple. For us to feel our best, we need to feel strong and clear minded. That will not happen eating a diet rich in saturated fats, heavy proteins and simple sugars. Your best bet for maintaining vitality and the desire to pursue your life with passion and drive is to avoid animal flesh, using it only as individually needed for strength, and to rely on plant protein for your daily dose of stamina.

A diet rich in saturated fats makes us worse than tired.

Lethargy and lack of stamina are the result of accumulated fats in and around the body. Our organs work much harder to function, exhausting our resources of energy. It gets worse. Saturated fat also accumulates just under the skin. Think about cleaning chicken before cooking. There is a layer of gummy, yellow fat under the skin's surface. We labor to remove every ounce of it because it is so unappealing and less than healthy. The same type of fat forms under our skin as we consume excessive amounts of saturated fats and animal proteins, particularly if we are more sedentary than active. What that means to us, besides heading down the path to coronary disease, is that we feel less, literally. The fat accumulates under the skin, making us less sensitive to touch. After a while, we spiral downward into depression and inertia about our lives, as life's little challenges overwhelm us.

You are not doomed to a life of lentils; however, splendid as they are. The choices available to us are as varied as they are delicious, including black turtle beans, adzuki beans, kidney beans, split peas, fava beans, white navy beans, cannellini, cranberry beans, chickpeas and yes, red, green, brown or black lentils, to name just a few. And it doesn't end there. Along with beans, there are bean by-products. Easy to prepare and requiring less cooking time, tofu and tempeh are the most popular and are part of the magical soy category that enchant us so. Soybeans, and thereby soyfoods, are rich in protein, contain a heart-nourishing oil containing some omega-3 fatty acids, contain isoflavones, phytochemicals with hormonelike effects that protect both men and women from certain forms of cancer, when eaten in moderate amounts. Whole soybeans can be tough on our tender tummies, so the brilliant Asian culture discovered many ways to process them, so we may enjoy the many benefits of these wonderful beans.

From miso, soy sauce and tamari, soymilk, tofu and tempeh, freshly picked and lightly cooked, soybeans are as delicious as they are beneficial to our vitality.

So now that I have convinced you to add beans to your diet, how do we make them less . . . musical? Simple. Follow these steps to delicious, silent bean dishes.

1. Rinse the dried beans well, soak for about 1 hour before cooking, drain them and discard the soaking water. You can skip the soaking process altogether, if you like. It doesn't affect cooking time and the flavor of the cooked dish is actually the richer for lack of soaking. Cooking beans in fresh water eliminates many intestinal difficulties.

2. Bring the beans to a boil over medium heat, uncovered, allowing any bubbles to cook away, rather than lodge in your tummy. Boil them for about 5 minutes before reducing the heat and covering.

3. Finally, add a bay leaf or a small piece of kombu (sea plant) to the water at the beginning of cooking. Both of these ingredients contain compounds that aid the body in breaking down the protein and fat that can cause digestive struggles with high fiber beans.

Oh, and you can forget protein powders, supplements and other forms of processed plant proteins. They are devoid of vital life-giving energy and depleting of passion. To find and maintain our passion for life, nutrients must be gleaned from the food we eat.

Whether you choose lentils, cannellini, split peas, black turtle, adzuki or black-eyed peas, beans may appear to be the humble food of peasants, but they are nothing short of food of the gods.

WHITE BEANS ALESSI

Alessi means "of the season." The simplicity of this dish will take your breath away. Cooked to tender perfection, silkily dressed in fruity olive oil, with salt and lemon juice enhancing their sweet quality, these beans make us strong and vital.

MAKES 3 TO 4 SERVINGS

½ cup dried cannellini or white navy beans,
   sorted, rinsed well and soaked for 1 hour
2 cups spring or filtered water
1 bay leaf or 1-inch piece kombu
2 to 3 cloves fresh garlic, peeled, left whole
Fruity olive oil, for drizzling
Sea salt
Juice of 1 lemon

Drain the beans, discarding the soaking water. Place the beans and fresh water in a heavy saucepan. Add the bay leaf and garlic. Bring to a boil, uncovered, over medium heat. Boil for 5 minutes, cover and reduce the heat to low. Simmer the beans until tender, but not mushy, about 45 minutes. Drain the remaining liquid from the beans, discard the bay leaf and transfer the beans to a mixing bowl.

Drizzle generously with a fruity olive oil and toss gently to coat the beans. Season to taste with salt and add the lemon juice. Stir gently to combine the ingredients and serve hot.

CANNELLINI BEANS WITH WILTED BITTER GREENS

The combination of delicate white beans with richly sautéed, strongly flavored bitter greens is simply perfect. With the astringent quality of the greens aiding in the digestion of the protein and fat of the beans, this dish nourishes us deeply, without overworking our systems, leaving us with plenty of energy for our lives.

MAKES 3 TO 5 SERVINGS

½ cup dried cannellini beans, sorted, rinsed
   well and soaked for 1 hour
2½ cups fresh spring or filtered water
1-inch piece kombu or 1 bay leaf
2 cloves fresh garlic, peeled, left whole
About 1 tablespoon extra-virgin olive oil
2 cloves fresh garlic, cut into thin slices
½ red onion, thinly sliced
Generous pinch red pepper flakes
Sea salt
1 small bunch broccoli rabe, rinsed well, cut
   into small pieces
3 to 4 lemon wedges, for garnish

Drain the beans, discarding the soaking water. Place the beans and fresh water in a heavy saucepan. Add the kombu and garlic. Bring to a boil, uncovered, over medium heat. Boil for about 5 minutes, cover and reduce the heat to low. Cook the beans until just tender, about 45 minutes. Drain away the remaining liquid from the beans, discard the kombu and garlic and set the beans aside.

Place the oil, garlic and onion in a deep skillet over medium heat. When the onion begins to sizzle, add the red pepper flakes and a pinch of salt and sauté for 1 minute. Stir in the broccoli rabe, season lightly with salt and sauté until limp and deeply green, about 4 minutes. Turn off the heat and gently stir in the beans until just combined. Transfer to a serving platter and serve with lemon wedges on the side.

WHITE BEAN STEW WITH PARSNIPS, SHALLOTS AND RED PEPPER

A lovely winter bean stew, this dish will keep you warm and toasty when the weather outside is frightful and even when it's not too bad. Yummy and delicately sweet, this stew will add color and flavor to any cold weather feast.

MAKES 3 TO 4 SERVINGS

1 cup dried Great Northern beans, sorted, rinsed well and soaked for 1 hour

3½ cups fresh spring or filtered water

1-inch piece kombu or 1 bay leaf

About 1 tablespoon extra-virgin olive oil

3 to 4 cloves fresh garlic, thinly sliced

4 to 5 shallots, peeled, quartered

Sea salt

1 red bell pepper, roasted over an open flame (page 57), peeled, seeded and diced

3 to 4 parsnips, diced

Grated zest of 1 lemon

1½ cups dry white wine

2 to 3 sprigs fresh flat-leaf parsley, finely minced

Drain the beans, discarding the soaking water. Place the beans and fresh water in a heavy saucepan. Add the kombu. Bring to a boil, uncovered, over medium heat. Boil for about 5 minutes, cover and reduce the heat to low. Cook the beans until just tender, about 45 minutes. Drain away the remaining liquid from the beans, discard the kombu and set the beans aside.

Place the oil, garlic and shallots in a deep skillet over medium heat. When the shallots begin to sizzle, add a pinch of salt and sauté for 2 to 3 minutes. Stir in the bell pepper, parsnips, lemon zest and a pinch of salt and sauté until just coated with oil. Add the wine and beans and season to taste with salt. Cover and cook until the parsnips are quite tender, about 20 minutes. Remove the cover and cook until any remaining liquid has reduced to a thick syrup. Remove from heat and stir in the parsley.

CHICKPEAS WITH PICKLED ONIONS

Protein can be tough on our tender tummies, leaving us tired and heavy. This recipe is the perfect remedy. Lightly sour, the quickly pickled onions complement the chickpeas perfectly, enhancing their sweet richness and adding just the right sparkle.

MAKES 3 TO 4 SERVINGS

Pickled Onion

1 red onion, cut into very thin half-moon
    pieces
Umeboshi plum vinegar, as needed
Mirin, as needed
Juice of ½ lemon

Chickpeas

½ cup dried chickpeas, sorted, rinsed well and
    soaked for 1 hour
2 cups fresh spring or filtered water
1-inch piece kombu or 1 bay leaf
3 tablespoons sesame tahini
2 teaspoons sweet white miso
2 teaspoons brown rice syrup
2 to 3 sprigs fresh flat-leaf parsley, minced

To pickle the onion: Place the onion in a shallow
bowl and add equal amounts of vinegar and mirin
to cover. Add the lemon juice and gently rub the
onion slices through your fingers. Set aside to
pickle for about 1 hour, tossing occasionally.

To prepare the chickpeas: Drain the beans, discarding the soaking water. Place the beans and
fresh water in a heavy saucepan. Add the kombu.
Bring to a boil, uncovered, over medium heat.
Boil for about 5 minutes, cover and reduce the
heat to low. Cook the beans until just tender,
about 45 to 60 minutes. Drain away the remaining liquid from the beans, reserving about 1 cup,
discard the kombu and transfer the beans to a
bowl.

Gently mix in the tahini, miso, rice syrup and
parsley until well combined, adding reserved
cooking liquid as needed to create a creamy sauce
for the beans.

To serve, drain the onion, gently squeezing any
excess liquid. Arrange on a platter. Toss cooked
chickpeas with sauce to coat and mound in the
center.

SPICY MOROCCAN CHICKPEAS

*Exotic, spicy and sultry just about sums up this delicious
side dish. The spices blend together to enhance the sweet
flavor of the chickpeas, while imparting a strong, vital
energy in us. Their natural sparkle lifts our spirits,
enhances our life force and fills us with the sheer joy of
living.*

MAKES 3 TO 4 SERVINGS

½ cup dried chickpeas, sorted, rinsed well and
    soaked for 1 hour
2 cups fresh spring or filtered water
1-inch piece kombu or 1 bay leaf
1-inch cinnamon stick
About 1 tablespoon extra-virgin olive oil
½ yellow onion, diced
Sea salt
1 small carrot, diced
1 to 2 stalks celery, diced
½-inch piece fresh ginger, grated, juice
    extracted
Pinch ground saffron
Generous pinch turmeric
Generous pinch cayenne
1 ripe tomato, diced
2 to 3 sprigs fresh flat-leaf parsley, finely
    minced

Drain the beans, discarding the soaking water.
Place the beans and fresh water in a heavy
saucepan. Add the kombu. Bring to a boil, uncov-

ered, over medium heat. Boil for about 5 minutes. Add the cinnamon stick, cover and reduce the heat to low. Cook the beans until tender, about 1 hour. When the beans are done, drain off any remaining liquid, discard the cinnamon stick and kombu and set the beans aside.

Place the oil and onion in a deep skillet over medium heat. When the onion begins to sizzle, add a pinch of salt and sauté for 1 to 2 minutes. Add the carrot, celery and pinch of salt and sauté for 2 minutes. Stir in the ginger juice and spices and season lightly with salt. Stir in cooked chickpeas and season to taste with salt. Remove from heat and stir in diced tomato. Transfer to a serving platter and sprinkle with the parsley.

≈≈ *Did You Know?* ≈≈
TURMERIC

Legend Turmeric's hot energy relieves joint pain, menstrual cramps and indigestion.

Fact Rich concentrations of potassium, phosphorous and magnesium make turmeric an ideal natural anti-inflammatory.

CHICKPEA SALAD WITH TOMATOES AND CHIPOTLE

Summertime calls for light, fresh food with a bit of spice to keep us cool. But we still need substance to feel satisfied. This bean salad fits the bill perfectly, with chickpeas, a creamy dressing, fresh juicy summer tomatoes and a touch of heat from the chipotle, just yummy.
MAKES 3 TO 4 SERVINGS

1-inch piece kombu
1½ cups dried chickpeas, sorted and rinsed
4½ cups spring or filtered water
⅓ cup sesame tahini
1 teaspoon sea salt
2 tablespoons freshly squeezed lime juice
2 teaspoons extra-virgin olive oil
2 teaspoons brown rice syrup
½ red onion, finely diced
1 tablespoon finely minced canned chipotle chile
½ teaspoon ground cumin
3 to 4 plum tomatoes, diced (do not peel or seed)
½ cup fresh cilantro, finely minced
½ cup shelled pumpkin seeds, lightly toasted, for garnish (see note below)

Place the kombu in a pressure cooker; add the beans and water. Bring to a boil, uncovered. Seal the lid and bring to full pressure. Reduce the heat to low and cook for 40 minutes. Allow the pressure to reduce naturally, open the lid and check the beans for tenderness. If done to your satisfaction, drain the beans and set aside. If still too hard, continue cooking (not under pressure) until tender. Transfer the beans to a mixing bowl.

Combine the tahini, salt, lime juice, oil and rice syrup in a bowl, whisking until smooth. Adjust the flavor to your taste. Set aside.

Mix the onion, chile, cumin, tomatoes and cilantro with the beans and stir in the dressing to coat. Transfer to a serving bowl and garnish with pumpkin seeds.

Note: To toast pumpkin seeds, heat a dry skillet over medium heat and toast the seeds, stirring, until they are slightly puffed and fragrant, about 5 minutes.

GREEN LENTIL SALAD

Spicy and peppery, yet humble and lightly sweet, sound perfect? Well, lentils aren't just pretty; these little beans are powerhouses of nutrition, all the essential ingredients needed for strength and endurance, with just the right touch of serenity.

MAKES 3 TO 4 SERVINGS

1-inch piece kombu or 1 bay leaf
½ cup Le Puy lentils, sorted and rinsed well
2 cups spring or filtered water
About 1 tablespoon extra-virgin olive oil
1 to 2 cloves fresh garlic, finely minced
Generous pinch red pepper flakes
Sea salt
2 to 3 shallots, finely diced
1 to 2 stalks celery, diced
5 to 6 leaves fresh basil, shredded
Juice of ½ lemon
½ ripe tomato, diced

Place the kombu on the bottom of a pot and top with the lentils. Add the water and bring to a boil, uncovered. Cover and reduce heat to low, cooking the lentils until tender but not mushy, about 35 minutes. When the lentils are tender, drain away any remaining cooking liquid, discard the kombu and set the lentils aside.

Place the oil, garlic and red pepper flakes in a skillet over medium heat. When the garlic begins to sizzle, add a pinch of salt and the shallots. Sauté until just translucent, about 1 minute. Stir in the celery and basil and sauté until shiny with oil. Stir in the lentils and season to taste with salt. Remove from the heat and stir in the lemon juice and tomato. Serve warm.

≈ *Did You Know?* ≈
CELERY

Legend Celery helps us to relax and manage stress more easily.

Fact A rich source of vitamin C, B6 and folic acid, celery contains an active ingredient that lowers blood pressure by reducing the level of hormones associated with stress.

SPICY GINGER DAHL

Beans and spices are like love and passion. On their own, they're okay, but together, they ignite. The calming and strengthening character of the protein in the beans becomes warm and powerful when enhanced by the exotic heat of spices.

MAKES 2 TO 3 SERVINGS

About 2 tablespoons extra-virgin olive oil
1 to 2 cloves fresh garlic, finely minced
3 to 4 slices fresh ginger, finely minced
½ yellow onion, diced
Sea salt
Generous pinch red pepper flakes
Generous pinch cumin
Generous pinch coriander
½ cup mung beans, sorted and rinsed well
2 cups spring or filtered water
2 to 3 sprigs fresh flat-leaf parsley, finely minced
4 to 6 pita breads, cut into wedges, toasted

Place the oil, garlic, ginger and onion in a heavy saucepan over medium heat. When the onion begins to sizzle, add a pinch of salt and sauté for 1 to 2 minutes. Add the red pepper flakes, cumin and coriander and sauté for 1 minute. Top with the mung beans and add the water. Bring to a boil, uncovered. Cover and reduce the heat to low. Cook the beans until quite tender, about 45 minutes. Season to taste with salt and cook for 5 minutes. Using a potato masher, crush the beans into a coarse purée. Transfer to a serving bowl and garnish with the parsley. Serve with the pita wedges.

BLACK-EYED HUMMUS

Spicy, creamy, richly flavored bean spreads are so lovely and so great for creating vitality and clarity of thought. The strength of protein joins up with hot spices and garlic to give us endurance and focus sharp as a laser, with enough courage to be tender.
MAKES 4 TO 5 SERVINGS

½ cup dried black-eyed peas, sorted and rinsed well

2 cups spring or filtered water

1 bay leaf

3 tablespoons extra-virgin olive oil

3 tablespoons sesame tahini

1 to 2 cloves fresh garlic, minced

Generous pinch ground cumin

Generous pinch chili powder

Juice of ½ lemon

Sea salt

2 to 3 sprigs fresh flat-leaf parsley, finely minced

Crackers, pita bread or whole-grain toast points, to serve

Place the beans and water in a heavy saucepan. Add the bay leaf. Bring to a boil, uncovered, over medium heat. Boil for about 5 minutes, cover and reduce the heat to low. Cook the beans until just tender, about 1 hour. Drain away the remaining liquid from the beans, discard the bay leaf and set the beans aside to cool.

When the beans are cooled to room temperature, place in a food processor with the remaining ingredients, except the parsley, adding salt to your taste. Purée until quite smooth. Adjust the seasonings to your taste, adding more spices or more lemon juice. Transfer to a serving bowl, stir in the parsley and serve at room temperature or chilled with crackers.

LEMON AND GINGER-SPICED ADZUKI BEANS

Lemon and spice and everything nice, that's what this dish is made of. Adzuki beans, red jewellike beans, have an uncanny ability to nourish our kidneys, the organs that take the hardest knocks, from morning coffee to overly long working hours to sugary sweets, all of which exhaust them, leaving us looking washed out, with no energy. This simple side dish restores our vitality and our passion for living.
MAKES 3 TO 4 SERVINGS

½ cup dried adzuki beans, sorted and rinsed well

2 cups spring or filtered water

1-inch piece kombu or 1 bay leaf

About 2 tablespoons extra-virgin olive oil

1 to 2 cloves fresh garlic, finely minced

2 shallots, finely minced

Sea salt

5 to 6 slices fresh ginger, finely minced

Grated zest of 1 lemon

Mirin

1 to 2 sprigs fresh flat-leaf parsley, finely
   minced

Juice of ½ lemon

Place the beans and water in a heavy saucepan. Add the kombu. Bring to a boil, uncovered, over medium heat. Boil for about 5 minutes, cover and reduce the heat to low. Cook the beans until just tender, about 45 minutes. Drain away the remaining liquid from the beans, discard the kombu and set the beans aside.

Place the oil, garlic and shallots in a skillet over medium heat. When the shallots begin to sizzle, add a pinch of salt and sauté until they are translucent, about 2 minutes. Stir in the ginger, lemon zest and a generous sprinkling of mirin. Season to taste with salt and sauté for 3 to 4 minutes, stirring constantly. Stir in the beans, adjust the seasonings to your taste and remove from the heat. Stir in the parsley and lemon juice and serve hot.

BLACK SOYBEAN-STUFFED CORNBREAD

Warming, nourishing and comforting, casseroles are like a warm embrace. In this case, we layer vitalizing cornbread with spicy black soybeans to create a deep heat and sparkling strength without weighing you down.

MAKES 4 TO 8 SERVINGS

Filling
About 1 tablespoon extra-virgin olive oil
1 to 2 cloves fresh garlic, thinly sliced
½ yellow onion, diced
Sea salt
Generous pinch red pepper flakes
2 cups cooked black soybeans
1 (10-ounce) can diced tomatoes, drained

Cornbread
2 cups whole wheat pastry flour
1 cup yellow cornmeal
2½ teaspoons baking powder
Generous pinch sea salt
⅓ cup light olive oil
⅔ to 1 cup plain soymilk
2 tablespoons finely minced fresh chives

Preheat the oven to 350°F and lightly oil and flour a deep-dish pie plate.

To make the filling: Place the oil, garlic and onion in a skillet over medium heat. When the onion begins to sizzle, add a pinch of salt and sauté for 1 to 2 minutes. Add the red pepper flakes and beans, stirring to combine ingredients. Add the tomatoes and bring to a low boil. Reduce heat to low and cook for 20 to 30 minutes, uncovered, stirring frequently. The mixture will naturally thicken slightly.

To make the cornbread: Combine the flour, cornmeal, baking powder and salt in a mixing bowl and whisk briskly. Add the olive oil and mix well. Slowly stir in the soymilk until you achieve a thick, spoonable batter. Fold in the chives.

Spoon half of the batter into the prepared pie plate. Top with the soybean mixture, covering the batter completely. Spoon the remaining batter over the soybean mixture, covering completely. Bake 35 to 40 minutes, until the center of the cornbread springs back to the touch. Remove from the oven and allow to cool for at least 15 minutes before slicing into wedges.

SOUTHWESTERN SUCCOTASH

A spicy take on a classic side dish, frozen lima beans ensure ease of preparation. Enlivened by the gentle heat of poblano chiles, the beans come to life, with crisp, fresh vegetables to make sure it doesn't get too hot to handle.

MAKES 4 TO 5 SERVINGS

1 (8-ounce) package frozen baby lima beans

3 to 4 ears fresh corn kernels or 8 ounces frozen corn kernels

About 2 tablespoons extra-virgin olive oil

1 tablespoon cumin seeds

1 red onion, diced

3 to 4 cloves fresh garlic, finely minced

Pinch sea salt

1 poblano chile, seeded, minced

1 red bell pepper, roasted over an open flame (page 57), peeled, seeded and diced

¼ cup spring or filtered water

½ cup plain soymilk

2 teaspoons white miso

3 to 4 sprigs fresh cilantro, finely minced

Bring a pot of water to a boil and cook the lima beans until just tender, about 6 minutes. Drain and transfer to a mixing bowl. In the same water, cook the corn for 30 seconds, drain and mix in with the beans.

Place the oil and cumin seeds in a skillet over medium heat. When the seeds begin to sizzle, cook, stirring, until toasted, about 3 minutes. Stir in the onion, garlic and salt and sauté for 2 to 3 minutes. Stir in the chile and bell pepper and sauté for 4 to 5 minutes. Add the water and soymilk, cover and bring to a boil. Reduce the heat to low and cook for 5 minutes. Add the lima beans and corn, cover and cook for 10 minutes. Remove a small amount of liquid and use to dissolve the miso. Stir the miso mixture into the bean mixture and simmer, uncovered for 2 to 3 minutes. Remove from the heat and stir in the cilantro. Transfer to a serving bowl and serve hot or warm.

SPICY BLACK BEAN CAKES WITH TOFU SOUR CREAM

These little bean cakes are a wonderful side dish, great for parties or on a buffet table. I love to serve them with a homemade spicy salsa, but a packaged salsa will work just as well, if you don't have the time to make your own.

MAKES 6 TO 9 SERVINGS

Spicy Black Bean Cakes

3½ cups cooked black turtle beans

5 to 6 fresh scallions, finely diced

½ roasted red bell pepper, roasted over an open flame (page 57), peeled, seeded and diced

5 to 6 sprigs fresh cilantro, finely minced

2 to 3 fresh garlic cloves, finely minced

1 to 2 tablespoons finely minced, seeded jalapeño chile

2 teaspoons ground cumin

½ pound firm tofu, finely crumbled

Sea salt

1 cup plus 2 tablespoons yellow cornmeal

Light olive oil, for frying

Tofu Sour Cream

½ pound firm tofu, crumbled

½ teaspoon sea salt

Splash umeboshi plum vinegar

Juice of ½ lemon

1 teaspoon brown rice syrup

Salsa, to serve

To make the bean cakes: Place the beans in a mixing bowl, and using a potato masher or a fork, crush them coarsely. Stir in the scallions, bell pepper, cilantro, garlic, chile, cumin and tofu, mixing well to combine. Stir in the salt and about 2 tablespoons of the cornmeal to help the cakes hold their shape. The mixture should be stiff.

Place about 1 cup cornmeal in a bowl. Form tablespoonfuls of the black beans into small cakes, about ½ inch thick and dredge in the cornmeal to coat. Place each cake on a plate; you should have 18 to 20 cakes.

Heat enough oil in a deep skillet over medium heat to generously cover the bottom. Working in small batches, fry the cakes until golden and crispy, turning them once to ensure even cooking. Drain on parchment paper and repeat with remaining cakes. You may want to place the fried cakes in a warm oven while cooking the rest.

To make the tofu sour cream: Place all the ingredients in a food processor and purée until smooth. Adjust the seasoning to taste and purée again. Arrange the bean cakes on a platter and spoon a small amount of salsa and tofu sour cream on top of each one.

CURRIED KIDNEY BEAN BURRITOS

A bit of a cultural mix, but the results are so wonderful, no one will notice. In addition to the traditional spices of Latin cooking, I've added a bit of curry for interest. A great side dish, festive buffet dish, school lunch or party snack, these burritos are real crowd pleasers, and did I mention that they're ready in 30 minutes?

MAKES 4 TO 6 SERVINGS

3 to 4 tablespoons extra-virgin olive oil
1 to 2 cloves fresh garlic, finely minced
1 medium red onion, finely diced
Sea salt
1 tablespoon finely minced, seeded jalapeño chile
3 to 4 fresh scallions, diced
1 teaspoon mirin
⅔ teaspoon curry powder
2 (10-ounce) cans diced tomatoes, well drained
2 (15-ounce) cans kidney beans, well drained
Juice of ½ fresh lime
2 to 3 sprigs fresh cilantro, finely minced
4 (6- to 8-inch) soft flour or corn tortillas
Salsa (optional)

Place the oil, garlic and onion in a skillet over medium heat. When the onion begins to sizzle, add a pinch of salt and sauté for 2 to 3 minutes. Stir in the chile, scallions, mirin and curry powder and sauté for 1 minute. Stir in the tomatoes and beans and season to taste with salt. Cover and bring to a boil. Reduce the heat to low and simmer for 10 to 15 minutes. Remove from the heat and stir in the lime juice and cilantro. Set the bean mixture aside to cool.

Preheat the oven to 275°F. Warm the tortillas in the oven for 3 to 4 minutes, just to soften. Spoon a generous amount of filling down the center of each tortilla and roll into cylinders. Serve sliced in half or whole, with salsa on the side, if desired.

LENTIL, RED PEPPER AND BASIL SAUTÉ

This is such a delicious way to serve lentils; they are slightly spicy, but with the sweetness of peppers and the earthy taste of the basil balancing the flavors perfectly, creating a symphony of tastes to delight your tongue.

MAKES 4 TO 5 SERVINGS

1-inch piece kombu
1 cup dried lentils, sorted and rinsed well
3 cups spring or filtered water
About 2 tablespoons extra-virgin olive oil
½ teaspoon cumin seeds
2 to 3 cloves fresh garlic, thinly sliced
1 yellow onion, thinly sliced into half-moon pieces
Sea salt
1 red bell pepper, roasted over an open flame (page 57), peeled, seeded and sliced into strips
3 to 4 tablespoons dry white wine
3 to 4 fresh scallions, diced
1 bunch fresh basil, leaves removed and coarsely chopped
Juice of ½ lemon
Cooked brown basmati rice, to serve

Place the kombu on the bottom of a pot and top with the lentils. Add the water and bring to a boil, uncovered. Cover and reduce the heat to low, cooking the lentils until tender, 45 to 50 minutes. Drain away any remaining cooking liquid, discard the kombu and set the lentils aside.

Place the oil and cumin seeds in a deep skillet over medium heat. Sauté for 2 minutes. Add the garlic, onion and a pinch of salt and sauté for 5 to 6 minutes, browning the onion slightly. Stir in the bell pepper and wine. Cover, reduce the heat to low and cook for 3 minutes. Stir in the scallions and lentils, cover and cook for 2 minutes. Remove from the heat and stir in the basil and lemon juice. Serve with rice.

WARM POTATO, SOYBEAN AND CUCUMBER SALAD

Fresh soybeans are just brilliant, truly. The problem is that most people think the only way to eat them is in the pod, as the traditional edamame. But there are many ways to eat these babies. This is just one.

MAKES 4 TO 5 SERVINGS

Salad
- 1 pound new or fingerling potatoes, unpeeled, cubed
- 1 cup frozen fresh (green) soybeans, thawed
- 1 red onion, thinly sliced into half-moon pieces
- 1 small cucumber, halved lengthwise, cut into very thin half-moon slices (peel only if the cucumber is not organic)

Dressing
- ¼ cup umeboshi plum vinegar
- 1 tablespoon finely minced fresh ginger
- 1 clove fresh garlic, finely minced
- 1 tablespoon stone-ground mustard
- 4 tablespoons extra-virgin olive oil
- 2 teaspoons brown rice syrup
- 1 teaspoon white miso

To make the salad: Bring a pot of water to a boil and cook the potatoes until just tender, about 12 minutes. Drain and transfer to a mixing bowl. In the same water, cook the soybeans until just tender, about 5 minutes. Drain and add to the potatoes. Finally, in the same water, boil the onion for 30 seconds. Drain and add to the potatoes. Fold in the cucumber.

To make the dressing: Whisk all the ingredients together until well combined. Adjust the seasonings to taste. Stir the dressing into the warm salad, tossing to coat. Serve warm.

BULGUR BEAN SALAD

Want to make a quick main course, using leftover beans? How about this richly flavored, protein-packed grain and bean salad? It's perfect for a light summer dinner, when chasing fireflies is far more important than cooking.

MAKES 4 TO 5 SERVINGS

2 cups spring or filtered water

1 cup bulgur

About 1 tablespoon extra-virgin olive oil

2 cloves fresh garlic, thinly sliced

1 small red onion, diced

Grated zest of 1 lemon

1 teaspoon dried basil

Sea salt

1 carrot, diced

1 cup sliced button mushrooms

1½ cups finely chopped broccoli rabe

Mirin

½ cup cooked kidney beans

½ cup cooked chickpeas

1 cup canned artichoke hearts, coarsely chopped

¼ cup oil-cured black olives, pitted, finely minced

2 slices (½ of 8-ounce package) baked tofu, diced

Bring the water to a boil and stir in the bulgur. Cover and turn off the heat. Allow to stand for 30 minutes. Fluff with a fork. Set aside.

Place the oil, garlic, onion, lemon zest and basil in a deep skillet over medium heat. When the onion begins to sizzle, add a pinch of salt and sauté for 2 to 3 minutes. Stir in the carrot and mushrooms, add a pinch of salt and sauté for 2 minutes. Stir in the broccoli rabe, a light seasoning of salt and a generous sprinkling of mirin. Sauté until the greens wilt, 5 to 6 minutes. Remove from the heat and stir in the beans, artichoke hearts, olives and tofu.

To serve, mound the bulgur on a platter and spoon the bean mixture over the top.

BLACK BEAN AND SQUASH STEW

I love this stew when the weather has turned chill. It's so warm and cozy and satisfying . . . and it doesn't make me feel heavy and lethargic—it makes me feel calm, centered and oh so strong.

MAKES 4 TO 5 SERVINGS

1 cup dried black soybeans, sorted, rinsed well and towel dried

1-inch piece kombu

3 cups spring or filtered water

About 2 tablespoons extra-virgin olive oil

2 to 3 cloves fresh garlic, thinly sliced

1 red onion, diced

1 tablespoon minced, seeded jalapeño chile

Sea salt

Generous pinch crushed red pepper flakes

1 teaspoon ground cumin

3 cups canned diced tomatoes

½ Kabocha or butternut squash, halved, seeded and cut into 1-inch pieces

1 cup dry white wine

1 cup spring or filtered water

2 teaspoons white miso

2 stalks celery, diced

3 to 4 sprigs fresh cilantro, finely minced

Place a stainless-steel skillet over medium-low heat and pan-toast the soybeans until they puff slightly and their skins split open. Place the kombu in a pressure cooker and place the soybeans on top. Add the water and bring to a boil, uncovered. Allow beans to cook at a high boil for 5 minutes. Seal the lid, bring to full pressure, reduce the heat to low and cook for 45 to 50 minutes. Remove from the heat and allow pressure to reduce naturally.

Place the oil, garlic, onion and chile in a deep skillet over medium heat. When the onion begins to sizzle, add a pinch of salt, the red pepper flakes and cumin and sauté for 2 to 3 minutes. Add the tomatoes, squash, wine and water. Cover and bring to a boil. Reduce the heat to low and cook until the squash is tender, about 35 minutes. Remove a small amount of broth and use to dissolve the miso. Stir the miso mixture into the cooking vegetables.

Drain the beans of any liquid, add them to the vegetables and simmer over low heat until any remaining liquid has evaporated. Remove from heat, stir in the celery and cilantro. Transfer to a serving bowl and serve hot.

FRIED TEMPEH WITH APRICOT MUSTARD

The sweet isn't as sweet without the bitter . . . at least that's what they say about life. I don't know about that, but sweet and bitter come together in this dish to make perfect harmony. The strong tempeh and hot mustard are softened and enhanced by the sweet tenderness of the apricot flavor, creating a stable, enduring energy.
MAKES 3 TO 4 SERVINGS

Fried Tempeh
Avocado or light olive oil, for frying
1 (8-ounce) block tempeh, cut into 1-inch triangles

Apricot Mustard
4 tablespoons stone-ground mustard
4 tablespoons unsweetened apricot preserves
2 teaspoons brown rice syrup
Grated zest of ½ lemon
1 teaspoon freshly squeezed lemon juice
Sea salt

1 to 2 sprigs fresh flat-leaf parsley, finely minced, for garnish

To fry the tempeh: Heat enough oil in a skillet over medium heat to generously cover the bottom. Add the tempeh and pan-fry until browned, turning once, 1 to 2 minutes per side. Drain on paper and set aside.

To make the sauce: Place all the ingredients in a small saucepan, adding salt to taste. Warm over low heat until the preserves and rice syrup thin, creating a thick sauce, about 1 minute. Do not let the mixture foam.

As soon as the sauce thins, stir in the tempeh to coat. Transfer to a serving platter and serve garnished with the parsley.

~~~~~~~~~~~~~~~~~~~~~~~~

FRIED TEMPEH AND WINTER VEGETABLE SALAD

When the weather outside is frigid, we need warming, hearty foods to keep us strong and vital. But if our food is too heavy, too rich, we feel lethargic, without energy. A dish like this one keeps us on our toes, with strength, endurance and vitality to spare.

MAKES 3 TO 4 SERVINGS

Fried Tempeh
Avocado or light olive oil, for frying
1 (8-ounce) block tempeh, cut into 1-inch triangles
Sea salt

Winter Vegetables
4 to 5 small cauliflower florets
1 small carrot, cut into ¼-inch thick rounds
4 to 5 small Brussels sprouts, trimmed and halved
½ red onion, cut into thin half-moon slices

Lemon Vinaigrette
¼ cup extra-virgin olive oil
Sea salt
2 tablespoons balsamic vinegar
2 teaspoons brown rice syrup
Grated zest of 1 lemon
Juice of ½ lemon

2 to 3 sprigs fresh flat-leaf parsley, finely minced

To fry the tempeh: Heat enough oil in a skillet over medium heat to generously cover the bottom. Add the tempeh and pan-fry until browned, turning once, 1 to 2 minutes per side. Drain on paper, sprinkle lightly with salt and set aside.

To cook the vegetables: Bring a pot of water to a boil and cook the cauliflower until crisp-tender, about 2 minutes. Remove with a slotted spoon or skimmer, drain and transfer to a mixing bowl. In the same water, cook the carrot until crisp-tender, about 2 minutes. Remove with a slotted spoon or skimmer, drain and add to the cauliflower. Next,

cook the Brussels sprouts until tender, about 7 minutes. Remove with a slotted spoon or skimmer, drain and add to the other vegetables. Finally, cook the onions, about 1 minute. Drain and mix in with the other vegetables. Set aside.

To prepare the vinaigrette: Whisk the ingredients together to combine. Adjust the flavors to your taste, slightly sweeter, more sour or saltier.

Add the tempeh to the vegetables, spoon the vinaigrette over top and toss gently with the parsley to coat the ingredients. Serve warm.

~~~~~~~~~~~~~~~~~~~~~~~

PAN-SEARED TEMPEH WITH ROSEMARY AND DRIED CHERRIES

A lovely winter main course in which savory and sweet come together, creating the perfect marriage of flavors. Crispy-fried tempeh completes this dish that your family and friends will love.

MAKES 4 TO 5 SERVINGS

> **Extra-virgin olive oil, for frying**
> **8 ounces tempeh, sliced into 2-inch rectangles**
> **2 teaspoons fresh rosemary leaves**
> **1 teaspoon coriander seeds**
> **2 cloves fresh garlic, peeled**
> **1 red onion, diced**
> **Sea salt**
> **½ cup dry red wine**
> **½ cup unsweetened dried cherries, coarsely chopped**
> **1½ cups spring or filtered water**

> **1 teaspoon kuzu, dissolved in small amount cold water**
> **2 tablespoons unsweetened cherry preserves**
> **Grated zest of ½ lemon**

Heat enough oil to cover the bottom of a skillet over high heat. Lay the tempeh slices in the hot oil and sear them, turning once to brown both sides. Set aside.

Place the rosemary, coriander and garlic in a mortar and grind them with a pestle into a paste. Set aside.

Place about 1 tablespoon of the oil and the onion in a deep skillet over medium heat. When the onion begins to sizzle, add a pinch of salt and sauté for 2 minutes. Add the wine and rosemary paste and sauté for 2 minutes. Add the cherries and water and season to taste with salt. Cover and cook for 7 to 10 minutes. Add the tempeh, cover and cook for 3 to 4 minutes. Stir in the dissolved kuzu and cherry preserves and cook, stirring, until a glaze forms over the dish. Transfer to a serving platter and sprinkle with the lemon zest.

CHERRIES

Legend Cherries aid in fertility.

Fact Cherries are a rich source of potassium, a key nutrient in the health and smooth functioning of the kidneys, which in Chinese medicine govern the health and smooth functioning of our reproductive organs.

≈≈≈≈≈≈≈≈≈≈≈≈≈≈≈≈≈

FRIED TOFU AND MARINATED VEGETABLE SALAD

Tofu, with its cooling character, provides us with strengthening protein, while relaxing any tension in our stressed muscles. When the body is relaxed, we open ourselves to possibilities, to creative thought, to life and our dreams.

MAKES 3 TO 4 SERVINGS

Avocado oil or light olive oil, for frying

4 ounces extra-firm tofu, cut into 2-inch cubes

½ cucumber, very thinly sliced into rounds (do not peel unless cucumber is not organic)

1 small carrot, cut into fine matchstick pieces

2 to 3 red radishes, very thinly sliced into rounds

¼ cup hempseed oil

2 teaspoons sea salt

Juice of 1 lemon

1 clove fresh garlic, finely minced

4 to 5 small broccoli florets, boiled 1 minute and drained

4 to 5 thin slices fresh daikon, cut into fine matchstick pieces, boiled 1 minute and drained

2 to 3 scallions, sliced into long, thin diagonal pieces

Preheat the oven to 250°F.

Pour 1 inch oil into a small saucepan over medium-low heat. When the oil is hot (you'll see patterns forming in the oil, known as "dancing"), turn the heat to high and fry the tofu, a couple of pieces at a time, until golden brown. Drain on paper and place in the warm oven.

Place the cucumber, carrot and radish in a mixing bowl. Whisk the hempseed oil, salt, lemon juice and garlic together and pour over the cucumber mixture, covering completely. Set aside to marinate for 15 minutes.

Just before serving (see note), mix the fried tofu, broccoli and daikon into the marinating vegetables, allowing the marinade to double as a dressing. Fold in the scallions and serve immediately as a warm salad.

Note: If you dress the salad too early, the lemon juice will discolor the broccoli and scallions, turning the dish bitter, so remember to dress the vegetables and tofu just before serving.

TOFU WITH MUSHROOMS AND CARROT

You know the saying . . . less is more. Simple foods, elegantly prepared, with little adornment are sometimes the most memorable. This is one of those recipes. It doesn't get easier . . . or more delicious. Sweet and satisfying, yet cooling and relaxing, this dish is not only wonderful but works in the body to soften, open and release tension.

MAKES 2 TO 3 SERVINGS

1 cup spring or filtered water
Soy sauce
1 teaspoon brown rice vinegar
1 teaspoon fresh ginger juice
4 ounces extra-firm tofu, cut into ¼-inch-
     thick slices
1 cup yellow cornmeal
2 tablespoons tan sesame seeds
Sea salt
Avocado or light olive oil, for frying
About 1 tablespoon extra-virgin olive oil
1 to 2 cloves fresh garlic, thinly sliced
2 to 3 shallots, thinly sliced
3 to 4 dried shiitake mushrooms, soaked until
     tender, drained and thinly sliced
1 small carrot, cut into fine matchstick pieces
¼ cup white wine
1 to 2 scallions, thinly sliced on the diagonal
4 lemon wedges, for garnish

Combine the water, 2 tablespoons soy sauce, vinegar and ginger juice in a shallow baking dish. Whisk to combine. Arrange the tofu in the mixture so that it is completely covered. Marinate for 10 to 15 minutes. Mix the cornmeal and sesame seeds together with a pinch of salt and set aside.

Preheat the oven to 250°F.

Heat about ½ inch avocado oil in a deep skillet over medium-low heat. When the oil is hot (you'll see patterns forming in the oil, known as "dancing"), dip the marinated tofu into the cornmeal mixture and fry until golden on both sides, turning once. Drain on paper and place in the warm oven.

Place the extra-virgin olive oil, garlic and shallots in a skillet over medium heat. When the shallots begin to sizzle, add a dash of soy sauce and sauté until translucent, about 2 minutes. Add the mushrooms, carrot and a light seasoning of soy sauce and stir to combine. Add the wine, cover and reduce the heat to low. Cook until the vegetables are tender, about 10 minutes. Remove from the heat and stir in the scallions.

To serve, arrange the tofu slices on a platter and mound the vegetables on top, with lemon wedges on the rim of the platter. Serve hot.

BROWN RICE VINEGAR

Vinegar traditionally made by the agricultural communities of Japan, it is composed of brown rice, koji (cultured rice), seed vinegar (from the previous year) and well water. Fermented for 9 to 10 months, this vinegar has a delicately sharp flavor.

FRIED TOFU WITH GINGER RELISH

When it comes to natural cooking, there's nothing quite like the richness of fried tofu. Golden brown and hearty, fried tofu serves us on so many levels, nourishing, satisfying our cravings for rich foods, releasing muscle tension in our shoulders and legs. Combining the relaxed energy of tofu with a strongly flavored, deeply vitalizing ginger relish, we get the added benefit of stimulated circulation.
MAKES 2 TO 3 SERVINGS

Fried Tofu
Avocado or light olive oil, for frying
4 ounces extra-firm tofu, cut into 1-inch
    cubes

Ginger Relish
About 1 tablespoon light sesame oil
1 to 2 cloves fresh garlic, finely minced
5 to 6 slices fresh ginger, finely minced
2 to 3 shallots, finely minced
Generous pinch cumin
Sea salt
6 to 8 leaves fresh basil, finely shredded or ½
    teaspoon dried basil

¼ red bell pepper, roasted over an open flame (page 57), peeled, seeded and finely diced

Brown rice vinegar

Preheat the oven to 250°F.

To fry the tofu: Heat enough oil in a skillet over medium heat to generously cover the bottom. Add the tofu and pan-fry until golden, turning once, 1 to 2 minutes per side. Drain on paper and place the tofu in the warm oven.

To make the relish: Place the oil, garlic, ginger and shallots in a skillet over medium heat. Add the cumin and a pinch of salt and sauté until caramelized, about 15 minutes, stirring occasionally. Season to taste with salt, stir in the basil and bell pepper and cook for 1 minute.

To serve, stir the tofu into the relish and transfer to a serving platter. Sprinkle lightly with rice vinegar and serve hot.

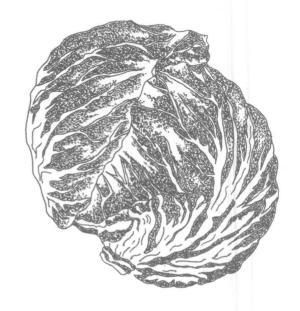

ASIAN TOFU SALAD WITH ROASTED PEANUTS

I love this salad, a one-dish meal that's light, fresh, but deeply satisfying. Smoky baked tofu is beautifully offset with crisp greens, sweet roasted peanuts and sensually sweet mango for just a hint of the tropics.

MAKES 4 TO 5 SERVINGS

> **About 3 tablespoons toasted sesame oil**
>
> **2 cloves fresh garlic, thinly sliced**
>
> **3 to 4 shallots, halved, thinly sliced into half-moon pieces**
>
> **5 to 6 thin slices fresh ginger, finely minced**
>
> **Grated zest of 1 lemon**
>
> **Soy sauce**
>
> **1 red bell pepper, roasted over an open flame (page 57), peeled, seeded and diced**
>
> **1 carrot, cut into fine matchstick pieces**
>
> **½ cup mirin**
>
> **1 (8-ounce) package baked tofu**
>
> **1 bunch watercress, finely diced**
>
> **Brown rice vinegar**
>
> **½ cup Valencia peanuts**
>
> **2 tablespoons brown rice syrup**
>
> **Pinch sea salt**
>
> **1 mango, peeled, pitted and thinly sliced, for garnish**

Place the oil, garlic, shallots, ginger and lemon zest in a deep skillet over medium heat. Add a splash of soy sauce and sauté for 2 to 3 minutes. Stir in the bell pepper, carrot and another splash of soy sauce and sauté for 2 to 3 minutes. Add the mirin, season lightly with soy sauce and reduce the heat to low. Cook the vegetables, uncovered, until the liquid has reduced to a thin syrup, 10 to 12 minutes. Stir in the tofu and lay the watercress on top. Cover and steam the watercress until just wilted, 1 to 2 minutes. Remove from the heat and stir in a sprinkle of vinegar.

Place the peanuts in a heat-resistant bowl. Bring the rice syrup and salt to a foaming boil over high heat. Pour over peanuts and stir well to coat. Immediately stir the peanuts into the vegetables.

Transfer to a serving platter and arrange the mango around the rim of the dish.

≈ *Did You Know?* ≈
TOFU

Legend Tofu relaxes and relieves tension in the body; in excess it can reduce libido in men. It was used in Buddhist monasteries to keep the monks' minds off matters of the flesh.

Fact A rich source of protein, unsaturated fat and vitamins and minerals, tofu contains high concentrations of phytoestrogens, compounds that mimic the properties of estrogen in the body, good for women but a bit too relaxing for men if eaten too often.

ASIAN VEGETABLES WITH TOFU AND COCONUT MILK

This spectacularly tasty dish can be the main course or a hearty appetizer. Either way, it'll win over just about anyone who has reservations about adding tofu to his diet.

MAKES 4 TO 5 SERVINGS

- 5 to 6 small cauliflower florets
- 5 to 6 small broccoli florets
- 2 tablespoons extra-virgin olive oil
- 2 to 3 cloves fresh garlic, thinly sliced
- 1 red onion, thinly sliced into half-moon pieces
- 4 to 5 slices fresh ginger, cut into fine matchstick pieces
- Generous pinch crushed red pepper flakes
- Soy sauce
- 6 to 8 dried shiitake mushrooms, soaked until tender and thinly sliced
- 8 to 10 snowpeas, strings removed, left whole
- 1 small Chinese or Japanese eggplant, quartered lengthwise and cut into 1-inch pieces
- 1 cup unsweetened coconut milk
- Mirin
- 4 to 8 ounces baked tofu, cubed
- 2 to 3 baby bok choy, quartered lengthwise
- 2 to 3 sprigs fresh cilantro, finely minced

Bring a pot of water to a boil and boil the cauliflower for 1 minute. Remove with a slotted spoon or skimmer, drain and set aside. In the same water, boil the broccoli for 1 minute. Drain and mix in with the cauliflower.

Place the oil, garlic, onion, ginger and red pepper flakes in a deep skillet or wok over medium heat. When the onion begins to sizzle, add a splash of soy sauce and sauté for 2 to 3 minutes. Stir in the mushrooms and a splash of soy sauce and sauté for 2 minutes. Stir in cauliflower and broccoli. Stir in the snowpeas and eggplant, along with the coconut milk. Season lightly with soy sauce and mirin, cover and cook over low heat until the vegetables are just tender, stirring occasionally, about 4 minutes. Stir in the tofu and bok choy, cover and cook until the bok choy is wilted, 2 to 3 minutes. Remove the cover and increase the heat to medium; cook until any remaining liquid has turned into a syrup. Remove from the heat and stir in the cilantro. Transfer to a serving platter.

CONFETTI RICE WITH BAKED TOFU

A great way to serve rice and tofu, it's so delicious, so easy to make, no one will miss the meat in the main course.

MAKES 4 TO 5 SERVINGS

Marinated Tofu
- ⅓ cup spring or filtered water
- 2 to 3 scallions, finely diced
- Generous pinch crushed red pepper flakes
- 3 tablespoons soy sauce
- 2 teaspoons Suzanne's Specialties Maple Rice Nectar
- 1 tablespoon toasted sesame oil
- 1 tablespoon light sesame oil
- 8 ounces extra-firm tofu, cut into ¼-inch-thick slices

Rice

About 1 tablespoon toasted sesame oil

2 to 3 cloves fresh garlic, thinly sliced

4 to 5 scallions, thinly sliced on the diagonal

1 red bell pepper, roasted over an open flame (page 57), peeled, seeded and diced

Soy sauce

1 carrot, finely diced

½ cup finely diced daikon

Brown rice vinegar

2 cups cooked brown basmati rice

2 to 3 scallions, thinly sliced on the diagonal, for garnish

To prepare the tofu: Combine all ingredients, except the tofu, in a small saucepan over low heat and cook for 1 to 2 minutes, to develop the flavors. Place the tofu in a shallow baking dish and pour the warm marinade over the top. Marinate for 10 to 15 minutes.

Preheat the oven to 450°F and drain the tofu slices, reserving the marinade. Place the tofu on a baking sheet and bake 15 to 20 minutes, until browned at the edges.

To make the rice: Meanwhile, place the oil, garlic, scallions and bell pepper in a deep skillet over medium heat. Stir in a splash of soy sauce and sauté for 1 minute. Stir in the carrot and daikon, season with soy sauce and sauté until the carrot is just tender, 3 to 4 minutes. Remove from the heat and stir in a generous splash of vinegar. Fold the vegetables into the rice and mound onto a serving platter.

Arrange the tofu over the rice mixture, spoon a small amount of the reserved marinade over the entire dish and sprinkle with the scallions.

SPICY TOFU WITH PINEAPPLE AND BOK CHOY

Fried spicy tofu takes center stage in this main course. Rich, a bit hot, with sweet pineapple and tender bok choy stir-fried with bell pepper and onions to create a symphony of flavors sure to please.

MAKES 4 TO 5 SERVINGS

Spicy Tofu

3 tablespoons soy sauce

2 tablespoons brown rice vinegar

1 tablespoon barley malt

2 tablespoons toasted sesame oil

1 tablespoon arrowroot

Generous pinch chili powder

1 pound extra-firm tofu, cut into 1-inch cubes

Light olive oil, for frying

Pineapple and Bok Choy

2 tablespoons toasted sesame oil

3 to 4 cloves fresh garlic, thinly sliced

2 tablespoons finely minced fresh ginger

1 medium red onion, thin half-moon slices

1 red bell pepper, roasted over an open flame (page 57), peeled, seeded and diced

Generous pinch crushed red pepper flakes

Soy sauce

6 to 7 baby bok choy, split lengthwise

2 cups ½-inch cubes fresh pineapple

2 to 3 scallions, thinly sliced on the diagonal, for garnish

To make the marinated tofu: Whisk all the ingredients except the tofu and oil together and set aside.

Pat the tofu cubes dry and place in the marinade for 10 minutes. Heat 1 inch of oil in a deep skillet over medium heat. Remove the tofu from the marinade, reserving the marinade, and pat dry. Fry until golden and crispy, turning once to ensure even cooking. Drain on paper and set aside.

To make the pineapple and bok choy: Place the oil, garlic, ginger, onion, bell pepper and red pepper flakes in a deep skillet over medium heat. Stir in a splash of soy sauce and sauté for 2 to 3 minutes. Add the bok choy and sauté until wilted, about 1 minute. Stir in the tofu and reserved marinade, stirring until a glaze coats the ingredients. Remove from the heat and stir in the pineapple. Transfer to a serving platter and serve garnished with the scallions.

RED CURRIED TOFU

There's something about the combination of curry and tofu that is just irresistible. Tofu's mild mannered character simply adores the hot, spicy nature of curry, making a simply delicious union.

MAKES 4 TO 5 SERVINGS

>   Avocado or light olive oil, for frying
>   8 ounces extra-firm tofu, cut into 1-inch
>   cubes
>   About 1 tablespoon extra-virgin olive oil
>   1 tablespoon red curry paste
>   ½ teaspoon chili paste
>   2 to 3 cloves fresh garlic, thinly sliced
>   1 medium red onion, sliced into thin half-
>   moon pieces
>   Soy sauce
>   1 carrot, cut into fine matchstick pieces

>   1 cup fine matchstick pieces fresh daikon
>   1 teaspoon ground coriander
>   ½ teaspoon ground turmeric
>   1 tablespoon brown rice syrup
>   1 (10-ounce) can diced no-salt-added
>   tomatoes
>   Grated zest of 1 lemon
>   2 cups cooked brown basmatic rice, to serve
>   2 to 3 sprigs fresh cilantro, finely minced, for
>   garnish

Heat about 1 inch oil in a deep skillet over medium heat. Fry the tofu cubes until golden and crisp, turning once to ensure even browning. Drain on parchment paper and set aside.

Place the olive oil, curry paste and chili paste in a deep skillet over medium heat. Cook, stirring, until the mixture is creamy, about 2 minutes. Add the garlic, onion and a dash of soy sauce and sauté until the onion is limp, about 2 minutes. Stir in the carrot, daikon and a dash of soy sauce and sauté for 2 minutes. Stir in the coriander, turmeric, brown rice syrup, tomatoes and lemon zest. Season to taste with soy sauce. Cover and bring to a boil. Reduce the heat to low and simmer until the carrot is tender, about 15 minutes. Stir in the tofu and simmer for 1 to 2 minutes.

To serve, mound the rice on a platter and spoon the tofu mixture over the rice. Sprinkle the cilantro over the top and serve hot.

≋ *Did You Know?* ≋
CITRUS ZEST

Legend Citrus fruit is a great source of vitamin C.

Fact True, but it's in the skin (zest) as well as the flesh, so to get the full benefit of the vitamin C, add grated zest to a dish. It's better to use organic citrus, as pesticides accumulate on the skin.

PAN-FRIED TOFU WITH SESAME WATERCRESS

Lightly fried, the tofu is just rich enough to be satisfying, without being oily. Paired with the peppery freshness of watercress, with a sweet and sour citrus dressing, you have created a great main-course tofu dish of varying flavors and textures sure to please.

MAKES 4 TO 6 SERVINGS

Tofu
Avocado or light olive oil, for frying
**8 ounces extra-firm tofu, cut into
½-inch-thick slices**

Vegetables
½ red onion, sliced into very thin rings
**1 bunch watercress, rinsed well and tips of
stems trimmed**
**2 teaspoons black sesame seeds, lightly pan-
toasted**
**1 teaspoon shelled hempseeds, lightly pan-
toasted**

Dressing
2 tablespoons sesame tahini
1 teaspoon umeboshi plum vinegar
1 teaspoon brown rice syrup
Grated zest of 1 lime
1½ teaspoons soy sauce
Spring or filtered water, as needed

Preheat the oven to 250°F.

To make the tofu: Heat about 1 inch oil in a deep skillet over medium heat. Fry the tofu slices until golden and crisp, turning once to ensure even browning. Drain on parchment paper and place in the warm oven, while preparing the rest of the dish.

To make the vegetables: Bring a pot of water to a boil. Add the onion and boil for 30 seconds. Remove with a slotted spoon or skimmer, drain and place in a mixing bowl. In the same water, boil the watercress until it just wilts, about 1 minute. Drain and cut into bite-size pieces. Add to the onion and mix to combine. Stir the sesame seeds and hempseeds into the vegetables and transfer to a serving platter. Arrange the tofu on top of the greens.

To prepare the dressing: Whisk all the ingredients together, adding water only to thin the dressing to desired consistency. Adjust seasoning to taste. Spoon dressing over warm salad and serve immediately.

TOFU AND APPLE CURRY WITH GOLDEN RAISINS

This hot, sweet tofu dish will win you raves. The spicy nature of curry is nicely offset by the delicate sweetness of the apples and raisins. One bite of this main course and no one will turn his nose up at tofu again.

MAKES 4 TO 6 SERVINGS

> About 5 tablespoons light olive oil
> ½ cup brown rice syrup
> 8 ounces extra-firm tofu, cut into ¼-inch-thick slices
> 2 tablespoons red curry paste
> 2 to 3 cloves fresh garlic, finely minced
> ½ red onion, finely diced
> Sea salt
> ¼ teaspoon ground cumin
> ¼ teaspoon ground cinnamon
> ½ cup golden raisins
> 2 Granny Smith apples, unpeeled, halved, cored and cut into ½-inch dice
> ½ cup dry white wine
> 2 cups cooked brown basmatic rice, to serve
> 2 to 3 sprigs fresh flat-leaf parsley, finely minced, for garnish

Place 4 tablespoons of the oil and the rice syrup in a skillet over medium heat. When the mixture begins to foam, lay the tofu slices in the skillet and cook until golden, turning once to ensure even browning. Transfer the tofu to a plate and set aside.

Place about 1 tablespoon oil and the curry paste in a deep skillet over medium heat. Cook, stirring, until the paste is creamy. Stir in the garlic, onion, a pinch of salt, cumin and cinnamon and sauté for 1 to 2 minutes. Stir in the raisins, apples, wine and a light seasoning of salt. Cook, stirring occasionally, until liquid has been absorbed and the apples are just tender, 5 to 7 minutes.

To serve, mound the rice on a platter, spoon the apple mixture over the rice and lay the tofu slices on top. Sprinkle with the parsley and serve immediately.

SOY SAUSAGE AND LENTIL SALAD

This is the loveliest casual main course for cold weather. Hearty and packed with protein, this slightly spicy dish will give you energy to burn and keep you warm and cozy all winter long.

MAKES 4 TO 5 SERVINGS

> 1-inch piece kombu
> 1 cup Le Puy lentils, sorted and rinsed well
> 3 cups spring or filtered water
> Soy sauce
> About 2 tablespoons extra-virgin olive oil
> 2 to 3 cloves fresh garlic, thinly sliced
> 1 red onion, diced
> Sea salt
> 1 carrot, diced
> 1 to 2 stalks celery, diced
> 1 cup diced butternut squash
> Grated zest of 1 lemon
> 6 ounces vegan soy sausage, sliced into ¼-inch-thick rounds
> ½ cup unsweetened apple juice

4 to 5 leaves kale, steamed until bright green and cut into bite-size pieces

Place the kombu in a heavy pot and add the lentils and water. Bring to a boil, uncovered, over medium heat. Boil for 5 minutes. Cover and reduce the heat to low and simmer the beans until just tender, about 45 minutes. Season to taste with soy sauce and cook for 5 minutes. When the lentils are done, drain off any remaining liquid, discard the kombu and set the lentils aside.

Place the oil, garlic and onion in a deep skillet over medium heat. When the onion begins to sizzle, add a pinch of salt and sauté for 1 to 2 minutes. Stir in the carrot, celery, squash, lemon zest and a light seasoning of salt and sauté for 2 minutes. Spread the vegetables evenly over the bottom of the skillet and lay the sausage rounds on top. Add the apple juice, season to taste with salt, cover and cook for 3 to 4 minutes. Remove the cover and allow any remaining liquid to reduce to a syrup.

To serve, arrange the kale on a serving platter, spoon the lentils over the kale and spoon the sausage mixture over the lentils.

GRILLED SOY SAUSAGE SANDWICHES WITH CARAMELIZED ONIONS

So it's a lazy Sunday afternoon and you want something casual, as you while away the day on the sofa with the paper—but you don't want to sacrifice taste. This should do it for you.

MAKES 2 TO 4 SANDWICHES

> **4 tablespoons extra-virgin olive oil**
> **6 to 8 yellow onions, thinly sliced into half-moon pieces**
> **Sea salt**
> **1 tablespoon barley malt**
> **½ teaspoon caraway seeds**
> **8 ounces vegan soy sausage, rolled into 3-inch logs**
> **4 to 8 thick slices whole-grain sourdough bread**
> **Stone-ground mustard**
> **2 ripe tomatoes, thinly sliced**

Place 2 tablespoons of the oil and the onions in a deep skillet over medium heat. Sauté the onions with a generous pinch of salt until they begin to wilt. Stir in the barley malt and caraway seeds, season lightly with salt and cook until the onions are quite limp and browned, as long as 25 minutes, stirring frequently.

When the onions are almost ready, place the remaining oil in a skillet over medium heat. Add the sausage and cook, turning frequently, until evenly browned. Remove from pan and allow to cool slightly so you can handle it.

Lay the bread on a dry work surface. Spread mustard on half the slices and lay the tomato slices on top of the mustard. Slice the sausage logs in half lengthwise and lay them on top of the tomatoes. Spoon onions over the sausage. Lay remaining bread slices on top and cut in half diagonally.

BARLEY MALT

A grain sweetener, it is made from sprouted barley cooked into a sweet syrup. The barley is steeped in water and germinated. After sprouting, the barley is heated to bring out the flavor and cooked until a thick syrup forms. A richly flavored sweetener reminiscent of molasses (but without the excessive simple sugars), barley malt contain dextrin, maltose, minerals and protein.

VIVACIOUS VEGETABLES

I remember the day I met Julia Child. Like anyone who has spent more than 30 seconds in the kitchen will tell you, it was awe-inspiring and I was just a little star-struck. Here she stood, the icon of all that is cooking, shaking my hand, smiling and asking about my specialty.

"So all you eat are vegetables?" she inquired, genuinely interested and perplexed. At first, all I could think was that she did a great imitation of Julia . . . but she *was* Julia and *I* was dumbstruck.

After recovering, I explained my chosen eating patterns and we talked food for a few more minutes before she was whisked away to another function.

Her words have stuck with me for years. Although she was perplexed by my chosen diet, my belief about the use of vegetables has not changed. For me, there can never be enough, and there is never any shortage of variety and interest to keep me inspired.

So what is it about vegetables that has me so enchanted, season to season, with no end in sight to this honeymoon state of culinary bliss? Plants have the most important job on Mother Earth; they work to supply the planet with oxygen as they purify the air of carbon dioxide, which they, in turn, absorb as a part of photosynthesis. Because we, as animals, take in oxygen and release carbon dioxide, plants make the perfect partner for humanity.

With an innate ability to transform light into usable energy, which they can store for later use, plants are our most significant source of vitality, as we consume their energy and convert it into fuel. Plants are the original source of protein, carbohydrates and other complex nutritional molecules, which means they contain within their humble seeds, stalks, stems, roots, leaves and flowers all the vital components necessary for animal life (which includes us) to thrive. Without plant life, our beautiful, fragile planet would be a barren, sterile sphere, lifeless and still.

Still not convinced to eat more plants? Then skip the science and picture the bustling activity of open-air markets, bins overflowing with the harvest of the land. From backyard gardens to busy farm markets, wherever fresh vegetables, fruits and herbs of the season are cultivated and shared, an engaging way of life is created, one that puts us back in direct contact with the planet we call home, from robust greens and delicate herbs to succulent tomatoes, strong, sweet roots and fresh seasonal fruits. If that doesn't inspire us, I'm not sure what will.

Planting your own garden, even if it's just a few herbs in containers, as well as making early morning trips to area farm markets, will give you a sense of abundance that is unparalleled. Even supermarkets feature locally grown fresh produce, as the demand for such lively freshness grows.

For me, the recipe is secondary to the choosing of ingredients, especially true with vegetables. No amount of culinary skill can revive vegetables that are bereft of their fresh vitality, even creating complex sauces and dressings as disguises. Freshly harvested, organic, locally grown vegetables are always my first choice and make up the majority of what I use—commercial and organic choices from outside my region are used solely to fill in the gaps. Over the years I have discovered that the handling of a vegetable in the kitchen, the actual preparation of it for a dish, is far less important to taste than the quality of it. Where and how it was grown, when it was harvested, how long it has taken to get from the farm to the cutting board

will impact a recipe far more dramatically than how you seasoned it. Cooking is only a bit player in the drama of the kitchen.

So how do you get the best-quality vegetables and fruits on your dining table? Shop where you know the food is freshest, a farm market, a cooperative market or better-quality supermarkets. Decide your final menu *after* you have shopped, not before. Free yourself to look for the most vital and beautiful produce you can find and build your delicious menu plans around them. Buy produce that is locally grown and organic (as much as possible), choosing the ingredients that look freshly harvested. Vegetables and fruits should look like they can jump out of the bin into your cart.

Thinking of vegetables in this manner will make the cooking of them an entirely different experience. Handling fresh, vital, living food is so inspiring you will *want* to cook. You will never tire of washing beautiful vegetables, as their vital colors blind you with jewellike vibrancy. Smell them, caress them, taste them in their raw form so that you become familiar with how they will behave in a dish. With this kind of insight into cooking vegetables, you will come to the realization that fresh, vital foods require very little effort and little enhancement. You will find that they stand best when left to their own devices, with just a little coaxing from sea salt, fresh herbs, excellent oils, nuts and seeds and a touch of lemon or vinegar. Complex cooking methods, heavy sauces and overwhelming preparation time will be a thing of the past in your fresh kitchen . . . with yummy results.

Cooking vegetables is the key to our vitality, to enlivening our being. With vegetables in our diet, anything is possible. Can you imagine a more delicious way to follow the path to your dreams?

ASPARAGUS WITH BLOOD ORANGES AND SHALLOTS

Not sure what seasonal means? This recipe should clear things right up, as the key ingredients are available only in the spring. Okay, okay, you can get asparagus anytime, but to have asparagus at its tender peak is a spring thing. And can you use regular oranges in place of splendid blood oranges? Sure, but in the spring, why would you? This dish lightens our energy, but with its depth of flavor is tremendously satisfying.

MAKES 4 TO 5 SERVINGS

> About 1 tablespoon extra-virgin olive oil
> 2 to 3 cloves fresh garlic, thinly sliced
> 8 to 10 shallots, peeled, quartered lengthwise
> Sea salt
> Grated zest of 1 lemon
> Mirin
> 1 bunch asparagus, tough ends snapped off
> 2 blood oranges, peeled, thinly sliced into
>   rounds and seeds removed
> Balsamic vinegar

Place the oil, garlic and shallots in a deep skillet over medium heat. When the shallots begin to sizzle, add a pinch of salt and sauté until the shallots are quite limp and beginning to color, about 4 minutes. Add the lemon zest, sprinkle generously with mirin and add the asparagus spears. Cover and reduce the heat to low. Cook until the asparagus is just tender and a vivid green. Remove from the heat and stir gently to combine.

Arrange blood oranges around the rim of a serving platter and spoon the asparagus and shallots into the center. Drizzle the entire dish with balsamic vinegar and serve immediately.

≈ Did You Know? ≈
ASPARAGUS

Legend Asparagus is said to be the perfect spring tonic, ridding the body of excess fluids accumulated over winter.

Fact Asparagus contains asparagine, an acidic compound that gives the veggie its characteristic flavor and is also a natural diuretic.

RED CABBAGE WITH CHESTNUTS

Sweet and savory, this colorful side dish is an autumn delight. Wonderfully satisfying, it has the delicate sweet taste of dried chestnuts balancing the refreshing crunch of red cabbage, all smothered in a light sour dressing, so we feel sated, relaxed, but not without sparkle.

MAKES 4 TO 6 SERVINGS

> About 1 tablespoon extra-virgin olive oil
> 2 to 3 cloves fresh garlic, thinly sliced
> 1 red onion, cut into thin half-moon slices
> Sea salt
> 1 cup dried chestnuts, soaked until tender and
>   pressure-cooked for 15 minutes
> Mirin
> Grated zest of 1 lemon
> ½ head red cabbage, finely shredded
> Juice of ½ lemon
> Brown rice vinegar

Place the oil, garlic and onion in a deep skillet over medium heat. When the onion begins to sizzle, add a pinch of salt and sauté for 2 to 3 minutes. Add the chestnuts, a generous sprinkle of mirin and the lemon zest and sauté for 1 minute. Cover, reduce the heat to low and simmer for 10 to 12 minutes. Add the cabbage, but do not stir in. Season lightly with salt, cover and simmer over low heat until the cabbage is wilted, but not mushy, 6 to 8 minutes. Remove from the heat and gently stir in the lemon juice and a light sprinkle of rice vinegar.

SAUTÉED CUCUMBERS WITH PEACHES

Never thought of sautéing cucumbers but only enjoying them in their crisp, fresh form? This luscious salad may just convince you that there's more to this summer favorite than being tossed with lettuce. The sweetness of the peaches makes this beautiful, delicate salad a real celebration of summer.

MAKES 4 TO 5 SERVINGS

About 1 tablespoon extra-virgin olive oil or
    avocado oil, plus extra for drizzling
    (optional)
1 red onion, cut into thin half-moon slices
Sea salt
1 large cucumber, very thin slices (do not peel
    unless cucumber is not organic)
2 to 3 ripe peaches, peeled, pitted and thinly
    sliced
Juice of 1 lemon
2 teaspoons brown rice syrup

4 cups salad greens, chilled
Fresh basil sprigs, for garnish

Place the oil and onion in a skillet over medium heat. When the onion begins to sizzle, add a pinch of salt and sauté until beginning to brown, 5 to 6 minutes. Stir in the cucumber and a light sprinkling of salt and sauté just until the cucumber begins to wilt, about 2 minutes. Stir in the peaches and sauté for 2 minutes. Remove from the heat; gently stir in the lemon juice and rice syrup. Serve warm on a bed of chilled salad greens, garnish with basil sprigs and finish with a drizzle of oil, if desired.

SHAVED FENNEL AND ARTICHOKE HEART SALAD

Aromatic and light, yet rich and strongly flavored, this salad is at its best in the spring and autumn, the two seasons yielding the most delicious fennel and artichokes. The flavors of the vegetables are so distinctive that just a touch of oil and lemon juice will perfect the dish.

MAKES 4 TO 5 SERVINGS

About 1 tablespoon extra-virgin olive oil, plus
    extra for drizzling
2 to 3 cloves fresh garlic, thinly sliced
1 red onion, cut into thin half-moon slices
Sea salt
6 to 8 fresh artichoke hearts, split lengthwise
    (see box)

1 small fennel bulb, tops trimmed, 2 to 3
    tablespoons leaves reserved and bulb
    very thinly shaved or sliced
Juice of 1 lemon

Place the oil, garlic and
onion in a deep skillet over
medium heat. When the
onion begins to sizzle, add a
pinch of salt and sauté until
the onion is quite limp, 3 to 4 minutes. Add the artichoke hearts, sprinkle lightly with salt, cover, reduce the
heat to low and cook until the artichoke
hearts are tender, 17 to 20 minutes. Remove
from the heat, stir in the fennel bulb and lemon
juice and adjust seasoning. Spoon onto a serving
platter and sprinkle reserved fennel leaves on top,
with a drizzle of extra-virgin olive oil. Serve
warm.

FRESH ARTICHOKE HEARTS

To prepare an artichoke heart, cut the stem of the
artichoke off at the base. Remove the outer leaves
of the artichoke by pulling them down so they
snap off. Using a sharp knife, cut the artichoke
crosswise, removing the remaining leaves, leaving
about a 1/2-inch-thick base to prevent discoloring.
With a small paring knife, trim the green leaf stubs
off the bottom of the base. Then trim the dark
green leaf stubs from the top of the base. Using a
melon baller, remove the hairy choke from the
base of the artichoke. Place the prepared artichoke
heart in a bowl of cold water that has had the juice
of 1 lemon mixed in to prevent discoloring.

WILD MUSHROOM CREPES

This requires a bit of effort, but worth every second when you taste the soft crepes filled with richly flavored mushrooms.

MAKES 6 TO 8 CREPES

Corn Crepes
¾ cup whole wheat pastry flour
¼ cup yellow cornmeal
Generous pinch sea salt
2 to 2½ cups plain soymilk
Avocado or light olive oil, for cooking

Wild Mushroom Filling
About 1 tablespoon extra-virgin olive oil
2 to 3 cloves fresh garlic, thinly sliced
1 yellow onion, cut into thin half-moon slices
Sea salt
2 teaspoons dried basil
6 to 8 dried shiitake mushrooms, soaked until tender and thinly sliced
2 cups cremini mushrooms, brushed free of dirt and thinly sliced
2 cups chanterelle mushrooms, thinly sliced
½ cup plain soymilk

Onion Gravy
½ sweet onion, finely diced
2 cups spring or filtered water
1½ teaspoons white miso
2 teaspoons kuzu, dissolved in small amount cold water

To make the crepes: Mix together the flour, corn-meal and salt in a bowl. Slowly mix in the soymilk to form a thin pancake batter. Set aside for 15 minutes before proceeding.

To make the filling: While the batter rests, place the oil, garlic and onion in a deep skillet over medium heat. When the onion begins to sizzle, add a pinch of salt and the basil and sauté for 2 to 3 minutes. Stir in all the mushrooms, season lightly with salt and sauté until the mushrooms release their juices and begin to reabsorb them. Add the soymilk, cover and reduce the heat to low. Simmer until the mushrooms are tender, about 15 minutes. Remove the cover, season to taste with salt and cook until all remaining liquid has been absorbed.

Lightly oil a small cast-iron skillet or crepe pan and heat over medium heat. Add ¼ cup of batter to the hot pan, turning the pan to coat evenly with batter. Cook until the edges loosen and the center of the crepe is covered with pinpoint bubbles. Gently flip the crepe and cook the other side until set, 1 to 2 minutes. Transfer to a kitchen towel to cool and cover with a towel to keep soft. Repeat with the remaining batter.

To make the gravy: Simmer the onion and water over low heat for 3 to 4 minutes. Remove a small amount of warm water and use to dissolve the miso. Stir the miso mixture into the onion mixture and simmer for 3 to 4 minutes. Stir in the dissolved kuzu and cook, stirring, until the gravy thickens slightly, about 3 minutes.

To assemble the crepes: Spoon some filling onto the center of a crepe and roll to close. Place, seam side down, on a platter. Repeat with the remaining crepes and filling. Serve crepes topped with the warm gravy.

BRAISED SCALLIONS WITH WILTED GREENS

One of the first signs that spring has sprung is the growth of tender green onions, or scallions. Although we can find these peppery "wild" onions anytime, they are at their spicy best in the spring, just in time to help us get our winter-weary energy motivated.

MAKES 3 TO 4 SERVINGS

> About 1 tablespoon extra-virgin olive oil
> About 1 tablespoon balsamic vinegar
> 1 bunch scallions, rinsed well, trimmed and left whole
> Sea salt
> Grated zest of 1 lemon
> 1 bunch wild spring greens (dandelion, arugula, watercress, nettle)
> Juice of 1 lemon

Place the oil and vinegar in a wide skillet over medium heat, with the scallions flat on top. Sprinkle with salt and lemon zest and cover. When you hear sizzling, shake the pan gently to distribute the oil evenly. Reduce the heat to low and simmer until the scallions are quite limp and beginning to brown, 3 to 5 minutes. Remove from the heat and transfer the scallions to a flat plate. Do not clean the pot, but return it to the stove. Slice the greens into bite-size pieces and add to the hot skillet. Cover and increase the heat to medium. Shake the pan gently and cook just until the greens wilt, 2 to 3 minutes. Remove from the heat and stir in the lemon juice. To serve, arrange the greens on a serving platter with scallions on top. Serve immediately.

BAKED ONION SLICES

Rich, sweet and packed with nutrition—especially hard-to-get essential fatty acids—this dish takes its place as one of the great side dishes for any dinner or buffet table. Plus you get the additional pleasure of feeding your loved ones the best food in its yummiest form.

MAKES 4 TO 8 SERVINGS

2 large red onions, sliced into ½-inch-thick
    rings
Extra-virgin olive oil
Sea salt
Mirin
4 to 5 sprigs fresh flat-leaf parsley, finely
    minced
Finely grated zest of 1 lemon
½ cup shelled hempseeds

Preheat the oven to 350°F.

Arrange the onion slices on a shallow baking sheet, avoiding overlap. Sprinkle generously with oil and sprinkle lightly with salt and mirin. Cover tightly with foil and bake for 40 minutes. Remove the foil and return to the oven and bake 7 to 10 minutes, until the onions are beginning to brown.

While the onions bake, combine the parsley and lemon zest until well mixed. Lightly pan-toast the hempseeds in a dry skillet over low heat. Mix them very well with the parsley and lemon zest. Season lightly with salt and mix well.

When the onions are ready, remove from oven and transfer to a serving platter. Mound the parsley mixture on each onion slice and serve.

ONION RINGS WITH WASABI DIPPING SAUCE

Onions rings can be a bit heavy and somewhat difficult to digest, but oh we do love them for their richness and the inherent sweetness of the onions. Well, here's a version that's sure to please, light and crisp with a spicy dipping sauce designed to aid in digesting the oil.

MAKES 4 TO 5 SERVINGS

Onion Rings
1 cup whole wheat pastry flour
Pinch sea salt
1 tablespoon kuzu, dissolved in a small bit of
    cold water
¾ to 1 cup dark beer or sparkling water
3 to 4 large yellow or red onions, sliced into
    thin rings
Avocado or light olive oil, for frying

Wasabi Dipping Sauce
1 cup spring or filtered water
1 tablespoon soy sauce
Juice of ¼ lemon
½ teaspoon wasabi powder

To make the onion rings: Combine the flour and salt in a bowl. Stir in the dissolved kuzu and slowly add the beer to create a thick batter (a bit thicker than pancake batter). Set aside for 15 minutes.

Preheat the oven to 250°F.

Separate the onion slices into individual rings. Heat 3 to 4 inches oil in a deep saucepan over medium heat. When the oil is hot, increase the heat to high, dip the onion rings, in batches, into the batter to coat and drop them carefully into the hot oil. When they are crisp and golden, remove from the oil and drain on paper towels. Transfer the fried onion rings to a baking sheet and place in the warm oven while frying the balance of the rings.

To make the dipping sauce: Whisk together the water, soy sauce and lemon juice. Mix the wasabi powder with a tiny bit of water to form a thick paste and place it under a glass cup for 2 to 3 minutes to increase the heat. Whisk the wasabi paste into the soy mixture to blend.

To serve: Arrange the onion rings on a platter with the dipping sauce on the side.

WASABI

A very potent root, comparable to horseradish in taste and heat, wasabi adds quite a kick to sauces, dressings and condiments or as an ingredient, so use it sparingly until you know its power.

RADISH, FENNEL AND DANDELION SALAD

This is the perfect spring salad, an incredible combination of intense flavors, with a delightfully crisp texture. The sweet-tart dressing gentles and enhances the tastes, while relaxing the liver and opening our energy to spring as beautifully as the opening crocus blossoms.

MAKES 4 TO 5 SERVINGS

Salad

3 to 4 red radishes, very thinly sliced
Umeboshi plum vinegar
About 1 tablespoon extra-virgin olive oil
2 to 3 cloves fresh garlic, thinly sliced
1 small fennel bulb, tops trimmed and bulb thinly sliced; 2 to 3 teaspoons leaves minced and reserved
Sea salt
Generous pinch red pepper flakes
1 bunch dandelion greens, rinsed very well, left whole
1 cucumber, thinly sliced on the diagonal (do not peel unless cucumber is not organic)

Dressing

¼ cup extra-virgin olive oil
Juice of 1 lemon
2 teaspoons brown rice syrup
3 to 4 sprigs fresh flat-leaf parsley, finely minced
Sea salt

To make the salad: Place the radishes in a shallow bowl and sprinkle generously with vinegar. Toss well and set aside to marinate for 10 to 15 minutes.

Place the oil, garlic and fennel bulb in a skillet over medium heat. When the fennel begins to sizzle, add a pinch of salt and the red pepper flakes and sauté until the fennel is just limp, about 2 minutes. Slice the dandelion into thin pieces and stir into the fennel with a light sprinkle of salt, and cook just until it wilts, about 1 minute. Remove from the heat.

Arrange the cucumber slices around the rim of a serving platter and mound the dandelion and fennel in the center. Drain the radishes and sprinkle over the top.

To make the dressing: Whisk all the ingredients together. Spoon over the top of the salad just before serving.

~~~~~~~~~~~~~~~~~~~~~~

ROASTED WINTER SQUASH WITH GARLIC

This is a yummy winter side dish. The sweetness of winter squash, in season, is without compare. Add to it the savory earthy flavor of garlic and the delicate sweet flavor just soars. It relaxes us, softening our tension, but with just a bit of vitality from that powerhouse of nutrition—garlic—to keep us on our toes.

MAKES 4 TO 6 SERVINGS

   1 medium butternut squash, seeded, cut into
      1-inch pieces (do not peel unless not
      organic)
   1 red onion, diced
   2 heads garlic, cloves peeled
   Grated zest of 1 lemon
   Extra-virgin olive oil
   Sea salt
   Balsamic vinegar
   3 to 4 sprigs fresh basil, leaves removed and
      shredded

Preheat the oven to 375°F.

Arrange the squash and onion in a large baking dish, avoiding overlap. Distribute the garlic cloves all through the dish. Sprinkle the lemon zest over the top. Drizzle generously with oil; sprinkle with salt and balsamic vinegar. Cover tightly and bake

for 45 minutes. Remove the cover and return to the oven for 7 to 10 minutes, until the vegetables are beginning to brown. Remove from the oven and gently toss everything with the basil. Serve hot.

~~~~~~~~~~~~~~~~~~~~~~

ROASTED SWEET POTATOES WITH APRICOTS AND CURRIED HEMPSEEDS

A sweet side dish that is the epitome of autumn, luscious, warming to the body, satisfying and oh so rich. With the addition of lightly toasted hempseeds, we add essential fatty acids that aren't called essential *for nothing.*

MAKES 4 TO 6 SERVINGS

   3 to 4 Garnet or Jewel sweet potatoes, cut into
      large chunks
   6 to 8 dried apricots, halved
   Extra-virgin olive oil
   Sea salt
   Grated zest of ½ lemon
   1 teaspoon curry powder
   ½ cup shelled hempseeds
   2 to 3 sprigs fresh flat-leaf parsley, finely
      minced

Preheat the oven to 375°F.

Arrange the sweet potatoes and apricots in a large baking dish, avoiding overlap. Drizzle generously with oil; sprinkle with salt and the lemon zest. Cover tightly and bake for 45 minutes.

Remove the cover and bake for 7 to 10 minutes, until the sweet potatoes are lightly browned.

While the sweet potatoes roast, heat the curry powder in a dry skillet over medium heat. Dry-toast the curry for 1 to 2 minutes, stirring. Reduce the heat to low and stir in the hempseeds. Heat, stirring constantly, until the curry turns from orange to a vivid yellow; it will return to a lovely orange color as it cools (see note).

To serve, sprinkle the sweet potatoes with the curried hempseeds and parsley.

CURRIED HEMPSEEDS

Toasted curried hempseeds can be transferred to a glass jar and cooled completely before sealing. It will last, in a sealed jar, for 1 to 2 weeks.

CARAMELIZED TURNIPS AND TOPS

There is nothing like the flavor of fresh vegetables, simply braised in olive oil, with the lightest of seasonings. Braising turnips draws all their luscious essence to the surface, intensifying their delicate bitter flavor and enhancing their character with the richness of olive oil.
MAKES 2 TO 4 SERVINGS

About 2 tablespoons extra-virgin olive oil
2 tablespoons balsamic vinegar
Sea salt
4 whole baby turnips with tops, rinsed very
   well and roots trimmed

4 to 5 cloves fresh garlic, peeled
Grated zest of 1 lemon
4 lemon wedges, for garnish

Place the oil, vinegar and a generous sprinkle of salt in a deep skillet over medium heat. Arrange the turnips in the oil, avoiding overlap. Add the garlic cloves and lemon zest. Cover and cook over medium heat. When you hear a sizzle, gently shake the pan to ensure that the oil mixture covers the bottom. Reduce the heat to low and cook until the turnips are tender, 20 to 25 minutes. Remove from the heat and arrange on a serving platter. Garnish with the lemon wedges.

Note: You may use whole large turnips in this recipe, but split them lengthwise, tops and all, and braise them, cut sides down, for the best results.

WATERCRESS SALAD WITH APPLES AND TANGERINES

A great autumn salad showcases the seasonal sweetness of apples and tangerines against the delicate spice of the watercress. A sturdy dish, this salad is a great addition to a buffet dinner. Its lighter energy makes it the perfect balance to a hearty autumn feast.
MAKES 4 TO 5 SERVINGS

Salad
1 bunch watercress, rinsed well and tips of
   stems trimmed
About 1 tablespoon extra-virgin olive oil

3 Granny Smith apples, unpeeled, halved, and
    thinly sliced

Sea salt

2 to 3 teaspoons brown rice syrup

3 to 4 tangerines, sectioned

Sesame Dressing

3 tablespoons sesame tahini

2 scallions, finely minced

Juice of 1 lemon

Sea salt

1 teaspoon brown rice syrup

Spring or filtered water, as needed

To make the salad: Coarsely chop the watercress and arrange on a serving platter.

Place the oil and apples in a skillet over medium heat. When the apples begin to sizzle, add a pinch of salt and sauté until just limp, 2 to 3 minutes. Add the rice syrup and stir just until apples are coated. Remove from heat and stir in the tangerines. Spoon the fruit over the watercress.

To make the dressing: Mix all the ingredients together, except the water, until smooth. Slowly add enough water to create a thin dressing. Drizzle over the salad and serve warm.

~~~~~~

STUFFED SQUASH BLOSSOM TEMPURA

A showpiece dish, this one will have them screaming for more. Beautiful zucchini blossoms are stuffed with a richly flavored rice filling, battered and quickly fried to create the most sensually decadent side dish. A bit of work? Yes, but worth it.

Zucchini blossoms are available only during summer and very early autumn, so get them while you can.

MAKES 4 TO 8 SERVINGS

Zucchini Blossoms

8 large zucchini blossoms, rinsed and patted
    dry

About 1 tablespoon extra-virgin olive oil

2 to 3 cloves fresh garlic, finely minced

½ yellow onion, diced

Sea salt

Generous pinch red pepper flakes

1 cup cooked short-grain brown rice

Tempura Batter

1 cup whole wheat pastry flour

Pinch sea salt

1 tablespoon kuzu, dissolved in a small bit of
    cold water

¾ to 1 cup dark beer or sparkling water

Avocado or light olive oil, for frying

3 to 4 sprigs fresh basil, leaves removed, finely
    shredded, for garnish

To prepare the blossoms: Clean the zucchini blossoms and then carefully remove the stamens. Try not to open the blossoms too much. Wrap the blossoms in a damp kitchen towel and set aside.

Place the olive oil, garlic and onion in a skillet over medium heat. When the onion begins to sizzle, add a pinch of salt and the red pepper flakes and sauté for 1 to 2 minutes. Stir in the rice and season lightly with salt. Sauté just until the onions are well incorporated into the rice. Remove from the heat and set aside to cool.

To make the batter: Combine the flour and salt in a bowl. Stir in the dissolved kuzu and slowly add enough beer to create a thick batter (a bit thicker than pancake batter). Set aside for 15 minutes.

Stuff each blossom with the rice mixture, taking care to stuff abundantly, but keeping the blossom as tightly closed as possible.

Preheat the oven to 250°F.

Heat 3 to 4 inches oil in a deep pot over medium heat. Check the tempura batter for thickness; if it thickens while it rests, whisk in a small amount of water to return it to the right consistency. When the oil is hot, increase the heat to high, dip each stuffed squash blossom in the tempura batter, covering completely, but not too thickly. Fry each blossom until golden brown and crispy. Transfer to parchment paper to drain and transfer the fried blossoms to a baking sheet and place in the warm oven until all are ready.

Arrange the squash blossoms on a platter and serve immediately, garnished with shredded basil.

DEEP-FRYING TIPS

You can tell when oil for deep-frying is hot and ready for frying by using one of these little tricks. Submerge the end of a wooden cooking spoon handle in the oil. If the handle creates lots of bubbles, the oil is ready. You may also splash a tiny bit of water into the oil. If it rises to the top and bursts, the oil is ready. Finally, you can drop a small bit of the food you will be frying into the oil. If it rises quickly to the top and browns, the oil is ready. Increase the heat to high when you add the food to be fried; this prevents a drop in the oil temperature, which will cause more oil to be absorbed into the food during frying.

RED ONION PICKLE

This sweet, spicy pickle is quick to make and incredibly versatile. Use in salads for an added kick, on sandwiches for something a little different, as a side dish to hearty meal or in a stir-fry for some added sparkle. Good for digestion, as well as delicious, this marinated pickle is something you'll want to keep around.

MAKES 2 TO 3 CUPS PICKLED ONIONS

> **2 to 3 red onions, cut into thin half-moon slices**
> **½ cup umeboshi plum vinegar**
> **Juice of 1 lemon**
> **½ cup mirin**

Bring a large pot of spring or filtered water to a boil. Quickly blanch the onions by dipping them into the water and immediately draining them.

Pat dry and place in a bowl. Add the vinegar, lemon juice and mirin and stir gently to combine. Set aside for 45 minutes to marinate before using. This light pickle will keep, refrigerated, for several days in a sealed jar, in its pickling liquid.

UMEBOSHI PLUM VINEGAR

The sour, salty liquid left over from the pickling process of umeboshi plums is used as a vinegar. It will lend a flavor similar to lemon juice and salt, but is prized in Asia for its alkalizing effects in the digestive tract.

TURNIP SALAD WITH ARUGULA

I used to hate turnips, much to the dismay of my dear husband, who adores them, but never got to eat them, because I wouldn't prepare them. Then I discovered that I hadn't really given them a chance and began a series of culinary experiments; here is one of the great successes.
MAKES 4 TO 6 SERVINGS

5 to 6 turnips, cut into chunks (do not peel
   unless not organic)
1 red onion, diced
¼ cup extra-virgin olive oil
3 tablespoons balsamic vinegar
Juice of 1 lemon
Sea salt
1 small cucumber, thinly sliced
1 bunch arugula, rinsed well and tips trimmed

Bring a pot of water to a boil and cook the turnips until just tender, but not mushy, 6 to 8 minutes. Remove with a slotted spoon or skimmer, drain and transfer to a mixing bowl. Cook the onion in the same water for 2 to 3 minutes, drain and add to the turnips. Drizzle with the oil, balsamic vinegar, lemon juice and a generous sprinkle of salt. Toss gently to combine.

Arrange the cucumbers and arugula haphazardly on a platter and top with the turnip salad. Serve warm or at room temperature.

Variation: A delightful way to serve this salad is to chill the cucumbers and arugula completely and top with the warm salad. The extremes in temperature make an interesting mouth feel.

OVEN-ROASTED SPRING VEGETABLES WITH GREMOLATA

With spring, we begin to think about lightening our cooking to accommodate the warmer weather that is on the way. As we transition to salad season, we still need the warmth of oven-roasting for those chilly mornings and nights. This dish is perfect to take us out of the winter doldrums to the fresh energy of spring.

MAKES 4 TO 6 SERVINGS

Vegetables
1 small leek, split lengthwise, rinsed well, cut into 1-inch pieces
2 cups whole baby zucchini, trimmed
2 cups whole baby pattypan squash
2 cups whole baby carrots
Extra-virgin olive oil
Sea salt

Gremolata
Grated zest of 2 lemons
1 small bunch flat-leaf parsley, stems trimmed, finely minced
Sea salt

6 to 7 red radishes, quartered, for garnish

Preheat the oven to 375°F.

To make the vegetables: Combine all the vegetables in a large mixing bowl. Drizzle generously with olive oil and sprinkle lightly with salt. Toss gently to coat the vegetables. Transfer to a shallow baking sheet and spread evenly, trying to avoid overlap. Bake, uncovered, stirring occasionally, for 40 to 45 minutes, until the vegetables are tender and browned.

While the vegetables are cooking, *make the gremolata:* Mix the lemon zest with the parsley, stirring in salt to taste.

When the vegetables are ready, stir the gremolata into them and transfer to a serving platter. Serve hot, garnished with the radishes.

≈≈ *Did You Know?* ≈≈
CARROTS

Legend Carrots make us feel grounded, centered and vital.

Fact Carrots are a rich source of vitamin A in the form of beta carotene, vitamin B6, thiamine, folic acid, vitamin C, potassium, magnesium and copper. Carrots are credited with many medicinal properties—diuretic, antianemic, tonic for the liver, maintenance of eyesight, appetite stimulant, reduction of colic to name a few, no wonder they make us feel so good.

TUSCAN SLAW

This lemony, light cabbage slaw, with just enough spice to keep you awake, is served on hot summer days in the Tuscan region of Italy. The dish takes the cooling energy of cabbage and the heat-releasing nature of hot spice and brings them together to help us beat the heat.

MAKES 4 TO 6 SERVINGS

½ head green cabbage, shredded
½ head red cabbage

2 small Belgian endive, shredded

½ small fennel bulb, trimmed and very thinly sliced

1 cucumber, peeled and thinly sliced

4 to 5 red radishes, thinly sliced

¼ cup hempseed oil or extra-virgin olive oil

3 to 4 cloves fresh garlic, thinly sliced

Generous pinch red pepper flakes

Sea salt

Juice of 1 lemon

Balsamic vinegar

10 to 12 oil-cured black olives

Bring a pot of water to a boil and cook the green cabbage for 2 minutes. Remove with a slotted spoon or skimmer, drain and transfer to a mixing bowl. In the same water, cook the red cabbage for 2 minutes. Drain and add to the green cabbage. Stir in the endive, fennel, cucumber and radishes.

Place the oil, garlic and red pepper flakes in a small saucepan and cook over low heat for 5 minutes, to infuse the oil with the flavors. Strain the oil through a fine sieve to remove the garlic and red pepper and pour over the cabbage mixture. Season lightly with salt, the lemon juice and a generous sprinkle of balsamic vinegar. Toss gently to combine. Serve warm or chilled, garnished with olives.

ITALIAN-STYLE COLLARD GREENS

Italian cooking and dark leafy greens are great partners. It seems that no meal is complete without a side serving of well-cooked, spiced, strongly flavored greens. This one puts an autumn favorite, collard greens, in the spotlight.

MAKES 4 TO 5 SERVINGS

About 1 tablespoon extra-virgin olive oil

3 to 4 cloves fresh garlic, thinly sliced

1 red onion, cut into thin half-moon slices

Sea salt

Generous pinch red pepper flakes

1 bunch collard greens, rinsed well and stem tips trimmed

Grated zest of 1 lemon

4 to 6 lemon wedges, for garnish

Place the oil, garlic and onion in a deep skillet over medium heat. When the onion begins to sizzle, add a pinch of salt and the red pepper flakes and sauté until the onion is quite limp and beginning to color, 3 to 4 minutes. Just before adding them to the skillet, slice the collard greens into bite-size pieces and stir them into the skillet with the lemon zest. Season lightly with salt and sauté until the collards are deep green and limp, about 4 minutes. Transfer to a serving platter and serve garnished with lemon wedges.

GREEK COUNTRY SALAD

My version of a Greek antipasto, this salad is a hearty first course, with lots of variety, flavors and textures. Serve it with crusty whole-grain bread and a hearty soup, for a satisfying light lunch on its own or as the starter course for any meal.

MAKES 4 TO 6 SERVINGS

1 cup orzo
1 red onion, finely diced
1 cucumber, peeled and diced
4 to 5 red radishes, diced
1 carrot, grated
4 to 5 sprigs fresh flat-leaf parsley, finely
   minced
½ cup coarsely chopped oil-cured black olives
1 red bell pepper, roasted over an open flame
   (page 57), peeled, seeded and diced
2 ripe tomatoes, diced (do not peel or seed)
½ cup extra-virgin olive oil, plus extra for
   drizzling (optional)
Juice of 1 lemon
Sea salt
¼ cup red wine vinegar
1 tablespoon brown rice syrup
Several leaves Romaine lettuce, rinsed,
   shredded, chilled

Bring a pot of water to a boil and cook the orzo al dente, about 6 minutes. Drain well, but do not rinse, and transfer to a mixing bowl. Stir in the onion, cucumber, radishes, carrot, parsley, olives, bell pepper and tomatoes and mix to combine.

Whisk the olive oil, lemon juice, a light seasoning of salt, vinegar and rice syrup together until well combined. Stir gently into the orzo mixture. Arrange the lettuce on a serving platter and mound the salad on top. Drizzle with more olive oil, if desired.

SAUTÉED MUSTARD GREENS WITH GARLIC

A simple side dish, this is quick to prepare, strongly flavored and a real attention getter. Calcium-rich greens join forces with vitality-producing garlic to create not only a delicious dish but one that keeps us strong and healthy.

MAKES 3 TO 4 SERVINGS

About 1 tablespoon extra-virgin olive oil
4 to 5 cloves fresh garlic, thinly sliced
1 yellow onion, cut into thin half-moon slices
Sea salt
1 bunch mustard greens, rinsed and stem tips
   trimmed
Brown rice vinegar

Place the oil, garlic and onion in a deep skillet over medium heat. When the onion begins to sizzle, add a pinch of salt and sauté until the onion is beginning to brown, about 5 minutes. Take care not to burn the garlic. Just before adding them to the pan, slice the greens into bite-size pieces and add them to the skillet, on top of the onions, but do not stir them in. Season lightly with salt, cover and cook just until the mustard greens are limp, about 4 minutes. Remove from the heat and drizzle lightly with vinegar. Stir well and serve immediately.

GARLIC

Legend In ancient Egypt, slaves were given daily doses of fresh garlic to increase their strength and endurance.

Fact The medicinal properties of garlic are the stuff of legend but grounded in fact. A natural source of allyl sulfide, a powerful antibioticlike compound, and allicin, a natural cholesterol-reducing agent, garlic creates strong blood to fuel us.

BRAISED ESCAROLE WITH APPLES

Long cooking adds a whole new dimension to the delicate bitter flavor that is the signature of escarole. Its strong flavor takes on more depth and is further enhanced by the sweetness of the apples. A great side dish for a hearty autumn feast, this is not only delicious but aids digestion and keeps our energy from stagnating.

MAKES 4 TO 8 SERVINGS

> **About 1 tablespoon extra-virgin olive oil**
> **2 to 3 cloves fresh garlic, thinly sliced**
> **1 red onion, cut into thin half-moon slices**
> **Sea salt**
> **Generous pinch red pepper flakes**
> **2 medium heads escarole, rinsed well and quartered lengthwise**
> **Dry white wine**
> **2 to 3 sweet apples, unpeeled, diced**
> **2 tablespoons brown rice syrup**
> **Juice of ½ lemon**

Place the oil, garlic and onion in a deep skillet over medium heat. When the onion begins to sizzle, add a pinch of salt and the red pepper flakes and sauté for 2 to 3 minutes. Spread the onion evenly over the bottom of the skillet and lay the escarole on top. Sprinkle lightly with salt and add enough white wine to just cover the bottom of the skillet. Cover and cook until escarole begins to brown, 15 to 20 minutes.

While the escarole cooks, place the apples, a pinch of salt and the rice syrup in a saucepan over medium-low heat. Cook, stirring constantly, until the rice syrup melts and coats the apples, about 3 minutes. The apples will still be crisp. Remove from the heat and stir in the lemon juice.

Transfer the escarole to a serving platter and top with the onion. Spoon apples over top and serve.

ARUGULA SALAD WITH SCALLION VINAIGRETTE AND RED GRAPES

A brilliant summer salad, filled with the abundance of the season, bitter arugula and fresh tomatoes join forces to keep our energy light and aid the body in releasing internal heat. We can stay cool as the cucumbers in this salad.

MAKES 4 TO 6 SERVINGS

Salad
1 bunch arugula, rinsed well and tips trimmed
1 cucumber, peeled and diced
2 ripe tomatoes, diced (do not peel or seed)
4 to 5 red radishes, diced
2 to 3 scallions, thinly sliced on the diagonal
2 to 3 cups red grapes

Scallion Vinaigrette
½ cup shelled hempseeds
2 to 3 scallions, diced
⅓ cup extra-virgin olive oil
3 tablespoons red wine vinegar
2 tablespoons balsamic vinegar
Sea salt

To make the salad: Arrange the arugula on a platter. Chill completely.

Combine the remaining vegetables and grapes in a mixing bowl. Set aside while making the vinaigrette.

To make the vinaigrette: Heat a dry skillet over low heat. Stir in the hempseeds and lightly toast until fragrant, about 3 minutes. Transfer the hempseeds to a suribachi (grinding bowl) and grind until half broken. Add the scallions and grind to a paste. Transfer to a small mixing bowl and add the oil, vinegars and a light sprinkle of salt. Whisk until well blended. Adjust the seasoning to taste. Fold the dressing into the vegetables and toss gently until well coated.

To serve, mound the vegetables onto the bed of chilled arugula.

GRILLED PORTOBELLO SANDWICH WITH CARAMELIZED ONIONS, CAPERS AND SUN-DRIED TOMATOES

Yummy and meaty, this sandwich will satisfy the most discriminating palate, from vegan to burger munchers. Packed with flavor, sensationally seasoned and hearty enough for a lumberjack, this sandwich is great for barbecues and picnics, when you want more than just the same old thing.

MAKES 6 SANDWICHES

Caramelized Onions
About 1 tablespoon extra-virgin olive oil
2 to 3 cloves fresh garlic, thinly sliced
5 to 6 red onions, cut into thin half-moon
   slices
Sea salt
Mirin
Generous pinch red pepper flakes
3 tablespoons capers, drained well (do not
   rinse)
8 to 10 dry-packed, sun-dried tomatoes,
   soaked until tender and diced
Juice of ½ lemon

Portobello Mushrooms
2 to 3 tablespoons extra-virgin olive oil or
   avocado oil
1 tablespoon balsamic vinegar
Generous pinch red pepper flakes
Sea salt

6 portobello mushrooms, stems removed, gills
   intact and brushed free of dirt

Extra-virgin olive oil
12 slices whole-grain sourdough bread
6 leaves fresh Romaine lettuce
1 container alfalfa sprouts (optional)

To make the onions: Place the oil, garlic and onions in a deep skillet over medium heat. When the onions begin to sizzle, add a pinch of salt, a generous dash of mirin and the red pepper flakes and sauté for 3 to 4 minutes. Add the capers and tomatoes, season lightly with salt and cook, stirring frequently, until the onions begin to caramelize, as long as 25 minutes. Remove from the heat, stir in the lemon juice and set aside to cool slightly before making the sandwiches.

To make the mushrooms: Preheat a grill to hot or warm a lightly oiled grill pan over medium heat.

Whisk together the olive oil, vinegar, red pepper flakes and a generous pinch of salt. Rub each mushroom thoroughly with the oil mixture. Grill on both sides until tender and lightly browned, 5 to 6 minutes per side. Set aside.

Preheat the grill to hot or warm a lightly oiled grill pan over medium heat.

To assemble the sandwiches: Brush one side of each slice of bread lightly with oil and grill, oil sides down, until lightly browned, about 2 minutes. Lay the bread slices, grilled sides up, on a dry work surface. Lay each lettuce leaf on a slice of the bread. Lay a whole portobello mushroom on top of the lettuce. Mound caramelized onion topping on each mushroom and top with sprouts, if desired. Lay the remaining slices of grilled bread on top and serve.

CURRIED VEGETABLE STRUDEL

Spicy sautéed vegetables wrapped in flaky pastry make the perfect starter course or cocktail party food. Strudels are easy to make, comforting in nature and absolutely delicious. With sweet root vegetables at the core, curry to enhance their nature with a bit of warmth and a soft pastry wrap, this strudel is the perfect party food.

MAKES 8 TO 10 SERVINGS

Strudel Dough
2 cups whole wheat pastry flour
Generous pinch sea salt
½ teaspoon baking powder
⅓ cup avocado or light olive oil
Spring or filtered water, as needed

Curried Vegetables
About 1 tablespoon extra-virgin olive oil
2 to 3 cloves fresh garlic, thinly sliced
1 red onion, diced
Sea salt
1 teaspoon curry powder
2 to 3 carrots, diced
1 to 2 parsnips, diced
1 to 2 small turnips, diced
¼ head green cabbage, diced
¼ head cauliflower, broken into very small florets
1 cup spring or filtered water
½ to 1 teaspoon kuzu, dissolved in small amount of cold water
½ cup shelled hempseeds

To make the dough: Combine the flour, salt and baking powder in a mixing bowl and whisk well.

Cut in the oil with a fork or a pastry cutter until the flour resembles the texture of wet sand. Slowly mix in the water, by tablespoonfuls, to create a soft dough that gathers but isn't sticky. Gather into a ball, cover with plastic wrap and set aside to rest while preparing the vegetable filling.

To make the vegetables: Place the oil, garlic and onion in a deep skillet over medium heat. When the onion begins to sizzle, add a generous pinch of salt and the curry powder and sauté for 2 to 3 minutes. Add the carrots, parsnips and a pinch of salt and sauté for 2 minutes. Stir in the turnips and a pinch of salt and sauté for 1 minute. Add the cabbage and cauliflower, season to taste with salt and sauté for 2 minutes. Add the water, cover and reduce the heat to low. Cook over low heat until the vegetables are quite tender, about 20 minutes. Stir in the dissolved kuzu and cook, stirring, until a thin, clear sauce forms, about 2 minutes. Set aside to cool.

Preheat the oven to 350°F and line a baking sheet with parchment paper. Roll the dough into a rectangular shape that is about ⅛ inch thick. Spoon the filling over the crust, leaving about 1 inch around the perimeter. Beginning on a short side, roll the dough around the filling, tucking the edges of the pastry in around the vegetables, as you roll, to prevent leaks. Lay the strudel, seam side down, on the lined baking sheet, and using a sharp knife, make slits in the top to mark portions, as well as to release steam. Brush the top lightly with oil and sprinkle with the hempseeds. Bake for 40 to 45 minutes, until the crust is lightly browned and firm to the touch and the filling is bubbling.

GARLIC-BRAISED KALE AND SUN-DRIED TOMATOES

Can't get your family to eat their green leafy vegetables? Then try this one on them. Rich with garlic and oil and just a touch of spice, there's nothing boring about this side dish.

MAKES 3 TO 4 SERVINGS

About 1 tablespoon extra-virgin olive oil
6 to 7 cloves fresh garlic, thinly sliced
1 red onion, diced
Sea salt
Generous pinch piccante spice (see note)
3 to 4 tablespoons diced, oil-packed sun-dried
 tomatoes, drained well
1 medium bunch kale, rinsed well
Grated zest of 1 lemon
½ cup spring or filtered water
2 tablespoons mirin
1 teaspoon balsamic vinegar
½ cup lightly toasted hazelnuts, coarsely
 chopped

Place the oil, garlic and onion in a deep skillet or wok over medium heat. When the onion begins to sizzle, add a generous pinch of salt and piccante spice and sauté for about 2 minutes. Stir in the sun-dried tomatoes. Remove the kale stems, dice and stir into the skillet. Slice the kale leaves into bite-size pieces and stir them and the lemon zest into the skillet. Season to taste with salt and sauté for 2 minutes. Add the water and mirin, cover and reduce the heat to low. Cook until the kale is quite wilted and a deep green, about 8 minutes. Remove from the heat and stir in the vinegar.

Transfer to a serving plate and garnish with the hazelnuts.

Note: Piccante spice is an Italian spice mixture available in specialty markets.

ROASTED BRUSSELS SPROUTS WITH GARLIC

When I was a kid, I picked Brussels sprouts out of every dish, no matter how my poor mother tried to enhance them. Now, I wonder what I was thinking. Their centering, relaxing energy and the vitality of garlic make Brussels sprouts a most wonderful balanced energy source.

MAKES 4 TO 5 SERVINGS

1 pound Brussels sprouts, trimmed and halved
2 to 3 cloves fresh garlic, minced
2 tablespoons extra-virgin olive oil
2 to 3 tablespoons capers, drained
½ cup mirin

Preheat the oven to 400°F.

Toss the Brussels sprouts with the garlic, oil and capers. Spoon the vegetables into a large baking dish, avoiding overlap. Sprinkle with the mirin, cover tightly and bake for 35 minutes or until the Brussels sprouts are tender. Remove the cover and bake for 10 to 15 minutes, until just beginning to brown. Remove from the oven and gently stir, coating the vegetables with the remaining thickened cooking liquid.

WINTER SALAD WITH HEMPSEED VINAIGRETTE

Anise-scented fennel joins forces with nutty hempseeds to create a powerfully yummy winter salad, but that's not the best part. Sure, vegetables are jam-packed with nutrients, fiber, vitamins and minerals, but by adding hempseeds, you get the added punch of essential fatty acids, omega-3 and omega 6. The perfect salad, I'd say.

MAKES 6 TO 8 SERVINGS

Salad
2 fennel bulbs
1 large head Romaine lettuce, rinsed well and hand shredded
2 heads friseé (curly endive), rinsed well and hand shredded
4 to 5 Belgian endives, halved lengthwise and thinly sliced lengthwise
5 to 6 red radishes, thinly sliced
1 small bunch flat-leaf parsley, finely minced

Hempseed Vinaigrette
⅓ cup shelled hempseeds
¾ cup extra-virgin olive oil
2 to 3 shallots, minced
¼ cup brown rice vinegar
2 tablespoons stone-ground mustard
Sea salt

To make the salad: Trim the fennel stalks flush with the bulbs and discard the stalks, reserving about 3 tablespoons of minced leaves. Halve the fennel bulbs, remove the cores and slice each half very thinly. Combine with the remaining vegetables and the parsley in a mixing bowl and set aside.

To make the vinaigrette: Heat a dry skillet over low heat and pan-toast the hempseeds until fragrant, 2 to 3 minutes. Transfer to a small bowl and set aside. Place the oil and shallots in a small saucepan and warm over low heat for 4 to 5 minutes. Remove from the heat and whisk in the vinegar, mustard, salt to taste and toasted hempseeds until smooth.

Spoon the vinaigrette over the vegetables and toss to coat. Serve immediately.

CRISPY ZUCCHINI CHIPS

A spectacular party dish, it's not too shabby as a starter for a special dinner for two, either. Lightly battered, so they fry up delightfully crispy, the zucchini slices are nicely balanced with lemon slices so that we can digest the oil with no problems.

MAKES 6 TO 8 SERVINGS

Avocado or light olive oil, for frying
1 cup whole wheat pastry flour
¼ cup yellow cornmeal
Sea salt
4 to 5 firm zucchini, sliced into paper-thin oblongs
2 lemons, sliced into paper-thin rounds

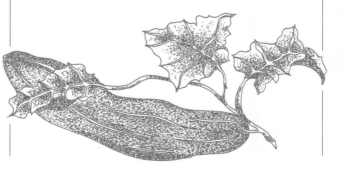

4 to 5 sprigs fresh flat-leaf parsley, finely
minced

8 to 10 sprigs watercress, stems trimmed to
make 3-inch sprigs

Put about 3 inches oil in a deep saucepan over medium-low heat. Line a baking sheet with parchment paper and preheat the oven to 250°F.

Mix the flour, cornmeal and a generous pinch of salt in a bowl. Add about one-third of the zucchini slices to the flour mixture and toss gently with your hands to coat. When the oil is hot, raise heat to high and fry the zucchini until crisp, about 2 minutes. Drain and arrange on lined baking sheet and place in the warm oven. Repeat with the remaining zucchini slices.

Dredge the lemon slices in the flour mixture and fry until golden, about 2 minutes. Drain and combine with the zucchini in the oven, keeping the oil hot.

Just before serving, toss the zucchini and lemon with the parsley and transfer to a serving platter. Quickly fry the watercress sprigs until crisp and mound them on the zucchini and lemon as a garnish.

≈≈≈ *Did You Know?* ≈≈≈
PARSLEY

Legend Eating parsley freshens the breath.

Fact Parsley is so rich in vitamin C, potassium and phosphorus that it freshens the breath by aiding in digestion.

SAUTÉED WILD MUSHROOMS WITH CHIVES, SHALLOTS AND CURRIED HEMPSEEDS

This dish is so great. The rich, earthy flavors of the mushrooms get just a subtle kick from the gentle curry flavor. If the delicious flavors aren't enough to start your engines, how about the essential fatty acids in the hempseeds? Decadent and *good for us is as good as it gets.*

MAKES 8 TO 10 SERVINGS

Vegetables
About 1 tablespoon extra-virgin olive oil plus
extra for brushing

2 to 3 cloves fresh garlic, thinly sliced

6 to 8 shallots, cut into thin half-moon slices

Sea salt

6 to 8 dried shiitake mushrooms, soaked until
tender and thinly sliced

10 ounces cremini mushrooms, brushed free
of dirt and thinly sliced

10 ounces chanterelle or oyster mushrooms,
trimmed

¼ cup mirin

Grated zest of 1 lemon

Juice of ½ lemon

1 small bunch fresh chives, minced

1 whole-grain sourdough baguette, sliced into
½-inch-thick oblongs

Curried Hempseeds
1 teaspoon curry powder

6 tablespoons shelled hempseeds

Pinch sea salt

To make the vegetables: Place the oil, garlic and shallots in a deep skillet over medium heat. When the shallots begin to sizzle, add a generous pinch of salt and sauté for 1 to 2 minutes. Add the shiitake mushrooms and a pinch of salt and sauté for 1 minute. Stir in the cremini and chanterelle mushrooms and a pinch of salt and sauté until the mushrooms begin to release their juices. Add the mirin and lemon zest and season lightly with salt. Cook, stirring frequently, until the mushrooms reabsorb their juices and begin to brown, 7 to 10 minutes. Remove from the heat and stir in the lemon juice and chives.

Preheat the oven to 375°F and line a baking sheet with parchment paper. Brush each slice of bread lightly with oil and bake until the edges are crisp and golden, about 10 minutes.

While the bread bakes, make the curried hempseeds: Heat a dry skillet over low heat. Dry-roast the curry powder for 2 minutes. Stir in the hempseeds and salt and dry-roast until the curry turns from orange to bright yellow, about 4 minutes. Cool and transfer to a small glass jar.

To serve, mound the mushrooms onto the bread and sprinkle generously with the hempseeds. Serve immediately.

Note: You will have more curried hempseeds than you need for this recipe. They will keep, sealed in a glass jar, for about 1 to 2 weeks.

FENNEL SALSA

Fresh and crisp, this salsa is like no other I have tasted. Salty and a bit peppery, with the richness of olives, it goes great with chips or toast points on a buffet or at a patio party. But the best part is that the strong energies of the salsa will make for a very social event.
MAKES 8 TO 12 SERVINGS

2 to 3 small fennel bulbs, stalks trimmed and finely diced

4 to 5 ripe tomatoes, diced (do not peel or seed)

½ cup oil-cured black olives, finely diced

3 to 4 sprigs fresh basil, leaves removed and finely diced

3 tablespoons extra-virgin olive oil

2 tablespoons capers, drained well (do not rinse)

Grated zest of 1 lemon

1 to 2 tablespoons balsamic vinegar

2 teaspoons umeboshi plum vinegar

Combine all the ingredients in a bowl, tossing well to coat the vegetables with the oil and vinegars. If more salt is needed for your taste, add it by the pinch and mix well. Cover and chill for at least 2 hours before serving to allow the flavors to develop.

Variation: In place of the umeboshi plum vinegar, you may use 2 teaspoons lemon juice and 1 generous pinch salt.

SICILIAN POTATO SALAD WITH OLIVES

A Sicilian summer classic, not potato salad as we, in America know it, this version is richly seasoned, wild with varying textures and perked up with herbs and the freshest hot weather vegetables. I love to serve this salad warm, with the flavors gently combining on the tongue.

MAKES 8 TO 10 SERVINGS

Salad

2 pounds fingerling, purple or new potatoes, unpeeled, cut into 2-inch cubes

Sea salt

10 to 12 ounces green beans, trimmed

1 small red onion, finely diced

10 to 12 green olives, pitted and quartered

10 to 12 oil-cured black olives, pitted and diced

3 to 4 tablespoons capers, well drained

3 to 4 ripe tomatoes, diced (do not peel or seed)

Dressing

⅔ cup extra-virgin olive oil

3 to 4 shallots, finely diced

¼ cup balsamic vinegar

Juice of ½ lemon

2 teaspoons brown rice syrup

3 to 4 sprigs fresh flat-leaf parsley, finely minced

2 to 3 sprigs fresh basil, leaves removed and finely diced

Sea salt

1 to 2 basil sprigs, for garnish

To make the salad: Bring a large pot of water to a boil. Add the potatoes, a pinch of salt and cook until the potatoes are just tender, 12 to 15 minutes. Remove with a slotted spoon or skimmer, drain and transfer to a mixing bowl. In the same water, cook the green beans until just tender, 2 to 3 minutes. Drain and add to the potatoes. Mix in the onion, olives and capers. Gently fold in the tomatoes. Set aside.

To make the dressing: Place the oil and shallots in a small saucepan over low heat and cook for 3 to 4 minutes to soften the shallots. Remove from the heat and whisk in the remaining ingredients, adding only a light seasoning of salt; remember the salty flavors of the olives and capers. Allow the dressing to cool for about 3 minutes before gently tossing it with the potatoes. Serve warm, garnished with the whole basil sprigs.

COLORFUL VEGETABLE BUNDLES

A special occasion side dish, because there's a bit of extra work involved. On those occasions when you're cooking with additional care, this is a beauty of a recipe to serve. Flavorful and lovely, this dish will definitely make vegetable lovers out of your guests.

MAKES 12 TO 15 BUNDLES

5 large carrots, cut into 5 × ½ × ¼-inch strips
About 2 pounds green beans, ends trimmed
1 to 2 daikons, cut into 5 × ½ × ¼-inch strips
1 to 2 leeks, outer leaves sliced into 12 to 15
   (5 × ½ × ¼-inch) strips
Extra-virgin olive oil
2 to 3 sprigs fresh basil, leaves removed and
   finely minced
Sea salt

Bring a pot of water to a boil. Cook the carrots until just tender, about 3 minutes. Remove with a slotted spoon or skimmer, drain and transfer to a plate. In the same water, cook the green beans until bright green and crisp-tender, 2 to 3 minutes. Remove with a slotted spoon or skimmer, drain and transfer to a plate. In the same water, cook the daikon until crisp-tender, 2 to 3 minutes. Remove with a slotted spoon or skimmer, drain and transfer to a plate. Quickly dip the leek strips in the boiling water just to soften them. Drain and transfer to a kitchen towel and pat dry.

Preheat the oven to 375°F and line a rimmed baking sheet with parchment paper.

To assemble, divide the vegetables equally into 12 bundles of equal number. Gently tie a leek strip around the center of each bundle to secure them.

Transfer the vegetable bundles to the lined baking sheet and brush lightly with olive oil. Sprinkle lightly with basil and salt and bake for 8 to 10 minutes, until the edges begin to brown.

≈ *Did You Know?* ≈
DAIKON

Legend Daikon is the eighth wonder of natural medicine—good for whatever ails us.

Fact A rich source of potassium and vitamin C, daikon also contains compounds used in phytotherapy to bring down fever, aid in the digestion of fat and protein, rid the body of toxins and work as a mild diuretic.

SUGAR SNAP PEAS WITH TOASTED HEMPSEEDS

A dish so simple, so light, you won't believe it's so delicious. And on top of that, we add the nutritional punch of essential fatty acids, complete protein, vitamins, minerals and amino acids that make hempseeds nature's perfect food.

MAKES 5 TO 6 SERVINGS

1 pound sugar snap peas, strings removed
2 teaspoons shelled hempseeds
1 teaspoon hempseed oil
Sea salt
Ground cinnamon

Bring a pot of water to a boil and cook the peas until crisp-tender, about 3 minutes. Drain, place on a kitchen towel and pat dry. Transfer to a mixing bowl and toss with the hempseeds, oil, a generous pinch of salt and a scant pinch of cinnamon.

CUCUMBER-WATERCRESS RELISH

Cool and refreshing, this relish is the perfect summer side dish on those days when we're wilting under heat and humidity. The crisp crunch of peppery watercress releases heat, while moisture-rich cucumbers keep us cool as, well, cucumbers.

MAKES 5 TO 6 SERVINGS

2 teaspoons mustard seeds
½ teaspoon fennel seeds
½ teaspoon black sesame seeds
¼ cup brown rice vinegar
3 tablespoons extra-virgin olive oil
1 tablespoon brown rice syrup
Sea salt
2 cups ¼-inch dice unpeeled cucumber (peel if not organic)
1 red onion, diced
Grated zest of 1 lemon
½ bunch watercress, rinsed well, diced and chilled

Heat a dry skillet over medium heat and toast the mustard, fennel and sesame seeds until the mustard seeds begin to pop, about 2 minutes. Transfer to a glass bowl. Whisk together the vinegar, oil, rice syrup and salt to taste. Mix in the toasted seeds and set aside.

Combine the cucumber, onion and lemon zest in a bowl and mix in the dressing. Set aside for at least 30 minutes to allow the flavors to develop. Just before serving, stir in the watercress.

RADICCHIO, GRAPEFRUIT AND ARUGULA SALAD

It doesn't get fresher than this. On hot sultry summer days, when we feel limp and wilted, this salad comes to our rescue with a moisture-rich, sweetly refreshing energy, a bit of bitter taste to relax our hot, cranky livers and beautiful color to delight our eyes.

MAKES 4 TO 6 SERVINGS

1 teaspoon shelled hempseeds
Sea salt
4 to 5 tablespoons balsamic vinegar
½ cup extra-virgin olive oil
2 ruby grapefruits, peeled, pith removed and thinly sliced
1 large head radicchio, hand shredded
1 medium bunch arugula, stems trimmed and hand shredded
½ cup oil-cured black olives, pitted

Heat a dry skillet over low heat. Stir in the hempseeds and a generous pinch of salt and lightly pan-toast for 2 to 3 minutes, taking care not to burn the seeds. Transfer to a small mixing bowl and whisk in the vinegar and olive oil. Season with salt to taste and whisk to combine.

Place the grapefruit in a bowl. Pour the dressing over the grapefruit and set aside to marinate for 15 minutes.

To serve the salad, combine the radicchio, arugula and olives in a bowl. Stir in the grapefruit and dressing, tossing gently to coat the salad with dressing. Serve at room temperature or chilled.

ITALIAN CHOPPED SALAD

Chopped salad is the greatest Italian food innovation since their last one. The idea of beautifully diced, seasonal vegetables smothered in a richly flavored dressing is about as brilliantly simple as recipes get. A few knife skills and you're on your way to a real crowd-pleasing side dish or salad course.

MAKES 4 TO 6 SERVINGS

Salad
2 small yellow summer squash, diced
2 small zucchini, diced
2 cups chopped red cabbage
5 plum tomatoes, diced (do not peel or seed)
2 heads Belgian endive, diced
2 cups chopped dandelion or arugula
1 cup cooked chickpeas

Dressing
⅓ cup extra-virgin olive oil
2 to 3 cloves fresh garlic, minced
3 to 4 shallots, minced
Grated zest of 1 lemon
Sea salt

Juice of ½ lemon
2 tablespoons balsamic vinegar

To make the salad: Bring a small pot of water to a boil and cook the yellow squash until just tender, about 2 minutes. Remove with a slotted spoon or skimmer, drain and transfer to a mixing bowl. Cook the zucchini in the same water until just tender, about 2 minutes. Remove with a slotted spoon or skimmer, drain and add to yellow squash. Cook the cabbage in the same water until just tender, about 2 minutes. Drain and add to the squash. Set aside to cool.

Mix in the tomatoes, endive, greens and chickpeas. Cover and chill while preparing the dressing.

To make the dressing: Place the oil, garlic, shallots, lemon zest and a light seasoning of salt in a small pan and cook over low heat for 3 to 4 minutes. Remove from the heat and whisk in the lemon juice and balsamic vinegar. Transfer to a glass bowl and set aside to cool.

Just before serving, stir the dressing into the salad, tossing to coat the vegetables.

BAKED BELGIAN ENDIVE WITH HAZELNUTS AND MISO

While many of us can purchase endive year-round, it's really best during the first crisp cold of autumn. Baked in a light miso sauce and sprinkled with toasted hazelnuts, this side dish or vegetable course has a light energy but with enough substance to sustain us during the chilly days of the season.

MAKES 8 TO 16 SERVINGS

8 medium Belgian endive, split lengthwise
¼ cup extra-virgin olive oil
2 tablespoons white miso, dissolved in a small
    amount of warm water
1 teaspoon mirin
Spring or filtered water, as needed
½ cup chopped toasted hazelnuts
Juice of ½ lemon
2 to 3 sprigs fresh flat-leaf parsley, finely
    minced, for garnish

Preheat the oven to 375°F.

Tightly pack the endive, cut sides up, in a baking dish. Mix together the olive oil, dissolved miso and mirin, whisking until smooth. Add a small amount of water to thin the sauce until spoonable. Spoon the sauce evenly over the endive halves. Cover tightly with foil and bake for 35 to 40 minutes. Remove the cover and bake for 7 to 10 minutes to brown the edges. Transfer the endive to a serving platter, squeeze the lemon juice over the top and sprinkle with the parsley.

SAUTÉED FENNEL AND CARROTS

Sweet and savory, this side dish is a great complement to any hearty meal. Traditionally used to aid in digestion, the fennel showcases the delicate sweet taste of the carrots, making for a calming energy that helps us assimilate nutrients.

MAKES 4 TO 6 SERVINGS

About 1 tablespoon extra-virgin olive oil
2 to 3 cloves fresh garlic, thinly sliced
½ yellow onion, cut into thin half-moon
    slices
Sea salt
1 large fennel bulb, stalks trimmed, 2 to 3
    tablespoons minced leaves reserved and
    bulb thickly sliced
3 to 4 carrots, cut into ¼-inch-thick oblong
    pieces
⅓ cup dry white wine
¼ cup spring or filtered water
1 tablespoon brown rice syrup

Place the oil, garlic and onion in a deep skillet over medium heat. When the onion begins to sizzle, add a pinch of salt and sauté for 2 to 3 minutes. Stir in the fennel bulb and a pinch of salt and sauté for 2 minutes. Stir in the carrots and a pinch of salt and sauté until just shiny with oil. Spread the vegetables evenly over the bottom of the skillet and add the wine, water and rice syrup. Sprinkle lightly with salt, cover and bring to a boil. Reduce the heat to low and cook until the carrots are soft, but not mushy, 12 to 15 minutes.

Remove the cover and cook until any remaining liquid reduces to a thick syrup. Stir gently to coat the vegetables with the syrup and transfer to a serving platter. Sprinkle with the fennel leaves and serve.

SPICY SWEET POTATOES

Nothing enhances sweet taste quite like its opposite, in this case, a bit of hot spice. Even better, the spice works in the body to turn the relaxed energy of the potatoes into long, enduring, calm stamina.

MAKES 3 TO 4 SERVINGS

2 medium Garnet or Jewel sweet potatoes, rinsed, unpeeled
2 tablespoons extra-virgin olive oil
1 teaspoon sea salt
⅛ teaspoon curry powder
⅛ teaspoon chili powder
⅛ teaspoon ground cinnamon
Juice of ½ lemon

Preheat the oven to 400°F.

Halve the sweet potatoes lengthwise, and then slice each half into 4 wedges. Transfer to a mixing bowl and drizzle with the oil. Toss the sweet potatoes to coat with oil. Sprinkle with the salt and spices, toss to coat and transfer the sweet potatoes to a shallow baking pan. Cover and bake in the center of the oven for 35 minutes. Remove the cover and bake about 15 minutes to brown the potatoes. Toss gently and return to the oven to brown evenly, about 5 minutes.

Carefully transfer the sweet potatoes to a serving platter, sprinkle lightly with lemon juice and serve.

ARUGULA AND ROASTED SQUASH SALAD

Sweet, roasted winter squash is balanced nicely against the delicate bitter flavor of astringent arugula, creating a balanced, relaxed energy, with brilliant focus.

MAKES 4 TO 5 SERVINGS

1 to 2 pounds butternut squash, halved, seeds reserved, cut into 1-inch cubes
Extra-virgin olive oil
Sea salt
⅛ teaspoon chili powder
1 tablespoon brown rice syrup
Juice of ½ lemon
2 bunches arugula, rinsed well and stems trimmed

Preheat the oven to 350°F.

Place the squash in a mixing bowl, drizzle lightly with oil and season to taste with salt. Toss gently to coat the squash and transfer to a shallow baking dish, avoiding overlap. Cover tightly and bake for 35 minutes. Remove the cover and bake for 7 to 10 minutes to brown.

While the squash bakes, rinse the squash seeds until they are free of the stringy membranes and towel dry. Place a small amount of oil, a generous pinch of salt, the chili powder and rice syrup in a skillet over medium heat. When the rice syrup foams, stir in the seeds and cook, stirring, until they begin to brown and are quite fragrant, 5 to 7 minutes.

Whisk together ⅓ cup olive oil, the lemon juice and salt to taste. Arrange the arugula on a serving platter, mound the squash on the arugula, sprinkle with the seeds and spoon the dressing over the top.

PARCHMENT-BAKED SWEET POTATOES

Wrapping the sweet potatoes in parchment seals in flavor and nutrients, resulting in buttery, tender mouthfuls and makes a neat little package of a side dish. The rosemary adds just the right touch of savory to make the sweetness just soar.

MAKES 5 TO 6 SERVINGS

3 to 4 medium sweet potatoes, unpeeled, cut into 2-inch chunks

Extra-virgin olive oil

Sea salt

2 to 3 sprigs fresh rosemary, leaves removed, or 1 teaspoon dried rosemary

Grated zest of ½ lemon

2 lemon halves

Preheat the oven to 375°F. Cut out 2 large, heart-shaped pieces of parchment paper, each one roughly the same size as your shallow baking pan.

Lay one sheet of parchment on each half of the pan. Divide the potatoes on half of each sheet of parchment. Drizzle lightly with oil, sprinkle lightly with salt, rosemary and lemon zest. Fold the remaining half of the parchment sheet over the potatoes, sealing the edges by folding them together over and over, creating two snug packages of sweet potatoes. Bake the packages for 35 to 40 minutes, until the potatoes are tender. You may check for doneness by opening a corner of one of the packages and checking a potato for desired tenderness. Transfer the packages to a serving platter and serve still wrapped to be opened at the table. Just after opening the packages, squeeze the juice of ½ lemon over each mound of potatoes.

ARUGULA SALAD WITH BRAISED ARTICHOKE HEARTS

A unique and robust salad, it's ideal for taking us from spring to summer. The delicate bitterness of the arugula is offset by the artichoke hearts, both working to relax our livers and keep us calm and cool. With the added nutrition of toasted hempseeds and oil, showcasing essential fatty acids, this is a salad to be reckoned with.

MAKES 4 TO 6 SERVINGS

6 tablespoons hempseed oil
2 heads garlic, halved lengthwise
Sea salt
1½ cups dry white wine
½ cup balsamic vinegar
2 sprigs fresh rosemary
2 sprigs fresh basil
2 sprigs fresh flat-leaf parsley
4 cups spring or filtered water
4 artichokes, halved lengthwise
¼ cup extra-virgin olive oil
1 small bunch arugula, rinsed well, stems
**   trimmed and hand shredded**
1 head frisée (curly endive), rinsed well and
**   hand shredded**
½ cup shelled hempseeds

Place 2 tablespoons of the hempseed oil in a large saucepan over medium heat. Lay the garlic heads in the pan, cut sides down. Cook for 5 to 7 minutes. Sprinkle lightly with salt and add the wine and vinegar. Cook until the liquid has reduced by half. Tie together the rosemary, basil and parsley and lay the bundle on top of the garlic. Add the water and bring to a boil. Add the artichokes, cover, turn off the heat and set aside to cool to room temperature.

When the liquid has cooled, remove 2 cups and transfer to a saucepan. (Re-cover the artichokes.) Cook the liquid over high heat until it has reduced to about ½ cup. Remove from the heat and stir in the remaining 4 tablespoons hempseed oil, the olive oil and salt to taste. Set aside.

To assemble the salad, arrange the greens in a mixing bowl. Remove the outer leaves from the artichokes and scoop out the inner hairy chokes. Slice the artichoke hearts thinly and add them to the greens. Toss with enough dressing just to coat the salad.

Heat a dry skillet over low heat and lightly pan-toast the hempseeds just until fragrant, about 3 minutes. Transfer to a small bowl and set aside.

Arrange the salad on a platter, drizzle with a little more dressing, sprinkle with a little of the hempseeds and serve the remaining dressing and hempseeds on the side.

≈≈ *Did You Know?* ≈≈
ARTICHOKES

Legend This flowering bud of a garden plant, artichokes were prized during the Renaissance for their aphrodisiac properties. Catherine de Medici brought them to France to ensure the success of her marriage to the king.

Fact This delicious bud is so nutrient rich, it only makes sense that it would gain the reputation of a love potion. It contains potassium, folic acid, magnesium, vitamin C, copper, iron, phosphorus, vitamin B6, niacin, calcium and pantothenic acid, as well as compounds that smooth the function of the liver. In addition, is there anything more sensual to eat with your lover?

DEEP-FRIED CAULIFLOWER WITH GARLIC OIL

Nothing, nothing, nothing is as satisfying (at least with food) as deep-frying. Crisp, light and oh so rich, just a few pieces and you're completely sated. And energizing? High heat and nourishing oil come together with the brilliant vitality of garlic to create a strengthening special occasion side dish.
MAKES 4 TO 6 SERVINGS

1 head cauliflower, broken into medium
    florets
2 tablespoons extra-virgin olive oil
3 to 4 cloves fresh garlic, thinly sliced
2 tablespoons brown rice vinegar
1 tablespoon sweet paprika
Sea salt

Batter
1 cup whole wheat pastry flour
1 teaspoon baking powder
Sea salt
1 teaspoon kuzu, dissolved in 3 tablespoons
    cold water
Spring or filtered water

Avocado or light olive oil, for deep-frying
2 to 3 sprigs fresh flat-leaf parsley, finely
    minced, for garnish

Bring a pot of water to a boil and cook the cauliflower until crisp-tender, about 4 minutes. Drain well and set aside.

Place the oil and garlic in a small saucepan over low heat and cook for 3 to 4 minutes to infuse the oil with garlic flavor. Strain the garlic out of the oil and whisk in the vinegar, paprika and salt to taste. Set aside to cool.

To make the batter: Whisk together the flour, baking powder and a generous pinch salt. Mix in the dissolved kuzu and enough water to make a batter like that for pancakes. Set aside for 15 minutes.

Preheat the oven to 250°F.

Heat 3 to 4 inches oil in a deep pot over medium heat. When the oil is hot, dip the cauliflower in the batter to coat. Increase heat to high. Fry, in batches, until golden and crisp, 2 to 3 minutes. Drain well and transfer to a parchment-lined baking sheet and place in a warm oven while frying the remaining batches.

To serve, arrange the cauliflower on a platter and drizzle with the garlic oil and garnish with the parsley. Serve immediately.

CHERRY TOMATO, MANGO AND SHALLOT SALAD

A light, fresh summer salad, with just enough rich flavor to keep us satisfied.

MAKES 3 TO 4 SERVINGS

2 tablespoons extra-virgin olive oil
3 to 4 shallots, finely minced
2 cloves fresh garlic, finely minced
Sea salt
12 to 14 cherry tomatoes, halved
2 to 3 sprigs fresh basil, leaves removed and shredded
1 small head butter lettuce, rinsed well and hand shredded
1 ripe mango, thinly sliced
Juice of ½ lemon

Place oil, shallots and garlic in a skillet over medium heat. When the shallots begin to sizzle, add a pinch of salt and sauté for 2 minutes. Lay the tomato halves cut-side down in the skillet, season lightly with salt and cook, uncovered, until tomatoes are tender, 3 to 5 minutes. Add the basil, stir gently to combine and set aside.

Arrange the lettuce on a platter with the mango slices in the center. Spoon the tomato and shallot mixture over top, drizzle with the lemon juice and serve.

SAUTÉED KALE WITH RED ONIONS

Lots of people aren't all that fond of dark leafy greens, but this gem of a recipe could change all that. With caramelized onions cooked to sweet perfection, a touch of garlic for energy and just a bit of lemon juice to make the dish sparkle, this side dish can't be beat.

MAKES 6 TO 8 SERVINGS

About 1 tablespoon extra-virgin olive oil
3 red onions, cut into thin half-moon slices
4 to 5 cloves fresh garlic, thinly sliced
Sea salt
Generous pinch red pepper flakes
Grated zest of 1 lemon
2 tablespoons brown rice syrup
2 medium bunches kale, rinsed well and stems trimmed
2 lemons, cut into 4 wedges each, for garnish

Place the oil, onions and garlic in a deep skillet over medium heat. When the onions begin to sizzle add a pinch of salt, the red pepper flakes and lemon zest and sauté until the onions begin to wilt. Add the rice syrup and reduce the heat slightly. Cook, stirring frequently, until the onions have browned, about 15 minutes.

Spread the onions evenly over the bottom of the skillet. Slice the kale into bite-size pieces and lay on top of the onions. Season lightly with salt, cover and cook over low heat until the kale is wilted and deep green but not mushy, about 5 minutes. Stir gently to combine the kale and onions and transfer to a serving platter. Serve with the lemon wedges.

LEMON-GINGER GLAZED CARROTS

A delicious sweet-and-sour side dish, with centering, grounding energy and loaded with essential fatty acids, the perfect accompaniment to any autumn meal. Just rich enough to get everyone's attention, and easy enough to make it a regular on your table.

MAKES 6 TO 8 SERVINGS

8 to 10 carrots, cut into 3 × ½-inch spears

Sea salt

3 tablespoons barley malt

2 tablespoons hempseed oil

1 tablespoon finely minced fresh ginger

Grated zest of 1 lemon

Juice of ½ lemon

2 to 3 sprigs fresh flat-leaf parsley, finely minced, for garnish

Place the carrots and a generous pinch of salt in a saucepan with enough water to half cover. Cover and bring to a boil over medium heat. Reduce the heat to low and cook until the carrots are just tender, about 10 minutes.

While the carrots cook, combine the barley malt, hempseed oil, ginger and lemon zest in a saucepan over low heat and cook until it foams. Remove from the heat. When the carrots are ready, drain well and toss with the ginger glaze to coat. Transfer to a serving bowl and sprinkle with the lemon juice and parsley just before serving.

PARSNIP-FENNEL PURÉE

Delicately sweet and peppery, this purée is a great spread on toasted bread, making the perfect autumn crostini. The savory fennel prevents the parsnip from becoming cloyingly sweet and the combination goes extremely well with a nice Chianti.

MAKES 3 TO 4 SERVINGS

2 to 3 parsnips, diced

1 fennel bulb, stalks trimmed flush with bulb and bulb diced

2 to 3 cloves fresh garlic, diced

Sea salt

1 tablespoon extra-virgin olive oil

2 to 3 sprigs fresh flat-leaf parsley, finely minced

Place the parsnips, fennel and garlic in a saucepan with water to just cover. Cover and bring to a boil. Add a generous pinch salt, re-cover and reduce the heat to low. Cook until the vegetables are very tender, 15 to 20 minutes. Drain the vegetables well and transfer to a food processor. Add the olive oil and salt to taste and purée until smooth. Transfer to a small bowl and fold in the parsley. Serve warm, as a side dish or a spread for toasted bread.

PARSLEY CABBAGE SALAD WITH ORANGE VINAIGRETTE

A delightfully light side dish, serve with a hearty meal, or on a buffet table to lend an air of simplicity to a feast.
MAKES 4 TO 5 SERVINGS

Salad
½ medium head green cabbage, finely shredded
1 small bunch flat-leaf parsley, finely minced
1 to 2 carrots, cut into fine matchstick pieces
4 to 5 scallions, thinly sliced on the diagonal

Orange Vinaigrette
¼ cup extra-virgin olive oil
2 to 3 cloves fresh garlic, finely minced
2 to 3 shallots, finely minced
Grated zest of 1 orange
Sea salt
Juice of 2 oranges
Juice of 1 lime

To make the salad: Bring a pot of water to a boil and cook the cabbage until crisp-tender, about 3 minutes. With a slotted spoon or skimmer, drain and transfer to a mixing bowl. Stir in the parsley. In the same boiling water, cook the carrots for 2 minutes. Drain and add to the cabbage mixture. Stir in the scallions and set aside to cool.

To make the dressing: Combine the oil, garlic, shallots, orange zest and a light sprinkle of salt in a small saucepan and cook over low heat for 4 to 5 minutes. Remove from the heat, whisk in the orange and lime juices and season to taste with salt.

To serve, toss the cabbage mixture with the dressing and serve warm or lightly chilled.

≈ *Did You Know?* ≈
CABBAGE?

Legend Cabbage cools fevers, hot flashes and relieves swelling from sprains and bruising.

Fact Vitamin C, potassium, folic acid and vitamin B6 in the cabbage work together to reduce inflammation and normalize hormonal function.

STIR-FRIED BOK CHOY WITH GARLIC AND GINGER

You can never eat enough greens, ever—but after a while, steamed or boiled greens can lose their appeal. Try this spicy, delicious side dish and I promise you'll just love your greens . . . and so will everybody else.
MAKES 3 TO 4 SERVINGS

2 to 3 tablespoons extra-virgin olive oil
2 to 3 cloves fresh garlic, thinly sliced
1 teaspoon finely minced fresh ginger
Generous pinch red pepper flakes
Sea salt
1 medium bunch bok choy, rinsed well and stem tips trimmed
Brown rice vinegar

Place the oil, garlic, ginger and red pepper flakes in a skillet over medium heat. As soon as the garlic begins to sizzle (do not let it burn), add a pinch of salt. Slice the bok choy into bite-size pieces and add to the skillet. Season lightly with salt and sauté until the bok choy wilts and turns a deep green, about 5 minutes. Remove from the heat and sprinkle lightly with rice vinegar. Transfer to a serving platter and serve immediately.

lightly with salt and add the red pepper flakes. Cook, stirring constantly, until a smooth paste forms. Stir in the green beans and cook, stirring, until coated, about 1 minute. Transfer to a serving platter and serve hot.

GARLIC FRENCHED GREEN BEANS

This dish is a summer knockout. Strongly flavored, but so delicious and easy to make, this dish will find its way to the table for as long as green beans hang from their vines.

MAKES 5 TO 6 SERVINGS

1 large head garlic
1 to 2 pounds green beans, tips trimmed
Extra-virgin olive oil
2 tablespoons spring or filtered water
Sea salt
Generous pinch red pepper flakes

Preheat the oven to 400°F. Slice the top off the garlic head and place in a small baking dish or on a square of foil. Drizzle lightly with oil and cover, or if using foil, wrap tightly. Bake about 1 hour, until very tender. Set aside to cool.

When the garlic has cooled enough to handle, squeeze the pulp from the cloves. You should have about 2 tablespoons. Set aside.

Bring a pot of water to a boil. Halve the green beans, lengthwise, and boil until crisp-tender, about 5 minutes. Drain well.

Place about 3 tablespoons oil, the garlic pulp and water in a skillet over medium heat. Season

BABY CARROTS AND ASPARAGUS WITH LEMON-MAPLE GLAZE

This is such a great side dish for spring, you'll wonder what you did before you knew about it. Colorful and dripping with sweet glaze, with light, yet grounded energy, it's as sweet as the crocus blossoms outside your window.

MAKES 5 TO 6 SERVINGS

1 pound baby carrots, with tops if available, left whole, rinsed very well
1 pound asparagus, tough ends snapped off
¼ cup extra-virgin olive oil
3 tablespoons Suzanne's Specialties Maple Rice Nectar
Sea salt
Grated zest of 1 lemon
5 to 6 lemon wedges, for garnish

Bring a small amount of water to a boil. Arrange the carrots in a steamer basket and steam over the boiling water until crisp-tender, about 10 minutes. Set aside. Steam the asparagus until crisp-tender, about 5 minutes. Arrange the carrots and asparagus on a serving platter.

Combine the oil, maple rice nectar, a generous pinch salt and the lemon zest in a small saucepan.

Cook over high heat until foaming. Remove from the heat and spoon the glaze over the cooked vegetables. Serve garnished with lemon wedges.

~~~~~~~~~~

TOMATO AND GREEN SALAD WITH SWEET LEMON DRESSING

As colorful as summer itself, this light-as-air salad is just dreamy, as a side dish or as a luncheon main course. Perfect for any al fresco feast, from a grilling party to a birthday celebration to a Wednesday night dinner in your garden.

MAKES 6 TO 8 SIDE SERVINGS OR 3 TO 4 MAIN COURSES

- 1 cup extra-virgin olive oil
- Juice of 2 to 3 lemons
- 4 tablespoons brown rice syrup
- Grated zest of 1 lemon
- Generous pinch red pepper flakes
- Sea salt
- 1 bunch watercress, rinsed well and stem tips trimmed
- 2 Belgian endive, bottoms trimmed and thinly sliced lengthwise
- 1 small bunch arugula, rinsed well and stem tips trimmed
- 4 ripe tomatoes, sliced into thin wedges
- 1 red onion, cut into very thin half-moon slices
- 1 (8-ounce) package baked tofu, cubed

Combine the oil, lemon juice, rice syrup, lemon zest, red pepper flakes and salt to taste in a small saucepan over low heat and warm for 3 minutes, whisking constantly. Remove from the heat, transfer to a heat-resistant bowl and set aside to cool.

Combine the greens on a platter and arrange the tomatoes and onion around the rim. Mound the tofu in the center. Chill the salad completely. Just before serving, spoon a small amount of dressing over the salad and serve the remaining dressing on the side.

~~~~~~~~~~

BROCCOLI WITH HEMPSEEDS AND CRUSHED RED PEPPER

Broccoli is a great staple vegetable, delicious, familiar and loaded with calcium, folic acid, vitamins and minerals. In this side dish, we up the ante just a little by adding the zippy vitality of red pepper and essential fatty acids with crunchy hempseeds.

MAKES 4 TO 5 SERVINGS

- ½ teaspoon sea salt
- 4 tablespoons shelled hempseeds
- ¾ teaspoon red pepper flakes
- 2 to 3 large stalks broccoli, cut into florets and stems peeled and thinly sliced
- 1 tablespoon hempseed oil

Heat a dry skillet over medium heat. Add the salt and dry-roast, stirring, for 2 to 3 minutes. Add the hempseeds and red pepper flakes and cook, stirring constantly, until fragrant, about 2 minutes. Transfer to a suribachi (grinding bowl) and grind with a pestle until a coarse meal forms. Set aside.

Bring a pot of water to a boil and cook the broccoli stems until crisp-tender, about 3 minutes. Remove with a slotted spoon or skimmer, drain well and place in a mixing bowl. In the same water, cook the broccoli florets until crisp-tender, 5 to 6 minutes. Drain well and add to the stems. Stir in the hempseed mixture to taste, add the oil and toss to combine. Transfer to a serving platter and serve warm.

ROASTED ASPARAGUS WITH FRESH FAVA BEANS AND MUSHROOMS

Spring means two things to me: lilacs blossoms and fresh fava beans, both of which are a delight beyond imagining. In this dish, we use smoky roasted asparagus to serve as the backdrop for the sautéed favas and mushrooms. Satisfying, but as light as spring itself, this is a side dish worth the work.

MAKES 4 TO 6 SERVINGS

½ cup spring or filtered water

6 dried shiitake mushrooms

1 shallot, finely minced

2 cloves fresh garlic, finely minced

Grated zest of 1 lemon

1 tablespoon balsamic vinegar

Sea salt

1 pound fresh fava beans, shelled (about 1 cup)

1 bunch asparagus, tough ends snapped off

About 1 tablespoon extra-virgin olive oil, plus extra for drizzling

2 slices (½ of 8-ounce package) baked tofu, cubed

2 to 3 sprigs fresh flat-leaf parsley, finely minced

Bring the water to a boil and add the mushrooms. Turn off the heat and cover. When the mushrooms are soft, remove and slice thinly, reserving the liquid. Return the mushrooms to the warm liquid, cover and set aside.

Place the shallot, garlic and lemon zest in a small bowl and add the vinegar and a pinch of salt. Toss to combine and set aside for 30 minutes.

Bring a pot of water to a boil and cook the fava beans until crisp-tender, about 3 minutes. Drain well and cool just enough to handle. Remove and discard the outer skins of each fava bean and place the beans in a mixing bowl.

Preheat the oven to 450°F. Arrange the asparagus on a shallow rimmed baking sheet. Drizzle generously with olive oil and sprinkle with salt. Roast the asparagus, uncovered, for about 20 minutes, until slightly browned and tender when pierced.

Place the oil and shallot mixture in a deep skillet over medium heat. When the shallot begins to sizzle, sauté for 1 to 2 minutes. Drain the shiitake mushrooms and stir into the shallot mixture, add a pinch of salt and sauté for 2 minutes, adding a little of the mushroom soaking liquid, if needed. Stir in the tofu and sauté for 2 minutes. Stir in the fava beans, season lightly with salt and toss to coat. Remove from the heat and stir in the parsley.

To serve, arrange asparagus on a platter and spoon the fava bean mixture over the top.

BROCCOLI WITH FENNEL

Broccoli is so everyday, we sometimes forget just how wonderful it can be. Rich in calcium, vitamin C and folic acid, this familiar beauty is also a great source of nutrients essential for health. Try this dressed-up version for variety.

MAKES 6 TO 8 SERVINGS

About 4 tablespoons extra-virgin
   olive oil
2 to 3 cloves fresh garlic, thinly sliced
3 to 4 shallots, thinly sliced
Sea salt
1 small fresh fennel bulb, stems removed,
   bulb thinly sliced, reserving 2 to
   3 tablespoons minced leaves
1 red bell pepper, roasted over an open flame
   (page 57), peeled, seeded and thinly sliced
   into ribbons
7 cups broccoli florets (2 to 3 heads)
½ teaspoon dried basil
½ teaspoon dried rosemary
⅔ cup spring or filtered water

Place about 2 tablespoons of the oil, the garlic and shallots in a deep skillet over medium heat. When the shallots begin to sizzle, add a pinch of salt and sauté until turning golden, 3 to 4 minutes. Add the fennel bulb, bell pepper and a pinch of salt and sauté until just beginning to wilt, 3 minutes. Add the broccoli, the remaining 2 tablespoons oil, the dried herbs and a light seasoning of salt and stir to coat. Add the water, cover and cook until the broccoli is crisp-tender, about 5 minutes. Remove the cover and allow any remaining liquid to cook away. Stir gently to combine the ingredients and transfer to a serving platter.

ROOT VEGETABLE MEDLEY WITH FRESH HERBS

I love to serve this dish for Thanksgiving dinner . . . you know, when all the relatives are dreading your "weird" food. It would be nice to have a family gathering where the only thing noticed is how wonderful the meal is, doncha' think?

MAKES 6 TO 8 SERVINGS

1 tablespoon chopped fresh thyme
1 tablespoon chopped fresh rosemary
1 tablespoon chopped fresh basil
3 cloves fresh garlic, finely minced
¼ cup extra-virgin olive oil
1 teaspoon sea salt
Grated zest of 1 lemon
10 to 12 baby beets, unpeeled, trimmed, left
   whole
4 medium turnips, quartered
4 medium rutabaga, quartered (do not peel,
   unless they've been waxed)
8 to 10 carrots, cut into 2-inch irregular
   pieces
8 to 10 parsnips, cut into 2-inch irregular
   pieces
10 to 12 small cipollini or pearl onions,
   peeled
⅓ cup spring or filtered water
2 tablespoons balsamic vinegar

Preheat the oven to 375°F.

Mix together the herbs, garlic, oil, salt and lemon zest in a large mixing bowl. Remove half of the mixture to a small bowl and set aside. Take 1 tablespoon of the mixture and transfer to a medium bowl and mix in the beets, tossing to coat. Arrange the beets in a corner of a large shallow baking dish. Toss the remaining vegetables with the herb mixture in the large bowl, stirring to coat. Arrange on the baking sheet with the beets, but do not mix together (the beets will color the other vegetables). Cover tightly and bake for 35 minutes. Remove the cover, toss the vegetables gently and bake for about 15 minutes, until browned.

Mix the water and vinegar with the remaining herb mixture and pour over the vegetables. Return to oven and bake, uncovered, for about 7 minutes, until the liquid evaporates and the vegetables are lightly glazed. Serve hot or at room temperature.

PEAS WITH CELERY ROOT

This lovely holiday side dish, is beautiful to serve. It has an earthy, slightly spicy taste and makes a delightfully different addition to any special occasion feast.
MAKES 6 TO 8 SERVINGS

1½ pounds celery root, peeled and cut into 2-inch dice
¼ cup extra-virgin olive oil
2 cloves fresh garlic, finely minced
2 to 3 shallots, diced

Sea salt
Grated zest of 1 lemon
½ cup dry white wine
16 ounces frozen petite peas

Bring a pot of water to a boil and cook the celery root until just tender, about 5 minutes. Drain well. Set aside.

Place the oil, garlic and shallots in a deep skillet over medium heat. When the shallots begin to sizzle, add a pinch of salt and the lemon zest and sauté for 2 to 3 minutes. Add the celery root, wine and a light seasoning of salt. Cover and cook over low heat for 5 minutes. Stir in the peas, season to taste with salt and cook, stirring occasionally, until the peas are tender and any remaining liquid has cooked away, about 5 minutes. Transfer to a serving bowl and serve hot.

CARROTS AND RUTABAGAS WITH LEMON

Earthy root vegetables have the sparkling zest of lemon juice added for vitality. This side dish will become a regular addition to any number of autumn meals—from the everyday to the most special of occasions.

MAKES 6 TO 8 SERVINGS

2 to 3 medium rutabaga, halved and sliced into matchstick pieces (do not peel, unless they've been waxed)

6 to 8 carrots, cut into matchstick pieces

¼ cup extra-virgin olive oil

3 tablespoons brown rice syrup

1 red onion, cut into thin half-moon slices

Sea salt

Grated zest of 1 lemon

Juice of 1 lemon

2 to 3 sprigs fresh flat-leaf parsley, finely minced

Bring a pot of water to a boil and cook the rutabaga until just tender, about 2 minutes. Remove with a slotted spoon or skimmer, drain well and transfer to a bowl. In the same water, cook the carrots until just tender, about 2 minutes. Drain well and mix with the rutabaga.

Place the oil, rice syrup and onion in a skillet over medium heat. When the onion begins to sizzle, add a generous pinch of salt and sauté for 2 to 3 minutes. Stir in the lemon zest, rutabaga, carrots and a light seasoning of salt. Cook, stirring occasionally, for 6 to 7 minutes. Remove from the heat, stir in the lemon juice and parsley and transfer to a serving bowl. Serve immediately.

APPLE-FILLED ACORN SQUASH WITH CURRIED HEMPSEEDS

The flavor of the curry powder enhances the sweetness of the apples and squash in this easy recipe.

MAKES 8 SERVINGS

About 4 tablespoons extra-virgin olive oil

1 large yellow onion, diced

2 cloves fresh garlic, finely minced

2½ teaspoons curry powder

Sea salt

2 Granny Smith apples, peeled, cored and diced

⅔ cup apple juice

1 tablespoon barley malt

½ cup dried currants

8 (1-inch-thick) acorn squash rings, unpeeled, seeded

2 to 3 sprigs fresh flat-leaf parsley, finely minced, for garnish

Curried hempseeds

Place about 1 tablespoon oil, the onion and garlic in a heavy skillet over medium heat. When the onion begins to sizzle, add 2 teaspoons of the curry powder and a generous pinch salt and sauté for 8 to 10 minutes, until the onion is quite soft. Stir in the apples, apple juice, barley malt and currants, season lightly with salt and sauté until all the liquid has evaporated, 6 to 8 minutes.

Preheat the oven to 350°F. Place 3 to 4 table-spoons oil and the remaining ½ teaspoon curry powder in a small skillet over medium heat. Sauté for 1 to 2 minutes, just long enough to flavor the oil. Transfer to a small cup and set aside.

Arrange the squash rings in a single layer on a lightly oiled shallow baking pan. Sprinkle lightly with salt and brush with the curry-flavored oil. Spoon the apple mixture into the center of the rings, filling abundantly. Drizzle lightly with curry oil and cover tightly.

Bake for 45 to 50 minutes, until the squash is tender when pierced with a skewer. Carefully transfer the squash rings, using a spatula, to a serving platter. Garnish with the parsley and curried hempseeds and serve hot.

BRUSSELS SPROUTS WITH PEARL ONIONS AND PINE NUTS

I know you don't think irresistible *when you think of Brussels sprouts, but with this recipe, you might be forced to reconsider. Delicious and easy to make, this is a splendid side dish for any special occasion—or any ordinary occasion, for that matter.*

MAKES 5 TO 6 SERVINGS

3 tablespoons extra-virgin olive oil
6 to 8 pearl onions, peeled
Sea salt
½ cup pine nuts
2 pounds Brussels sprouts, halved
½ cup spring or filtered water

½ cup dry white wine
2 to 3 sprigs fresh flat-leaf parsley, finely minced
Tofu sour cream (page 137)

Place the oil and onions in a skillet over medium heat. When the onions begin to sizzle, add a generous pinch salt and sauté until the onions are limp and beginning to brown, about 5 minutes. Stir in pine nuts and stir to coat. Add the Brussels sprouts and season lightly with salt. Add the water and wine, cover and cook until the Brussels sprouts are tender, 10 to 12 minutes. Season lightly with salt and cook, uncovered, until any remaining liquid has evaporated.

Stir the parsley and enough tofu sour cream to coat the Brussels sprouts, reserving the balance for garnish. Transfer the Brussels sprouts to a serving platter, and serve the remaining tofu sour cream on the side for use as desired.

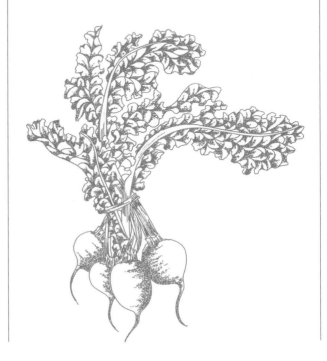

GREEN BEANS AND SHIITAKE MUSHROOMS

Summer and green beans go together so well we can hardly imagine warm weather without them. This upscale (but oh so easy to make) dish will grace the table of any midsummer night's feast with elegance and delicious delicacy.

MAKES 8 TO 9 SERVINGS

4 tablespoons extra-virgin olive oil

3 to 4 shallots, thinly sliced

2 to 3 cloves fresh garlic, thinly sliced

Sea salt

Generous pinch red pepper flakes

8 to 10 fresh shiitake mushrooms, stems removed and thinly sliced

2 pounds green beans, tips trimmed

⅔ cup dry white wine or spring or filtered water

Place the oil, shallots and garlic in a deep skillet over medium heat. When the shallots begin to sizzle, add a pinch of salt and the red pepper flakes and sauté until the shallots are limp, about 2 minutes. Stir in the mushrooms and a pinch of salt and sauté for 2 to 3 minutes. Place the green beans on top of the shallot mixture and add the wine and a light seasoning of salt. Cover, reduce the heat to low and cook until the green beans are crisp-tender, about 7 minutes. Remove the cover and increase the heat to medium, cooking until any remaining liquid has evaporated. Stir gently to combine and transfer to a serving bowl.

SHIITAKE MUSHROOMS

Legend Shiitake mushrooms relax muscle tension and reduce high blood pressure and cholesterol levels.

Fact A high concentration of potassium is the reason the mushrooms affect these conditions.

WHOLE ROASTED SWEET POTATOES WITH SWEET CURRY GLAZE

A great holiday, or any day, side dish, I like to choose well-shaped sweet potatoes for this dish, so they look especially pretty on the table. With their sweet taste enlivened by the delicately spicy flavor of the curry, these humble, centering sweet potatoes give us a grounded vitality to get us through the holiday rush.

MAKES 4 SERVINGS

½ cup extra-virgin olive oil

2 tablespoons brown rice syrup

1½ teaspoons curry powder

Generous pinch ground cinnamon

Generous pinch sea salt

4 small sweet potatoes, washed well

Preheat the oven to 375°F.

Combine the oil and rice syrup in a small saucepan over low heat and cook for 3 to 4 min-

utes. Stir in the curry powder, cinnamon and salt and cook for 2 minutes. Set aside.

Pierce sweet potatoes all over with a fork and place directly on the center oven rack. Bake the sweet potatoes for about 1 hour, until tender when pierced with a skewer or fork. Remove from the oven and cut a slit, lengthwise, in the top of each potato. Using oven mitts to protect your hands, gently squeeze each potato from the ends forcing the slit open. Spoon the curried oil into each slit, arrange the sweet potatoes on a platter and drizzle any remaining oil over top. Serve immediately.

ORANGE-SCENTED SWEET POTATO PUREE WITH NUTTY STREUSEL

This is one of my favorite Thanksgiving side dishes. I love to take a commonly served food, like sweet potatoes, and put my own unique twist on it. In this beautiful holiday dish, I add the crunch of a streusel topping to the comforting creaminess of pureed sweet potatoes for a unique blend of textures.
MAKES 6 TO 8 SERVINGS

3 to 4 pounds sweet potatoes, washed well

Nutty Streusel
⅓ cup whole wheat pastry flour
⅓ cup whole almonds, ground into a coarse meal
⅓ cup pecan pieces, ground into a coarse meal
Pinch sea salt

3 tablespoons barley malt
¼ cup avocado or light olive oil

Filling
⅓ cup fresh orange juice
2 tablespoons brown rice syrup
2 tablespoons extra-virgin olive oil
Grated zest of 1 orange
Sea salt

Preheat the oven to 375°F. Pierce the sweet potatoes all over with a fork and place directly on the center oven rack. Bake the sweet potatoes for about 1 hour, until tender when pierced with a skewer or fork.

While the sweet potatoes bake, *make the streusel:* Combine all the ingredients in a mixing bowl and stir, blending until moist clumps form. Set aside.

Remove the sweet potatoes from the oven and cool just enough to handle. Increase the oven temperature to 400°F and lightly oil a 13 × 9-inch baking dish (I like oval here).

To make the filling: Peel and transfer the sweet potatoes to a mixing bowl and mash. Stir in the orange juice, rice syrup, oil, orange zest and a light seasoning of salt. Mix well.

Spread the sweet potato purée evenly in the prepared dish, smoothing the top surface. Crumble the streusel dough over the purée. Bake for 30 to 25 minutes, until the streusel is crisp and lightly browned. Cool for 5 to 10 minutes before serving.

HEARTS OF LETTUCE SALAD WITH APPLES

As summer fades into autumn, salads can lose their appeal. One more tomato and lettuce salad will send you over the edge. This elegant beauty can take you right into cooler weather with its hearty dressing and the addition of crisp, seasonal apples.
MAKES 8 TO 10 SERVINGS

Salad
1 red onion, cut into very thin rings
5 hearts romaine lettuce, trimmed and halved lengthwise
2 Granny Smith apples, unpeeled, cut into ¼-inch dice
1 cup lightly toasted hazelnuts
½ cups dried currants

Dressing
1 cup extra-virgin olive oil
2 to 3 cloves fresh garlic, finely minced
½ red onion, finely diced
¼ cup apple cider
3 tablespoons brown rice syrup
1½ teaspoons sea salt
½ teaspoon ground nutmeg
½ teaspoon ground ginger
½ teaspoon red pepper flakes
Grated zest of 1 lemon
Juice of 1 lemon

To make the salad: Place the onion rings in a bowl and cover them with very cold water. Set aside for 30 minutes.

Cut each romaine half into 3 large wedges and press them gently to fan them. Arrange them on a serving platter. Drain the onion and arrange them on top of the lettuce.

To make the dressing: Combine all the ingredients except the lemon juice in a small saucepan over low heat and warm through. Remove from the heat and whisk in the lemon juice. Set aside to cool to room temperature.

To serve, spoon the dressing generously over the lettuce and onion. Sprinkle the apples, currants and hazelnuts over the top and serve with the remaining dressing on the side.

SALAD OF AUTUMN GREENS AND POMEGRANATE

Salads don't have to disappear from our tables just because the weather cools; they just have to change with the seasons to be at their delicious best, lifting our energy and keeping us refreshed as we move from season to season.
MAKES 6 TO 8 SERVINGS

Tangerine Dressing
¾ cup fresh tangerine juice
1 tablespoon grated tangerine zest
2 tablespoons brown rice syrup
¾ cup extra-virgin olive oil
2 to 3 tablespoons balsamic vinegar

⅔ teaspoon sea salt

Generous pinch ground cinnamon

Salad

1 head escarole, rinsed well and hand
   shredded

1 large bunch watercress, rinsed well and
   stems trimmed

3 to 4 Belgian endive, halved lengthwise and
   sliced into thin slivers

Seeds of 2 pomegranates

½ cup pecan pieces, lightly toasted, coarsely
   chopped

To make the dressing: Place the tangerine juice and zest and rice syrup in a small saucepan over medium heat. Cook until reduced to ¼ cup, about 5 minutes. Transfer to a mixing bowl. Whisk in the oil, vinegar, salt and cinnamon. Set aside.

To make the salad: Place the greens in a mixing bowl. Spoon the dressing over the greens and toss to coat. Transfer the salad to a platter and sprinkle with the pomegranate seeds and pecan pieces.

POMEGRANATES

To eat or serve a pomegranate, simply split the fruit open and extract the edible seeds, discarding the skin. Be careful not to crush the seeds, because the juice can stain. An easy way to remove any peel fragments is to place the seeds in water; the white parts and immature seeds will float to the top.

Slightly tart and delicately sweet pomegranate is a most delicious snack or addition to a salad or oven-roasted vegetables.

BUTTERNUT SQUASH WITH CRANBERRIES

This is a take on a traditional Shaker recipe used all during the autumn and winter, when vegetables grew scarcer and creativity with simple ingredients ruled. This vegan side dish is a splendid addition to a simple dinner, a casual buffet or a brunch.

MAKES 4 TO 5 SERVINGS

1 to 2 pounds butternut squash, peeled,
   seeded and cut into 1-inch cubes

Sea salt

1 cup fresh or frozen cranberries

3 tablespoons brown rice syrup

1 tablespoon extra-virgin olive oil (optional)

Grated zest of 1 orange

2 to 3 orange slices, for garnish

Place the squash in a saucepan with 2 inches of water. Cover and bring to a boil. Add a generous pinch of salt, reduce the heat to low and cook for 20 minutes. Add the cranberries, season lightly with salt and cook, uncovered, until they burst open and are soft, 10 to 15 minutes. Increase the heat to high and cook away any remaining liquid.

Transfer the squash and cranberries to a food processor and add the rice syrup, oil, if using, and orange zest. Purée until smooth. Transfer to a serving bowl and garnish with the orange slices.

ROASTED ASPARAGUS WITH MUSHROOM FRICASSEE

Nothing intensifies the flavor of asparagus like roasting. In this elegant spring starter course, the softening energy of mushrooms combines with the light, refreshing energy of asparagus to help us to feel as fresh as a spring breeze.
MAKES 4 TO 5 SERVINGS

1 pound asparagus, tough ends snapped off
About 1 tablespoon extra-virgin olive oil, plus extra for drizzling
Sea salt
Grated zest of 1 lemon
3 to 4 shallots, thinly sliced
2 to 3 cloves fresh garlic, thinly sliced
10 to 12 ounces assorted wild mushrooms (cremini, chanterelle, shiitake), thinly sliced
½ cup mirin
2 to 3 sprigs fresh flat-leaf parsley, finely minced
Juice of ½ lemon

Preheat the oven to 375°F.

Arrange the asparagus in a single layer in a rimmed baking pan. Drizzle with olive oil and sprinkle generously with salt and the lemon zest. Bake, uncovered, for 10 to 12 minutes, until just tender.

While the asparagus bakes, place 1 tablespoon oil, the shallots and garlic in a deep skillet over medium heat. When the shallots begin to sizzle, add a pinch of salt and sauté for 2 to 3 minutes. Add the mushrooms and sauté until browned, about 5 minutes. Cover, reduce the heat to low and simmer the mushrooms for 3 to 4 minutes. Remove the cover, increase the heat to medium and add the mirin and a light seasoning of salt. Cook until mirin is absorbed, 2 to 3 minutes. Remove from the heat and stir in the parsley.

To serve, arrange the asparagus on a large platter and spoon the mushrooms over the top. Drizzle with the lemon juice.

ROASTED AUTUMN VEGETABLES

Without a doubt, the easiest and most delicious way to prepare vegetables in cooler weather is oven roasting. The intense heat of the oven draws the natural sugars of the vegetables to the surface, making them mouthwateringly yummy. Their comforting heartiness keeps us toasty warm all through the chilly days of autumn and winter.
MAKES 6 TO 8 SERVINGS

3 to 4 medium sweet potatoes, unpeeled, cut into 2-inch irregular pieces
2 pounds Brussels sprouts, trimmed
1 large fennel bulb, stalks trimmed, bulb halved and cut into thick wedges
5 to 6 large carrots, quartered lengthwise
3 to 4 parsnips, quartered lengthwise
1 medium daikon, cut into 2-inch irregular pieces
Extra-virgin olive oil
Barley malt

Sea salt
1 small bunch fresh chives, finely minced
Juice of ½ lemon

Preheat the oven to 375°F.

Place the sweet potatoes, Brussels sprouts, fennel, carrots, parsnips and daikon in a mixing bowl. Drizzle generously with oil and barley malt and season lightly with salt. Toss well to coat the vegetables. Transfer to a large baking dish, avoiding overlap (you may need two pans). Cover tightly and bake for 40 minutes, until the vegetables pierce easily with a fork. Remove the cover and bake for 10 to 15 minutes to brown the vegetables. Remove from the oven, toss gently with the chives and lemon juice, transfer to a serving platter and serve hot.

GREEN BEANS WITH PEARS

As summer fades to autumn and crisp, cool days become the norm, we begin to change our eating and cooking styles. During this short season of late summer, green beans begin to fade, as sweet tree fruit comes into its fullness to carry us through the winter. In this gentle salad, we bring the seasons together to create a sweetly satisfying side dish.

MAKES 6 TO 8 SERVINGS

2 pounds haricot verts (or very slender green
   beans), trimmed, left whole
¼ cup extra-virgin olive oil
3 to 4 tablespoons balsamic vinegar
2 to 3 sprigs fresh flat-leaf parsley, finely
   minced
2 to 3 shallots, finely minced

2 to 3 cloves fresh garlic, finely minced
Grated zest of 1 lemon
1 cup finely minced basil leaves
2 teaspoons white miso
4 small ripe pears, unpeeled, halved and cut
   into very thin lengthwise slices
1 cup coarsely chopped walnut pieces, lightly
   pan-toasted (page 81)

Bring a pot of water to a boil and cook the beans until crisp-tender, 5 to 6 minutes. Drain well and set aside.

Mix together the oil, vinegar, parsley, shallots, garlic, lemon zest, basil and miso, whisking briskly until smooth.

Place the green beans, pears and walnuts in a mixing bowl. Mix in the dressing and transfer to a serving bowl.

≈ *Did You Know?* ≈
BASIL

Legend Eating basil can relieve migraine headaches and upset stomachs.

Fact Basil is a rich source of potassium, phosphorus and magnesium in ratios that can aid in the relief of both these ailments.

SPECTACULAR POT PIE

In this splendid recipe, I combine strengthening root vegetables, centering ground vegetables with some protein from tofu. Smothered in a richly flavored sauce and encased in a flaky crust, it's a perfect one-dish casual dinner, served with a crisp, fresh salad.

MAKES 8 TO 10 SERVINGS

Filling
About 1 tablespoon extra-virgin olive oil
1 yellow onion, diced
2 to 3 cloves fresh garlic, thinly sliced
Soy sauce
**6 to 8 cremini mushrooms, brushed free of
    dirt, thinly sliced**
2 to 3 stalks celery, diced
2 carrots, diced
¼ cup dry white wine
1 pound extra-firm tofu, cut into 2-inch cubes
½ cup frozen petite peas, thawed
⅓ cup walnut pieces, coarsely chopped
½ cup spring or filtered water
2 to 3 teaspoons dried basil
½ teaspoon chili powder
**1 tablespoon kuzu, dissolved in 3 to 4
    tablespoons cold water**

Pastry
1½ cups whole wheat pastry flour
½ cup yellow cornmeal
Pinch sea salt
¼ cup avocado or light olive oil
¼ cup cold spring or filtered water

Olive oil, for brushing

Preheat the oven to 350°F. Lightly oil a deep-dish glass pie plate.

To make the filling: Place the oil, onion and garlic in a deep skillet over medium heat. When the onion begins to sizzle, add a dash of soy sauce and sauté for 2 minutes. Stir in the mushrooms, celery and a dash of soy sauce and sauté until the mushrooms release their juices. Stir in the carrots. Add the wine, season lightly with soy sauce, cover and reduce the heat to low and simmer for 5 to 7 minutes. Add the tofu, peas and walnuts, stir gently, add the water, basil and chili powder and cook for 5 minutes. Season to taste with soy sauce and stir in the dissolved kuzu, cook, stirring, until the liquid turns into a clear, thick glaze. Set aside.

To make the crust: Combine the flour, cornmeal and salt in a mixing bowl. Cut in the oil with a fork or pastry cutter until the dough is the texture of wet sand. Slowly add the water, mixing until the dough gathers together into a soft ball, not too sticky, not too dry.

Divide the dough in half and roll each piece between parchment paper to a round that is about 2 inches larger than the pie plate. Fit one dough round into the pie plate, without stretching, letting the excess hang over the side. Pierce in several places with a fork. Spoon the filling into the shell. Place the other dough round over top of the filling. Trim the excess to within ½ inch of the rim of the pie plate. Fold the bottom shell edge up over the top edge and crimp decoratively to seal the edges. Cut deep slits in the top crust to allow steam to escape. Brush lightly with olive oil and bake for 50 to 55 minutes, until the filling is bubbling and the crust is firm and lightly browned. Remove from the oven and cool to warm before slicing.

SAVORY ROOT VEGETABLE COBBLER WITH CHIVE BISCUITS

Need a great recipe for a casual dinner party? Nothing too fancy, but delectable and satisfying? Oh, and it should be easy to make, too? Look no further. This savory cobbler makes a beautiful presentation and is so delicious, you'll love making it as much as you'll love eating it.
MAKES 6 SERVINGS

Filling
About 2 tablespoons extra-virgin olive oil
1 yellow onion, diced
2 to 3 cloves fresh garlic, thinly sliced
Sea salt
2 to 3 stalks celery, diced
1 small winter squash, seeded and diced
2 small turnips, diced
2 carrots, diced
1 (2-ounce) package dried porcini
    mushrooms, soaked until tender and diced,
    soaking liquid reserved
8 to 10 dried shiitake mushrooms, soaked
    until tender and diced, soaking liquid
    reserved
¾ teaspoon ground cumin
1 cup plain soymilk
1 cup frozen petite peas, thawed
3 to 4 fresh chives, finely minced
1 to 2 tablespoons whole wheat pastry flour

Chive Biscuits
2 cups whole wheat pastry flour
2 teapoons baking powder
½ teaspoon sea salt
⅓ cup finely minced fresh chives
6 tablespoons avocado or light olive oil
½ to ⅔ cup Eden Rice & Soy Blend or plain
    soymilk

To make the filling: Place the oil, onion and garlic in a deep pot over medium heat. When the onion begins to sizzle, add a pinch of salt and sauté until the onion begins to color, 4 to 5 minutes. Add the celery, squash, turnips, carrots and a pinch of salt and sauté for 2 to 3 minutes. Add the mushrooms, their soaking liquid and cumin. Cover and reduce the heat to low. Simmer until the vegetables are almost cooked, 10 to 15 minutes. Add the soymilk, season to taste with salt, stir in the peas and cook for 5 minutes. Stir in the chives and flour, and cook, stirring constantly, until the mixture thickens, about 5 minutes. Divide the mixture evenly among 6 (2-cup) soufflé cups or baking dishes. Set aside while preparing the biscuits.

Preheat the oven to 350°F.

To make the biscuits: Combine the flour, baking powder, salt and chives in a mixing bowl. Cut in the olive oil with a fork until the texture of wet sand. Slowly add the rice and soy blend to create a soft, but not sticky, dough.

Turn the dough out onto a lightly floured surface and knead just until it holds together, 1 to 2 minutes. Divide the dough into 6 equal pieces and pat each one into a round slightly smaller than the soufflé dishes. Place a biscuit on top of the filling in each soufflé dish, allowing some filling to show around the edges. Place the dishes on a large baking sheet. Bake for 18 to 20 minutes, until filling is bubbling and the biscuits golden. Remove them from the oven and allow to stand for 5 minutes before serving.

SPECTACULAR SEA VEGETABLES

Sea plants? Spectacular? Absolutely. We all think of sea vegetables as seaweed, those slimy, slick fronds that wrap around our ankles as we wade into the sea for a dip. While that may not be the most exciting part of our trip to the beach, sea plants are a most exciting part of a healthy diet.

Mineral-rich and strongly flavored, sea vegetables are so packed with nutrients that we need only a mere dab . . . just a small portion to reap the many benefits. Exotic sea plants are more than just unique. Rich in protein, calcium, vitamins and minerals, these strong vegetables are essential to maintaining strong, well-balanced blood. Small amounts of these dense nutrients ensure that we nourish our organs with essential nutrients for health. With sea vegetables, our liver, pancreas, kidneys and intestinal tract, our greatest filtering organs, are kept vital, working smoothly and efficiently to keep us healthy and toxin-free.

If the nutrients aren't enough to draw you to these exotic, strongly flavored vegetables, then maybe this will. Sea plants have, as one of their jobs, the task of cleansing the water around them of toxins, providing a healthy environment for the sea life so dependent on them for nutrients. Great filters, sea plants use their rich minerals to do the job. Of course, man's commitment to pollution may place sea plants on the fast track to extinction. When water grows too toxic, the plants cease to thrive, hence we have fewer sea plants wrapping around our ankles as we frolic at the seaside. Where they can grow, however, we find clean, pure water and rich sea life only. And, of course, sea vegetables for eating are harvested from only clean waters.

Think about it. Sea vegetables have been used for years in spa treatments, in wraps, baths, facial treatments and rubdowns. Used for everything from a basic detox treatment to more dramatic relief of fluid retention . . . to total body wraps to tone and firm the skin . . . to the current rage of rubbing cellulite with sea plants to rid the body of orange peel skin, sea plants have long been prized for their ability to cleanse, strengthen and beautify the body.

By eating these powerful pollution fighters, we ease the struggle to rid our system of the many toxins with which it is bombarded on a daily basis, from bus exhaust to junk food. Sea plants provide us with essential vitamins and minerals, helping maintain well-balanced blood, which in turn nourishes our various organs, keeping them strong in their work to maintain our health.

So the next time you see a bowl of sea vegetables, don't turn up your nose. Instead, fill a small plate and nosh your way to better health.

NORI ROLLS WITH BAKED TOFU AND GREENS

It's hard to imagine sea plants as trendy, but with nori, it's true. Delicate nibbles of strongly flavored foods, spicy dipping sauces, tart pickles all come together to make the perfect snack food or starter to a meal.

MAKES 16 PIECES

1 small carrot, sliced into long strips
1 bunch watercress, rinsed and ends trimmed
2 sheets toasted sushi nori
2 slices (½ of 8-ounce package) baked tofu, sliced into strips
Prepared spicy dipping sauce, to serve

Bring a small pot of water to a boil. Add the carrot and boil until crisp-tender, about 2 minutes. Remove with a slotted spoon or skimmer, drain and set aside. In the same water, boil the watercress until just wilted, about 2 minutes. Drain and set aside.

To assemble the rolls, place the nori, shiny side down, on a sushi mat or kitchen towel. On the edge closest to you, arrange half the watercress and 2 to 3 carrot strips, making a row of filling that covers the nori, from edge to edge. Place 2 to 3 strips baked tofu on top of the watercress, again, the width of the nori. Using the mat as a guide, roll the nori around the filling, pressing gently as you roll, creating a tight cylinder. Wrap the mat completely around the roll and squeeze any excess liquid from the filling. Set aside. Make another roll with the remaining ingredients.

Using a sharp knife, slice each nori roll into 8 equal pieces. Arrange on a platter and serve with a spicy dipping sauce.

BAKED TOFU

You can purchase packaged baked tofu in natural foods stores and some supermarkets. To bake it yourself, cut extra-firm tofu into about ¼-inch slices and marinate in a mixture of soy sauce, water and ginger juice for about 10 minutes. Drain and bake in a 400°F oven for about 10 minutes per side, until golden brown.

NORI PACKAGES

Nori and tofu are great partners. Mild-mannered tofu works as the "bread" in these little starters, with almond butter and miso as the richly flavored filling. Holding it all together is the strong taste of toasted nori, the perfect wrapping paper for these beautiful packages.

MAKES 2 SERVINGS

4 (⅓-inch-thick) slices tofu, halved
2 tablespoons almond butter
2 tablespoons barley miso
½ sheet nori, cut into ½-inch strips

Bring a pot of water to a boil and cook the tofu for 3 minutes. Drain well and pat dry. Set aside to cool.

Mix the almond butter and miso together, combining completely.

To assemble, spread the miso mixture over 2 slices of the tofu. Place the remaining 2 tofu slices over the miso mixture, making sandwiches. Moisten the nori strips and wrap each sandwich crosswise, holding them together.

Variation: For even more richness, use packaged baked tofu in place of the mildly flavored boiled tofu.

NORI ROLLS WITH ASPARAGUS

Nothing like a little sushi to lighten things up for spring. In this beautiful tribute to warmer weather, we use soba noodles in place of rice with lightly sautéed asparagus to help us feel refreshed after a long winter.
MAKES 24 PIECES

10 ounces soba noodles

3 sheets toasted sushi nori

About 1 tablespoon extra-virgin olive oil

6 asparagus spears, tough ends snapped off

Soy sauce

1 red bell pepper, roasted over an open flame (page 57), peeled, seeded and sliced

Divide the soba into six small bundles and, using cotton string, tie each bundle as close to the ends as possible. Bring a pot of water to a boil and cook the noodles until al dente, about 11 minutes. Drain well and rinse thoroughly. Spread the noodles on a damp towel so that they lay straight, wrapping the towel around them, so they do not dry out.

Place the oil and asparagus in a skillet over medium heat. When the asparagus begins to sizzle, season lightly with soy sauce and sauté until crisp-tender, about 5 minutes. Set aside to cool.

Place a sheet of sushi nori, shiny side down, on a bamboo mat or kitchen towel. Take 2 bundles of the noodles and slice off the end that was tied, from the string to the end. Spread the noodles lengthwise on the nori, edge to edge, leaving some nori exposed closest to and farthest from you. Lay 2 spears of asparagus on the noodles close to you, with some red pepper ribbons next to them. Using the mat as a guide, roll the nori around the filling, jellyroll style, creating a tight cylinder. Repeat with remaining ingredients to create three rolls.

Using a wet knife, slice each nori roll into 8 equal pieces. Arrange, cut side up, on a platter. Dot each piece with a dash of soy sauce and serve.

TEMPURA NORI SQUARES

My mother used to say that anything deep-fried created a party atmosphere, and she was right. Light and just rich enough, as well as loaded with minerals and vitamins as only sea vegetables can be, this easy-to-prepare appetizer or great starter course will win you rave reviews at your next party.
MAKES 4 TO 6 SERVINGS

Dipping Sauce
1 tablespoon freshly grated ginger juice
2 teaspoons soy sauce
1 teaspoon mirin
6 tablespoons spring or filtered water
2 scallions, finely minced

3 sheets toasted sushi nori
Avocado or light olive oil, for frying

Tempura Batter
½ cup whole wheat pastry flour
¼ cup yellow cornmeal
Pinch sea salt
1 tablespoon kuzu, dissolved in a small amount of cold water
About ½ cup dark beer

To make the dipping sauce: Combine all the ingredients in a small bowl. Set aside.

Cut the nori sheets into 3-inch squares or triangles, or both. Set aside, covered with a dry towel (to prevent the nori from curling).

Heat 2 to 3 inches oil over low heat until hot enough to fry (the oil is ready when patterns form, known as "dancing"). Preheat the oven to 250°F.

While the oil heats, *make the batter:* Combine the flour, cornmeal and salt in a mixing bowl. Stir in the dissolved kuzu and enough beer to make a batter that is slightly thicker than pancake batter.

When you are ready to fry, increase the heat to high. Dip one piece of nori at a time into the batter and drop gently into the hot oil. Cook, turning once, until golden brown, 1 to 2 minutes. Drain on a parchment-lined baking sheet and keep the fried nori in the warm oven while frying the remaining pieces.

Serve the tempura nori with the dipping sauce on the side.

HIZIKI WITH BURDOCK, BROCCOLI RABE AND LEMON

This powerful, delicious side dish has it all, graceful beauty, a bit of spice, dramatic strength and a sweet flavor, with just a touch of bitter.
MAKES 2 TO 3 SERVINGS

½ cup loosely packed, dried hiziki, rinsed well and soaked until softened
Soy sauce
Mirin
About 1 tablespoon extra-virgin olive oil
1 small burdock, cut into fine matchstick pieces
Generous pinch red pepper flakes

½ small bunch broccoli rabe, rinsed well and
  thinly sliced
Grated zest of ½ lemon
Sea salt
Juice of ½ lemon

Place the hiziki in a small saucepan and add a light
sprinkle of soy sauce and mirin. Add enough
water to half cover and bring to a boil, uncovered,
over medium heat. Cover, reduce the heat to low
and cook until the hiziki is tender and the liquid
has been absorbed, about 30 minutes. Set aside.

When the hiziki is nearly done, place the oil,
burdock and red pepper flakes in a skillet over
high heat. When the burdock sizzles, sauté until it
is well coated with oil, 1 to 2 minutes. Stir in the
broccoli rabe and lemon zest and season lightly
with salt. Sauté until the rabe is bright green and
wilted, about 3 minutes. Remove from the heat
and stir in the hiziki and lemon juice, tossing to
combine. Serve immediately.

≈≈ Did You Know? ≈≈
HIZIKI

Legend Eating hiziki creates strong shiny hair with
no split ends.

Fact The quality of our hair is determined by the
healthy functioning of our intestinal tract. Hiziki
is rich in trace minerals, calcium and in a keratin-
like protein that aids in the creation of the health
of our hair.

HIZIKI CAVIAR ON DAIKON ROUNDS

*For me there is nothing remotely cool about salty fish
eggs, but that's me. For most people, caviar conjures up
visions of beautiful people, glamorous affairs, Bentleys
and summers in the Hamptons. Mix this nutrient-rich
sea plant with rich sautéing, white wine, plenty of garlic,
and serve atop crisp, peppery daikon and you have the
perfect "glam" first course.*

MAKES 4 SERVINGS

About 2 tablespoons extra-virgin olive oil
3 to 4 cloves fresh garlic, finely minced
3 to 4 shallots, finely minced
½ cup loosely packed, dried hiziki, rinsed
  well, soaked until softened and finely
  diced
Dry white wine
Soy sauce
8 (¼-inch-thick) rounds fresh daikon
1 to 2 scallions, thinly sliced on the diagonal
¼ roasted red bell pepper (page 57), finely
  minced

Place the oil, garlic and shallots in a deep skillet
over high heat. When the shallots sizzle, sauté for
1 to 2 minutes. Stir in the hiziki and reduce the
heat to medium. Sauté for 1 minute. Add enough
white wine to half cover the ingredients, sprinkle
lightly with soy sauce, cover and bring to a boil.
Reduce the heat to very low and simmer until all
the wine has been absorbed into the hiziki, the
longer the better, 40 to 45 minutes. Stir occasionally to prevent scorching.

Bring a pot of water to a boil and cook the daikon until just crisp-tender, about 3 minutes. Drain well and set aside to cool.

To serve, mound the hiziki mixture on the daikon rounds and top with the scallions and bell pepper. Serve warm or at room temperature.

Note: You will have hiziki left over. You can make more daikon rounds (about 20 total) or serve the hiziki as a side dish.

HIZIKI SPIRALS

A delicious side dish and elegant to serve, this is a great way to introduce sea vegetables to those who may be a bit hesitant to try them. Calcium-rich hiziki makes this as good for us as it is tasty.
MAKES 5 TO 6 SERVINGS

Crepes
1 cup whole wheat pastry flour
1 tablespoon arrowroot
Sea salt
1 teaspoon baking powder
About 1 cup spring or filtered water
Light olive oil, for cooking

Hiziki Filling
½ cup dried hiziki, rinsed well, soaked until softened and minced
Soy sauce
Mirin
Spring or filtered water
About 1 tablespoon light sesame oil
2 cloves fresh garlic, minced

½ yellow onion, diced
2 to 3 scallions, finely minced

To make the crepes: Combine the flour, arrowroot, a pinch of salt and baking powder in a small mixing bowl. Slowly mix in enough water to make a thin, pancakelike batter. Set aside for 15 minutes. Brush oil in a small skillet or crepe pan over medium-low heat. Add 2 to 3 tablespoons of batter, turning the pan to create an even, thin round. Cook until the crepe easily lifts off the pan. Turn and cook the other side until it releases. Turn the crepe out onto a dry kitchen towel and place another towel over it. Repeat with remaining batter.

While the crepes cool, *make the filling:* Place the hiziki in a small saucepan. Add a light seasoning of soy sauce and mirin and enough water to just cover. Cover and bring to a boil over medium heat. Reduce the heat to low and cook until the hiziki is tender and all liquid has been absorbed, 30 to 35 minutes.

While the hiziki cooks, place the oil, garlic and onion in a skillet over medium heat. When the onion begins to sizzle, add a dash of soy sauce and sauté until the onions are quite limp and beginning to brown, 7 to 10 minutes. Stir the hiziki and scallions into the onions. Transfer to a mixing bowl and set aside to cool to room temperature.

To assemble, lay a crepe on a dry work surface. Spoon 2 to 3 tablespoons of filling across each crepe and roll, jelly-roll style, into firm cylinders. Slice each cylinder into 2-inch pieces. Arrange, cut sides up, on a platter and serve.

HIZIKI-TOFU CROQUETTES

Strongly flavored sea vegetables can be a bit exotic for some people's tastes. Try this side dish on those less adventurous diners. Packed with vegetables and tofu and gently fried, these are delicious.

MAKES 5 SERVINGS

Croquettes
½ block extra-firm tofu, crumbled
¼ cup dried hiziki, rinsed well, soaked until softened and diced
Spring or filtered water
Soy sauce
Mirin
1 carrot, diced
¼ cup diced burdock
¼ cup shelled hempseeds
Sea salt
¼ cup whole wheat pastry flour, if needed
Avocado or light olive oil, for frying

Dipping Sauce
1 tablespoon freshly grated ginger juice
Generous pinch red pepper flakes
3 tablespoons soy sauce
1 teaspoon mirin
1 teaspoon fresh lemon juice
3 tablespoons spring or filtered water

5 romaine lettuce leaves
1 small cucumber, cut into very thin diagonal slices

To make the croquettes: Place the tofu in a mixing bowl and mash with a fork to create a coarse paste.

Place the hiziki in a small saucepan with enough water to just cover. Season lightly with soy sauce and mirin, cover and bring to a boil over medium heat. Top with the carrot and burdock. Reduce the heat to low and cook until all the liquid has been absorbed, 30 to 35 minutes. Stir in the hempseeds and a pinch of salt and mix together to create a stiff consistency, using the pastry flour as necessary to achieve a consistency that can be shaped into 1-inch spheres. Set aside.

Heat 2 to 3 inches oil in a deep pot over medium heat. When the oil is hot, increase heat to high and gently drop 3 to 4 croquettes into the oil. Cook until golden and crisp on the outside, about 3 minutes. Drain on parchment paper and repeat with remaining hiziki mixture.

To make the sauce: Whisk all the ingredients together in a small bowl. Adjust seasoning to your taste.

To serve, arrange the lettuce leaves on 5 individual salad plates and distribute the cucumber slices evenly among the plates. Divide the croquettes among the plates and drizzle with the sauce.

HIZIKI WITH CORN AND SCALLIONS

Sea vegetables are without compare in their nutritional value. Mineral rich and loaded with vitamins, these strong-tasting plants are essential to our health and well-being, although an acquired taste for some. Dishes that balance their strength with naturally sweet vegetables take sea vegetables from required to desired.

MAKES 4 TO 6 SERVINGS

½ cup dried hiziki, rinsed well and soaked
   until softened
Spring or filtered water
Soy sauce
Mirin
Generous pinch red pepper flakes
About 1 tablespoon extra-virgin olive oil
2 cloves fresh garlic, thinly sliced
2 shallots, thinly sliced
5 to 6 scallions, thinly sliced on the diagonal
1 carrot, cut into fine matchstick pieces
½ cup fresh or frozen corn kernels
½ cup fresh or frozen peas

Place the hiziki in a small saucepan with enough water to just cover. Season lightly with soy sauce, mirin and red pepper flakes, cover and bring to a boil over medium heat. Reduce the heat to low and cook until all the liquid is absorbed, 30 to 35 minutes.

When the hiziki is nearly ready, place the oil, garlic and shallots in a skillet over medium heat. When the shallots begin to sizzle, add a dash of soy sauce and sauté for 2 minutes. Add the remaining vegetables, season lightly with soy sauce and mirin and sauté until the carrot is just crisp-tender, about 3 minutes. Stir in the hiziki. Transfer to a serving platter and serve hot.

MARINATED ARAME AND ROOT VEGETABLE SALAD

Delicate and a bit more mild-mannered than hiziki, arame is no shrinking violet. Rich in vitamins A and D, folic acid, trace minerals and other essential nutrients, arame joins forces with stamina-producing root vegetables to create a vitalizing salad.

MAKES 3 TO 4 SERVINGS

½ cup arame, rinsed well and set aside to
   soften (do not soak)
Mirin
Freshly squeezed lemon juice
Soy sauce
Extra-virgin olive oil
1 to 2 cloves fresh garlic, thinly sliced
1 teaspoon sea salt
2 tablespoons balsamic vinegar
½ yellow onion, cut into thin half-moon slices
1 small carrot, cut into fine matchstick pieces
1 small parsnip, cut into fine matchstick
   pieces
½ cup thinly sliced fennel bulb
2 to 3 sprigs fresh flat-leaf parsley, finely
   minced
2 to 3 leaves fresh red leaf lettuce, trimmed,
   arranged on a plate and chilled

Place the arame in a small, deep bowl. Cover completely with equal amounts of mirin, lemon juice, soy sauce and oil. Set aside to marinate for at least 30 minutes.

Place about 1 tablespoon oil, the garlic, salt and vinegar in a deep skillet over medium heat. Layer the onion, carrot, parsnip and fennel in the skillet and cover. When you hear the vegetables begin to sizzle, reduce the heat to low and allow the vegetables to simmer in the juices until tender, gently shaking the pan occasionally, about 30 minutes. Drain the arame, discarding the marinade. Remove the vegetables from the heat and stir in the arame, parsley and a light drizzle of lemon juice. Mound the salad on the chilled greens and serve.

ARAME TURNOVERS

Tender, flaky pastry wraps around richly flavored arame to create a tempting side dish. The mild-mannered phyllo dough gentles the strong taste of the arame, which is nicely balanced with sweet vegetables. A dreamy dish designed to enliven your energy.

MAKES 2 TO 4 SERVINGS

½ cup dried arame, rinsed well and
    set aside to soften (do not soak)
Spring or filtered water
Soy sauce
Mirin
2 shallots, thinly sliced
1 small carrot, cut into fine matchstick pieces
¼ cup fresh or frozen corn kernels
3 sheets phyllo dough, thawed

Extra-virgin olive oil
¼ cup toasted almonds, ground into fine meal

Place the arame in a small saucepan with enough water to half cover. Add generous dashes of soy sauce and mirin. Bring to a boil over medium heat. Cover, reduce the heat to low and simmer for 15 minutes. Layer the shallots, carrot and corn over the arame and re-cover. Simmer until all the cooking liquid has been absorbed into the dish.

Preheat the oven to 350°F and line a baking sheet with parchment paper.

Cut the phyllo sheets lengthwise into four equal strips. Lay one phyllo strip on a dry work surface, covering the remaining phyllo with a damp towel. Brush the phyllo strip with oil and sprinkle with some of the ground almonds. Lay another strip on top, brush with oil and sprinkle with some of the ground almonds. Lay a third sheet on top. Spoon about 3 tablespoons of the arame mixture onto one corner. Fold the phyllo around the filling as you would fold a flag, forming a layered triangle. Place on lined baking sheet. Repeat with remaining phyllo and filling to make four turnovers.

Before baking, brush each turnover lightly with oil and bake for 15 to 20 minutes, until the phyllo is crisp and golden brown.

ARAME WITH FRIED TEMPEH

Arame is a mild-tasting sea plant, but don't let that fool you. Arame is rich in minerals, vitamins and other essential nutrients. Its delicate taste makes it perfect for salads and side dishes for those who may not be used to the strong flavor of sea vegetables.

MAKES 3 TO 4 SERVINGS

Tempeh
**1 cup arame, rinsed well and set aside to
    soften (do not soak)**
Spring or filtered water
Soy sauce
Mirin
Light olive oil, for frying
4 ounces tempeh, cut into small triangles

Dressing
3 to 4 tablespoons stone-ground mustard
2 teaspoons sesame tahini
2 teaspoons brown rice syrup
1 teaspoon soy sauce
1 tablespoon brown rice vinegar
Spring or filtered water

6 red radishes, thinly sliced
2 to 3 scallions, thinly sliced on the diagonal
**1 red bell pepper, roasted over an open flame
    (page 57), peeled, seeded and diced**

To make the tempeh: Place the arame in a small saucepan with enough water to half cover. Season lightly with soy sauce and mirin, cover and bring to a boil. Reduce the heat to low and simmer until all liquid has been absorbed, about 20 minutes.

While the arame cooks, heat enough oil to cover the bottom of a skillet over medium heat. When the oil is hot, pan-fry the tempeh until golden, turning once to brown evenly. Drain on parchment paper and set aside.

To make the dressing: Combine all the ingredients, except water, and whisk until smooth. Slowly add enough water to make a smooth dressing. Adjust seasonings to taste.

Transfer the arame to a mixing bowl and stir in the radishes, scallions, bell pepper and tempeh. Fold in the dressing and stir to coat. Serve warm or at room temperature.

ARAME CABBAGE ROLLS

A lovely side dish, the delicately sweet flavor of cabbage balances the strong flavor of arame, making an interesting combination. I like this dish in the autumn, when cooler weather just begs for heartier fare.

MAKES 6 SERVINGS

Arame cabbage rolls
6 large cabbage leaves
**1 cup arame, rinsed well and set aside to
    soften (do not soak)**
Spring or filtered water
Soy sauce
Mirin
Light sesame oil
¼ cup fresh or frozen corn kernels
¼ cup diced winter squash
¼ cup diced carrots

Gravy

1 cup spring or filtered water

½ yellow onion, cut into thin half-moon slices

6 to 7 button mushrooms, brushed free of dirt and thinly sliced

Soy sauce

2 teaspoons kuzu, dissolved in small amount cold water

2 to 3 scallions, thinly sliced on the diagonal, for garnish

To make the cabbage rolls: Bring a pot of water to a boil and boil the cabbage leaves until just tender, about 3 minutes. Drain and lay flat on a plate to cool.

Place the arame in a small saucepan with enough water to half cover and a light seasoning of soy sauce, mirin and sesame oil. Layer the corn, squash and carrots on top of the arame. Bring to a boil, covered, over medium heat. Reduce the heat to low and simmer until the liquid has been absorbed, about 25 minutes.

Assemble the cabbage rolls by laying each leaf flat on a dry work surface. Spoon one-sixth of the arame filling onto the center of each leaf and fold and roll the cabbage to enclose the filling. Place, seam sides down, in a skillet. Arrange the rolls so that they fit snugly in a deep skillet. Add ¼ inch water to the skillet, cover and bring to a boil over medium heat. Reduce the heat to low and simmer until the cabbage is soft, about 15 minutes. Carefully transfer the cabbage rolls to a serving platter and cover loosely to keep warm.

To make the gravy: Combine the water, onion and mushrooms in a saucepan. Season lightly with soy sauce and bring to a boil, covered, over

medium heat. Reduce the heat to low and cook until the onions are soft, about 12 minutes. Stir in the dissolved kuzu and cook, stirring, until the gravy thickens and turns clear, about 3 minutes. Spoon the gravy over the cabbage rolls and garnish with scallions.

ARAME CUCUMBER SALAD

Because arame is partially cooked before drying, it tenderizes very easily. In this dish, we eliminate the cooking and simply marinate it for a cooling, mineral-rich salad that is the perfect summer side dish.

MAKES 4 TO 5 SERVINGS

1 cup arame, rinsed well and set aside to soften (do not soak)

2 teaspoons soy sauce

2 teaspoons umeboshi plum vinegar

1 tablespoon mirin

1 tablespoon toasted sesame oil

Grated zest of 1 lemon

1 medium cucumber, thinly sliced on the diagonal

3 to 4 scallions, thinly sliced on the diagonal

4 to 5 red radishes, thinly sliced

1 red bell pepper, roasted over an open flame (page 57), peeled, seeded and sliced into thin ribbons

1 small bunch watercress, rinsed well, coarsely chopped

Place the arame in a bowl and toss with the soy sauce, vinegar, mirin, oil and lemon zest. Set aside to marinate for 30 minutes.

Mix the arame with the remaining ingredients, adjust the seasonings to taste and chill thoroughly before serving.

Legend Cucumber facial masks make for flawless skin.

Fact Cucumbers contain potassium, vitamin C and folic acid in a combination that creates properties of purifying, cooling and relaxing.

KOMBU WITH SPICY ROOT VEGETABLES

Strengthening root vegetables, stir-fried to crisp perfection are splendid on their own, vitalizing, grounding, sweetly satisfying. Add to them the minerals and trace elements of kombu to create a side dish that keeps your focus on your dream.

MAKES 2 TO 3 SERVINGS

About 1 tablespoon light sesame oil
1 (6-inch piece) kombu, soaked until softened and cut into thin slices
Generous pinch red pepper flakes
Soy sauce
Mirin
1 small leek, split lengthwise, rinsed well, thinly sliced on the diagonal
½ cup fine matchstick pieces daikon
½ cup fine matchstick pieces carrot
½ cup thinly sliced rounds of fresh lotus root
Juice of ½ lemon
1 to 2 sprigs fresh flat-leaf parsley, minced

Heat the oil in a deep skillet over medium heat. Stir in the kombu and red pepper flakes. Add generous dashes of soy sauce and mirin and sauté for 2 to 3 minutes to infuse the kombu with rich flavor.

Stir in the leek and a dash of soy sauce. Sauté for 2 minutes. Stir in the daikon, carrot and lotus root, season lightly with soy sauce and stir-fry until the carrots are crisp-tender, 3 to 4 minutes. Remove from the heat and stir in the lemon juice and parsley.

SHIO KOMBU

Salty and slightly spicy, used to create vitality and to tone the reproductive system, this condiment is one of the strongest ways to eat your sea vegetables. Cooked slowly over low heat, the kombu grows rich, its nutrients concentrating to their peak, nourishing you to perform at your peak.

MAKES 4 TO 6 SERVINGS

3 (4-inch) pieces kombu, soaked until softened, sliced into 1-inch pieces
6 tablespoons soy sauce
2 tablespoons mirin
Generous pinch chili powder
Spring or filtered water

Place the kombu on the bottom of a small heavy pot. Add the soy sauce, mirin and chili powder. Add enough water to generously cover. Cook the kombu, uncovered, over very low heat until all the liquid has been absorbed into the kombu, 25 minutes to 1 hour. This dish is best for you when eaten in very small amounts, 2 to 3 slices per serving. Shio kombu will keep, refrigerated, for up to 2 weeks. Allow to come to room temperature before eating.

KOMBU SHOYU PICKLES

Pickles are an essential part of a healthy diet. They aid us in the process of assimilating nutrients from the rest of our food. The process of pickling is a lost art that would serve us well to be resurrected. Give this simple recipe a try and you'll be hooked.

MAKES 15 TO 20 SERVINGS

½ cup soy sauce
1 cup spring or filtered water
1 (8-inch) piece kombu, cut with scissors into
   1-inch pieces
1½ cups thinly sliced carrots
5 to 6 thin slices fresh ginger

Bring a pot of water to a boil and sterilize a 1½ quart jar by boiling for 5 minutes. Drain and cool to room temperature.

Place all the ingredients in the sterilized jar, cover loosely with cheesecloth and set in a cool place to pickle for 3 days. After 3 days, the pickles are ready to eat. Eat 1 to 2 pieces per serving. Covered tightly and refrigerated, the pickles will keep for 2 to 3 weeks.

DLT SANDWICHES

A strongly flavored take on the fat-laden BLT, Shep Earhardt of Maine Coast Sea Vegetables taught me this recipe. Jam-packed with flavor and interesting textures, this unique sandwich is great for casual lunches or picnics.

MAKES 6 TO 12 SERVINGS

About 1 tablespoon extra-virgin olive oil
1 cup dried dulse
12 slices whole-grain sourdough bread
Stone-ground mustard
6 leaves Romaine lettuce, rinsed well
2 fresh tomatoes, thinly sliced

Place the oil in a skillet over medium heat. Add the dulse and pan-fry, stirring constantly, until coated with oil and crisp, about 4 minutes. Drain on parchment paper and set aside.

To make the sandwiches, lay 6 slices of the bread on a dry work surface and spread with mustard. Lay a lettuce leaf on each slice; top with the tomatoes. Divide the dulse evenly among the 6 sandwiches and lay the remaining slices of bread on top. Slice diagonally and serve.

FRESH CORN SALAD

A North American sea plant, dulse is rich in magnesium and potassium, making it just perfect for this summer salad, when warm weather makes us perspire more, losing precious minerals that we need to replace to stay vital and healthy.

MAKES 3 TO 4 SERVINGS

Salad
4 ears fresh corn
1 carrot, cut into fine matchstick pieces
**3 stalks broccoli, cut into small florets and
    stems thinly sliced**
**1 cup dulse, soaked for 5 minutes and
    shredded**

Dressing
¼ cup extra-virgin olive oil
2 to 3 shallots, finely minced
2 cloves fresh garlic, finely minced
Sea salt
2 to 3 scallions, thinly sliced on the diagonal
Juice of 1 lemon
2 tablespoons balsamic vinegar

To make the salad: Bring a pot of water to a boil and cook the corn for 2 to 3 minutes. Remove with tongs, drain and set aside to cool. In the same water, boil the carrot until crisp-tender, about 2 minutes. Remove with a slotted spoon or skimmer, drain and transfer to a mixing bowl. In the same water, cook the broccoli florets and stems until crisp-tender, about 4 minutes. Drain and add to the carrot.

Using a sharp knife, remove the kernels from the cobs and stir into the carrot and broccoli. Fold in the dulse.

To make the dressing: Place the oil, shallots and garlic in a small saucepan over medium heat. When the shallots begin to sizzle, season lightly with salt and simmer for 4 to 5 minutes. Remove from the heat and whisk in the scallions, lemon juice and vinegar to combine ingredients. Pour the dressing over the vegetables and stir to coat. Serve warm.

≋ *Did You Know?* ≋
CORN

Legend It makes us happy, active and gregarious and is good for fertility.

Fact The only cereal grain native to America, corn is high in lysine, folic acid and fiber, which help us to feel vital and digest efficiently. Corn kernels are actually fertilized ovaries, hence the fertility legend.

DESIRABLE DESSERTS

Desserts have snuggled their way into our hearts, inspiring our deepest affections. Interestingly, the prime role dessert plays in our memories and in family traditions is a relatively recent phenomenon in the serving of a meal.

Our evolution of nourishment is one of grains, beans and essential crops, with meat, fish, dairy products and eggs playing secondary roles. Our culinary history is a fable of bread and wine, of aristocracy and impoverishment, of abundance and famine.

Dessert as a separate course has taken place only in the last few centuries. Before that, distinctions between sweet and savory flavors were less distinct, with meats and grains paired with fruits and sweets in the most common of dishes, from steamed puddings to pies. In ancient times, dessert-type dishes were served in between, and sometimes with, savory courses. For instance, a banquet said to be served in Pompeii, had, as its final course, molded sweet cream, assorted cakes, boar's head, and fricassee of wild duck.

On most occasions, sweet cakes and creamy puddings were served alongside meat and other savory side dishes. It wasn't until sixteenth-century England that dessert evolved to the end of the meal, as refined diners retired to another room for sweet wines, tarts, marmalades, preserved fruit and marzipan treats.

But it was the French who took dessert to the level of importance we enjoy today. Banquets were served in two principal courses. It wasn't until the table was completely cleared,

"de-served," that sweets were brought out to end the spectacle of dining.

Today, dessert takes on varying degrees of importance around the world. Italy and France have elevated dessert to a fine art. In Germany and Asia, dessert is, on many occasions, served outside the meal completely. In Budapest's and Vienna's opulent coffeehouses, cakes and other desserts are enjoyed throughout the day.

So, do we indulge? Do we forbid it? Do we sneak it? Do we brazenly serve it after a meal, enjoying every sensual bite? What do we do about this glorious affair with sweets?

Truth is, dessert can serve or destroy us. We know, without question, that sweet taste suppresses appetite, while salty, savory foods will spark it. Consuming dessert at the close of a meal signals us that it's time to stop eating, which explains why desserts in Europe are small, just a bite or two to cap off a satisfying meal and send your brain the message that you have had enough food.

I have long held to the belief that good-quality, fresh, homemade desserts actually serve us in our quest for better health—and not just because I love them so. Sweet taste is, above all others, the flavor we most love and crave. Why? Because sweet taste relaxes our bodies, relieves tension and, most important, makes us deliriously happy. If that's not enough for you, try this. Eating good-quality desserts on a regular basis keeps us satisfied within our diet, preventing binge eating, so we actually eat less.

There is bad news though. Good-quality desserts aren't easy to come by. You won't be hitting the drive-through window or convenience store to pick up a grain-sweetened, organic apple pie. You'll need to make these kinds of desserts at home, because desserts made from refined sugar, white flour, dairy products, artificial sweeteners, colorings, additives and chemicals will destroy your health faster than just about anything.

There's good news, too. Desserts made from whole, fresh ingredients are easy to make, are worth the effort and, in many ways, have more in common with a healthy bowl of soup than with calorie-dense, sugar-loaded, chemical-laced junk food. You don't need to be a rocket scientist or Martha Stewart to create luscious, tempting desserts for your family and friends. There are basic skills to learn—but once mastered, the world is your . . . uh . . . tartlet. Dessert making allows us to tap into our deepest well of passion for cooking and nourishing.

Not a fan of the school of thinking that dessert is an alchemy as complicated as brain surgery, I have always contended that the best bakers, whether home chef or pro, work from that well of passion. When you love making desserts, you will create the most wonderful, decadent, delicious treats imaginable. Master the basic skills, understand the ingredients and then throw caution to the wind, allowing your sensual, creative nature to guide your hand. Your results will be intoxicating.

But what about these illusive skills? Any book on baking and desserts can describe basic techniques of pastry making. When to whisk, when to knead, how to fold, mix and combine are all fundamental to baking.

Most of all, relax and take joy in the creation of dessert. Remember that stressed spelled backwards is . . . desserts.

INGREDIENTS

Study your ingredients; grow familiar with their textures, flavors and reactions to each other. Watch their behavior as you mix, whisk and knead them. See how they respond to your touch. Lose yourself in the sensations, delight in aromas, taste essences, raw and cooked; watch the ingredients reveal themselves to you; listen to their whispers. Enjoy the process as much as you enjoy the dessert itself. Remember that when you are creating whole, natural desserts, the only variable is in the ingredients. The techniques, the tried-and-true methods of dessert making, do not change. Only the ingredients have been altered to accommodate the desire to create dishes that will nourish us, body and soul. For your desserts to be as delicious as they can be, rely only on the finest quality . . . the freshest seasonal fruits, the purest extracts, organic soy and nut milks, fresh organic flours and sweeteners, pure sea salt, organic nuts and seeds and cold-pressed, organic oils. Nothing but the best you can find, and afford, should make it to your mixing bowl . . . and into your body.

Listed below are some of the ingredients that I use to create desserts.

Flour

I use only whole-wheat pastry flour when baking cakes, cookies, pie crusts, pastries, muffins, tortes, cupcakes, or other baked treats. A finer grind of flour than regular whole wheat flour (which is great for breads), it results in a lighter end product. I very rarely use white flour, bleached or unbleached, in my baking. It is highly refined and compromised, nutritionally deficient and really tough on the digestive tract.

Always whisk dry ingredients together to create air in the batter. Mix dry and wet ingredients separately and then simply fold them together until blended. This trick helps you avoid overmixing, which will most assuredly remove air from the batter, leaving you with a heavy, tough dough. Also, remember that whole grain loves moisture, so overmixing will cause the flour to saturate itself. So much for a light, springy cake!

Fats

To create moist textures in your pastries, you need to introduce some kind of fat or fat substitute. Conventional baked goods rely on milk, cream, eggs, butter, margarine, or artificial fat additives. Because I choose not to cook with any of those foods, I needed to find viable alternatives. I use avocado oil, hempseed oil (see page 232) and light olive oil. However, when adapting recipes, you will need to adjust liquid when using oil. Simply cut back equally on other liquids to accommodate the liquid of the oil—you will see more of that in the recipes.

Zest

Adding citrus zest to a recipe is one of the best ways I have found to add flavor to desserts that may be lacking because of diminished fat content. The zest is the colored part of the outer skin of lemons, oranges and other citrus fruits. Citrus zest adds tangy zip to fruit compotes, sauces, cakes, pastries and puddings. Since zest only has a mild sweet zing to it, you can pretty much use it as you desire.

Egg Substitutes

Eggs are used in desserts for two reasons: to leaven and/or to bind. With that in mind, eliminating them can create leaden pastries and cakes—not good. There are a couple of alternatives to eggs in dessert making. For leavening, you may simply add 1 teaspoon of baking powder for every egg in the recipe. (You want to look for nonaluminum baking powder; the products are clearly marked.)

In recipes in which eggs act as binders, I have simply substituted 1 teaspoon kuzu or arrowroot for each egg and have been quite successful. For custards or flan, a combination of agar flakes and kuzu has proved most satisfying in providing a firm, creamy pudding. Usually 1 teaspoon of each—kuzu and agar flakes—is enough to yield the firmest, creamiest custards.

Nuts

Nuts are a wonderful addition to healthful desserts for many reasons. Their fat content gives desserts a rich, distinctive flavor and their texture adds an interestingly appealing crunch. To get the best flavor from nuts, simply roast them lightly before use, the lower the oven temperature, the more flavorful the nuts. For instance, I roast pecans at 275°F for about 20 minutes to bring forth their delicate flavor. A too-high roasting temperature will result in bitter flavor. Pan-roasting nuts yields a more delicate flavor and is the method I prefer on most occasions.

Sweeteners

Now the real issue—sweeteners. The best-quality sweeteners I have found are grain based. Barley malt and brown rice syrup are the sweeteners I choose most often. The beauty of grain sweeteners is that they are complex sugars, not simple sugars, so they are released into the blood slowly, providing fuel for the body instead of the rush and crash we get from simple sugars. They are also not all that refined a product; they are simply whole grains, inoculated with a fermenting agent and then cooked until they reduce to a syrup.

Rice syrup yields a delicate sweetness with no aftertaste that is very satisfying. It is the perfect sweetener for most cakes, pastries, cookies and puddings. Barley malt has a stronger taste, much like molasses, so I reserve its use for desserts, that complement that kind of flavor, like spice cakes, carrot cakes and squash custards.

I rarely use honey, maple syrup or fruit sweeteners, again, because they are simple sugars and also because they have such a strong sweet taste. Grain sweeteners yield a lovely sweet taste, so there is no point in compromising for me. However, these are great sweeteners to use if grain sweeteners are unavailable or if you are making the transition from conventional, sugary desserts to healthier treats.

When using grain sweeteners, remember that they are liquid, so you will need to adjust your recipes to accommodate them. In adapting, I have found that substituting ½ cup of rice syrup for every 1 cup of sugar in a recipe yields a lovely sweet pastry.

So go . . . off with you . . . the world of sweets awaits you.

HAZELNUT CAKE

I can't imagine why Mother Nature created any other nut after the hazelnut. Rich, delicately flavored and moist, hazelnuts add depth of flavor and tenderness to any recipe. In this cake, they help create a tender, moist crumb and nutty flavor without compare.

MAKES 8 TO 10 SERVINGS

Hazelnut Cake

2½ cups whole wheat pastry flour

2 teaspoons baking powder

Generous pinch sea salt

¼ teaspoon ground cinnamon

1 teaspoon pure hazelnut or vanilla extract

⅓ cup avocado or light olive oil

½ cup brown rice syrup

½ to 1 cup vanilla soymilk

½ cup finely ground, lightly toasted hazelnuts

Mocha Glaze

1 cup nondairy, grain-sweetened chocolate chips

¼ cup vanilla soymilk

1 tablespoon brown rice syrup

1 tablespoon grain coffee

Preheat the oven to 350°F and lightly oil and flour a standard Bundt pan.

To make the cake: Combine the flour, baking powder, salt and cinnamon in a mixing bowl. Whisk briskly to impart air into the flour. Stir in the hazelnut extract, oil and rice syrup. Slowly mix in enough soymilk, stirring constantly, to create a smooth, pourable batter. Fold in the hazelnuts. Spoon the batter evenly into the prepared pan. Bake for 35 to 45 minutes, until the top of the cake springs back to the touch. Allow to cool in the pan for 10 minutes before inverting onto a wire rack to cool completely.

To make the glaze: Place the chocolate chips in a heat-resistant bowl. Combine the soymilk, rice syrup and grain coffee in a small saucepan and whisk briskly to dissolve the coffee. Cook over medium heat until the mixture reaches a high foam. Pour over the chocolate and whisk to create a smooth, satiny glaze.

Slip a piece of parchment paper under the wire rack holding the cake. Spoon the glaze over the cake, allowing it to run down the sides. Wait a few minutes and repeat, coating the cake with several layers of mocha glaze.

Note: To grind hazelnuts or other nuts, place in a food processor and pulse until ground into a fine meal. Do not process too much or you will have nut butter.

LINZER BAR COOKIES

Jam-filled, nutty cookies, based on the decadently rich linzer tortes. These bite-size jewellike treats make any occasion special.

MAKES 16 TO 18 SQUARES

½ cup avocado or light olive oil

½ cup brown rice syrup

¼ cup barley malt

1 teaspoon pure vanilla extract

1 teaspoon ground cinnamon

Grated zest of 1 lemon

Generous pinch sea salt

1 cup coarse almond meal

¾ cup arrowroot powder

¾ cup whole wheat pastry flour

½ teaspoon baking powder

½ cup unsweetened raspberry or strawberry preserves

Preheat the oven to 350°F and lightly oil and flour a 9-inch-square baking pan.

Place the oil, rice syrup, barley malt and vanilla in a saucepan over low heat, and cook, stirring, until loose. Remove from the heat and pour into a mixing bowl. Whisk in the cinnamon, lemon zest and salt. Mix in the almond meal, arrowroot, flour and baking powder, stirring to create a stiff dough.

Press half the dough firmly into the prepared pan. Spoon preserves evenly over the dough, right to the edges. Crumble the remaining dough over the preserves, covering completely. Bake for 30 to 35 minutes, until the dough is firm to the touch and the preserves are bubbling. Transfer the pan to a wire rack to cool completely before cutting into 1-inch squares.

STRAWBERRY COUNTRY TART

During that brief period of paradise when strawberries are in season, you must figure out ways to make them part of your daily diet. They are simply too wonderful, too sensual and too fleeting to let them pass you by. This casual tart showcases this splendid fruit in all its early summer glory.

MAKES 8 TO 10 SERVINGS

Pastry

1½ cups whole wheat pastry flour

Generous pinch sea salt

½ teaspoon baking powder

Generous pinch cinnamon

⅓ cup light olive oil

Spring or filtered water

Filling

1 quart strawberries, quartered

2 tablespoons arrowroot

Generous pinch sea salt

2 tablespoons avocado or light olive oil
4 tablespoons brown rice syrup
Grated zest of 1 lemon

½ cup Suzanne's Specialties Strawberry Rice
   Nectar, for glazing

Preheat the oven to 350°F and line a baking sheet
or pizza pan with parchment paper.

To make the pastry: Whisk the flour, salt, baking
powder and cinnamon in a mixing bowl. Using a
fork or a pastry cutter, cut the oil into the flour
mixture until it is the texture of wet sand. Slowly
add water, 1 tablespoon at a time, mixing until the
dough gathers into a soft, pliable ball, not too
sticky or too dry. Knead 3 to 4 times just to gather
the dough into a ball. Wrap in plastic wrap and set
aside.

To make the filling: Combine the strawberries,
arrowroot, salt, oil, rice syrup and lemon zest in a
bowl. Mix well, folding gently to coat all ingredients. Set aside.

Roll the dough out between two sheets of
parchment paper into a large round disk, about ⅛
inch thick. Transfer the dough to the prepared
pan. Spoon the filling onto the dough, leaving
about 2 inches of dough exposed around the
edge. Fold and pinch the edge of the dough up
over the filling, leaving the center exposed, creating an open-faced, circular, homestyle tart (known
as a galette). Bake for 35 to 40 minutes, until the
crust is golden and firm and the fruit is tender
and bubbling. (If the crust seems to be browning
too quickly, cover loosely with foil for 10 to 15
minutes.)

Remove the tart from oven and transfer to a
wire rack. Place about ½ cup strawberry rice nectar in a small saucepan and cook over high heat

until it foams. Spoon the glaze evenly over the
outer crust. Allow to stand for 10 minutes before
slicing into wedges.

FIG MOONS

*I make this wonderful cookie in the autumn, to celebrate
fig season. At their freshest best in cooler weather, figs are
sweet, sensual and richly satisfying with little enhancement. The filling is encased in a soft pastry, making for
the perfect sweet treat.*
MAKES 20 TO 24 COOKIES

Pastry
2 cups whole wheat pastry flour
Generous pinch sea salt
½ teaspoon baking powder
Pinch ground cinnamon
¼ cup avocado or light olive oil
¼ to ⅓ cup soymilk

Filling
20 to 24 fresh figs, trimmed and coarsely
   chopped
3 tablespoons brown rice syrup
Pinch sea salt
Grated zest of 1 lemon
2 to 3 tablespoons soymilk
1 to 2 tablespoons kuzu, dissolved in small
   amount cold water

Preheat the oven to 350°F and line a baking sheet
with parchment paper.

To make the pastry: Whisk the flour, salt, baking
powder and cinnamon in a mixing bowl. Using a
fork or a pastry cutter, cut the oil into the flour

mixture until it resembles the texture of wet sand. Slowly add soymilk, 1 tablespoon at a time, mixing until the dough gathers into a soft, pliable ball, not too sticky or too dry. Knead 2 to 3 times just to gather the dough into a ball. Wrap in plastic wrap and set aside.

To make the filling: Combine the figs, rice syrup, salt, lemon zest and soymilk in a saucepan over medium-low heat. Cook, stirring frequently, until the figs are soft, about 15 minutes. Stir in the dissolved kuzu and cook, stirring, until the mixture thickens, about 3 minutes.

Roll out the dough between two sheets of parchment paper into a rectangle that is about ⅛ inch thick. Using a 3-inch cookie cutter or glass, cut round shapes in the dough. Place a teaspoon of fig filling on one side of each round and fold over, creating a half moon. Seal the edges of each half moon with a fork, pressing them together to create a decorative edge. Place each cookie on the lined baking sheet. Repeat with the remaining ingredients, re-rolling the dough as necessary.

Bake the cookies for 20 to 28 minutes, until they are firm to the touch and the edges are lightly browned. Remove from the oven and transfer to a wire rack to cool completely.

Variation: For added zip, cook some rice syrup until it foams and spoon it over each cookie as a sticky glaze.

COCONUT DREAMS

Every year on my birthday, my mother would give me the option of a cake or these light-as-air, delightful cookies. My choice never varied. When I changed my eating patterns, I worked feverishly to duplicate these babies. The results are just wonderful.

MAKES 18 TO 24 COOKIES

Cookies
1½ cups whole wheat pastry flour
Generous pinch sea salt
1 teaspoon baking powder
½ cup unsweetened shredded coconut
¼ cup avocado or light olive oil
⅓ cup brown rice syrup
1 teaspoon pure vanilla extract
⅓ to ½ cup vanilla soymilk

Glaze
¼ cup almond amasake
¼ to ⅓ cup vanilla soymilk
2 teaspoons brown rice syrup
2 teaspoons kuzu, dissolved in small amount cold water
1 cup unsweetened shredded coconut, lightly toasted (see note below)

Preheat the oven to 350°F and line a baking sheet with parchment paper.

To make the cookies: Whisk together the flour, salt and baking powder in a mixing bowl. Mix in the coconut, oil, rice syrup and vanilla extract, stirring to combine. Slowly add enough soymilk, stirring, to create a soft, pliable dough. Do not overmix.

With moist hands, roll the dough into 1-inch spheres and arrange about 1 inch apart on the lined baking sheet. Bake for 13 to 15 minutes, until the cookies are firm, but still yield easily to touch. The cookies should still be soft when removed from the oven. Allow to stand, undisturbed on the baking sheet, for 5 minutes before transferring to a wire rack to cool completely.

To make the glaze: Place the amasake, soymilk and rice syrup in a small saucepan over low heat and warm through. Stir in the dissolved kuzu, and cook, stirring constantly, until the mixture thickens, about 3 minutes. Cover and set aside.

To finish the cookies, slip a piece of parchment paper under the wire cooling rack. Loosen the glaze with a whisk, if needed. Spoon over the cookies to coat and mound the coconut on top of each one.

Note: To toast the coconut, spread on a small baking sheet and bake at 350°F until light golden brown, 2 to 3 minutes. Keep an eye on the coconut, as it can burn quickly.

SESAME COOKIES

My husband is a pure-blooded Sicilian and loves all the treats that are a part of that rich culture. His favorite dessert is light and crispy, not too sweet sesame-coated cookies. After many failed attempts, I got them just the way he likes them. Enjoy!

MAKES 18 TO 24 COOKIES

2 cups whole wheat pastry flour
Generous pinch sea salt
1 teaspoon baking powder
Scant pinch cinnamon
¼ cup unsweetened shredded coconut
¼ cup avocado or light olive oil
⅓ cup brown rice syrup
1 teaspoon pure vanilla extract
¼ to ⅓ cup vanilla soymilk
About 1 cup tan sesame seeds

Preheat the oven to 350°F and line a baking sheet with parchment paper.

Whisk together the flour, salt, baking powder and cinnamon in a mixing bowl. Mix in the coconut, oil, rice syrup and vanilla. Slowly add enough soymilk, stirring, to create a soft, pliable dough. Do not overmix.

With moist hands, roll the dough into 1-inch spheres. Place the sesame seeds in a small bowl. Roll each cookie in the sesame seeds, covering completely. Arrange the cookies about 1 inch apart on the lined baking sheet. Bake for 18 to 21 minutes, until the cookies are firm to the touch. Allow to stand, undisturbed, on the baking sheet for about 5 minutes. Transfer to a wire rack to cool completely. The cookies will turn crisp as they cool.

≈ *Did You Know?* ≈
SESAME

Legend Sesame seeds are great for improving romance in our lives.

Fact Sesame seeds contain nutrients and compounds said to have antiarthritic and emollient properties, beneficial for nervous system and blood circulation. When we're flexible, easily stimulated and sensitive to touch, romance is a way of life.

~~~~~~~~~~~~~~~~~~~~~~~~~~~

NIPPLES OF VENUS

Chocolate and vanilla are like love and marriage. They just go together . . . and in these little bites, they are the perfect match. Rich, moist vanilla cookies with just a dab of decadent chocolate—yum.

MAKES 18 TO 24 COOKIES

Cookies
2 cups whole wheat pastry flour
Generous pinch sea salt
1 teaspoon baking powder
Scant pinch ground cinnamon
½ cup unsweetened shredded coconut
¼ cup avocado or light olive oil
⅓ cup brown rice syrup
1 teaspoon pure vanilla extract
¼ to ⅓ cup vanilla soymilk

Chocolate Glaze
⅔ cup nondairy, grain-sweetened chocolate chips, plus 18 to 24 chips, for garnish
¼ cup vanilla soymilk
1 teaspoon Suzanne's Specialties Chocolate Rice Nectar

Preheat the oven to 350°F and line a baking sheet with parchment paper.

To make the cookies: Whisk together the flour, salt, baking powder and cinnamon in a mixing bowl. Mix in the coconut, oil, rice syrup and vanilla. Slowly add enough soymilk, stirring, to create a soft, pliable dough. Do not overmix.

With moist hands, roll the dough into 1-inch spheres and arrange about 1 inch apart on the lined baking sheet. Bake for 15 to 18 minutes until firm, but still tender. Immediately transfer to a wire rack to cool completely.

To make the glaze: Place the chocolate chips in a heat-resistant bowl. Place the soymilk and chocolate rice nectar in a small saucepan and bring to a rolling boil. Pour over the chocolate chips and whisk to create a smooth, shiny glaze.

Using a small spoon, dab a small bit of glaze on the center of each cookie and press a chocolate chip into the center of the glaze, creating the nipple.

Note: You will have more chocolate glaze than you will need, but it will keep, refrigerated, for about 1 week. You'll need to loosen it before using.

~~~~~~~~~~~~~~~~~~~~~~~~~~~

SHEILA'S LACY WAFERS

My dear friend Sheila Davidson is famous for her exquisitely beautiful holiday cookies. A tin of her jewel-like treats is simply the best gift you can get. On occasion, she grants me the great privilege of working with her on a baking day. This great cookie is the result. You'll love it and won't reserve it for special occasions. It'll be a regular.

MAKES 30 TO 40 COOKIES

Cookies
¼ cup avocado or light olive oil
¼ cup brown rice syrup

¼ cup barley malt

⅓ cup whole wheat pastry flour

½ cup quick rolled oats

¼ cup very finely chopped almonds or walnut pieces

¼ teaspoon pure vanilla or almond extract

Chocolate Filling

1 cup nondairy, grain-sweetened chocolate chips

2 teaspoons Suzanne's Specialties Chocolate Rice Nectar

¼ cup vanilla soymilk

Preheat the oven to 350°F and line a baking sheet with parchment paper.

To make the cookies: Place the oil, rice syrup and barley malt in a small saucepan over low heat and cook, stirring, until loose. Remove from the heat and transfer to a mixing bowl. Stir in the flour until smooth. Fold in the oats, nuts and vanilla, mixing well.

Drop the batter, by ¼ teaspoonfuls onto the lined baking sheet, spacing 2 inches apart. Bake for 8 to 10 minutes, until golden brown. Cool on the baking sheet for 1 minute. Carefully peel cookies from the parchment paper and set aside to cool.

To make the filling: Place the chocolate chips in a heat-resistant bowl. Bring the chocolate rice nectar and soymilk to a rolling boil over high heat. Pour over the chocolate chips and whisk until shiny and smooth.

Select pairs of similar-size cookies to make sandwiches. Spread the flat side of one cookie with the chocolate glaze and press its partner's flat side to the chocolate, making a sandwich. Place on parchment paper to allow the chocolate to set. Repeat with the remaining cookies and chocolate.

CHOCOLATE-DIPPED BISCOTTI

These double-baked crisp cookies are just the best for dipping in strong espresso . . . or tea for the more delicate of heart. Cocoa powder, chocolate chips and chocolate glaze make these delicious cookies a chocolate lover's dream.

MAKES 24 TO 30 BISCOTTI

Biscotti

1⅔ cups whole wheat pastry flour

⅓ cup unsweetened cocoa powder

2 teaspoons baking powder

Generous pinch sea salt

Scant pinch ground cinnamon

⅓ cup hempseed or light olive oil

½ cup brown rice syrup

1 teaspoon pure vanilla extract

½ to ⅔ cup vanilla soymilk

8 ounces nondairy, grain-sweetened chocolate chips

Ganache

1 cup nondairy, grain-sweetened chocolate chips

2 teaspoons Suzanne's Specialties Chocolate Rice Nectar

¼ cup vanilla soymilk

Preheat the oven to 350°F and line a baking sheet with parchment paper.

To make the biscotti: Whisk together the flour, cocoa, baking powder, salt and cinnamon in a mixing bowl. Mix in the oil, rice syrup and vanilla, stirring to combine. Slowly add soymilk, stirring, to create a soft, pliable dough. Fold in the chocolate chips to incorporate them into the dough. Divide the dough in half and, with moist hands, form each half into a log about 10 inches long and 2 inches wide. Bake for 30 to 35 minutes, until the top of each log is firm. Allow to stand on the baking sheet for 2 minutes. Carefully transfer each log to a dry cutting board, and using a sharp serrated knife, slice each log into ¾-inch-thick slices. Lay the slices, cut sides up, on the baking sheet and bake for 3 minutes. Turn the slices so the other cut sides are up and bake for 3 to 4 minutes, until the cookies are crisp. Allow to cool completely on the baking sheet.

To make the ganache: Place the chocolate chips in a heat-resistant bowl. Combine the chocolate rice nectar and soymilk in a small saucepan and bring to a rolling boil over high heat. Pour over the chocolate chips and whisk to form a smooth, shiny ganache.

Dip one half of each biscotti into the ganache and place on parchment paper. Allow to stand until the ganache sets. You can also place the ganache in a squeeze bottle and drizzle over each cookie.

Note: Hempseed oil is high in an albuminlike protein (like egg whites) and helps prevent the biscotti from crumbling when slicing.

LEMON-NUTMEG SHORTBREADS

Just crisp enough to be light, just chewy enough to be satisfying, with just a hint of lemon flavor to keep them sparklingly delicious.
MAKES 12 COOKIES

½ cup whole wheat pastry flour
½ cup semolina flour
2½ tablespoons arrowroot
¼ teaspoon nutmeg
Pinch ground cinnamon
Pinch sea salt
½ cup avocado or light olive oil
⅓ cup brown rice syrup
1 teaspoon pure vanilla extract
Grated zest of 1 lemon

Preheat the oven to 350°F and line a baking sheet with parchment paper.

Whisk together the flours, arrowroot, nutmeg, cinnamon and salt in a mixing bowl. Add the oil, rice syrup, vanilla and lemon zest, and mix until dough begins to come together.

Turn the dough out onto parchment paper, gather into a ball and flatten into a disk with your hands. Cover with a second sheet of parchment paper and roll the dough into a rectangle, ¼ inch thick. Using a sharp knife, slice the dough into 2-inch squares. Carefully transfer cookies to the lined baking sheet. Bake for 15 to 18 minutes, until firm to the touch and just beginning to color at the edges. Transfer to a wire cooling rack to cool completely.

Variation: For added richness, cook ½ cup brown rice syrup until it foams and drizzle over the cooled cookies.

CHOCOLATE CHUNK, ORANGE AND HAZELNUT COOKIES

I love these babies. Loaded with chocolate bits, hazelnut pieces and laced through with just a hint of chocolate, they are a cookie lover's dream.

MAKES 20 TO 24 COOKIES

1¼ cups whole wheat pastry flour
½ teaspoon baking powder
Pinch sea salt
1 teaspoon pure vanilla extract
⅓ cup avocado or light olive oil
½ cup brown rice syrup
2 tablespoons grated orange zest
½ to ⅔ cup soymilk
1 cup nondairy, grain-sweetened chocolate chips
1½ cups hazelnuts, lightly toasted, skins removed and coarsely chopped (see box)

Preheat the oven to 350°F and line 2 baking sheets with parchment paper.

Whisk together the flour, baking powder and salt in a mixing bowl. Stir in the vanilla, oil, rice syrup and orange zest. Slowly add the soymilk, stirring to create a soft, spoonable dough. Fold in the chocolate chips and hazelnuts.

Drop the dough by heaping tablespoonfuls onto lined baking sheets, spacing 2 inches apart. Press the dough to flatten slightly. Bake for 13 to 15 minutes, until just firm to the touch and beginning to brown. Do not overcook or the cookies will harden as they cool. Transfer the cookies to a wire cooling rack to cool completely.

HAZELNUTS

To roast hazelnuts, place the nuts on a baking sheet, taking care to make only one layer. Roast for about 10 minutes until fragrant. Remove from the oven and transfer the hazelnuts to a paper sack. Seal and allow to steam in the sack for 15 minutes. Transfer the hazelnuts to a towel and rub gently to remove the skins.

PECAN CRESCENTS

I love to serve these cookies in the autumn, with a lovely side dish of fresh, crisp pears. The marriage of cool pear slices and warm cookies are just the sweetest way to welcome the cool weather of the season.
MAKES 24 TO 30 COOKIES

Cookies
1 cup whole wheat pastry flour
½ teaspoon baking powder
Pinch sea salt
½ teaspoon ground cinnamon
¾ cup pecans, lightly toasted
1 teaspoon pure vanilla extract
½ cup avocado or light olive oil
¼ cup brown rice syrup

Glaze
⅔ cup brown rice syrup
¼ cup fine pecan meal (see note below)

Preheat the oven to 350°F and line a baking sheet with parchment paper.

To make the cookies: Combine the flour, baking powder, salt, cinnamon and pecans in a food processor and pulse until a coarse meal forms. Transfer to a mixing bowl and stir in the vanilla, oil and rice syrup, mixing until the dough comes together.

Take 2 teaspoons of dough in your hands and roll into a 2½-inch log. Lay on lined baking sheet and bend to a crescent shape, pinching the ends to a taper. Repeat with remaining dough, spacing the cookies about 1 inch apart.

Bake for 18 to 20 minutes, until the cookies are just firm to the touch. Allow to cool on the bak-ing sheet for 5 minutes before transferring them to a wire rack to cool completely.

To make the glaze: Bring the rice syrup to a foaming boil, remove from the heat and stir in the pecan meal. When the cookies have cooled, roll them in the pecan syrup to coat. If the syrup thickens while you're working, place the pan over low heat to loosen.

Note: To make pecan meal, lightly toast pecans, place in a food processor and pulse to create a fine meal.

GIANT CHOCOLATE COOKIES

If you love chocolate—and who doesn't?—then these treats are for you. Richly flavored with cocoa powder and laced through with whole nuts and chocolate chips, these cookies are a delicious, decadent indulgence.
MAKES 18 TO 24 COOKIES.

Cookies
1⅓ cups whole wheat pastry flour
⅔ cup unsweetened cocoa powder
1 teaspoon baking powder
Pinch sea salt
Generous pinch cinnamon
Scant pinch chili powder
⅓ cup avocado or light olive oil
1 teaspoon pure vanilla extract
½ cup brown rice syrup
½ to ⅔ cup vanilla soymilk
¼ cup unsweetened shredded coconut

1 cup nondairy, grain-sweetened chocolate chips

1 cup pecan pieces, lightly roasted

Chocolate Glaze

¼ cup nondairy, grain-sweetened chocolate chips

2 to 3 tablespoons soymilk

1 teaspoon Suzanne's Specialties Chocolate Rice Nectar

Preheat the oven to 350°F and line 2 baking sheets with parchment paper.

To make the cookies: Whisk together the flour, cocoa, baking powder, salt, cinnamon and chili powder. Stir in the oil, vanilla and rice syrup. Slowly add the soymilk, stirring, to create a soft dough. Fold in the coconut, chocolate chips and pecan pieces. Mix well to incorporate the nuts and chocolate within the dough. Drop by 2 tablespoonfuls, 2 inches apart onto lined baking sheets, pressing and shaping the cookies into rounds.

Bake for 18 to 21 minutes, until the cookies are just firm to the touch. Allow to cool on the baking sheets for 5 minutes. Transfer to wire cooling racks to cool completely.

To make the glaze: Place the chocolate chips in a heat-resistant bowl. Place the soymilk and chocolate rice nectar in a small saucepan and bring to a rolling boil. Pour over the chocolate chips and whisk to create a smooth, shiny glaze. Using a fork, drizzle the chocolate over the tops of the cookies.

≋ *Did You Know?* ≋
CHOCOLATE

Legend Known as a "food of the gods," chocolate is synonymous with love and romance.

Fact Cultivated since the Mayan and Aztec cultures, cocoa was said to be a gift of the gods, sent to bring fortune and strength. Cocoa is rich in phenylethylamine, which produces the same euphoria as being in love.

CHOCOLATE WALNUT COOKIES

I love making these cookies for the holidays. They're so delicious, but not too heavy; rich, but small—so your tongue is teased to chocolate satisfaction.

MAKES 24 TO 36 COOKIES

Cookies
1⅓ cups whole wheat pastry flour
⅔ cup unsweetened cocoa powder
½ teaspoon baking powder
Pinch sea salt
Generous pinch ground cinnamon
⅓ cup avocado or light olive oil
⅓ cup brown rice syrup
¼ cup barley malt
1 teaspoon pure vanilla extract
¼ to ½ cup vanilla soymilk
½ cup finely minced walnut pieces
24 to 36 whole walnut pieces

Chocolate Glaze
½ cup nondairy, grain-sweetened chocolate
   chips
2 to 3 tablespoons vanilla soymilk
2 tablespoons Suzanne's Specialties Chocolate
   Rice Nectar
Scant pinch cinnamon

Preheat the oven to 350°F and line 2 baking sheets with parchment paper.

To make the cookies: Whisk together the flour, cocoa, baking powder, salt and cinnamon in a mixing bowl. Stir in the oil, rice syrup, barley malt and vanilla. Slowly add the soymilk, stirring, to create a soft, pliable dough. Fold in the minced walnut pieces.

Roll tablespoons of dough into spheres and place about 1½ inches apart on lined baking sheets. Press a whole walnut into the center of each cookie. Bake for 15 to 18 minutes, until the cookies have puffed and are just firm to the touch. Do not overbake or the cookies will harden as they cool. Transfer the cookies to a wire rack to cool.

To make the glaze: Place the chocolate chips in a heat-resistant bowl. Place the soymilk, chocolate rice nectar and cinnamon in a small saucepan and bring to a rolling boil. Pour over the chocolate chips and whisk to create a smooth, shiny glaze. Using a fork, drizzle the chocolate over the cookies.

GERMAN SPICE COOKIES

These cookies are so wonderful. They're perfect any time—on a lazy Sunday, a chilly autumn afternoon, a special occasion or a holiday feast.

MAKES ABOUT 24 COOKIES

1½ cups whole wheat pastry flour
½ teaspoon baking powder
Pinch sea salt
½ teaspoon ground ginger
Generous pinch ground cinnamon
Scant pinch nutmeg
1 teaspoon pure vanilla extract
⅓ cup avocado or light olive oil

⅓ cup barley malt

¼ cup brown rice syrup

¼ to ⅓ cup vanilla soymilk

½ cup finely ground blanched almonds (see note, below)

Preheat the oven to 350°F and line 2 baking sheets with parchment paper.

Whisk together the flour, baking powder, salt, ginger, cinnamon and nutmeg in a mixing bowl. Stir in the vanilla, oil, barley malt and rice syrup. Slowly mix in the soymilk, stirring, to create a soft, formable dough. Fold in the almonds.

Roll tablespoonfuls of dough into spheres and place them about 2 inches apart on the lined baking sheets. Press gently to form disks. Bake for 15 to 18 minutes, until the cookies puff slightly and are just firm to the touch. Transfer to a wire rack to cool completely.

Note: You can purchase blanched almonds or blanch them yourself. Bring a small pot of water to a boil and cook almonds for 5 minutes. Drain and cool. Simply slip skins off almonds.

GINGER CAKE WITH APRICOT STICKY SAUCE

Sweet and spicy make a great match, bringing out the best in one another. The spicy flavors make the sweet seem sweeter and the sweet taste showcases the depth of flavor in the earthy spices. This perfect early autumn dessert marries a richly flavored spice cake with the last apricots of summer.

MAKES 9 TO 10 SERVINGS

Sauce

6 to 8 fresh apricots, diced

1 cup dried apricots, diced

3 tablespoons brown rice syrup

¼ cup fresh orange juice

¼ cup vanilla soymilk

Pinch sea salt

Grated zest of 1 lemon

Ginger Cake

2½ cups whole wheat pastry flour

1 tablespoon baking powder

Generous pinch sea salt

4 teaspoons ground ginger

1 teaspoon ground cinnamon

¼ teaspoon ground allspice

1 tablespoon grain coffee, dissolved in 1 cup hot spring or filtered water

½ cup avocado or light olive oil

½ cup brown rice syrup

¼ cup barley malt

1½ teaspoons pure vanilla extract

½ to 1 cup vanilla soymilk

2 tablespoons finely grated fresh ginger

2 cups coarsely minced walnut pieces

Preheat the oven to 350°F and lightly oil and flour a standard Bundt pan or 12 giant muffin cups (to make individual cakes).

To make the sauce: Combine all the ingredients in a heavy saucepan over medium heat. Bring the sauce to a boil, uncovered. Cover, reduce the heat to low and simmer until the dried apricots are soft, about 25 minutes. Remove cover and cook, stirring occasionally, until the sauce thickens slightly. Set aside to cool.

To make the cake: Whisk together the flour, baking powder, salt, ground ginger, cinnamon and allspice. Mix in the dissolved coffee, oil, rice syrup, barley malt and vanilla. Slowly add the soymilk, stirring, to create a smooth, spoonable batter. Fold in the fresh ginger and walnuts.

Spoon the batter evenly into the prepared pan. Bake for 35 to 45 minutes, until the top springs back to the touch. (Smaller cakes will require a little less baking time.) Allow to cool in the pan for about 10 minutes. Loosen the cake from the pan side with a butter knife and invert it onto a plate to cool completely.

To serve, place a wedge of cake on an individual dessert plate and spoon some of the sauce over the top.

PEACH BREAD WITH ORANGE GLAZE

One of the best things about summer is fresh, succulent peaches so lush with sweet juice that they intoxicate us for the short time we can enjoy their luscious presence in our lives. This bread showcases their brilliance splendidly.
MAKES 8 TO 10 SERVINGS

Bread
3 cups coarsely chopped peaches
3 tablespoons fresh orange juice

⅔ cup Suzanne's Specialties Raspberry Rice Nectar
Sea salt
3 cups whole wheat pastry flour
2½ teaspoons baking powder
⅓ cup avocado or light olive oil
⅔ cup coarsely chopped walnuts
⅔ cup rolled oats
½ to 1 cup soymilk

Orange Glaze
⅔ cup brown rice syrup
Grated zest of 1 orange

Preheat the oven to 350°F and lightly oil and flour a standard Bundt pan.

To make the bread: Purée 1 cup of the peaches in a food processor and place in a saucepan with the orange juice, raspberry rice nectar and a pinch of salt. Cook over low heat for 5 minutes. Set aside to cool.

Whisk together the flour, baking powder and a pinch of salt. Mix in the peach mixture, oil, walnuts, oats, remaining chopped peaches and enough soymilk to create a smooth, spoonable batter. Spoon into the prepared pan. Bake for 50 to 60 minutes, until the top of the bread springs back to the touch. Allow to cool in the pan for about 10 minutes. Loosen the bread from the pan side with a butter knife and invert it onto a plate to cool completely before glazing.

To make the glaze: Heat the rice syrup and orange zest in a saucepan until it foams. Spoon the glaze over the bread in thin layers to coat.

ORANGE COFFEE CAKE WITH CHOCOLATE-PECAN STREUSEL

Absolutely decadent . . . but not so rich that you can't enjoy a healthy slice. The hint of orange so enhances the chocolate that it's intoxicating. The pecans are just the right level of richness to create the perfect combo. Don't forget the omega-3 essential fatty acid in the hempseeds. Talk about having your cake and eating it, too!
MAKES 10 TO 12 SERVINGS

Streusel
1½ cups FruitSource granulated sweetener

1 tablespoon ground cinnamon

6 tablespoons avocado or light olive oil

1½ cups coarsely chopped lightly toasted pecan pieces

2 teaspoons shelled hempseeds

1 cup nondairy, grain-sweetened chocolate chips

Cake
3 cups whole wheat pastry flour

1 tablespoon baking powder

Generous pinch sea salt

¾ cup avocado or light olive oil

⅔ cup brown rice syrup

1 teaspoon pure vanilla extract

Grated zest of 1 orange

1½ cups whipped silken tofu (see note below)

¼ cup fresh orange juice

½ to 1 cup vanilla soymilk

Preheat the oven to 350°F and lightly oil and flour a 13 × 9-inch baking pan.

To make the streusel: Whisk the sweetener and cinnamon together to blend. Add the oil and mix with a fork to create small, moist clumps. Mix in the pecans, hempseeds and chocolate chips. Set aside.

To make the cake: Whisk together the flour, baking powder and salt in a mixing bowl, whisking briskly to impart air into the batter. Mix in the oil, rice syrup, vanilla, orange zest, tofu and orange juice. Slowly add soymilk, stirring, to create a smooth, spoonable batter. Spoon half the batter evenly into the prepared pan. Sprinkle half the streusel over the batter. Spoon the remaining batter over the streusel and carefully spread evenly. Sprinkle with remaining streusel.

Bake for 20 minutes. Loosely cover with foil, so the topping doesn't brown too quickly, and bake for 20 minutes more. Remove the foil and bake for 15 to 20 minutes, until the cake springs back to the touch. Allow to cool for 10 to 15 minutes before slicing.

Note: For whipped silken tofu, simply purée in a food processor or blender until smooth.

BLOOD ORANGE TART WITH CARAMEL GLAZE

When they're in season, blood oranges rule. I put them in salads, add their luscious juice to sauces, or simply munch on them. When I want to showcase their stunning beauty and delicious flavor, I make this tart.

MAKES 10 TO 12 SERVINGS

Pastry
1½ cups whole wheat pastry or kamut flour
Pinch sea salt
⅓ cup avocado or light olive oil
Cold spring or filtered water

Orange Custard
2 cups soymilk
1 cup plain amasake
1 teaspoon pure vanilla extract
2 tablespoons brown rice syrup
⅓ cup freshly squeezed blood orange juice
2 teaspoons freshly squeezed lemon juice
Grated zest of 1 blood orange
3 tablespoons kuzu, dissolved in small amount blood orange juice

Blood Orange Topping
6 to 8 blood oranges
½ cup brown rice syrup

Preheat the oven to 350°F and lightly oil an 11-inch tart pan with a removable bottom.

To make the pastry: With a fork, mix the flour, salt and oil in a bowl until it forms the texture of wet sand. Slowly add water, 1 tablespoon at a time, mixing just until the flour gathers into a smooth ball of dough. Knead 3 to 4 times just to gather the dough together. Roll the dough out between two sheets of parchment paper into a circle 1 inch larger than the pan. Fit the dough into the pan, without stretching, gently pressing it into all the curves of the pan. Cut the excess crust flush with the top of the rim. Pierce in several places with a fork. Cover loosely with foil and bake for 7 minutes. Remove the foil and bake for 7 to 8 minutes, until the crust is firm and lightly browned. Set aside to cool.

To make the custard: Combine the soymilk, amasake, vanilla extract and rice syrup in a saucepan over low heat. Cook until warmed through. Add the orange juice, lemon juice and orange zest to the pan and cook for 1 minute. Stir in the dissolved kuzu, and cook, stirring, until the mixture thickens, 3 to 4 minutes. Spoon into a heat-resistant bowl and cover with plastic wrap. Set aside to cool.

When the crust and custard have cooled to room temperature, loosen the custard with a whisk. Spread evenly in the pie shell, filling abundantly.

To make the topping: Peel the oranges, removing all the white pith. Cut the oranges into thin slices; remove any seeds. Arrange the orange slices over the custard in concentric circles, covering completely. Remove the tart from the pan. Bring the rice syrup to a boil over high heat, cooking until it foams. Spoon over the orange tart to cover the fruit completely, allowing the glaze to run over the sides. Allow to stand for 10 to 15 minutes before slicing into wedges.

VANILLA FLAN

There's nothing quite like a light, delicately sweet flan to end any meal, from a casual weeknight dinner to a holiday feast fit for royalty. Don't let its elegant presentation intimidate you; it doesn't get easier than this one.

MAKES 4 TO 5 SERVINGS

Flan

1½ cups vanilla soymilk

2 teaspoons brown rice syrup

Grated zest of 1 lemon

1 vanilla bean, split lengthwise, pulp
   removed

Pinch sea salt

2 tablespoons agar flakes

1 tablespoon kuzu, dissolved in small amount
   cold water

Glaze

5 tablespoons barley malt

1 tablespoon brown rice syrup

½ teaspoon pure vanilla extract

1 teaspoon freshly squeezed lemon juice

Fresh mint leaves or seasonal berries, to
   decorate

Lightly oil 4 or 5 (5- to 6-ounce) custard cups or ramekins.

To make the flan: Place the soymilk, rice syrup, lemon zest, vanilla pulp, salt and agar in a saucepan over low heat. Cook, stirring frequently, until the agar dissolves, about 20 minutes. Stir in the dissolved kuzu, and cook, stirring, until the mixture thickens, about 3 minutes. Spoon the mixture into the prepared cups. Set aside at room temperature

for 20 minutes. Place in the refrigerator until firmly set, about 1 hour.

Before serving, invert the ramekins onto individual serving plates.

To make the glaze: Combine the barley malt, rice syrup and vanilla extract in a saucepan over medium heat. Bring to a rolling boil. Remove from the heat, whisk in the lemon juice and cool for 1 to 2 minutes. Whisk to loosen and spoon over each flan. Serve decorated with mint leaves.

≈≈≈ *Did You Know?* ≈≈≈
AGAR

Legend This odorless, flavorless sea vegetable can keep you "regular."

Fact Composed of several species of red seaweed, agar is made by boiling and filtering the seaweed, leaving its polysaccharide status intact. Then it's filtered and neutralized with sodium bicarbonate. The fiber and sodium bicarbonate work together to create a mild laxative.

CHOCOLATE AND COCONUT PECAN TART

Chocolate, chocolate and more chocolate, and if that's not enough to tempt you with this special occasion dessert, we added coconut and pecans for some richness. This decadently luscious treat is one of life's great pleasures.

MAKES 10 TO 12 SERVINGS

Pastry

1½ cups whole wheat pastry flour
6 tablespoons unsweetened cocoa powder
¼ cup FruitSource granulated sweetener
Pinch sea salt
⅓ cup avocado or light olive oil
¼ to ⅓ cup vanilla soymilk

Filling

2 cups soymilk
½ cup plain amasake
¼ cup Suzanne's Specialties Chocolate Rice Nectar
1 teaspoon pure vanilla extract
Scant pinch cinnamon
Pinch sea salt
1 to 2 tablespoons kuzu, dissolved in small amount cold water
1¼ cups nondairy, grain-sweetened chocolate chips, plus some extra for garnish
¾ cup unsweetened shredded coconut
1½ cups pecan halves, lightly toasted

Preheat the oven to 350°F and lightly oil an 11-inch tart pan with a removable bottom.

To make the pastry: With a fork, mix the flour, cocoa, sweetener, salt and oil in a bowl until it is the texture of wet sand. Slowly add soymilk, 1 tablespoon at a time, mixing just until the flour gathers into a smooth ball of dough. Knead 3 to 4 times just to gather the dough together. Roll the dough out between two sheets of parchment paper into a circle 1 inch larger than the pan. Fit the dough into the pan, without stretching, gently pressing it into all the curves of the pan. Cut away the excess crust flush with the top of the rim. Pierce in several places with a fork. Cover loosely with foil and bake for 7 minutes. Remove the foil and bake for 7 to 8 minutes, until the crust is firm and lightly browned. Set aside to cool.

To make the filling: Combine the soymilk, amasake, chocolate rice nectar, vanilla, cinnamon and salt in a saucepan over low heat. Cook until hot. Stir in the dissolved kuzu, and cook, stirring, until the mixture thickens, about 3 minutes. Stir in the chocolate chips and whisk briskly until they melt and the mixture becomes silky smooth. Remove from the heat and fold in the coconut.

Remove the pie shell from the pan and place on a serving platter. Spoon the filling evenly into the pie shell and smooth with a spoon. Arrange a ring of chocolate chips around the rim and the pecans in a decorative pattern over the filling. Chill the tart for about 1 hour before serving.

Note: This tart is delicious served on a pool of raspberry coulis, as the bite of the raspberries enhances the richness of the tart and yet prevents cloying sweetness.

PEAR-GINGER STRUDEL

With autumn comes the joy of baking. No more heat and humidity means we can turn on the oven again. With autumn comes sweet, crisp pears. The ginger complements the sensuality of this seasonal fruit. I love to serve this strudel warm, with a scoop of nondairy "ice cream" on the side.

MAKES 6 TO 8 SLICES

3 tablespoons arrowroot

¼ teaspoon ground nutmeg

2 teaspoons ground ginger

Generous pinch sea salt

¼ cup avocado or light olive oil, plus extra for brushing

1 teaspoon pure vanilla extract

½ cup diced unsweetened dried pears or apples

¼ cup Suzanne's Specialties Maple Rice Nectar

6 ripe Bartlett pears, peeled and cut into ½-inch dice

Grated zest of 1 lemon

12 sheets fresh phyllo pastry, thawed

⅔ cup ground blanched almonds (see note, page 233)

Preheat the oven to 350°F and line a baking sheet with parchment paper.

Whisk the arrowroot, nutmeg, ginger and salt together in a small bowl. Combine the oil, vanilla, dried pears, maple rice nectar, fresh pears and lemon zest in another bowl. Mix well. Stir the arrowroot mixture into the pear mixture, stirring to coat. Cover and set aside.

Lay the phyllo sheets on a flat, dry surface, covered with a damp towel. Take one sheet and lay it on a dry work surface (remember to cover the remaining phyllo with the damp towel). Brush the phyllo sheet lightly with oil and sprinkle with about 1 tablespoon of the almonds. Repeat with remaining phyllo sheets, oil and remaining almonds, but do not brush the final sheet with oil or top with almonds.

Spoon the pear filling over the phyllo, leaving about 1 inch of dough exposed all around the edges. Beginning at one of the short sides, roll the phyllo around the filling, tucking in the edges as you roll, creating a firm cylinder. Transfer to the lined baking sheet. Using a sharp knife, cut deep slits in the strudel, indicating slices and allowing steam to escape. Lightly brush the strudel with oil.

Cover the strudel loosely with foil and bake for 15 minutes. Remove the foil and bake for 20 to 25 minutes, until the filling is soft and the pastry is lightly browned and crisp. Transfer to a wire rack to cool for 10 minutes before slicing.

≈ *Did You Know?* ≈
GINGER

Legend Ginger is one of the world's most prized aphrodisiacs.

Fact High in potassium, as well as having other medicinal properties, ginger is an overall tonic, antiseptic, diuretic, digestive cleanser and it improves circulation. Ginger makes us feel vital; no wonder it improves our love life.

~~~~~~~~~~~~~~~~~~~~~~~~

FRIED BANANAS IN CARAMEL SAUCE

Imagine the softly sensual flesh of bananas wrapped in a light, crisp batter, smothered in a sweet caramel sauce, lovely and just a bit decadent. Sound too good to be true? Think again.

MAKES 4 TO 6 SERVINGS

Batter
1½ cups whole wheat pastry flour
Pinch sea salt
1 teaspoon baking powder
Scant pinch cinnamon
¼ cup unsweetened shredded coconut
1 to 1½ cups sparkling water

Caramel Sauce
½ cup soymilk
½ cup brown rice syrup
½ cup barley malt
Juice of ¼ fresh lemon

Avocado or light olive oil, for frying
4 to 6 ripe bananas, cut into ¼-inch-thick
    diagonal slices

To make the batter: Whisk all the dry ingredients together in a mixing bowl. Slowly mix in the sparkling water to create the consistency of pancake batter. Cover loosely and set aside.

To make the sauce: Place the soymilk, rice syrup and barley malt in a small saucepan over medium heat. Bring to a boil, reduce the heat to low and cook until the syrup has reduced and thickened, about 15 minutes. Remove from the heat and whisk in lemon juice. Set aside.

Preheat the oven to 250°F.

Place about 2 inches oil in a deep skillet over medium heat. When the oil is hot, increase the heat to high, dip the bananas, in batches, in the batter to coat completely and fry until golden and crispy, turning once to ensure even browning. Drain on parchment paper. Transfer to a parchment-lined baking sheet and place the bananas in the warm oven until all the frying is completed.

To serve, mound the bananas on individual serving plates and spoon a generous amount of caramel sauce over the top. Serve immediately.

~~~~~~~~~~~~~~~~~~~~~~~~

SPICE CAKES WITH POACHED PEARS

There's something about spice cakes and crisp pears that's so comforting and soothing. The earthy flavors of spice lift the delicate sweetness of the pears to intoxicating heights and make a great autumn dessert to grace any table.

MAKES 8 SERVINGS

Poached Pears
1 bottle sparkling wine or asti spumante
½ cup brown rice syrup
1 (2-inch) piece fresh ginger, thinly sliced
2 to 3 cinnamon sticks
Grated zest of 1 lemon
Pinch sea salt
4 medium pears, peeled, halved and cored

Spice Cakes
2 cups whole wheat pastry flour
2 teaspoons baking powder

Generous pinch sea salt
¾ teaspoon ground cinnamon
¼ teaspoon ground nutmeg
¼ teaspoon ground cloves
⅓ cup avocado or light olive oil
1 teaspoon pure vanilla extract
⅔ cup brown rice syrup
½ to 1 cup vanilla soymilk

Caramel Sauce
1 cup vanilla soymilk
½ cup brown rice syrup
Pinch sea salt
Juice of ¼ lemon

To poach the pears: Place the wine, rice syrup, ginger, cinnamon sticks, lemon zest and salt in a saucepan and bring to a boil over medium heat. Add the pears, reduce the heat to low and simmer until the pears are just tender, 10 to 15 minutes. Drain liquid off and set the pears aside to cool. Slice each pear half, lengthwise, into thin wedges, not all the way to the top, creating a fan.

Preheat the oven to 350°F and lightly oil 8 (1¼-cup) custard cups or ramekins. Place a pear half in each oiled cup and press delicately to fan the slices.

To make the cakes: Whisk together the flour, baking powder, salt, cinnamon, nutmeg and cloves in a mixing bowl. Stir in the oil, vanilla and rice syrup. Slowly add the soymilk, stirring, to create a smooth, spoonable batter. Spoon the batter into prepared cups over the pears, filling each one to just over halfway. Place the cups on a baking sheet. Bake for 25 to 30 minutes until a toothpick inserted into each cake comes out clean. Remove from the oven and cool for 5 minutes before inverting the cakes onto dessert plates. Any pear pieces that stick to the cups can

be carefully removed and replaced on the cake tops.

To make caramel sauce: Combine soymilk, rice syrup and salt in a saucepan over medium heat. When the mixture boils, reduce the heat to low and cook until it reduces by half. Remove from the heat and whisk in the lemon juice. Spoon over each cake and serve hot.

CINNAMON-CHOCOLATE BROWNIES

Nothing enhances the richness of cocoa quite like cinnamon. It seems to lift the seductive taste of chocolate onto our palate, enchanting us with the dance of flavors. These brownies are brilliant, from a casual dinner to a buffet party to an al fresco brunch or lunch.

MAKES 16 SMALL BROWNIES

Brownies
1½ cups whole wheat pastry flour
1 teaspoon baking powder
Pinch sea salt
1 teaspoon ground cinnamon
6 ounces nondairy, grain-sweetened chocolate chips
¼ cup avocado or light olive oil
½ cup brown rice syrup
1 teaspoon pure vanilla extract
¼ cup vanilla soymilk
1 cup coarsely chopped pecan pieces

Chocolate Ganache
1 cup nondairy, grain-sweetened chocolate chips
¼ cup vanilla soymilk
2 teaspoons Suzanne's Specialties Chocolate Rice Nectar
Scant pinch ground cinnamon

Preheat the oven to 350°F and lightly oil an 8-inch-square baking dish. Dust with unsweetened cocoa powder instead of flour.

To make the brownies: Whisk together the flour, baking powder, salt and cinnamon. Combine the chocolate chips, oil, rice syrup, vanilla and soymilk in a saucepan over low heat. Whisking constantly, heat until smooth. Fold the chocolate mixture into the flour mixture, stirring to create a smooth batter. Fold in the pecans. Spoon into the prepared pan. Bake for 25 to 35 minutes, until a toothpick inserted into the center comes out clean. Set aside to cool.

To make the ganache: Place the chocolate chips in a heat-resistant bowl. Combine the soymilk, chocolate rice nectar and cinnamon in a saucepan and bring to a boil. Pour over the chocolate chips and whisk until smooth. Spoon the ganache evenly over the brownies and set aside until it sets a bit. Using a wet knife, cut the brownies into squares.

CHOCOLATE LAYER CAKE

Can you think of anything that makes an occasion more special than a luscious, fancy, decadent chocolate cake? Me, neither!

MAKES 8 TO 10 SLICES

Cake
3¾ cups whole wheat pastry flour
1 cup unsweetened cocoa powder
1 tablespoon baking powder
Generous pinch sea salt
Generous pinch cinnamon
Scant pinch chili powder

1 teaspoon pure vanilla extract

¾ cup avocado or light olive oil

1 cup brown rice syrup

2 teaspoons brown rice vinegar

⅔ to 1 cup vanilla soymilk

Mocha Frosting

1 tablespoon instant grain coffee

2 teaspoons pure vanilla extract

10 ounces nondairy, grain-sweetened
   chocolate chips

2 cups almond amasake

1 tablespoon Suzanne's Specialties Chocolate
   Rice Nectar

2 to 3 tablespoons kuzu, dissolved in small
   amount cold water

1 cup slivered almonds, lightly pan-toasted
   (page 81)

Preheat the oven to 350°F and lightly oil 3 (9-inch-round) cake pans. Instead of flour, dust the pans with unsweetened cocoa powder to avoid white deposits on your cakes. Cut three pieces of parchment paper the size of the inside of the cake pans and lightly oil them. Lay one in each prepared pan.

To make the cake: Whisk the dry ingredients briskly in a mixing bowl. Stir in the vanilla, oil, rice syrup and vinegar. Slowly add the soymilk, stirring, to create a smooth, satinlike cake batter. Spoon the batter evenly into the prepared pans. Bake for 40 to 45 minutes, until the top of the cakes spring back to the touch or a toothpick comes out clean. Cool in the pans on a wire cooling rack for 5 to 7 minutes. Invert and turn out the cakes onto plates to cool completely.

To make the frosting: Combine all the ingredients, except the kuzu, in a small saucepan over low heat. Cook, stirring constantly, until the chocolate melts and becomes smooth. Stir in the dissolved kuzu, and cook, stirring, until the mixture thickens, about 3 minutes. Cover loosely and set aside to cool before frosting the cakes.

To assemble the cake, examine each layer to find the most perfect one. Set it aside. Using a sharp knife, shave the tops off two of the remaining cakes, creating flat tops. Place one on a serving platter. Spread a layer of frosting, about ¼ inch thick, over the top of the cake, but not over the sides. Lay the second flat layer on top of the frosting and spread another layer over the top of the cake. Lay the final layer on top and smooth the remaining frosting over the top and side of the cake. Sprinkle with the almonds.

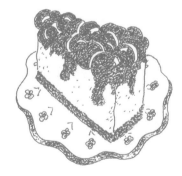

UPSIDE-DOWN APRICOT TART

At the end of summer, apricots are juicy and so incredibly sweet. You can just eat them on their own, enjoying their sensual soft flesh, or you can bake them into this decadent tart.

MAKES 8 TO 10 SLICES

Apricot Filling
¾ cup brown rice syrup
3 tablespoons avocado or light
    olive oil
Pinch sea salt
2 tablespoons vanilla soymilk
9 fresh apricots, halved

Cake
1 cup whole wheat pastry flour
¾ cup semolina flour
1 teaspoon baking powder
Pinch sea salt
1 teaspoon pure vanilla extract
⅓ cup avocado or light olive oil
⅓ cup brown rice syrup
⅓ to ½ cup vanilla soymilk

Preheat the oven to 350°F.

To make the filling: Place the rice syrup, oil, salt and soymilk in a 10-inch ovenproof skillet over medium heat. Stirring occasionally, cook the syrup until it foams. Reduce the heat to low and cook for 5 to 7 minutes. Turn off the heat and carefully place the apricot halves, rounded side down, close together in the syrup.

To make the cake: Whisk together the flours, baking powder and salt in a mixing bowl. Stir in the vanilla, oil and rice syrup. Slowly add the soymilk, stirring, to create a smooth, spoonable batter. Carefully spoon the batter over the apricot halves, covering them completely. Bake for 35 to 40 minutes until the center of the cake springs back to the touch.

Allow to cool in the skillet for 10 minutes. Run a knife around the rim of the skillet to loosen the cake. Invert onto a plate. If any apricot halves stick to the skillet, carefully lift them out and replace them on the cake. Cool completely before cutting.

FRESH PINEAPPLE POACHED IN CINNAMON SYRUP

A light, yet satisfying dessert . . . just perfect at the end of a rich, hearty meal or during hot summer weather when you just want something sweet and juicy.

MAKES 6 TO 7 SERVINGS

1½ cups spring or filtered water
¾ cup brown rice syrup
3 cinnamon sticks, snapped in half
Pinch sea salt
5 to 6 thin slices fresh ginger
½ lemon, halved
1 large pineapple, peeled, halved lengthwise,
    quartered, core removed and cut into ¾-
    inch-thick slices
Fresh mint or seasonal berries, for decoration

Combine the water, rice syrup, cinnamon sticks, salt, ginger and lemon in a large, heavy saucepan over medium heat. Cover and bring to a boil, reduce the heat to low and simmer for 10 minutes to develop the flavors. Add the pineapple, cover and simmer over low heat, stirring occasionally, until the pineapple is translucent, about 7 minutes.

Transfer the pineapple and syrup to a bowl and refrigerate until chilled through, about 2 hours. Serve the pineapple in individual dessert bowls, with the chilled syrup over the top, decorated with mint.

≈≈≈ *Did You Know?* ≈≈≈
PINEAPPLE

Legend Pineapple on the table is a sign that you are a welcome guest.

Fact Pineapple was difficult to ship and was so rare that hosts placed it on the table for only special guests. What should make your guests feel special is the bromelin, a digestive enzyme that eases our ability to assimilate foods, so it's welcome in our tummies, too.

HAZELNUT, CHOCOLATE AND STRAWBERRY TORTE

Rich, delicious and oh so decadent—with strawberries, velvety ganache, and crunchy hazelnuts—this is the perfect celebration dessert. Make any occasion special with this gorgeous dessert.

MAKES 8 TO 10 SERVINGS

Cake

1¼ cups hazelnuts, toasted and skins removed (page 229)
1 cup whole wheat pastry flour
½ teaspoon baking powder
Pinch sea salt
¼ cup avocado or light olive oil
⅓ cup brown rice syrup
    vanilla soymilk

Ganache

2 cups nondairy, grain-sweetened chocolate chips
⅔ cup vanilla soymilk
2 tablespoons Suzanne's Specialties Chocolate Rice Nectar
1 teaspoon pure vanilla extract

1 pint fresh strawberries, tops removed and thinly sliced, reserving one whole

Preheat the oven to 375°F and lightly oil and flour a 9-inch-round cake pan. Cut a piece of parchment paper the size of the bottom of the pan, lightly oil it and place on the bottom of the pan.

To make the cake: Place the hazelnuts in a food processor and pulse to make a fine meal. Transfer to a mixing bowl and stir in the flour, baking powder and salt. Mix in the oil and rice syrup. Slowly add the soymilk, by tablespoonfuls, to create a smooth, spoonable batter. Spoon evenly into the prepared pan. Bake for 25 to 30 minutes, until the top of the cake springs back to the touch. Allow to cool in the pan for 10 minutes. Run a knife around the rim between the cake and the pan to loosen it. Invert the cake onto a plate and set aside to cool completely. Using a sharp, serrated knife, split the cake in half crosswise, making 2 thin layers.

To make the ganache: Place the chocolate chips in a heat-resistant mixing bowl. Bring the soymilk, chocolate rice nectar and vanilla to a rolling boil. Pour over the chocolate chips. Whisk until a smooth, silky texture forms. Cover with plastic, and chill until it thickens, about 1 hour.

To assemble, place one cake layer, cut side up, on a serving plate. Spread one-third of the ganache over the cake. Arrange strawberry slices, reserving some for garnish, in concentric circles to cover the ganache. Spread another one-third of the ganache over the cut side of the other cake layer. Gently press the cake, ganache side down, onto the strawberries, creating a thick layer of chocolate and strawberries in the center.

Spread the remaining ganache over the top of the cake. Press remaining strawberry slices in concentric circles to decorate the top edge of the torte. Take the reserved whole strawberry and from the stem end, slice lengthwise to the tip, leaving the stem edge attached. Press gently to fan slices and place in the center of the cake.

CAPUCCINO MOUSSE

Light and frothy, this rich chocolate mousse is a chocolate lover's dream. Not too heavy, but with just the right hint of decadence to keep you satisfied.

MAKES 4 TO 6 SERVINGS

- 1 cup almond amasake
- 1 tablespoon grain coffee granules
- 1 cup vanilla soymilk
- 1 teaspoon pure vanilla extract
- 1 teaspoon mirin
- 2 tablespoons agar flakes
- 2 tablespoons brown rice syrup
- 1½ cups nondairy, grain-sweetened chocolate chips
- ½ cup slivered almonds, lightly toasted

Whisk together the amasake, grain coffee, soymilk, vanilla, mirin and agar in a saucepan until well combined. Place over low heat, and cook, stirring frequently, until the agar dissolves, about 20 minutes. Stir in the rice syrup and chocolate chips, and cook, stirring constantly, until the chocolate melts and the mixture turns satiny smooth. Transfer to a glass bowl and cover with plastic wrap. Set aside at room temperature for 25 minutes and then chill until set, 30 minutes.

To serve, loosen the mousse with a whisk or hand blender, whipping until light and smooth. Spoon the mousse into individual dessert cups and sprinkle with the almonds.

COCONUT CAKE

A taste of cool breezes and warm tropical sun are yours with this moist, light cake. A simple vanilla cake, with coconut for added moisture and sweetness, smothered in a coconut frosting that'll have you dancing to a reggae beat, whether you're on a tropical isle or a city patio.

MAKES 8 TO 12 SERVINGS

Cake
2 cups whole wheat pastry flour
1 cup semolina flour
1 tablespoon baking powder
Generous pinch sea salt
1½ teaspoons pure vanilla extract
½ cup avocado or light olive oil
½ cup brown rice syrup
¼ cup freshly squeezed lime juice
Grated zest of 1 lime
¼ cup unsweetened coconut milk
⅔ to 1 cup soymilk
½ cup unsweetened shredded coconut

Coconut Frosting
2 cups vanilla soymilk
3 tablespoons brown rice syrup
1 cup unsweetened shredded coconut
2 to 3 tablespoons kuzu, dissolved in small
    amount of cold water

Preheat the oven to 350°F and lightly oil and flour a standard Bundt pan.

To make the cake: Whisk together the flours, baking powder and salt in a mixing bowl. Mix in the vanilla, oil, rice syrup, lime juice and zest and coconut milk. Slowly add the soymilk, mixing to form a smooth, spoonable batter. Fold in the coconut and spoon the batter evenly into the prepared pan. Bake for 35 to 45 minutes, until the top of the cake springs back to the touch or a toothpick inserted comes out clean. Allow to cool in the pan for 5 to 7 minutes. Invert the cake on a serving platter and set aside to cool completely before frosting.

To make the frosting: Place the soymilk, rice syrup and ½ cup of the coconut in a saucepan over medium-low heat. When the mixture is warmed through, stir in the dissolved kuzu and cook, stirring constantly, until the mixture thickens, about 3 minutes. Transfer to a bowl, cover and chill completely.

To frost the cake, loosen the frosting with a whisk and spoon over the cake to cover. Sprinkle with the remaining coconut and serve.

Note: You can lightly oven-toast the garnish coconut for a bit of color contrast.

CHOCOLATE SESAME CUPS

Everybody loves a little decadent candy during the holiday season. Skip the commercial, sugar-laced, fat-laden stuff and make these simple jewels for yourself. You'll be delighted with the results and your guests' hearts, and hips, will thank you.

MAKES 18 CUPS

½ cup dried currants
1 cup boiling water
8 ounces nondairy, grain-sweetened chocolate chips
2 tablespoons brown rice syrup
Scant pinch ground cinnamon
3½ tablespoons sesame tahini

Lightly oil 18 candy molds or petit four cups.

Soak the currants in the boiling water for 5 minutes. Drain, pat the currants dry and finely chop.

Melt the chocolate chips with the rice syrup, cinnamon and 3 tablespoons of the tahini in a metal bowl set over a pot of simmering water; stir until smooth. Remove from the heat and fold in the currants.

Spoon the chocolate mixture into the prepared cups. Decorate the tops by dipping the end of a toothpick into the remaining tahini and swirling into the tops of each cup. Refrigerate until ready to serve.

MINI PUMPKIN BREADS

Autumn and pumpkin bread are like a passionate affair, all spicy and sweet. On a chilly autumn evening, these little breads make you feel warm and cozy all over.

MAKES 6 TO 8 MINIATURE LOAVES

Bread
2½ cups whole wheat pastry flour
2 teaspoons baking powder
Generous pinch sea salt
¾ teaspoon ground cinnamon
½ teaspoon ground nutmeg
2 cups canned unsweetened puréed pumpkin
1½ teaspoons pure vanilla extract
½ cup avocado or light olive oil
½ cup Suzanne's Specialties Maple Rice Nectar
¼ cup barley malt
1 teaspoon finely minced fresh ginger
1 teaspoon brown rice vinegar
½ to 1 cup vanilla soymilk

Caramel Glaze
1 cup Suzanne's Specialties Maple Rice Nectar
2 tablespoons vanilla soymilk
Scant pinch cinnamon

Preheat the oven to 350°F and lightly oil and flour 5 × 3 × 2-inch loaf pans.

To make the bread: Whisk together the flour, baking powder, salt, cinnamon and nutmeg in a mixing bowl. Stir in the pumpkin, vanilla, oil, maple rice nectar, barley malt, ginger, and rice vinegar. Slowly stir in the soymilk to create a smooth, spoonable batter. Spoon the batter evenly in the prepared pans. Place the pans on a baking sheet. Bake for 35 to 45 minutes, until the center of each bread springs back to the touch or a toothpick inserted into loaves comes out clean. Allow to cool in the pans for 5 minutes. Loosen the loaves from the pans and transfer to a wire rack to cool completely.

To make the glaze: Bring all the ingredients to a rolling boil. Reduce the heat to low and cook for 5 to 7 minutes, to thicken the glaze. Spoon over the breads and allow the glaze to set for 30 minutes before serving.

PERSIAN BAKED FIGS

Is there anything more sensual and inviting than fresh figs? Reserve this sweet temptation for those intimate evenings when you have only each other on your mind. It's nice to serve these warm, with a scoop of nondairy vanilla ice cream.

MAKES 2 SERVINGS

¼ cup golden raisins
¼ cup dried apricots
¼ cup dried cherries
Warm spring or filtered water
4 ripe fresh figs
2 tablespoons brown rice syrup
Grated zest of 1 orange

Scant pinch ground cinnamon
Pinch sea salt
4 tablespoons mirin
2 tablespoons orange flower water
1 tablespoon pine nuts, coarsely chopped

Place the raisins, apricots and cherries in warm water to just cover for 15 minutes, to plump the fruit. Drain well.

Preheat the oven to 350°F.

Split the figs in half lengthwise and scoop out the flesh, leaving a thin shell. Mince the flesh and mix with the dried fruit. Coarsely chop all the fruit together. Spoon the fruit mixture into the fig shells and arrange in a shallow baking dish.

Whisk together the rice syrup, orange zest, cinnamon, salt, mirin and orange water. Pour over the figs, cover tightly with foil and bake for 20 minutes. Remove the foil, baste the figs and bake, uncovered, 5 to 7 minutes until the liquid becomes a thick syrup.

To serve, arrange 4 fig halves on 2 individual dessert plates. Spoon the syrup from the baking dish over the figs and sprinkle with the pine nuts.

≈≈ *Did You Know?* ≈≈
FIGS

Legend Figs have been prized since ancient times for creating unparalleled strength and stamina.

Fact Nutrients in figs are more concentrated than in most other plant foods; they contain potassium, magnesium, iron, copper, calcium, sodium, phosphorus, vitamin B6, pantothenic acid, riboflavin, thiamine and zinc. High in fiber, they aid in efficient elimination.

HEALTHY KIDS

Have you been thinking about making healthier choices for your family, but the thought of all the turned-up noses at the table, all the whining, all the meals that get trashed because no one will eat them is more than you can bear?

How do you create healthy meals that are friendly, familiar and delicious? Well, the cooking is the easy part. The hard part comes with convincing the family, especially the kids, that you aren't turning into the food police, that enjoying meals isn't a thing of the past, that healthy food isn't weird. A daunting task in this slick, advertising-driven world—but not impossible.

What has worked for me has been saying nothing. That's right, nothing, at least nothing that my family would find alarming. I simply try new things, prepare them deliciously and present them as a new adventure at dinner. On most occasions, this works, but I'd be less than honest if I told you I had never experienced an evening where I sat at an empty table staring at untouched platters of new ideas. It's a way to find out what will work and what won't.

I also have had great success by involving my family in the choices. Sure, it's more work for me to cook this way, but if my family isn't worth the work, I can't think of who else might be. So, we shop together, even prepare ingredients together, so that when the meal is placed on the table, everyone feels a part and the weirdness has been replaced by a sense of adventure and a willingness to try new things.

When it comes to children, how we nourish them is essential to the people that they will become in the world. Sugar, chemicals, junk food, drive-through meals, instant, processed foods may be easier . . . and may be what is marketed to them, but as parents, we have a responsibility to rise above all of the white noise and nourish our children to be whole, healthy adults with social consciences. And that begins with the food choices they see *us* make. Habits learned at home are habits our children will take out into the world. Kids aren't born craving junk food; it's a learned habit.

We live in a world where cooking is the last thing on people's minds, where sitting down to relaxed dinners as a family is a rare treat instead of a daily occurrence. To create healthy, strong children, we need to reverse that trend. We need to return to the kitchen, cook daily meals, commune around the table with our children, teaching them the social graces that come with eating together— sharing, justice and communication, to name a few. I know, I know, this is not the news we want. We want to hear that we can have it all, careers, family, tons of outside activities. The truth is that we can have a lot, but not *all*. It's time to reprioritize our lives and put our families' health first. And that begins in the kitchen.

And if you need more motivation than simple love of your children, just watch the evening news or *Oprah*. You'll hear endless reports by experts talking about the health of modern children. Our kids are growing fat, lethargic and dramatically unhealthy. Obesity and juvenile diabetes, as well as type 2 diabetes are rising at alarming rates among our young. One study revealed the terrifying news that this generation of children may be the first in history to not live as long as their parents. The cause won't surprise you. A diet high in saturated fat, simple sugars, chemicals, processed food, fast food and drive-through are wreaking the same havoc on our kids' health as on ours. Trust me, the Golden Arches are leading us all right to the

Pearly Gates a lot sooner . . . and with more misery . . . than we'd like to think.

I know it's hard. Our schools take subsidies for much-needed supplies from fast-food chains, who in turn, get placement in the cafeterias and vending machines. Even the little ladies with hairnets dishing out mystery food gave our kids healthier options than fast-food kiosks. Our children are bombarded, with advertising, marketing, free toys and games, dancing clowns and promotions with popular children's movies. And just like us, they're seduced by colorful packaging and promises of happiness.

It's time to take our children's health out of the hands of fast-food chains and video game manufacturers. Having preteenage kids with plaque-clogged arteries, heart disease, excess weight, early-onset puberty, diabetes, attention deficit disorder, cancer, lethargy and lack of vitality is a national heartbreak. Our children are our future. Will we create kids who are the result of an artificial environment, the result of pollution, fast food and lack of physical exertion? Or will we create a future of healthy, strong, vital and socially conscious people who respect nature and each other? Only we can decide.

So how do we feed our kids, have them enjoy it and not send them to school with weird food, so they become freaks among their peers? Well, it takes a bit of creativity, juggling and effort, but the results will be more than worth it when you look into the clear eyes of your vibrant children and know in your heart that they are fit, happy and adjusted—and that you had a small hand in it through the food you put on the table.

Here are just a few recipes to get you started, but as the adventure continues, try out some of the others you find appealing throughout the book.

FALAFEL WITH SESAME SAUCE

A great lunch or dinner for older kids. Rich, with just a touch of spice, this recipe is packed with protein to keep them strong and healthy, and delicious enough to keep them satisfied.

MAKES 3 TO 4 SANDWICHES

Falafel

3 cloves fresh garlic, finely minced

3 cups cooked or canned chickpeas

2 teaspoons ground cumin

2 teaspoons ground coriander

1 teaspoon sweet paprika

1 teaspoon turmeric

2 teaspoons sea salt

Spring or filtered water

1 to 2 scallions, minced

2 to 3 fresh flat-leaf parsley sprigs, finely minced

Whole wheat pastry flour, as needed

Sesame Sauce

3 to 4 tablespoons sesame tahini

Juice of 1 lemon

½ to 1 teaspoon sea salt

1 teaspoon brown rice syrup

Spring or filtered water

3 or 4 large whole wheat pita breads

Shredded iceberg or romaine lettuce

2 ripe tomatoes, diced

8 ounces purchased hummus or homemade (page 254)

To make the falafel: Place the garlic, chickpeas, spices and salt in a food processor and purée until smooth, adding a small amount of water as necessary to make a thick paste. Add the scallions and parsley and pulse until well combined. Adjust the seasoning to your children's taste. Transfer the mixture to a bowl and add enough flour to make a dough that holds its shape, but isn't too dry. Shape into 1½-inch spheres.

You can either bake or deep-fry the falafel. Choose the method of cooking based on your children's needs and health. To bake, place on a parchment paper-lined baking sheet and bake at 375°F until crisp on the outside. To deep-fry, heat 3 to 4 inches avocado or light olive oil in a deep saucepan over medium heat. Increase the heat to high and add the falafel and fry until golden brown and crispy.

To make the dressing: Whisk all the ingredients until smooth in a small bowl, adjusting seasoning to taste and add water to create a thick, creamy sauce.

To serve, lay a pita on a dry work surface. Lay 3 falafel, shredded lettuce and diced tomato on the center of the pita. Spoon some of the hummus over the top and then add the sesame dressing. Roll, jelly-roll style, and wrap in foil for ease of eating.

MEDITERRANEAN BULGUR SALAD

A great light grain salad that can be carried as a school lunch in a container. Delicious and not odd looking, older kids will really enjoy this one, especially our girls, because they are calorie conscious.

MAKES 5 TO 6 SERVINGS

    4 cups spring or filtered water
    2 cups bulgur
    Pinch sea salt
    1 cup finely minced fresh flat-leaf parsley
    ¼ cup finely minced fresh mint
    2 ripe tomatoes, diced (do not seed or peel)
    2 to 3 scallions, minced
    1 medium cucumber, diced
    Juice of 2 lemons
    ¼ cup extra-virgin olive oil
    ½ cup minced black olives (optional)

Bring the water to a boil. Stir in the bulgur and salt, cover and turn off the heat. Allow to stand for 15 minutes, undisturbed. Fluff with a fork and transfer to a mixing bowl. Mix in the remaining ingredients, seasoning to taste with salt. Chill completely before serving.

TOFU BUNDLES

This is a really great way to get your kids to try tofu. Easy to make, richly flavored, with plenty of calories from fat and protein to ensure healthy growth and development, this fun dish is sure to please young ones.

MAKES 2 SANDWICHES

    1 (8-ounce) package flavored baked tofu
    2 tablespoons almond butter
    2 tablespoons barley miso
    ½ teaspoon brown rice syrup
    2 scallions, roots trimmed, halved lengthwise,
       blanched for 30 seconds and drained

Lay the tofu slices on a dry work surface.

Mix the almond butter, miso and rice syrup together to create a thick paste. Spoon a thick layer on 2 pieces of the tofu, covering completely. Lay the 2 remaining tofu slices on top and press gently to seal. Tie one scallion strip around the tofu pieces crosswise and one strip around it lengthwise, tying like a bundle. Repeat with the other tofu bundle.

SAUTÉED VEGETABLE FOCACCIA

Vary the vegetables to fit your family's taste and add nondairy soy cheese to turn it into a veggie pizza.
MAKES 6 TO 8 SQUARES

> **About 1 tablespoon extra-virgin olive oil**
> **2 to 3 cloves fresh garlic, thinly sliced**
> **1 red onion, thinly sliced into half-moon pieces**
> **Sea salt**
> **Generous pinch red pepper flakes (optional)**
> **1 zucchini, cut into thin matchstick pieces**
> **1 yellow summer squash, cut into thin matchstick pieces**
> **4 to 5 ripe tomatoes, thinly sliced (do not seed or peel)**
> **1 small bunch broccoli rabe, rinsed well, finely cut**
> **1 whole wheat focaccia**

Preheat the oven to 350°F.

Place the oil, garlic and onion in a deep skillet over medium heat. When the onion begins to sizzle, add a pinch of salt and the red pepper flakes and sauté for 2 minutes. Stir in the zucchini, yellow squash and a pinch of salt and sauté for 2 minutes. Stir in the tomatoes and broccoli rabe and season lightly with salt. Sauté until the vegetables are limp and tender.

While the vegetables are cooking, warm the focaccia in the oven for 5 to 6 minutes. To serve, cut into squares and mound the vegetables on each square.

HUMMUS WRAPS

A milder flavored hummus, this is absolutely great for school lunches and after-school snacks. Protein-rich, delicious and easy to make, hummus can be served like this, or sent to school with fresh vegetables or organic chips for dipping.
MAKES 4 TO 5 HALF WRAPS

> *Hummus*
> **2 to 3 cloves fresh garlic, minced**
> **2 cups cooked or canned chickpeas**
> **Grated zest and juice of 1 lemon**
> **⅓ cup sesame tahini**
> **1 teaspoon ground cumin (optional)**
> **¼ cup extra-virgin olive oil**
> **½ to 1 teaspoon sea salt**
> **2 to 3 sprigs parsley, finely minced**
> **Spring or filtered water**
>
> *Wraps*
> **2 to 3 whole wheat soft tortillas or pita halves**
> **Romaine lettuce leaves**
> **Alfalfa sprouts**
> **Sliced tomatoes**

To make the hummus: Combine all the ingredients, except the water, in a food processor, adjusting the salt to your children's tastes. Pureé until smooth, adding water if the mixture seems too thick for your taste.

To assemble the wraps: Lay 1 soft tortilla on a dry work surface and place lettuce, sprouts and tomato slices on one side of the tortilla. Spoon the hummus generously over the vegetables, and roll, jelly-roll style, securing with a toothpick. Repeat with the remaining tortillas. Slice each wrap in half crosswise to serve.

TORTILLA CHIPS AND ROASTED TOMATO SALSA

Worried about high-fat, junk food snacks? Keep organic chips on hand (remember that corn chips are so much healthier than potato chips). Serve with this incredible salsa and watch them drool at the thought. When you have the time, turn snacktime into a party by frying your own tortillas. It makes any occasion just a little special.

MAKES 5 TO 6 SERVINGS OF SALSA AND CHIPS

Salsa
10 to 12 plum tomatoes, quartered lengthwise (do not peel or seed)
8 shallots, peeled
5 cloves fresh garlic, peeled
Sea salt
2 poblano chiles, soaked in very hot water for 10 minutes and drained
Grated zest and juice of 1 lemon
1 sprig fresh rosemary, leaves stripped off the stems
2 tablespoons extra-virgin olive oil
¼ teaspoon brown rice syrup

Tortilla Chips
6 to 8 soft corn tortillas
Avocado or light olive oil, for frying
Sea salt

Preheat the oven to 325°F.

Arrange the tomato pieces on a baking sheet. Sprinkle the shallots and garlic over the tomatoes. Sprinkle with sea salt. Roast for 1 to 1½ hours, until the tomatoes are beginning to dry. Do not let them burn or blacken. Cool the tomatoes and peel. Finely mince the tomatoes, shallots and garlic. Transfer to a mixing bowl.

Remove the stems from the chiles and split them lengthwise. Remove the seeds and finely mince.

Mix the chiles, lemon zest and juice, rosemary, oil, rice syrup and salt to taste into the tomato mixture. Mix well and allow to stand for about 1 hour before serving.

To make the tortilla chips: Cut each tortilla into 8 to 10 wedges. Heat about 1 inch of oil in a deep skillet over medium heat. When the oil is hot (patterns will form, known as "dancing"), increase the heat to high and quickly fry the chips until crisp, 1 to 2 minutes. Drain on parchment paper and sprinkle lightly with salt.

Note: While this salsa takes time to make, it will keep, refrigerated for about 5 days, so you can make it ahead.

NOODLES WITH TOFU AND VEGETABLES

This is an easy-to-make and easy-to-present main-course dinner idea. Most kids love noodles and, more than you think, kids will try tofu, if it's delicious. Try this well-balanced meal of complex carbohydrates, protein and vegetables to keep your young ones strong and vital.

MAKES 3 TO 4 SERVINGS

About 1 tablespoon extra-virgin olive oil

3 to 4 thin slices fresh ginger, finely minced

1 red onion, cut into thin half-moon slices

Soy sauce

6 to 7 button mushrooms, brushed free of dirt and thinly sliced

1 carrot, cut into fine matchstick pieces

1 small bunch bok choy, thinly sliced on the diagonal

2 to 3 slices (4 to 6 ounces) baked tofu, cubed

2 teaspoons brown rice syrup

8 ounces whole wheat udon noodles

Juice of ½ lemon

2 to 3 sprigs fresh flat-leaf parsley, finely minced

Place the oil, ginger and onion in a deep skillet over medium heat. When the onion begins to sizzle, add a dash of soy sauce and sauté for 1 to 2 minutes. Stir in the mushrooms and sauté until the mushrooms release their juices, about 2 minutes. Stir in the carrot, bok choy and a light seasoning of soy sauce. Stir in the tofu and rice syrup and season with soy sauce to taste. Sauté until the bok choy is wilted and crisp-tender.

While the vegetables are sautéing, bring a pot of water to a boil and cook the udon al dente, about 12 minutes. Drain and rinse well.

Stir the noodles into the tofu and vegetables; stir in the lemon juice and transfer to a serving platter. Sprinkle with the parsley and serve immediately.

Note: Vary the vegetables to your family's taste. You can leave out the tofu if necessary, but you lose the protein punch.

TOFU POCKETS WITH CURRIED VEGETABLES

It's a bit complicated and takes some effort, but this dish is brilliant and, in my experience, well loved. I have yet to have anyone turn up their noses at this one. Vary the vegetables, adjust the spices and have fun with it. You might want to create a spicy or sweet dipping sauce as a side dish.

MAKES 8 FULL-SIZE POCKETS

Tofu
Avocado or light olive oil, for frying

1 pound extra-firm tofu

Dashi
4 to 5 cups spring or filtered water

3 tablespoons soy sauce

3 to 4 slices fresh ginger

2-inch piece kombu

Curried Vegetables

About 1 tablespoon extra-virgin olive oil

1 teaspoon curry powder

2 cloves fresh garlic, finely minced

½ red onion, finely minced

Sea salt

Mirin

½ cup finely minced butternut squash

½ cup fresh or frozen corn kernels

To make the tofu: Place about 3 inches oil in a deep pot over medium heat.

While the oil heats, cut the tofu diagonally into 4 triangles. Cut the 4 triangles in half, making them half as thick. Make a deep slit along the long side of each triangle, making a pocket. When the oil is hot (patterns will form, known as "dancing"), increase the heat to high and fry a few tofu triangles until crisp and golden, 2 to 3 minutes. Drain on parchment paper and repeat with remaining tofu until all the triangles are fried. Set aside.

To make the dashi: Combine all the ingredients in a deep pot and bring to a boil. When the dashi boils, add the fried tofu and reduce the heat to low. Cook the tofu for 25 minutes, drawing any excess oil out.

While the tofu cooks, *prepare the vegetables:* place the oil and curry powder in a skillet over medium heat and sauté the curry powder for 1 to 2 minutes. Stir in the garlic, onion and a pinch of salt. Sauté for 1 to 2 minutes. Add a dash of mirin, the squash and corn. Season to taste with salt and sauté until the squash is tender, about 7 minutes. Set aside to cool.

Set the tofu aside until cool enough to handle. Spoon the curried vegetable mixture into each pocket, filling abundantly. Arrange on a serving platter and serve hot.

AUSTRIAN CHOCOLATE CAKE

So what to do for that special occasion now that you're making healthier choices for your family? No sweat. Try this delicious cake and watch them rave.

MAKES 8 TO 10 SERVINGS

Cake

4 cups whole wheat pastry flour

1½ cups unsweetened cocoa powder

½ cup unsweetened shredded coconut

4 teaspoons baking powder

Generous pinch sea salt

½ teaspoon ground cinnamon

⅔ cup avocado or light olive oil

1 cup brown rice syrup

2 teaspoons brown rice vinegar

1 to 2 cups vanilla soymilk

Frosting

1 cup soymilk

2 cups amasake

2 tablespoons Suzanne's Specialties Chocolate Rice Nectar

Pinch sea salt

1 teaspoon pure vanilla extract

3 tablespoons kuzu, dissolved in small amount cold water

2½ cups nondairy, grain-sweetened chocolate chips

1½ cups unsweetened shredded coconut

1 cup lightly toasted, coarsely chopped pecans

Preheat the oven to 350°F and lightly oil 3 (9-inch-round) cake pans. Instead of flour, dust the pans with unsweetened cocoa powder to avoid white deposits on your cakes.

To make the cake: Whisk together the dry ingredients in a mixing bowl. Stir in the oil, rice syrup and vinegar. Slowly add the soymilk, mixing to create a smooth, spoonable cake batter. Spoon the batter evenly into the prepared pans. Bake for 35 to 40 minutes, until the center of the cakes spring back to the touch or a toothpick inserted in the centers comes out clean. Allow to cool in the pans for 10 minutes. Transfer to a wire rack and cool completely.

To make the frosting: Combine the soymilk, amasake, chocolate rice nectar, salt and vanilla in a saucepan over medium heat. When the liquid is warmed through, stir in the dissolved kuzu, and cook, stirring until the mixture thickens, about 3 minutes. Stir in chocolate chips, stirring until the mixture thickens and turns satiny smooth. Fold in the coconut. Transfer to a heat-resistant bowl and cover. Set aside until firm, about 15 minutes.

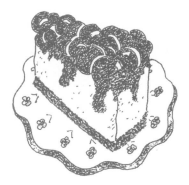

To assemble the cake, examine each layer to find the most perfect one. Set it aside. Using a sharp knife, shave the tops off the two remaining cakes, creating flat tops. Place one on a serving platter. Spread a layer of frosting, about ¼ inch thick, over the top of the cake, but not over the sides. Lay the second flat layer on top of the frosting and spread another layer of frosting over the top of the cake. Lay the final layer on top and smooth the remaining frosting over the top and sides of the cake. Press the pecans over the top of cake. If you have any left over, press them into the sides.

CINNAMON BAKED APPLES

Nothing says autumn quite like turning on the oven and popping in a tray of baked apples. With cinnamon complementing the natural sweetness of the apples, this is a dessert that will become a regular part of your autumn menu plans.

MAKES 6 SERVINGS

6 large Golden delicious apples

2 cups coarsely chopped pecans

¼ cup Suzanne's Specialties Maple Rice Nectar

3 tablespoons barley malt

1 teaspoon ground cinnamon

Pinch nutmeg

Pinch sea salt

2 tablespoons avocado or light olive oil

1 cup spring or filtered water

Preheat the oven to 350°F.

Peel the skin off the top quarter of each apple. Using a melon baller, scoop out the core and seeds, leaving the bottom of the apple intact. Stand the apples in a square baking dish.

In a skillet, lightly pan-toast the pecan pieces over medium heat. Add the maple rice nectar, barley malt, cinnamon, nutmeg, salt and olive oil. Cook, stirring constantly, until the mixture foams. Spoon the pecan mixture into the opening of each apple, filling completely. Pour the water into the pan around the apples. Bake for 35 to 45 minutes, until the apples pierce easily with a skewer.

RICE PUDDING WITH SPICES

One of my favorite desserts, I am always looking for ways to add variety to one of our most basic comfort foods. In this version, I add a variety of spices, which, against the mild backdrop of the rice lifts the sweetness to new heights.
MAKES 6 TO 8 SERVINGS

4 cups vanilla soymilk

1 cup plain amasake

1 cup Arborio rice (do not rinse)

⅔ cup brown rice syrup

1 teaspoon pure vanilla extract

Generous pinch sea salt

¼ cup dried currants

¾ teaspoon ground cinnamon, plus an extra pinch

½ teaspoon ground cardamom

½ teaspoon ground nutmeg

⅛ teaspoon ground allspice

½ cup slivered almonds, toasted

3 tablespoons FruitSource granulated sweetener

Combine the soymilk, amasake, rice, rice syrup, vanilla and salt in a heavy saucepan over medium heat. Cook, stirring constantly, until the mixture boils. Stir in the currants, ¾ teaspoon cinnamon, the cardamom, nutmeg and allspice; reduce the heat to low and cook, covered, stirring often, until the rice is creamy and the pudding thickens, about 1 hour.

Place the almonds, pinch of cinnamon and sweetener in a hot skillet over medium heat and pan-toast just until the almonds are coated. Transfer to a small bowl to cool and set aside.

Spoon the pudding into individual dessert cups or wineglasses and sprinkle with the almonds.

CHERRY CRUMBLE PIE

Summer's fresh juicy cherries deserve only the best showcase. With a flaky crust and a luscious crunchy topping, these jewels of hot weather really shine.

MAKES 8 TO 10 SERVINGS

Crust

1 cup whole wheat pastry flour
½ cup semolina flour
Pinch sea salt
Pinch ground cinnamon
8 tablespoons avocado or light olive oil
Spring or filtered water

Filling

6 cups pitted fresh cherries
2 tablespoons avocado or light olive oil
Pinch sea salt
½ cup Suzanne's Specialties Strawberry Rice Nectar
Grated zest of 1 lemon
3 tablespoons arrowroot

Topping

1 cup rolled oats
¾ cup whole wheat pastry flour
Pinch sea salt
¾ teaspoon ground cinnamon
½ cup slivered almonds
¾ cup brown rice syrup
½ cup avocado or light olive oil

Preheat the oven to 375°F and lightly oil a 9-inch deep-dish pie plate.

To make the crust: Combine the flours, salt and cinnamon in a mixing bowl. Using a fork, cut in the oil until it is the texture of wet sand. Slowly add water, 1 tablespoon at a time, mixing until the dough gathers together. Knead two to three times just to gather it into a ball. Roll out the dough between two sheets of parchment paper into a thin circle that is about 1 inch larger than the pie plate. Remove the top sheet of parchment paper and invert the crust onto the pie plate. Without stretching, fit the crust into the plate, allowing the excess crust to hang over the sides of the dish. Pierce in several places with a fork and bake for 5 to 7 minutes, to prevent the crust from becoming soggy. Set aside to cool.

To make the filling: Combine all the ingredients, except the arrowroot, in a saucepan over low heat. Stirring frequently, cook until the cherries begin to soften, 5 to 7 minutes. Remove from the heat and stir in the arrowroot. Spoon the filling into the partially baked shell.

To make the topping: Combine the oats, flour, salt, cinnamon and almonds in a mixing bowl. Stir in the rice syrup and oil to create a crumbly texture. Using your hands, crumble the topping over the cherry filling, covering completely.

Cover loosely with foil and bake for 30 minutes. Reduce the heat to 350°F and remove the foil. Bake for about 10 minutes, until filling is bubbling and the topping is golden brown.

RISE AND SHINE!

Your mother was right, at least about this one. The most important meal of the day is the first one. Skip breakfast and you set yourself up for a trying day . . . at the very best. But wait, start your day with food that doesn't serve you and you set yourself up for a trying day . . . at the very best. So, what to do?

Let me explain the chemistry, if you will, of breakfast. Here's how it works. Think of your afternoon. Your energy begins to flag; you feel like a nap would be in order. This is a pretty normal reaction. Your body needs to rest, to move with its rhythms. Your energy is moving inward and downward, as the day draws to a close. Your body is beginning the process of gathering its resources so that when you sleep, it can rejuvenate you for the next day. Working against those rhythms—not getting enough sleep on a regular basis, eating very close to bedtime (so that your organs are working all night to digest your snacks), working less than natural hours—cause you to become chronically tired, never waking rested. You're cranky and no fun at the start of the day, dragging your sorry butt out of bed and through the day, just praying for the moment when you can crawl back under the covers.

When you rest properly in the night, your body's energy moves to a place of dormancy, pure rest, so you can recharge your batteries. On these occasions, you wake refreshed and ready to face the day. Now it's time to break the fast, literally. Your body has taken no food while it has slept and has rebalanced all of your systems, blood chemistry, metabolism. Now you get to choose how you'll spend the rest of your day. Will you ride a roller coaster of highs and lows; will you exhaust your system at first bite, so to speak? Or will you create long, enduring, even, clear energy to sail through the challenges that are daily life?

If you're starting your day with bacon and eggs, drive-through breakfast sandwiches, hard bagels, donuts, toaster pastries, breakfast bars and coffee, well, I'd rather you skipped the idea of breakfast completely. At least you'd have a fighting chance of getting through the day with some energy left. But wait? Am I nuts? Don't these choices give us lots of protein and carbohydrates, energy we need to burn? Get real. What typical American breakfast choices give us is acid indigestion, among other things. Typical choices contain dense or empty calories, using our body's energies in the most inefficient ways, leaving us tired, lethargic and cranky, with clogged arteries, chaotic blood chemistry and brain fog, not to mention extra poundage.

So what's for breakfast? For us to feel well and strong through the day, we need to begin with food that is deeply nourishing and easy to digest, but we'll get to that. The good news is that all the breakfast ideas here, while somewhat exotic, are so incredibly vitalizing, you'll wonder why you didn't try them before. The bad news is that you have to prepare these breakfasts yourself. Sorry, it's back to the kitchen. I do live in the real world. I know we're all busy, but in order for you to meet the challenges of daily life you need to be at the top of your game, thinking clearly, feeling strong and centered. Drive-through breakfast sandwiches just won't nourish you the way you need to be nourished by real food.

Try preparing and eating healthy breakfasts for at a week. You'll see a difference. You'll have more energy and feel happier and calmer, so will your family. With more balanced food as the first nourishment of the day, you'll all feel better, able to cope. Wouldn't it be lovely to know that the early morning chaos that is the signature of how most people begin their day is completely avoidable with just a bit of effort? Wouldn't you love to leave the house in a good mood, rather than grumbling and overwhelmed before you've even begun? It's possible. It all begins in the kitchen.

SOFT GRAIN PORRIDGE

Soft grain porridge is one of the loveliest breakfast foods. Creamy, smooth and easy to digest, soft cereal porridge is delicious, varied and easy to prepare. You can cook it in the morning, while getting ready for the day or even overnight for a warming and strengthening breakfast.
MAKES 3 TO 4 SERVINGS

> 1 cup short-grain brown rice, millet, barley or
>   other whole grain, rinsed well
> ½ cup fresh or frozen corn kernels
> 5 cups spring or filtered water
> Pinch sea salt
> 2 to 3 sprigs fresh parsley, finely minced

Place the grain, corn and water in a heavy pot and bring to a boil, loosely covered. Add a pinch of salt, cover, reduce heat to low and cook, stirring occasionally, until the grain is quite creamy and the liquid has been absorbed, about 1 hour for brown rice, 1½ hours for barley and 30 minutes for millet and quinoa. Stir in the parsley and serve.

PORRIDGE

Soft grain porridge can be made from any whole or cracked grain, rice, wheat, barley, quinoa, oats, rolled oats, amaranth, teff, corn, or bulgur. For shorter cooking time, use leftover cooked grain. Add water to generously cover the grain, bring to a boil, add a pinch of salt, cover and cook over low heat until the liquid has been absorbed, about 25 minutes.

Remember to vary the grain and add diced vegetables like onion, carrot and winter squash to create variety and delicate sweet flavor. And for those with a real sweet tooth, add a small handful of raisins at the beginning of cooking or a touch of brown rice syrup when you serve the porridge.

SWEET POLENTA

One of my favorite breakfast cereals, polenta is quick, creamy and delicately sweet. It's so wonderful, I could eat it every day.
MAKES 3 TO 4 SERVINGS

> 2½ cups vanilla soymilk
> 2 tablespoons Suzanne's Specialties Raspberry
>   Rice nectar
> Pinch sea salt
> ½ cup yellow corn grits

Place all the ingredients in a saucepan over medium heat. Cook, whisking constantly, until the mixture boils. Reduce the heat to low and cook, whisking frequently, until the grits thicken and the center pops and bubbles, about 25 minutes. Spoon the polenta into individual serving bowls.

Variations: When they are in season, I love to stir fresh raspberries into this cereal at the end of cooking, or sprinkle them on top of each bowl. You may also add ¼ cup raisins at the beginning of cooking to create a sweeter taste. Finally, stir in some lightly toasted chopped pecans or hempseeds for some protein and extra energy.

CINNAMON PANCAKES WITH MAPLE RICE SYRUP

My husband makes what are arguably the best pancakes on earth. Okay, maybe I'm not entirely objective, but give these babies a try on a lazy Sunday morning and see for yourself.

MAKES 10 PANCAKES

> 1 cup whole wheat pastry flour
> 1 teaspoon baking powder
> Generous pinch ground cinnamon
> Pinch sea salt
> 1 cup soymilk
> 1 teaspoon umeboshi plum vinegar
> Light olive oil
> Suzanne's Specialties Maple Rice Nectar, for
>   serving

In a medium bowl, whisk the dry ingredients very briskly for about 1 minute. In another bowl, whisk the soymilk, vinegar and 1 tablespoon oil

until well blended. Mix the wet ingredients into the dry ingredients, whisking briskly for 1 minute to make a spoonable batter.

Lightly oil a griddle or skillet and warm over medium heat. Spoon the batter onto the hot griddle, using ¼ cup for each pancake, and cook until golden and bubbles form. Flip each pancake and cook until golden. Serve smothered in maple rice nectar.

Variation: Use ¾ cup whole wheat pastry flour with ¼ cup spelt flour, cornmeal or buckwheat flour to create different versions of the basic pancake.

BLUEBERRY-CORN GRIDDLE CAKES

A simply super summer breakfast for those weekend mornings when life is slow and easy. Served with blueberry rice syrup, this breakfast showcases the season's best at its best.

MAKES ABOUT 24 PANCAKES

> 1½ cups whole wheat pastry flour
> ½ cup yellow cornmeal
> 1 teaspoon baking powder
> Generous pinch sea salt
> Grated zest of 1 lemon
> 1 teaspoon brown rice vinegar
> 2 tablespoons light olive oil, plus extra for
>   cooking
> 1 to 2 cups vanilla soymilk
> 1¼ cups fresh blueberries, sorted and rinsed
>   well

Suzanne's Specialties Blueberry Rice
   Nectar

In a bowl, whisk together the flour, cornmeal, baking powder and salt. Mix in the lemon zest, rice vinegar and 2 tablespoons oil. Slowly mix in enough soymilk to make a thin batter. Fold in the blueberries.

Lightly oil a griddle or skillet and warm over medium heat. Spoon the batter onto the hot griddle, using about ¼ cup for each pancake, and cook until golden and bubbles form. Flip each pancake and cook until golden. Serve smothered in blueberry rice nectar.

GOLDEN SQUASH GRIDDLE CAKES

The golden color of these lovely little pancakes will surely bring sunshine to your table on cold winter mornings.

MAKES ABOUT 24 PANCAKES

- 1 cup whole wheat pastry flour
- ¼ cup semolina flour
- 1 teaspoon baking powder
- Generous pinch sea salt
- Generous pinch ground cinnamon
- 1 teaspoon umeboshi plum vinegar
- 2 tablespoons light olive oil, plus extra for cooking
- 1 cup puréed cooked butternut squash
- ½ to 1 cup vanilla soymilk

⅓ cup finely chopped pecans
Suzanne's Specialties Maple Rice Nectar

In a bowl, whisk together the flours, baking powder, salt and cinnamon. Mix in the vinegar, 2 tablespoons oil and the squash. Slowly mix in enough soymilk to make a thin batter. Fold in the pecans.

Lightly oil a griddle or skillet and warm over medium heat. Spoon the batter onto the hot griddle, using ¼ cup for each pancake, and cook until golden and bubbles form. Flip each pancake and cook until golden. Serve smothered in maple rice nectar.

MISO SOUP

I know what you're thinking. Soup for breakfast? Yep. Try it for a few mornings. You'll feel calm, centered, nourished and ready for the day. The miso works in the intestines to create strong, friendly bacteria so that your body works efficiently throughout the day. Add to it the minerals of sea plants and the vitality of fresh vegetables and you have a winning combination.

MAKES 3 TO 4 SERVINGS

- 3 cups spring or filtered water
- 1 (3-inch) piece wakame, soaked until tender and thinly sliced
- ½ yellow onion, thinly sliced into half-moon pieces
- ⅓ cup green head cabbage, finely shredded
- ½ carrot, sliced into fine matchstick pieces
- 1½ teaspoons barley or brown rice miso
- 1 to 2 scallions, thinly sliced on the diagonal, for garnish

Place the water and wakame in a saucepan over medium heat, cover and bring to a boil. Add the onion, cabbage and carrot, cover, reduce the heat to low and simmer until the vegetables are tender, about 10 minutes. Remove a small amount of hot broth and use to dissolve the miso. Stir the miso mixture into the soup and simmer, uncovered, 2 to 3 minutes to activate the enzymes in the miso. Serve garnished with the scallions.

Notes: Vary the vegetables daily to ensure proper nutrition and inspiration.

When purchasing miso, look for one that has been aged for a minimum of 18 months. This is miso that has the strongest nutritional value to you.

BOILED SALAD

There's nothing quite like fresh vegetables in the morning. Broccoli before noon? Sure. Eating lightly cooked vegetables in the morning is so refreshing—you have to try this. The light, crisp nature of this kind of dish in the morning puts a spring in your step.
MAKES 3 TO 4 SERVINGS

> 1 carrot, cut into thin oblong slices
> 1 cup green beans, tips trimmed
> 1 cup cauliflower florets
> 1 cup broccoli florets

Bring a pot of water to a rolling boil. Cook the carrot until crisp-tender, about 2 minutes. Remove with a slotted spoon or skimmer, drain and transfer to a mixing bowl. In the same water, cook the green beans until crisp-tender, about 3

minutes. Remove with a slotted spoon or skimmer, drain and add to the carrot. In the same water, cook the cauliflower until crisp-tender, about 3 minutes. Remove with a slotted spoon or skimmer, drain and add to the carrot and green beans. Finally, in the same water, cook the broccoli until bright green and crisp-tender, about 3 minutes. Drain and add to carrot, green beans and cauliflower.

Gently toss the vegetables to combine and serve.

Notes: Vary the vegetables, but keep them on the lighter side, Chinese cabbage, head cabbage, dark leafy greens, daikon. Avoid harder, heavier vegetables, as they take too long to cook.

You may also toss the boiled salad with brown rice vinegar, umeboshi plum vinegar or lemon juice to add a bit more sparkle.

LEMONY CHINESE CABBAGE PICKLE

Another of my husband's breakfast specialties is light pickle dishes. Pickled foods ensure smooth intestinal function and strength, and when kept light and crisp, can be a delightful treat in the morning, with a clean, refreshing taste. Trust me . . .
MAKES 3 TO 4 SERVINGS

> 4 to 5 leaves Chinese cabbage, finely shredded
> ½ cup fresh daikon, cut into fine matchstick pieces
> Juice of 1 lemon
> Grated zest of 1 lemon
> 1½ tablespoons sea salt

Place the vegetables, lemon juice and zest in a mixing bowl and toss to combine. Stir in the salt and begin rubbing vegetables through your fingers to incorporate it into the surface of the vegetables. You will notice that liquid will release from the vegetables as they wilt. Place a small plate on top of the vegetables, with a light weight on top of the plate. Press the vegetables for 20 minutes.

Remove the weight and gently squeeze any remaining liquid from the vegetables. Transfer to a serving plate and serve immediately. This dish will keep, refrigerated, for 2 to 3 days.

HEMPSEED GOMASHIO

A delicious condiment so packed with nutrients that you'll think you've begun your day with rocket fuel. Hempseeds are one of the world's greatest sources of the essential fatty acid omega-3 and are over 30 percent complete protein. Just a sprinkle a day of this powerful condiment on grains or vegetables will give you energy to burn.
MAKES ABOUT 6 TABLESPOONS CONDIMENT

1 teaspoon sea salt
6 tablespoons shelled hempseeds

In a dry skillet over low heat, dry-roast salt for 3 minutes. Stir in the hempseeds and roast, stirring constantly, for 2 to 3 minutes, until fragrant. Transfer to a glass jar and cool completely before sealing. This condiment will keep for 2 to 3 weeks.

BANANA NUT MUFFINS

Great for a brunch or lazy weekend, these moist, delicately sweet muffins will find their way to your table quite often. Easy, light and laced through with nuts, they're energizing and easy to digest. Beautiful!
MAKES 12 STANDARD OR 24 MINI MUFFINS

2½ cups whole wheat pastry flour
½ cup semolina flour
Pinch sea salt
2½ teaspoons baking powder
Pinch ground cinnamon
⅓ cup light olive oil
½ cup brown rice syrup
1 teaspoon pure vanilla extract
2 to 3 very ripe bananas, mashed
½ to 1 cup soymilk
½ cup coarsely chopped pecan pieces

Preheat the oven to 350°F and lightly oil and flour a 12-cup standard or 24-cup mini muffin pan.

In a bowl, whisk together the flours, salt, baking powder and cinnamon. Stir in the oil, rice syrup, vanilla and bananas. Slowly mix in enough soymilk to make a smooth, spoonable batter. Fold in the nuts. Spoon the batter evenly into prepared muffin cups. Bake for 25 to 30 minutes, until the tops of the muffins spring back to the touch or a toothpick inserted in the center comes out clean. (Mini-muffins will take less time. Check at 20 minutes.)

CRANBERRY-PECAN BREAD

Warm quick breads, fresh from the oven, can you think of a nicer way to begin a lazy weekend? This nutty, richly flavored bread is perfect on a chilly morning.

MAKES 1 LOAF, 8 TO 10 SLICES

2 cups whole wheat pastry flour
2 teaspoons baking powder
Generous pinch sea salt
½ teaspoon ground cinnamon
Pinch ground nutmeg
Grated zest of 1 lemon
½ cup light olive oil
½ cup brown rice syrup
1 cup silken tofu
1 teaspoon pure vanilla extract
½ to 1 cup vanilla soymilk
1 cup chopped fresh cranberries or ⅔ cup
    unsweetened dry cranberries
⅓ cup chopped prunes
½ cup finely chopped pecans

Preheat the oven to 350°F and lightly oil and flour a 9 × 5-inch loaf pan.

In a bowl, whisk together the flour, baking powder, salt, cinnamon and nutmeg. Stir in the lemon zest. In a small bowl, whisk the oil, rice syrup, tofu and vanilla until smooth. Stir the tofu mixture into the flour mixture. Slowly mix in enough soymilk to make a smooth, spoonable cake batter. Fold in the cranberries, prunes and pecans.

Spoon the batter into the prepared pan. Bake for 45 to 55 minutes, until the top springs back to the touch and a toothpick inserted in the center comes out clean. Remove from the oven and allow to stand in the pan for 10 minutes before inverting onto a cooling rack.

≈ Did You Know? ≈
CINNAMON

Legend Cinnamon can relieve cold hands and feet, but aggravate menopausal hot flashes.

Fact One of the world's oldest known spices, cinnamon contains stimulantlike compounds that aid in improving circulation by creating internal heat . . . so warm hands and feet, but more intense hot flashes.

PUMPKIN MUFFINS

Rich, fragrant and moist, these hearty muffins are delicious and will keep you in a holiday mood long after the tinsel has been packed away. They provide a cozy comfort for those long winter days ahead.

MAKES 12 STANDARD OR 24 MINI MUFFINS

2 cups whole wheat pastry flour
½ cup almond meal
2 teaspoons baking powder
Generous pinch sea salt
1 teaspoon ground cinnamon
¼ teaspoon allspice
Scant pinch ground cloves
½ cup light olive oil
¼ cup Suzanne's Specialties Maple Rice Nectar
¼ cup brown rice syrup

1 cup puréed canned or fresh pumpkin
½ to 1 cup vanilla soymilk
½ cup chopped blanched almonds

Preheat the oven to 350°F and lightly oil and flour a 12-cup standard or 24-cup mini muffin pan.

In a bowl, whisk together the flour, almond meal, baking powder, salt, cinnamon, allspice and cloves. Mix in the oil, maple rice nectar, rice syrup and pumpkin. Slowly mix in enough soymilk to make a smooth, spoonable batter. Fold in the almonds.

Spoon the batter evenly into prepared muffin cups. Bake for 25 to 30 minutes, until the tops of the muffins spring back to the touch. Allow to cool for 5 minutes before removing the muffins from the pan. Cool completely on a wire rack. (Mini-muffins will take less time to bake. Check at 20 minutes.)

CINNAMON APPLE MUFFINS

Moist, delicately sweet muffins for an easy start to a lazy weekend or as a light, sweet treat for an autumn brunch. There are lots of apple desserts out there, but this is one of my favorites.
MAKES 12 MUFFINS

2 cups whole wheat pastry flour
½ cup semolina flour
2 teaspoons baking powder
Generous pinch sea salt
Generous pinch ground cinnamon

Scant pinch ground nutmeg
Grated zest of 1 lemon
⅓ cup light olive oil
½ cup brown rice syrup
1 teaspoon pure vanilla extract
½ to 1 cup vanilla soymilk
2½ cups ¼-inch diced, unpeeled Granny Smith apples
½ cup coarsely chopped pecans

Preheat the oven to 350°F and lightly oil and flour a 12-cup standard muffin pan.

Whisk together the flours, baking powder, salt, cinnamon and nutmeg. Stir in the lemon zest, oil, rice syrup and vanilla. Slowly mix in enough soymilk to make a smooth, spoonable batter. Fold in the apples and pecans.

Spoon the batter evenly into the prepared muffin cups. Bake for 25 to 35 minutes, until the tops spring back to the touch or a toothpick inserted in the centers comes out clean. Allow to cool for 5 minutes before removing the muffins from the pan. Cool completely on a wire rack.

≋ *Did You Know?* ≋
APPLES

Legend An apple a day keeps the doctor away.

Fact Apples are rich in pectin, a compound that helps control cholesterol and blood sugar, as well as improving intestinal function.

PEACH, CANTALOUPE AND HONEYDEW MEDLEY

It doesn't get easier than this one, and during the heat of summer, that is exactly what we want. Normally, I'm not a big fan of fruit first thing in the morning, as it affects blood chemistry dramatically. But sometimes, on a special occasion, the lush sensuality of seasonal fruit is just what the doctor ordered.

MAKES 4 TO 5 SERVINGS

2 to 3 ripe peaches, halved, pitted, peeled and cut into bite-size pieces

½ cantaloupe, halved, seeded, peeled and cut into bite-size pieces

½ honeydew, halved, seeded, peeled and cut into bite-size pieces

Pinch sea salt

Juice of 1 lemon

Juice of 1 orange

3 to 4 tablespoons Suzanne's Specialties Strawberry Rice Nectar

Combine the fruit in a mixing bowl. Whisk together the lemon and orange juice and strawberry rice nectar. Spoon the juice mixture over the fruit and toss gently to coat. Transfer to a serving bowl and serve warm or chilled.

≈ *Did You Know?* ≈
PEACHES

Legend Eating peaches makes for better sex.

Fact Rich in vitamin C, moisture, magnesium and folic acid, peaches aid in smooth kidney function, which in Chinese medicine governs our sexual health. The Chinese were so fascinated with the peach's texture and sweetness, legend formed around the sensual nature of the fruit.

SCRAMBLED TOFU WITH SOY SAUSAGE PATTIES

A great main course for a brunch, this breakfast comes together so quickly that it's a great way to start just about any day.

MAKES 3 SERVINGS

About 3 tablespoons extra-virgin olive oil

½ small leek, split lengthwise, rinsed well and sliced on the diagonal

Sea salt

5 to 6 button or cremini mushrooms, brushed free of dirt and thinly sliced

1 small carrot, cut into fine matchstick pieces

½ red bell pepper, roasted over an oven flame (page 57), peeled, seeded and finely diced

Generous pinch turmeric

2 to 3 scallions, thinly sliced on the diagonal

10 ounces extra-firm tofu, coarsely crumbled

Spring or filtered water

9 slices vegan soy sausage

1 small bunch kale, stem tips trimmed

Place about 1 tablespoon of the oil and the leek in a deep skillet over medium heat. When the leek begins to sizzle, add a pinch of salt and the mushrooms. Sauté until the mushrooms begin to release their juices, about 3 minutes. Stir in the carrot, bell pepper, turmeric and a light seasoning of salt. Stir in the scallions and tofu. Sauté for 1 to 2 minutes and season to taste with salt. Add a small amount of water, cover and steam for 3 to 4 minutes. Remove the cover and stir well to loosen the tofu and combine the ingredients. Transfer to a serving bowl and cover loosely.

Wipe out the skillet and return it to the stovetop. Add enough of the remaining oil to cover the bottom of the skillet and place over medium heat. Add the soy sausage to the hot oil and cook, turning once, until golden brown, about 2 minutes per side. Drain on parchment paper.

Bring a medium pot of water to a boil and cook the kale until bright green and crisp-tender, 2 to 3 minutes. Drain and slice into bite-size pieces.

To serve, mound the tofu and greens on individual plates, with 3 sausage patties each.

SCRAMBLED TOFU FLORENTINE

This is such a delicious way to serve tofu. It's one of my favorite brunch dishes, particularly when I have to satisfy a variety of tastes and have skeptics in the group. You know the ones, if it's good for you, it must taste just awful. This one gets them every time, especially with a side of home fries.

MAKES 3 TO 4 SERVINGS

> About 1 tablespoon extra-virgin olive oil
> ½ yellow onion, finely diced
> Sea salt
> 1 small carrot, finely diced
> 1 to 2 stalks celery, finely diced
> 1 tablespoon mirin
> 1 pound extra-firm tofu, coarsely crumbled
> ¼ teaspoon ground turmeric
> ½ bunch arugula, cut into bite-size pieces
> ½ cup shredded soy or rice mozzarella, preferably vegan
> 2 to 3 sprigs fresh flat-leaf parsley, finely minced

Place the oil and onion in a deep skillet over medium heat. When the onion begins to sizzle, add a pinch of salt and sauté for 1 to 2 minutes. Stir in the carrot and celery and cook, stirring, until shiny with oil. Add the mirin, tofu and turmeric and stir well, incorporating the turmeric throughout the dish. Cover, reduce the heat to low and cook for 3 to 4 minutes. Stir in the arugula and soy cheese, cover and cook for 1 minute. Turn off the heat and allow to stand until the cheese melts, 2 to 3 minutes. Stir well to combine and serve garnished with the parsley.

WAKAME WITH SCRAMBLED TOFU

I love this for breakfast on those weekends when we'll be more active, hiking, biking or otherwise out doing lots of summer playing. Served with whole-grain toast and tea, this mineral-rich, high-protein breakfast dish is a great way to start the day.

MAKES 4 TO 5 SERVINGS

About 1 tablespoon extra-virgin olive oil
1 yellow onion, cut into thin half-moon slices
Soy sauce
½ cup wakame, soaked until tender and finely diced

5 to 6 button mushrooms, brushed free of dirt and thinly sliced
½ cup fresh or frozen corn kernels
1 carrot, cut into fine matchstick pieces
1 pound extra-firm tofu, coarsely crumbled
1 teaspoon turmeric
2 small bunches parsley, finely minced

Place the oil and onion in a skillet over medium heat. When the onion begins to sizzle, add a dash of soy sauce and sauté until the onion is translucent, about 3 minutes. Stir in the wakame, mushrooms, corn, carrot and a dash of soy sauce and sauté for 2 to 3 minutes. Add the tofu and turmeric, season lightly with soy sauce and sauté until the tofu is warmed through, about 4 minutes, adding a small amount of water if the tofu sticks. Remove from the heat and stir in the parsley.

IT'S A PARTY!

Healthy celebrations . . . if this seems like an oxymoron to you, you're in for the surprise of your life. Holidays and special occasions—birthdays, graduations, marriages, anniversaries, christenings—allow us to gather with family and friends, surround ourselves with those we love to celebrate our traditions, our heritage, the seasons and life.

These special times give us a much-needed respite from our hectic daily lives and routines, creating a space for us to relax and rejoice. I don't know about you, but I can't think of any celebration that doesn't, in some way, revolve around food and nourishing each other.

As a longtime vegan, I have always faced the challenge of creating a comfortable, inviting atmosphere for my nonvegetarian friends, so that I never impose my chosen path on anyone else. My challenge is rare, however, with it more often being the reverse; the nonvegetarian host wondering what in the world to prepare for the tree hugging, sprout eaters on their guest list. Don't laugh, you know I'm right.

So how do you throw a party that's remembered for its delicious food and relaxed atmosphere? How do you put on a soiree that leaves your guests breathless and you still able to sleep at night, knowing how well you have nourished them? It's so easy you'll wonder why you never did it before.

Deep inside all of us is a five-star chef, with a touch of Martha Stewart. We all envision the perfect bash or dinner party being served at a beautifully set table. We are dying to be the calm, collected host who has created the ultimate gathering.

PARTY PLANNING

A party can be quite daunting. Hosting a "healthy" one can really throw you a curve. Worries about things turning out right are increased dramatically, as you imagine people preferring a root canal to your healthy menu.

Well, breathe out. Creating a lovely party evening is not as complicated as you like to think. With a bit of thought, you can host a stylish event that you will actually enjoy. Party planning is exactly that, planning. From choosing the date to creating the menu, thoughtful planning is the difference between an event that sails along effortlessly and an event that leaves you wondering why you have to entertain all your stupid friends anyway. Just relax.

It's so easy to plan a party that is as delicious as it is truly nourishing. From nonalcoholic beverages to munchies this chapter is full of ideas, including My Thanksgiving Dinner, Without the Bird, to get you started and then you can come up with your own inventions.

From elegant holiday meals to casual buffet parties, it's so very easy to create a festive atmosphere, and if you play your cards right, no one will be the wiser that the food is as good for them as it is just plain good.

PARTY SCHEDULE

When I plan a party, I make a list—it's the only time in my life that I do. From the centerpieces or decorations to music, I write down everything that must be done and begin at the beginning. What do I want this gathering to look like? Is there a theme or an occasion to celebrate? How many friends will gather together? For me, I like smaller groups, so I can be with everybody and not miss anyone, but every now and again, a huge bash is in order. With a small number, I can manage the cooking easily; cleanup won't take six days; the party will maintain a sense of intimacy, but be exciting at the same time. With a huge amount of guests, I have to let go of details and think about foods and beverages that can be pulled together without lots of stress and just go with the flow of the group. Either way, I think in terms of a countdown to the big evening. Once the date is chosen, a timeline begins to fall into place for me.

■ *One month ahead:* I set the date, giving me plenty of time to send out invitations, decide if I will need any help. With all of our busy schedules, the more notice I can give guests, the better. Then I sort of forget about it all for a couple of weeks.

■ *One week before the party:* I plan my menu, looking at availability of food of the season and designing my meal or buffet around what will be freshest and most delicious. Once that's completed, I shop for all my nonperishables, wine, place cards, candles, and decorations I may want to use. I also take the time to clean and press any linens I might be using, so I don't have to worry about it at the last minute.

■ *Two days before the party:* I clean the house and begin getting it ready for the party. I buy and arrange the flowers. From simple sprays of flowers to beautiful trays with three perfect pears or a few candles with seasonal greens, the centerpieces are meant to complement the table, not overshadow the food and guests. Finally, I finish most of the shopping, all the perishables that will come together to create the meal.

▪ *The day before the party:* This is the most important for me. I pick up the final ingredients—fresh bread, any delicate herbs or very perishable items. I spend a good part of the day preparing any dishes that can be worked on ahead of time—hors d'oeuvres, desserts, preparing ingredients for assembly into dishes the next evening. I set the table the night before the party and usually arrange for a take-away dinner, so that I don't have to stop work to prepare a meal at home.

▪ *The morning of the party:* I set out all my serving platters and utensils, matching dishes to recipes, based on textures, colors and presentation. I relive my restaurant training and prep all ingredients that I will be using to create the meal, placing them in containers in the refrigerator until I am ready to cook. From mincing garlic to toasting nuts, the more I can do ahead, the calmer I will be as the time draws near for me to prepare for the party.

▪ *The afternoon of the party:* I cook whatever dishes can be prepared ahead and clean up the kitchen. If the kitchen is neat and orderly, then I'll be calm and cool when I get ready to make the last-minute dishes as my friends arrive. If all goes well, I give myself plenty of time to relax, take a hot bubble bath and get ready for the big night.

▪ *Just before the magic hour:* I return to the kitchen to begin preparation of the more delicate dishes of the evening, along with the assembly of others, adding finishing touches where needed. About 30 minutes before the party is set to begin, I light the candles, turn on the music, open the wine and make one final sweep of the room to check on everything. By the time the guests arrive, my kitchen and I are calm and ordered, ready to enjoy the evening.

My Thanksgiving Dinner, Without the Bird

Creamy Mushroom Soup
Golden Sweet Potato Biscuits

Artichoke Salad with Greens and Figs

Kabocha Squash with Wild Rice Stuffing
Maple Glazed Brussels Sprouts and Roots
Cranberry Chutney

Streusel-Topped Pumpkin Pie

Holidays can be challenging on many levels, but if you really want to throw your family into a tailspin, tell them that a vegetarian, or worse, a vegan, will be joining you for Thanksgiving. My most amusing conversations have come from the panicked inquiries of hosts wondering what in the world to cook for me on the one day of the year seemingly dedicated to the consumption of poultry.

Well, the truth is that Thanksgiving is my favorite holiday to host. The harvest is in; the abundance of our fields is in full, lush ripeness and the weather has cooled enough to inspire me to light the oven once again. And I suppose I like a challenge. I love putting a delicious and elegant meal on the table and watching my guests enjoy it and not realize, until the very end, that they haven't missed the meat.

While any combination of dishes can work for your own unique Thanksgiving feast, this is my favorite. In fact, it's become our very own tradition. This menu can be adapted to other holidays or special occasions.

CREAMY MUSHROOM SOUP

Nothing accents the delicate sweetness of the Golden Sweet Potato Biscuits or kicks off a great feast, quite like a creamy, rich soup. And this one is just amazing, biscuits or not, feast or not.

The recipe can be doubled.

MAKES 4 TO 5 SERVINGS

> **About 1 tablespoon extra-virgin olive oil**
> **1 to 2 cloves fresh garlic, diced**
> **1 yellow onion, diced**
> **Sea salt**
> **2 to 3 Yukon Gold potatoes, peeled and diced**
> **6 to 8 dried shiitake mushrooms, soaked in 1 cup water until tender and thinly sliced, soaking water reserved**
> **10 to 12 ounces button mushrooms, brushed free of dirt and thinly sliced**
> **¼ cup mirin**
> **4 cups plain soymilk**
> **1 tablespoon sweet white miso**
> **2 to 3 sprigs fresh flat-leaf parsley, finely minced, for garnish**

Place the oil, garlic and onion in a soup pot over medium heat. When the onion begins to sizzle, add a pinch of salt and sauté for 2 to 3 minutes. Stir in the potatoes and a pinch of salt and sauté for 2 minutes. Stir in the mushrooms and a pinch of salt and sauté for 1 minute. Add the shiitake soaking water, mirin and soymilk, cover and bring to a boil. Reduce the heat to low and cook until the mushrooms are quite tender, about 25 minutes. Remove a small amount of hot broth and use to dissolve the miso. Stir the miso mixture into soup and cook over very low heat, uncovered, for 3 to 4 minutes to activate the enzymes in the miso. Serve garnished with the parsley.

GOLDEN SWEET POTATO BISCUITS

Lusciously moist and delicately sweet, these biscuits will quickly become a tradition on your holiday table.

MAKES ABOUT 16 BISCUITS

> **1¼ cups whole wheat pastry flour**
> **½ cup semolina flour**
> **2 teaspoons baking powder**
> **Generous pinch sea salt**
> **Generous pinch ground cinnamon**
> **3 to 4 tablespoons light olive oil**
> **⅓ cup unsweetened apple juice**
> **1 cup smoothly mashed, cooked sweet potato**
> **2 tablespoons Suzanne's Specialties Maple Rice Nectar**
> **⅓ cup coarsely chopped pecan pieces**

Preheat the oven to 375°F and line a baking sheet with parchment paper.

Combine the flours, baking powder, salt and cinnamon in a mixing bowl and whisk briskly. With a fork, cut in the oil until the mixture is the texture of wet sand. Add the apple juice, sweet potato and maple rice nectar, mixing to form a soft dough. Fold in the pecans, working to incorporate them into the dough.

Turn the dough out onto a floured surface and knead in just enough flour so the dough loses its stickiness. With floured hands, press the dough into a ⅔-inch-thick rectangle. Using a glass or cookie cutter, cut the dough into 16 biscuits, reforming dough as needed to use it all. Arrange the biscuits about 1 inch apart on the lined baking sheet. Bake for 15 to 18 minutes, until the biscuits puff slightly and they spring back to the touch or a toothpick inserted comes out clean.

Transfer to a serving plate and serve hot.

ARTICHOKE SALAD WITH GREENS AND FIGS

A more festive and elegant salad is not to be had. Light and fresh, but rich enough to be decadent, this is a symphony of flavors and textures that makes any occasion just a bit more special.

The recipe can be doubled.

MAKES 5 TO 6 SERVINGS

Artichokes
About 1 tablespoon extra-virgin olive oil
2 to 3 cloves fresh garlic, thinly sliced
1 red onion, cut into thin half-moon slices
Sea salt
8 to 10 marinated artichoke hearts, split in half lengthwise
1 red bell pepper, roasted over an open flame (page 57), peeled, seeded and sliced into thin ribbons

Dressing
Juice of 2 limes
¼ cup extra-virgin olive oil
2 teaspoons umeboshi plum vinegar
2 teaspoons Suzanne's Specialties Maple Rice Nectar
Generous pinch freshly ground black pepper

Salad
2 bunches watercress, stem tips trimmed
8 to 10 fresh figs, split lengthwise
2 to 3 scallions, thinly sliced on the diagonal, for garnish

To make the artichokes: Place the oil, garlic and onion in a skillet over medium heat. When the onion begins to sizzle, add a pinch of salt and sauté for 1 minute. Stir in the artichoke hearts and bell pepper and sauté just until heated through, about 2 minutes.

To make the dressing: Whisk together the lime juice, oil, vinegar, maple rice nectar and pepper, adjusting the seasonings to taste.

To make the salad: Arrange the watercress on a platter, with figs around the rim. Spoon the artichoke heart mixture over the top and drizzle lightly with the dressing, serving the remaining dressing on the side for those who want to use more. Sprinkle with scallions and serve immediately after dressing.

KABOCHA SQUASH WITH WILD RICE STUFFING

Ah, finally, the centerpiece dish of the feast. It seems that tradition dictates that something be "stuffed," so some very clever vegetarians came up with the idea of baking the stuffing in a hearty, sweet winter squash. Since then, many variations on the theme have emerged, each more delicious. Here's one of mine.

MAKES 8 TO 10 SERVINGS

Squash
3 tablespoons extra-virgin olive oil
2 tablespoons barley malt
Sea salt
2 medium Kabocha squash, tops removed,
jack-o-lantern style and seeds removed
Spring or filtered water, as needed

Stuffing
¾ cup wild rice, rinsed very well
1½ cups spring or filtered water
Sea salt
About 1 tablespoon extra-virgin olive oil
2 to 3 cloves fresh garlic, finely minced
1 red onion, finely diced
1 to 2 stalks celery, diced
8 ounces tempeh, coarsely crumbled
½ teaspoon dried basil
½ cup pine nuts
½ cup dry white wine
2 to 3 cups firmly packed, shredded whole-
grain sourdough bread
1 to 2 cups freshly squeezed orange juice

Preheat the oven to 375°F.

To make the squash: Whisk together the oil, barley malt and a pinch of salt in a small bowl. Using your fingers, rub the mixture over the outsides and insides of the squash. Place the squash in a baking dish, replacing the caps. Add about ½ inch water to the baking dish. Cover with foil and bake until the squash pierces easily with a fork, but is still firm, about 45 minutes.

While the squash bakes, *make the stuffing:* Place the wild rice and water in a heavy pot and bring to a boil over medium heat. Add a pinch of salt, cover, reduce the heat to low and cook until all the liquid has been absorbed and the rice is tender, about 35 minutes. Set aside.

Place the oil, garlic, and onion in a skillet over medium heat. When the onion begins to sizzle, add a pinch of salt and sauté for 2 to 3 minutes. Stir in the celery and sauté for 1 minute. Stir in the tempeh and basil and sauté until the tempeh begins to brown, about 5 minutes. Add the pine nuts and wine and season to taste with salt. Cover and cook for 5 to 7 minutes. Remove the cover and cook until all liquid has been absorbed.

Place the bread in a mixing bowl and add the rice, sautéed vegetables and tempeh. Slowly add orange juice, mixing well until a soft stuffing forms. Don't make it too wet.

Stuff each squash abundantly and replace in the baking dish. Lay the caps in the baking dish next to squash, not on top. Cover with foil and bake until the squash is quite tender, 35 minutes to 1 hour, depending on the size of the squash. Allow squash to cool for about 10 minutes before transferring to a serving platter.

Note: Extra stuffing can be pressed into an oiled baking dish and cooked, covered for 35 to 40 minutes. Remove cover and brown the top before serving.

MAPLE-GLAZED BRUSSELS SPROUTS AND ROOTS

It seems that Thanksgiving tradition calls for sweetly glazed vegetables and these will never disappoint.
MAKES 6 TO 8 SERVINGS

> 2 pounds Brussels sprouts, tips trimmed, Xs cut into the bottoms of each
> 2 red onions, cut into thick wedges
> 2 to 3 sweet potatoes, split lengthwise and cut into ½-inch-thick half-moons
> 2 tablespoons extra-virgin olive oil
> Sea salt
> Grated zest of 2 lemons
> ½ cup dry white wine
> 3 tablespoons Suzanne's Specialties Maple Rice Nectar
> Juice of ½ lemon
> 2 to 3 sprigs fresh flat-leaf parsley, finely minced

Preheat the oven to 350°F.

Place all the vegetables in a mixing bowl and add the oil, a generous sprinkling of salt, the lemon zest, wine and maple rice nectar. Mix well to coat. Arrange the vegetables in a large baking dish, avoiding overlap. Cover with foil and bake until the vegetables are tender, about 45 minutes. Remove the foil and bake for 10 to 15 minutes, until the vegetables are browned and the liquid has turned to a syrup. Remove from the oven and squeeze the lemon juice over the top. Sprinkle with parsley and toss gently to coat. Serve hot.

CRANBERRY CHUTNEY

No sweet jelled sauces out of a can for your loved ones, not when a fresh cranberry chutney is this easy to make. And because you can prepare it the day before, everyone wins.

MAKES 6 TO 8 SERVINGS

12-ounce package fresh cranberries, rinsed
　　well
1 to 2 Granny Smith apples, peeled and diced
Grated zest of 1 orange
Juice of 1 orange
½ cup unsweetened dried apricots
1 teaspoon grated fresh ginger
1 teaspoon ground cinnamon
½ teaspoon pure vanilla extract
Pinch sea salt
3 to 4 tablespoons barley malt

Place all the ingredients, except the barley malt, in a saucepan and bring to a boil over medium heat. Cover and reduce the heat to low. Simmer until most of the liquid has been absorbed, about 25 minutes. Remove the cover and add barley malt to taste. Cook, uncovered, over low heat until the barley malt thickens, 10 to 12 minutes. Cool to room temperature and transfer to container with a lid. Seal tightly and chill completely. Before serving, bring the chutney to room temperature.

STREUSEL-TOPPED PUMPKIN PIE

What's Thanksgiving without pumpkin pie? Not the same, truly. Give this one a try for a twist on a traditional favorite.

MAKES 8 TO 10 SERVINGS

Filling
2 cups puréed canned or fresh cooked
　　pumpkin
Pinch sea salt
1 cup plain amasake
1 cup vanilla soymilk
1 teaspoon pure vanilla extract
½ cup brown rice syrup
Generous pinch ground cinnamon
Scant pinch allspice
3 tablespoons agar flakes
2 tablespoons kuzu, dissolved in small amount
　　cold water

Crust
1½ cups whole wheat pastry flour
Pinch sea salt
¼ cup avocado or light olive oil
Spring or filtered water

Streusel Topping
1½ cups whole wheat pastry flour
Pinch sea salt
¼ teaspoon ground cinnamon
¼ teaspoon ground nutmeg
½ cup finely chopped pecans
2 tablespoons avocado or light olive oil
3 to 4 tablespoons brown rice syrup

Preheat the oven to 350°F and lightly oil a deep-dish glass pie plate.

To make the filling: Place all the ingredients, except the kuzu, in a saucepan over low heat. Cook, whisking frequently, until the agar is dissolved, about 20 minutes. Whisk in the dissolved kuzu and cook, stirring, until the mixture thickens, about 3 minutes. Set aside.

To make the crust: Combine the flour and salt in a mixing bowl. With a fork, cut in the oil until the mixture is the texture of wet sand. Slowly add water, 1 tablespoon at a time, mixing until dough gathers into a ball. Roll out between 2 sheets of parchment paper, creating a thin circle that is about 1 inch larger than the pie plate. Transfer the circle to the pie plate and fit into the crevices without stretching, allowing the excess to hang over the sides of the pan. Fold the excess crust up over the rim and using your fingers, crimp into a decorative edge. Pierce in several places with a fork and bake for 12 minutes. Cool to room temperature.

Spoon the filling evenly into the crust and set aside.

To make the streusel: Combine the flour, salt, cinnamon and nutmeg in a mixing bowl. Fold in the pecans, oil and rice syrup and mix until a crumbly mixture forms. Sprinkle generously over the pumpkin filling, covering completely.

Place the pie on a baking sheet and cover loosely with foil. Bake for 25 minutes. Remove the foil and bake for 30 to 35 minutes, until the edges of the filling are set and the topping is browned and crunchy. Transfer the pie to a cooling rack and allow to stand for 15 to 30 minutes before slicing.

Nonalcoholic Beverages

So what do you serve the guest that chooses not to imbibe? Are they doomed to parties with nothing more than sparkling water with slices of lemon? Hardly. Check these out.

MIMOSAS

I know what you're thinking . . . mimosas? Aren't they champagne and orange juice? Well, in fact, they are. And lovely, but for those guests choosing not to drink alcohol, try this delicious alternative.

MAKES 1 DRINK

Chilled fresh orange juice
Chilled sparkling water
Freshly squeezed lime juice, to taste
Orange slices, for garnish

Mix together equal amounts of orange juice and sparkling water, with a light squeeze of lime juice. Whisk and serve. Serve garnished with orange slices. Note that these must be mixed to order, as they will get flat and tasteless if made too far in advance.

PASSIONFRUIT PUNCH

Traditionally, this is a rum-based punch, and you can surely make it that way. That'll get the party started, but for those guests who choose not to drink alcohol, this version has all the sensuality but none of the punch that goes with drunk.

MAKES 6 DRINKS

1 cup freshly squeezed orange juice
1 cup freshly squeezed grapefruit juice
12 to 14 ounces fresh or frozen passionfruit juice
1 vanilla bean, split lengthwise
Ice cubes

Place the juices in a blender. Scrape the pulp from the vanilla pod and add to the blender. Blend until the pulp is incorporated into the juices. Fill 6 glasses with ice and pour the punch over top.

Variation: For a creamy punch, add crushed ice and ½ cup vanilla soymilk to the blender mixture and purée until smooth. Serve immediately.

SANGRIA

It's hard to make this one taste authentic without real wine, but if you truly want to create a sangria that anyone can enjoy, try this variation.

MAKES 8 SERVINGS

3 cups nonalcoholic red wine
1½ cups natural lemon-lime soda
1½ cups freshly squeezed orange juice
Juice of 1 lemon
Juice of 1 lime
½ cup unsweetened cherry juice
1 teaspoon pure orange extract
¼ cup Suzanne's Specialties Strawberry Rice Nectar
16 lime slices
16 lemon slices
8 orange slices, halved

Whisk together the wine, soda, juices, orange extract and strawberry rice nectar in a bowl. Add half the lime, lemon and orange slices and set aside for 30 minutes, for flavors to develop.

To serve, fill 8 large wineglasses with ice and pour the sangria over top, garnishing with the remaining fruit slices.

COSMOPOLITAN

I know, I know. How very Sex and the City. *These are just as delicious as the alcohol versions, but without compromise to your judgment—so you'll remember whom you're going home with when the party ends!*
MAKES 8 TO 10 DRINKS

1¼ cups freshly squeezed orange juice
½ teaspoon pure orange extract
1¼ cups unsweetened cranberry juice
¼ cup Suzanne's Specialties Raspberry Rice Nectar
½ cup freshly squeezed lime juice
4 cups chilled sparkling water

Whisk together all the ingredients and pour evenly into champagne flutes or martini glasses (no reason to avoid the glassware just because you don't want the alcohol).

The Party Food

Parties can encompass everything from elegantly served dinners to casual buffet gatherings to snacks and drinks to dessert and tea. These recipes give you just a sample of the creative variety available to you.

From finger food to elegant main courses, healthy offerings can be as sensual, delicious and fabulously beautiful as anything you can imagine on your table. So party on.

CABBAGE SPRING ROLLS

A wonderful finger food, perfect for a buffet or for a casual snacks and drinks get-together. I serve these with a spicy dipping sauce for some added sparkle.
MAKES 12 TO 14 EGG ROLLS, 24 TO 28 SERVINGS

Rolls
About 1 tablespoon extra-virgin olive oil, plus extra for cooking
2 to 3 cloves fresh garlic, finely minced
1 yellow onion, finely diced
Soy sauce
1 to 2 stalks celery, diced
1 carrot, cut into fine matchstick pieces
4 cups finely shredded green head cabbage
1 cup fresh or frozen corn kernels
Mirin
12 to 14 eggless egg roll wrappers

Dipping Sauce
½ cup unsweetened orange marmalade
2 tablespoons freshly squeezed orange juice
1 tablespoon brown rice vinegar
1 tablespoon umeboshi plum vinegar
1 teaspoon fresh ginger juice
½ teaspoon soy sauce
1 tablespoon brown rice syrup
Generous pinch chili powder

To make the rolls: Place the oil, garlic and onion in a deep skillet over medium heat. When the onion begins to sizzle, add a dash of soy sauce and sauté for 1 to 2 minutes. Stir in the celery and carrot and sauté for 1 minute. Stir in the cabbage, cover and steam for 1 minute, until it begins to wilt.

Remove the cover and add a light seasoning of soy sauce. Sauté until the cabbage is quite limp, 2 to 3 minutes. Stir in the corn and a light seasoning of mirin and sauté until any liquid has been absorbed.

Lay an egg roll wrapper on a dry work surface with one corner facing you. Spoon 2 to 3 table-spoons of the filling across the wrapper, close to you, but leaving the corner exposed so you can fold it over. Fold the two side corners and the cor-ner closest to you over the filling. Roll, jelly-roll style, forming a cylinder. Moisten the remaining corner and seal the roll. Lay, seam side down, on a dry surface. Repeat the process with remaining filling and wrappers.

To make the dipping sauce: Combine the all ingredients in a small saucepan and cook over low heat, whisking, for 2 to 3 minutes. Adjust the sea-sonings to taste and cook 1 minute. Set aside to cool.

Brush a large skillet generously with oil and place over medium-high heat. Cook the spring rolls until golden and crispy, turning as needed to ensure even browning.

To serve, slice the spring rolls in half crosswise, on the diagonal. Arrange on a platter with the dipping sauce on the side. Serve immediately.

SPICY WHITE BEAN-TOMATO PATE

A great special occasion starter, served with elegant toast points or crackers, this is also great at a picnic or any other outdoor celebration. Mound it in a bowl and serve it with delicious whole-grain bread.

MAKES 2 TO 3 CUPS

About 1 tablespoon extra-virgin olive oil
2 to 3 cloves fresh garlic, finely minced
1 red onion, finely diced
Sea salt
Generous pinch red pepper flakes
2 cups cooked cannellini beans
⅓ cup oil-packed sun-dried tomatoes, diced
Grated zest of 1 lemon
Juice of ½ lemon
Generous pinch dried basil
2 to 3 leaves Romaine lettuce, left whole
1 sprig fresh flat-leaf parsley, finely minced
Crackers, pita or toast points, for serving

Place the oil, garlic and onion in a deep skillet over medium heat. When the onion begins to siz-zle, add a pinch of salt and the red pepper flakes and sauté for 1 to 2 minutes. Add the beans, toma-toes and lemon zest, season to taste with salt and cook, stirring, for 1 to 2 minutes.

Transfer the bean mixture to a food processor. Add the lemon juice and basil and purée until smooth. (If the mixture is too thick, add 1 to 2 tablespoons olive oil or water to loosen. The olive oil will create a much richer pate than the water.)

To serve, lay the lettuce leaves around the rim of a platter. Mound the pate in the center and sprinkle with the parsley. You may also press the pate into a shallow bowl for a more casual presentation. Serve with crackers.

~~~~~~~~~~~~~~~~~~~~~~~~~~~~~~~~~~~

CONFETTI BLACK BEAN SALAD

Not a more festive bean salad to be had. Spicy and sweet, with loads of finely diced, seasonal vegetables laced through, this yummy dish is ideal for casual get-togethers, large groups or any outdoor gathering. Lots of ingredients, but trust me, the more the merrier for this party on a plate!

MAKES 8 TO 10 SERVINGS

About 2 tablespoons extra-virgin olive oil

2 cloves fresh garlic, finely minced

1 tablespoon finely minced fresh ginger

1 red onion, diced

Sea salt

1 teaspoon dried cumin

½ teaspoon ground coriander

Generous pinch red pepper flakes

2 cups fresh or frozen corn kernels

1 red bell pepper, roasted over an open flame (page 57), peeled, seeded and diced

1 yellow bell pepper, roasted over an open flame, peeled, seeded and diced

2 to 3 scallions, thinly sliced on the diagonal

2 tablespoons stone-ground mustard

2 tablespoons brown rice syrup

Grated zest of 1 lemon

3 cups cooked black turtle beans

2 tomatoes, diced (do not peel or seed)

2 to 3 sprigs fresh flat-leaf parsley, finely minced, for garnish

Place the oil, garlic, ginger and onion in a deep skillet over medium heat. When the onion begins to sizzle, add a pinch of salt, the cumin, coriander and red pepper flakes and sauté for 2 to 3 minutes. Add the corn, bell peppers and scallions, season lightly with salt and sauté for 1 minute. Stir in the mustard, rice syrup and lemon zest, stirring to coat. Fold in the beans and tomatoes, adjust the seasoning to taste and stir gently to combine ingredients. Transfer salad to a serving bowl and sprinkle with parsley.

~~~~~~~~~~~~~~~~~~~~~~~~~~~~~~~~~~~

CURRIED PAN-FRIED TEMPEH

A great main course, served simply and elegantly with a side salad, crisp bread and a simple soup, you have the makings of a lovely dinner party. You can also slip these into pita bread with shredded lettuce and tomato slices and you have a spicy, casual lunch.

MAKES 4 TO 6 SERVINGS

About 1 tablespoon extra-virgin olive oil, plus extra for frying

16 ounces tempeh, cut into 1½- to 2-inch pieces and then split to make them half as thick

½ cup dry white wine

6 to 8 shallots, finely minced

Soy sauce

Grated zest of 1 to 2 lemons

4 teaspoons curry powder

2 to 4 sprigs fresh flat-leaf parsley, finely minced

Place enough oil in a deep skillet over high heat to generously cover the bottom. When the oil is hot (patterns will form, known as "dancing"), pan-fry the tempeh until golden, turning once to ensure browning. Drain on parchment paper and wipe out the skillet.

Place about 1 tablespoon oil, the wine and shallots in the skillet over medium heat. When the shallots begin to sizzle, add a sprinkling of the soy sauce, lemon zest and curry powder and sauté until shallots begin to color, about 4 minutes. Lay the tempeh on top of the shallots, cover, reduce the heat to low and simmer for 2 to 3 minutes to infuse the tempeh with the curry flavor. Remove the cover and stir gently to combine. Transfer to a serving platter and sprinkle lightly with parsley.

FAVA BEAN AND CHICKPEA SALAD WITH PITA POINTS

A very traditional Middle Eastern dish that I fell in love with on first taste. Simple, elegant and make-your-knees-buckle yummy, this simple bean salad is packed with protein and rich enough to satisfy any taste. For luncheons or on a buffet, this will become a fixed item in your repertoire.

MAKES 5 TO 6 SERVINGS

½ cup dried fava beans, sorted and rinsed well
4 cups spring or filtered water
½ cup dried chickpeas, sorted and rinsed well
2 bay leaves
½ red onion, finely diced
2 to 3 sprigs fresh flat-leaf parsley, minced
Sea salt
Freshly ground black pepper
Extra-virgin olive oil, for drizzling
Juice of 1 lemon
8 ounces purchased hummus or homemade (page 254)
Sweet paprika
3 to 4 whole wheat pita breads

Place the fava beans in a small saucepan with 2 cups of the water. Place the chickpeas in another small saucepan with the remaining 2 cups water. Drop a bay leaf into each pot and bring both to a boil, uncovered, over medium heat. Boil, uncovered, for 5 minutes. Cover, reduce the heat to low and cook until the beans are just tender, about 1 hour. Remove the bay leaves and drain away any remaining liquid. Transfer the fava beans and chickpeas to a mixing bowl. Stir in the onion, parsley, salt and pepper to taste, a generous drizzle of oil and the lemon juice. Gently mix to combine.

Spread the hummus evenly over a flat plate. Mound the fava bean and chickpea mixture onto the center of the hummus. Sprinkle lightly with paprika and drizzle with more olive oil.

Cut each pita into 8 triangular wedges and place in a basket. Eat the salad with the pita points.

SLICED AVOCADOS WITH BLACK OLIVE VINAIGRETTE

Until this dish, I have to honestly say that I was not a fan of avocado, but after tasting this combination, I was hooked. You will be, too. It's a great starter to serve in place of a salad.

MAKES 8 SERVINGS

Vinaigrette

¼ cup extra-virgin olive oil

4 teaspoons balsamic vinegar

1 teaspoon red wine vinegar

2 to 3 tablespoons black olive paste

2 shallots, finely minced

1 tablespoon finely minced fresh basil

Pinch sea salt

Salad

4 ripe avocados

2 bunches watercress, rinsed well, stems trimmed, cut into bite-size pieces

To make the vinaigrette: Whisk all the ingredients in a small bowl, adjusting the seasonings to your taste. It should be strong and slightly salty. Set aside.

To make the salad: Halve, pit and peel the avocados. Thinly slice them lengthwise, keeping them intact. Divide the watercress among 8 salad plates. Using a spatula, carefully transfer an avocado half onto each plate, pressing gently to fan the slices. Spoon the dressing over each plate and serve at room temperature or chilled.

Note: Black olive paste can be purchased in Italian and specialty markets.

≋ *Did You Know?* ≋
AVOCADOS

Legend The perfect food, avocados create energy and vitality.

Fact The fat in avocados is monounsaturated and polyunsaturated, and they contain numerous enzymes to ease digestion of protein and fat, making it great for the stomach and intestines.

WINTER SALAD WITH MUSTARD SEED VINAIGRETTE

Summer salads are a snap . . . crisp lettuce and toma-toes . . . yum. But how to achieve that elegant, light, fresh taste during the winter months? Here's how, with this great starter course.

MAKES 6 TO 8 SERVINGS

About 1 tablespoon extra-virgin olive oil
1 fennel bulb, stalks trimmed and bulb thinly sliced lengthwise

Dressing
¼ cup mustard seeds
¼ cup extra-virgin olive oil
¼ cup red wine vinegar
2 teaspoons balsamic vinegar
2 tablespoons stone-ground mustard
1 shallot, finely minced
Sea salt

2 small heads friseé or escarole, rinsed well and hand-shredded
6 Belgian endive, split lengthwise and very thinly sliced lengthwise
3 to 4 sprigs fresh flat-leaf parsley, finely minced, for garnish

Place the oil in a skillet over medium heat. Add the fennel slices and cook, stirring frequently, until they just begin to wilt, 5 to 7 minutes.

To make the dressing: Dry-roast the mustard seeds in a small skillet for 1 to 2 minutes. Transfer to a mixing bowl. Whisk in the oil, vinegars, mus-tard, shallot and salt to taste. Whisk briskly to combine.

Arrange the frisée and endive on a serving plat-ter. Spoon the fennel over the top and drizzle generously with the salad dressing. Sprinkle with parsley and serve immediately.

RED PEPPER BRUSCHETTA

What's a party without bruschetta? Boring. Simple to make, easy to eat and so incredibly delicious and beauti-ful that just placing the platter on the buffet gets the party started.

MAKES 6 SERVINGS

About 1 tablespoon extra-virgin olive oil
½ red onion, very thinly sliced into half-moon pieces
Sea salt
1 large red bell pepper, roasted over an open flame (page 57), peeled, seeded and thinly sliced
2 to 3 stalks broccoli rabe, finely chopped
5 to 6 fresh basil leaves, finely shredded
6 (½-inch-thick) diagonal slices whole-grain sourdough bread
6 cloves fresh garlic, halved lengthwise

Preheat the oven to 400°F and line a baking sheet with parchment paper.

Place the oil and onion in a skillet over medium heat. When the onion begins to sizzle, add a pinch of salt and sauté for 2 to 3 minutes. Stir in the bell pepper and broccoli rabe, season lightly with salt and sauté just until the rabe wilts. Turn off the heat and stir in the basil.

Arrange the bread on a baking sheet and bake until crisp, about 5 minutes. Remove the bread from oven and rub 2 garlic clove halves over one side of each slice of bread. Mound the vegetables on each slice of bread and serve immediately.

PESTO PIZZA WITH ARTICHOKE HEARTS

A festive dish fancy enough to work at a cocktail party, it's casual enough for an evening of snacks and old movies.

MAKES 2 CUPS PESTO AND 6 TO 8 SERVINGS PIZZA

Fresh Basil Pesto
1 cup pine nuts or walnuts
½ cup extra-virgin olive oil
2 cloves fresh garlic, thinly sliced
2 cups loosely packed fresh basil leaves
2 teaspoons white miso
1 teaspoon umeboshi plum vinegar
2 teaspoons brown rice syrup
Spring or filtered water

Pizza
1 (10-inch) loaf whole wheat focaccia
1 (6-ounce) jar marinated artichoke hearts, drained and thinly sliced
½ cup finely minced oil-cured black olives
Generous pinch red pepper flakes
Extra-virgin olive oil, for drizzling

1 ripe tomato, thinly sliced into rounds (do not peel or seed)
1 to 2 cups shredded vegan soy mozzarella

Preheat the oven to 350°F and line a baking sheet with parchment paper.

To make the pesto: Place the pine nuts, oil, garlic and basil in a food processor and purée until smooth. Add the miso, vinegar and rice syrup and purée until smooth. Slowly add water to achieve the desired consistency. Do not thin too much.

To make the pizza: Spread about ¾ cup of the pesto in a thin layer evenly over the focaccia. Top with the artichoke hearts and olives and sprinkle with red pepper flakes. Drizzle lightly with oil. Arrange the tomato slices over the top of the pizza and sprinkle with the soy mozzarella.

Bake for 15 to 20 minutes, until the cheese melts. Remove from the oven and transfer to a dry work surface. Cut into squares.

Note: The balance of unused pesto can be frozen or used in another recipe within 24 hours.

CREOLE-STYLE HUMMUS WITH PITA CHIPS

This is a slightly different take on a classic bean favorite. A bit spicy, this version of hummus will get everyone's attention but not send them to the bar looking to put out the fire.

MAKES 3 TO 4 CUPS HUMMUS

Hummus
2 cups cooked chickpeas
½ cup extra-virgin olive oil
½ cup sesame tahini
Juice of 1 lemon
1 teaspoon brown rice syrup
3 cloves fresh garlic, minced
1 teaspoon ground cumin
½ teaspoon chili powder
½ teaspoon freshly ground black pepper
½ teaspoon ground ginger
Sea salt
Spring or filtered water

Pita Chips
4 whole wheat pita breads
Extra-virgin olive oil, for drizzling
Sweet paprika

To make the hummus: Place all ingredients, except the salt and water, in a food processor and purée until smooth. Season to taste with salt, adjust the other seasonings and puree, slowly adding water to achieve a creamy consistency.

To make the pita chips: Preheat the oven to 375°F and line a baking sheet with parchment paper. Slice each pita bread into 8 triangular wedges and arrange on the lined baking sheet. Drizzle with olive oil and sprinkle lightly with paprika. Bake for 10 to 12 minutes, until crisp. Transfer to a basket.

Transfer the hummus to a serving bowl, and serve with the pita chips on the side.

TOMATILLO, CORN AND OLIVE SALSA WITH TORTILLA CHIPS

A lovely twist on a classic—let's just say it's not just any old salsa.

MAKES ABOUT 3 CUPS SALSA AND 32 CHIPS

Salsa
2 cups fresh or frozen corn kernels
4 to 5 tomatillos, husks removed
½ red onion, finely diced
2 to 3 cloves fresh garlic, finely minced
1 green bell pepper, roasted over an open
    flame (page 57), peeled, seeded and diced
1 jalapeño chile, roasted oven an open flame,
    peeled, seeded and minced
Sea salt
½ cup coarsely minced green olives
¼ cup extra-virgin olive oil
3 tablespoons red wine vinegar

Tortilla chips
Avocado or light olive oil, for frying
5 to 6 soft corn tortillas, cut into triangular
    wedges
Sea salt

To make the salsa: Bring a small pot of water to a boil. Add the corn and cook for 1 to 2 minutes. Remove with a slotted spoon or skimmer and drain well. Transfer to a mixing bowl. In the same water, cook the tomatillos for 5 minutes, drain, dice and add to the corn.

Mix in the onion, garlic, bell pepper, chile, salt to taste, olives, oil and vinegar. Mix well to combine. Allow to stand about 1 hour before serving to allow flavors to develop.

To make the tortilla chips: Heat about 1 inch of oil in a deep skillet over medium heat. When the oil is hot (patterns will form, known as "dancing"), increase the heat to high and quickly fry the chips until crisp, 1 to 2 minutes. Drain on parchment paper and sprinkle lightly with salt.

Place the salsa in a serving bowl, with chips on the side.

Note: You may substitute organic corn chips in place of frying your own.

SUGAR 'N' SPICE KUMQUATS

In this slightly exotic buffet treat, hot spice is nicely off-set with delicate sweet taste, showcasing the bittersweet nature of the kumquat. Pop one of these in your mouth for a taste sensation.

MAKES ABOUT 20 SERVINGS

6 tablespoons brown rice syrup
Pinch sea salt
1 tablespoon chili powder
35 to 40 kumquats

Place the brown rice syrup, salt and chile powder in a small saucepan. Cook over medium-low heat until the mixture foams.

Arrange the kumquats on a wire cooling rack with parchment paper underneath. Pour the foaming rice syrup quickly over kumquats, letting the excess drip onto the paper. If the rice syrup thickens, simply warm through again to thin. Allow the kumquats to stand for 15 to 20 minutes to set glaze before transferring them to a platter.

ITALIAN NUT COOKIES

No casual party would be complete without cozy, homey cookies on the buffet. My mother used to make these classics for impromptu gatherings where the atmosphere was more relaxed. Here's my take on her recipe.

MAKES ABOUT 24 COOKIES

Cookies
2 cups whole wheat pastry flour
½ cup semolina flour
⅓ cup unsweetened cocoa powder
2 teaspoons baking powder
½ teaspoon ground cinnamon
Pinch sea salt
½ cup light olive oil
½ cup brown rice syrup
½ to 1 cup vanilla soymilk
½ cup coarsely chopped pecans
½ cup coarsely chopped walnuts

Chocolate Glaze
1 cup nondairy, grain-sweetened chocolate chips
¼ cup vanilla soymilk
3 tablespoons Suzanne's Specialties Chocolate Rice Nectar

Preheat oven to 350°F and line a baking sheet with parchment paper.

To make the cookies: Whisk together the flours, cocoa, baking powder, cinnamon and salt. Mix in the oil and rice syrup. Slowly add the soymilk, mixing to create a soft dough that will hold its shape. Fold in the nuts. Using moist hands, form the dough into 1-inch spheres and arrange on the lined baking sheet.

Bake for 18 to 20 minutes, until the cookies are just firm but still slightly soft. Allow to cool for 2 to 3 minutes on baking sheet. Transfer to a wire rack and cool completely.

To make the glaze: Place the chocolate chips in a heat-resistant bowl. Place the soymilk and chocolate rice nectar in a small saucepan and bring to a rolling boil. Pour over chocolate chips and whisk to form a smooth, satinlike glaze.

Slip a piece of parchment paper under the rack of cookies. Spoon the glaze over each one, letting the glaze run over the sides. Allow to stand, undisturbed, until the glaze begins to set. Transfer to a serving platter. These cookies will keep, in a sealed container, for several days.

BIBLIOGRAPHY

I am inspired by the brilliance of many people around me and owe much of my wisdom to their teaching and experience. Without them and their generous sharing, I would not be doing what I am doing in the world.

Conrad, Chris. *Hemp: Lifeline to the Future*. Novato, CA: Creative Xpressions Publications, 1994.

Erasmus, Udo. *Fats that Heal, Fats that Kill*. Burnaby, Canada: Alive Books, 1993.

Kimbrell, Andrew (editor). *Fatal Harvest*. Washington, Covello, London: Island Press, 2000.

Kushi, Michio. *How to See Your Health: Book of Oriental Diagnosis*. New York: Japan Publications, Inc., 1980.

Lu, Henry C. *Chinese Natural Cures*. New York: Black Dog & Leventhal, Inc., 1994.

Ohsawa, Georges. *You Are All Sanpaku*. New York: Citadel, 1965.

————. *Zen Macrobiotics*. Los Angeles, CA: Ohsawa Foundation, Inc., 1965.

Rose, Richard. *The HempNut Health and Cookbook*. Santa Rosa, CA: HempNut, Inc., 2000.

Veith, Ilza. *The Yellow Emperor's Classic of Internal Medicine*. Berkeley, CA: University of California Press, 1949.

Weil, Andrew, M.D. *Eating Well for Optimum Health*. New York: Alfred A. Knopf, 2000.

RESOURCE GUIDE

Knowing how hard it is to get people back to the kitchen, I don't want you to feel discouraged about finding some of the more exotic ingredients that I use throughout the recipes. So, no more excuses, here's where you can find everything you'll need, starting with me!

Christina Enterprises, Inc.
christinacooks.com
800-939-3909
Recipes, information, newsletters, daily tips and lots of fun

Pearl Soymilk
www.pearlsoymilk.com
415-956-7750
Created by Kikkoman International, Pearl Soymilk is made from certified organic soybeans and flavored with the finest ingredients. In four flavors, Original, Creamy Vanilla, Green Tea and Tropical Delight.

Kuhn-Rikon Corp.
www.kuhnrikon.com
European cookware and kitchen accessories of the finest quality, including Duromatic pressure cookers, Duroply everyday stainless steel cookware, Durotherm thermal cookware and an extensive line of kitchen utensils.

Bob's Red Mill Natural Foods
www.bobsredmill.com
800-349-2173
An extensive line of more than 400 whole grain and grain-based products, including a full organic line, gluten-free products, whole grain mixes, dried beans and spices . . . whole, natural foods for every meal of the day.

Living Harvest Conscious Nutrition
www.livingharvest.com
800-848-2542
Makers of certified organic shelled hemp seeds, hemp seed oil and hemp protein powder, plus other fine hamp-based products, rich sources of fatty acids and other nutrients, in the perfect balance for our good health.

Pacifica Culinaria, Inc.
pacificaculinaria.com
800-622-8880
Fine cold-pressed avocado oil and other condiments

Suzanne's Specialties, Inc.
suzannesspecialties.com
800-762-2135
Brown rice syrup, original and flavored, plus other natural sweeteners

INDEX